William Blake
His Life and Work

By the same author

William Morris his life and work

JACK LINDSAY

William Blake

HIS LIFE AND WORK

GEORGE BRAZILLER
NEW YORK

Published in 1979 by George Braziller, Inc.
Copyright © 1978 by Jack Lindsay
Originally published by Constable and Company Ltd, London

All rights reserved.
For information address the publisher:
George Braziller, Inc.
One Park Avenue
New York, 10016

ISBN: 0–8076–0913–7   LC: 78–24639
Printed in Great Britain
First Edition

To Edith Sitwell

Edith, whose name but yours
      here spelled devoutly,
though I've been lucky in poets
      whose hand touched mine,
Tristan and Paul,
      Pablo and Dylan:
all the voices rhyme as these words
      go spilling out,

go echoing always through
      my caverned mind,
and you are there, in the curving
      and the returning,
momentary and eternal,
      your voice I hear
as the spiral closes and opens,
      your face is clear

both here and there, in the centre
      outside time
which chimes at time's heart
      as you bend your head
with a distant smile saying all
      that can be said

since before it was written
      you read this book
and here are living, I write
      not in memorial
but in thanksgiving:
      such has been my luck

            Jack Lindsay

Contents

Illustrations

William Blake. Portrait by Phillips (*National Portrait Gallery*) *frontispiece*

between pages 46 and 47

Blake at Hampstead, 1825; drawing by John Linnell (*Fitzwilliam Museum*)

'Blake in his fiery youth'; drawing by Catherine Blake (*Fitzwilliam Museum*)

Catherine Blake, about 1802; drawing by Blake (*Tate Gallery*)

Flaxman modelling bust of Hayley; painting by George Romney (*National Portrait Gallery*)

Fuseli, self-portrait; black and white chalk, 1780–90 (*Victoria and Albert*)

Samuel Palmer, self-portrait; about 1826 (*Ashmolean Museum*)

Blake and Varley; pencil drawing by Linnell (*Fitzwilliam Museum*)

Title page to *Europe* (*British Museum*)

Jerusalem, frontispiece (*British Museum*)

The Human Abstract from *Songs of Experience* (*British Museum*)

'Oberon and Titania'; drawing by Robert Blake (*British Museum*)

Blake's room at Fountain Court; drawing by Frederick Shields (*Central Library, City of Manchester*)

between pages 206 and 207

'Albion Arose'; engraving by Blake about 1800 (*British Museum*)

Engraving by James Heath of painting by Francis Wheatley of Gordon Riots (*British Museum*)

Foreword

I first read Blake in 1917–18 and was deeply affected by him. Besides the Sampson text, I came to know the Yeats-Ellis edition and read the books of Ellis, Swinburne, Berger. My world-view, such as it was, was provided by Shakespeare, Dostoevsky, Blake. In the 1920s I became a disciple of my father, the artist Norman Lindsay, who, under the shock of the war, had developed his Nietzschean philosophy into a sort of homespun Neoplatonism, in which the artist, creator of form, arrested the ceaseless fall of spirit in a contracting or disintegrating universe. In this period I wrote a little book on Blake (1927, with an enlarged edition, 1929) and an essay on Blake's metric for an edition of the *Poetical Sketches* by Eric Partridge's Scholartis Press. Through these works I came to know Thomas Wright, who asked me to address a meeting in a chapel at Bunhill Fields on the 1928 anniversary of Blake's death. A little later I met Mary Butts and talked with her about her ancestor.

I mention these facts to show how far back goes my interest in Blake. And through the years I have kept returning to him and seeking to revalue him in terms of the problems thrown up by my own development, though I have written little on him except for a few essays or reviews. (A booklet on him which I wrote for the New York Critics Group was prevented from appearing by the war; in 1975 I scripted a programme of his works at the Mermaid Theatre.) This book, then, has behind it a deep concern for Blake which goes back some sixty years. I do not write as someone interested in Blake from the outside, but as someone for whom he has been a vitally formative influence throughout life.

In the post-war years the number of books on Blake has steadily grown, especially in America, and there is now a large body of commentary, much of it of considerable value. I must acknowledge my debt to many devoted critics, but above all to David Erdman, who has done far more than anyone else to show how closely and deeply Blake's work is linked with the events and developments of his world. Other debts are brought out in the Notes.

Despite the vast amount of commentary on Blake, the only full-scale critical biography is still that of Mona Wilson (1927, revised in 1948). There is G. E. Bentley's *Blake Records* with its very useful collection of documents and materials; but it is a work for the scholar, not the general reader. For this reason I have chosen to put my study in biographical form, seeking to bring to bear the deepened critical understanding of his work on the extended knowledge that we now have of his life and reactions. In any event I feel that in a Life one can most concretely show the full interaction of a writer or artist with his world, while at the same time doing one's best to define his specific contribution in all its personal and aesthetic aspects.

Here at the outset I should like briefly to indicate the main sources on which we have to rely apart from letters and the like. J. T. Smith had known him for some forty years when he wrote down his recollections in *Nollekens and his Times*; he was generally reliable but was never close to Blake. Malkin's essay of 1806 records many things that Blake had told him; and Crabb Robinson's diary gives important accounts of Blake's conversation in his old age. But the men on whom we rely mainly for information knew Blake only superficially in his later years. Frederick Tatham compiled his account less than a year after Blake's widow died (that is, in late 1832). He wrote without checking anything, and where we can check him we find him seeking at all costs to fit Blake into a scheme of conventional piety. The young artists, the Ancients, who gathered round Blake in those last years, also wanted to fit him into acceptable patterns of visionary wisdom. Alan Cunningham in the first edition, 1830, of his *Lives of Painters, Sculptors, Architects*, presented Blake as madly composing poetry by night and sanely engraving by day, though in his second edition he added a more sympathetic account in the vein of the Ancients. The first serious Life was by Alexander Gilchrist (1828–61), who, in the later 1850s, did his best to collect reliable information and collate the testimonies of Blake's surviving acquaintances. After his early death at the age of thirty-three, his wife Anne completed the work. Inevitably they took over much of the sentimentalising trend of his informants. Their work, then, and the various reminiscences of the Ancients, which include Tatham's account, must be treated critically. For this reason it is important for the reader to know the source of any story about Blake.

I should like to make some general observations on the nature of Blake's creative achievement. His universe is so complex that it is easy to lose one's way up some tempting side-path in the rich landscape of his symbols. In writing his life one has a particularly difficult task in saying just enough, not too little or too much, of the ways in which he transforms experience in poetry and art.

First, we may claim that in him there came to a head the millenary and apocalyptic traditions of Christianity, which over the centuries had tended to revive at moments of extreme crisis and which the church in its established forms always found it difficult or impossible to control or contain. In these traditions (in which the forms of mystery-religion were used to express the desperate hopes of the enslaved and oppressed masses of the Roman Empire) the demand for a total change in society was powerfully expressed. Ancient mystery-religion was an adaptation to a developed class-society of the forms, ideas, and emotions of the passage-rite of initiation. The experience of ordeal, terror, loss and isolation was linked with the ritual-release of rebirth, of regeneration, of emergence on to a new level of living. In normal time the pattern could be limited to the individual existence, which was thus given a sense of value and significance, enabling it to carry on in a society which failed to be regenerated. But in times of crisis there was a return to the mass-element, to the demand that society itself be reborn and purified of its divisions and injustices. The last great period in which millenary emotions could be gathered and liberated on a wide scale and with a powerful relevance to the historical situation was that of the French Revolution. That period was the watershed between the old communal ways of life and the alienated world of bourgeois industrialism that was to follow. Men were aware of violent forces breaking down the old ways and precipitating new forms of organisation, but the labouring masses were only in the embryonic stages of being compacted into an industrial proletariat.

Millenary hopes were widespread and vigorous in the 1790s: Blake stands out as the supreme voice of the people at this decisive moment of change. He shared many ideas with other millenarians, and the hopes he expressed had many links with the militant forms of religious protest arising during the Cromwellian revolution. He carried on the traditions of the Ranters and Antinomians, seeking to apply them to a much more complicated and advanced world. But if that were all, he would be only an interesting and curious figure like Richard Brothers or Joanna Southcott. He was, however, also a great poet and was able to grasp all that was implied by the millenary

demands, and to apply it with ever-deepening comprehension to the
entangled situation in which he found himself.

He thus drew on a variety of dissident religious idioms, from that of the
Antinomians, who totally rejected the law and felt that by doing so they
moved at once into a sinless pastoral world where the lion lay down with the
lamb, to that of the millenarians who looked for some violent and shattering
event, a world-end that would overthrow all existing power-forms and
divisions. But because for Blake God was no more than a Man and the
purification or rebirth of the universe was to come about 'by an improvement
of sensual enjoyment', all that is most incisive and creative in his thought or
expression is directed towards life on earth, towards society and the individuals composing it, and not to other-worldly spheres. Inevitably many
ambiguities and difficulties arise when a religious idiom is thus used, and
Blake, by the nature of his situation, did not want to confront them except
intuitively and symbolically. But the extreme originality of his definitions
appears precisely in his huge struggle to secularise millenary religion without losing what was vital and inspiring in it: that element which had kept
alive in men, through years of hopeless division, a belief in an ultimate
brotherhood and equality, and which had given that belief a great uniting
force at crucial moments of change.

Blake uses the religious idiom because there was no other idiom in his
day that could affirm human unity with the fullness and depth that he
required. All the 'progressive' idioms of the period were keyed to bourgeois
needs, even when stretched to the limits, as in such concepts as those of
Paine's plebeian democracy or Godwin's abstract anarchism. Blake wanted
to go decisively beyond all such positions and to banish division and disintegration from every sphere of social and individual experience. The immediate political struggle then took on a deep human meaning by being viewed
and valued always in the focus of the full implications of the demand for
human unity. Blake's criterion was that everything which makes for division
is evil. The thirst for unity, which is never wholly quenched, proves that
men were once in an undivided state. (He has glimpses of the idea that this
stage was that of tribal society: a stage which has haunted men in a class-
society as a dream of a Golden Age or happy pastoral existence—the actual
level of development being glamorised in terms of the fresh potentialities
opening up in the divided society, which that society cannot truly realise, but
limits or distorts in various ways.) The only worthwhile goal for men can be
the regaining of the stage of brotherhood and freedom on a new, secure level.

So Blake devotes all his great poetic and analytic powers, first to defining and then to attacking the elements of division which operate in every form of activity or expression, unable to eradicate the desire for unity yet obstructing it all along the line. He defines this situation in aphoristic statements, in lyrics, and in his prophetic books. Unable to do without Biblical elements to give his imagery and symbols a point of reference to the culture of his world, he yet tears them away from their original contexts, which do not suit his message, and incorporates them in a myth-world of his own, so that Adam and Eve, Moses and Jesus, play their parts in a universe where events and values are determined by his own symbolic creations, Los and Urizen, Enitharmon and Vala, and the countless others.

Thus he explores all the relationships in his world, social, political, scientific, personal and sexual, as well as cultural, in order to show how the forces of division (the human Fall) have entered into all of them and how the counter-forces struggle to reverse the process. He is particularly interested in the science of fallen or divided man, which reflects his alienated condition even more sharply than his art, since its sets out directly his relation to the cosmos and reduces all nature (including his own) to mechanical forces and impacts. Such a gigantic voyage of exploration was without parallel, and it can be understood that Blake had to create a language of his own to embody his findings.

His task was thus twofold. He had to work out a philosophy of development and to depict concretely the patterns of historical movement. Every truly human moment is one in which the integrative elements are stronger than the divisive ones. Such a moment then brings together in open struggle the elements seeking to repeat the Fall and those aspiring to unity. It includes both the immediate experience and the comprehensive historical background, the forces of good and evil which are battling inside the individual experience. Hence the many simultaneities in Blake of the existential moment and the complex patterns of history unfolded in time. He comes closest to a direct statement of his dialectical system in his accounts of single, double, triple and fourfold vision, in his concept of contraries as necessary for progression, and in his descriptions of the social and psychological states named Beulah and Eternity, in which resolutions of the conflict of opposites are achieved, in temporary or stable forms. In thus grappling so fully and consistently with the problem of development he outdistances all the thinkers of his world apart from his younger contemporary Hegel. What Hegel achieved with all the rigours of philosophic method and terminology,

Blake achieved as a poet with his symbolic constructions. But his central concept (that men must and could and would transcend all the existing contradictions of their divided society and selves) made his ultimate kinship rather with the Marx of the 1844 Manuscripts. As no poet before or since, he was a total revolutionary.

Blake's attempt to set out all the essential movements of integration and disintegration brought a new dimension into the human consciousness. Poets like Virgil, Dante, or Milton had summed up many fundamental aspects of their society and had sought to make sense of the movement of history. But we cannot find in their work the Blakean concept of human unity, even though it operates at a subterranean level in determining their ultimate values. Only Blake brings the issue out into the open, so that it penetrates everywhere. In a new way he addresses *all men*.

So far we have discussed his content. Equally original and significant is the form that he worked out. Any of the old systems of verse could not but have fettered and finally drained the life-blood from his images and concepts. He needed a new form, oratorical in the sense he gives the term, yet clearly rhythmical in its organisation: concentrated and yet expanding in strength and vividness with the growth of the theme. He had antecedents such as the prose-poem, but he created something fundamentally new in his form, which now and then knits itself into lyric flight, but in the main consists of common speech achieving a new set of balances and unbalances, driving on in polyphonic variations and capable of release in symphonic crescendoes. The poetry had to evoke the all-round man who would be the inhabitant of a world of unity and freedom, so it was no accident that Blake could sing his own lyrics and that he carried his poetic imagery over into his pictorial art. He was both artist and craftsman, a prophet and yet a man who claimed no powers which would not be common property in a truly human society.

He was thus the first truly modern poet, and it is only with the twentieth century, indeed with the second half of it, that he has come fully into his own. First seen as a fascinating oddity, then with Rossetti and his group beginning to grasp something of his poetic insight and intensity, and with Swinburne praising him for his deep-going rebelliousness, he was at last recognised as a poet with a valid universe of his own, a fellow of the *Symbolistes*. But the full maturing of the crisis with which he had fiercely grappled was needed before the relevance of his complex messages could be realised; the terrible reality of his vision was brought home by two world wars and by the working out on a world scale of the conflicts, inner and outer, which he had defined. Other artists or poets have had to wait varying lengths of time before their contribution could be properly grasped; but none of them has had anything like the history of Blake and his work. To create that work he had to struggle to feel himself at the heart of the life-process, involved and responsible for everything that was happening, and yet to be torn apart in deep isolation, afraid of everything. The resulting tension kept him at the heart of the deep and wide changes going on in human life, and yet distanced him from it all. The vision of reality thus evolved was both too close and too distant for the men of his world and of the next few generations to get truly inside it. The tension was so great that it might well have torn him to pieces. Somehow, he managed always in the last resort to overcome the rending and crushing forces, and to set down effectively the pattern of his inner conflicts, which can now be seen as the pattern of all men struggling to become human in a world of thickening alienations.

Every reader interested in Blake should possess the Nonesuch edition of the complete poetry and prose, edited by Keynes, Erdman's edition of the poems with notes by W. H. Stevenson, or the Penguin edition of the poems edited by Alicia Ostriker. To one or other of these should be added the complete reproduction of the illuminated books edited by Erdman (Oxford University Press) and available at a low price. Finally I should like to thank Ms Christine Bernard for reading my MS and making suggestions for the better ordering of the material.

Jack Lindsay

Early Years, 1757–78

William Blake was born in the late autumn of 1757, the son of James Blake, hosier and haberdasher, at 28 Broad Street. This was a busy part of London, and William remained London-centred all his life, even more so than Hogarth or Dickens. 'I behold London; a Human awful wonder of God!' That was his late judgement and the basis of it was laid in his childhood. 'Infinite London's awful spires.' Round the corner was Carnaby Market where the slaughter-house with its lowing cattle numbered women among its butchers. Nearby, in the burial-grounds of Pawlett's Garden, stood St James's Workhouse, big enough to take in three hundred poor folk, spinning and weaving under harsh supervision; if they fell sick they were moved to an infirmary close to Broad Street. A short stroll down Marshall Street led to Golden Square with its grass plots and gravel walks cut off by iron rails, and a royal statue in the middle. The child looked through the rails at the forbidden greenery, and Golden Square provided later one of his models of Jerusalem, the redeemed earth.

There was an air of cosmopolitan gentry, with some streets given over to the French, who had their own places of worship (as in Hogarth's *Noon*), and at times foreign legations took houses round the Square. There were chapels of Anabaptists, Independents, Presbyterians and, not far off, the parish church of St James in Piccadilly. Many artists lived in the area. Angelica Kauffmann lived in Golden Square from 1769 to 1881; in Broad Street lived both the stipple-engraver Bartolozzi (from 1868 to 1874), and the engraver James Heath, with whom Blake was to work; and Fuseli lived at No 1, Poland Street between 1771 and 1781.[1]

James Blake seems to have been the son of another James, of Rotherhithe, a rather low-lying area south of London Bridge; he was bound as a draper's apprentice in 1737 for seven years. He lived from 1744 to 1753 at 5 Glass-house Street, where his brother John had moved the year before; in 1753 he moved to 28 Broad Street, having married Catherine Harmitage (or

Armitage) on 15 October 1752 in St George's Chapel, off Hanover Square, which was used for hasty weddings (fifteen others were solemnised on the same day) though two years later an Act of Parliament forbade the practice. James was about twenty-nine, his bride a year older. Their house, previously occupied by the Armitages, stood at the corner of Broad and Marshall Streets. It was valued at £21, with varying proportional rates, till 1782 when James protested at the revaluation of £30. There were four floors and a basement, a narrow stair-well leading to the sleeping quarters above. The first floor was taken up by a low-ceilinged room about twenty feet square (once divided into two or three rooms) with two fireplaces and a window. In all, three windows looked into Broad Street, while on the other side a window on each floor had been bricked up.

About nine months after the marriage the first child was born: a son James, on 10 July 1753, baptised in the parish church. A second son, John, born on 12 March 1755, seems to have died an infant. William arrived on 28 November 1757, and was baptised on 11 December, his father then being in his thirty-sixth year. A fourth son, born on 20 March 1760, was named John; Richard, born 19 June 1762, seems to have died an infant. Then, on 7 January 1764 a daughter, Catherine Elizabeth was born. The sixth and last son, Robert, was born on 4 August 1767.[2]

Thus William grew up with two older brothers and a younger brother and sister, in cramped but not uncomfortable quarters, child of a lower-middle-class tradesman. The accounts we have of the parents come from Blake's late acquaintances and are worth citing as long as we see them as conventionalised versions of passing remarks that he made in old age. The father was a hosier, 'of respectable Trade & easy habits & seems to have been well to do, of moderate desires, moderate enjoyments, & of substantial worth; his disposition was gentle, a lenient & affectionate Father, always more ready to encourage than to chide'. Mrs Blake 'has been represented as being possessed of all those Endearing Sympathies, so peculiar to maternal tenderness'. The eldest son James, who inherited the business in 1784, was 'an honest, unpretending shopkeeper in an old-world style', continuing to wear knee-breeches, worsted stockings and buckles, and concerned only with money; he was conventional; but though in general a humble, matter-of-fact man, 'he had his spiritual and visionary side too; would at times *talk Swedenborg*, talking of seeing Abraham and Moses'. Outsiders thought him a bit mad, like William, though 'a mild madman instead of wild and stormy'. He looked on William as 'wilful, misguided, wholly in the wrong track;

while the latter despised him for his grovelling, worldly mind'. Despite these comments it is clear that William remained on good terms throughout his life with the others of the family, apart from John.

We may assume that the family was religiously inclined, though certainly they were not Swedenborgians. One account makes the father a Moravian of the Fetter Lane Chapel. This seems likely in view of William's later views, for the Moravians stressed the Lamb and the freedom of the regenerated, and had something like veneration for the sexual organs. Mr Blake is called 'devout'. But though he was buried in the dissenters' cemetery, Bunhill Fields, he had his children baptised in the parish church. Perhaps although he dissented he shrank from making a definite break. Certainly from early years Blake would have heard the Bible read, and no doubt also *Pilgrim's Progress*. He came early to know Milton's poems. We have some stories of his childhood, which he told to the admiring group of young artists in his old age. They show how he looked back on his childhood: family tales of the sort likely to be told any imaginative child and losing nothing in the retelling over the years.[3]

Crabb Robinson records Blake's wife as saying to him, 'You know, dear, the first time you saw God was when you were four years old, and He put His head to the window, and set you a-screaming.' Gilchrist has two tales. On Peckham Rye, by Dulwich Hill, aged eight or ten, Blake saw a tree filled with angels. He told of the vision at home and only through his mother's intercession escaped a thrashing from his father, for telling a lie. Again, one summer morn, he saw haymakers at work with angelic figures walking among them. One day a traveller (apparently in the shop) was telling of a foreign city. 'Do you call *that* splendid?' William broke in. 'I should call a city splendid in which the houses were of gold, the pavement of silver, the gates ornamented with precious stones.' He was already familiar with the Book of Revelation.

His wanderings were to the south of the river, over Westminster Bridge to St George's Fields, scene of the Wilkite demonstrations in the 1760s; then to the village of Newington Butts and through open fields and hedgerows or to Dulwich, with hilly Sydenham to the south and Blackheath to the east. Favourite later rambles led along lane and footpath to Blackheath or over Dulwich and Norwood hills, through the old town of Croydon, to the meadows of Walton-upon-Thames. Such walks provided Blake with a contrast to the crowded London streets. For all his talk against Nature in later years he early imbibed a deep and abiding love of all natural scenes and creatures, for tree and flower and the sunlight of the open fields.

The story of his mother's intercession reminds us of the *Songs of Innocence*, where it is the mother who finds the little boy lost by the father, or comforts the black child longing for the father-god's love. But his father must in fact have been rather indulgent. 'Like the Arabian Horse, he [William] is said to have so hated a Blow that his Father thought it most prudent to withhold from him the liability of receiving punishment. He picked up his Education as well as he could. His talent for Drawing manifested itself as spontaneously as it was premature, he was already sketching.' We are told that his mother privately encouraged him to draw, then his father 'began to be pleased with the notice which his son obtained'. He consulted an eminent artist, but was deterred by the fee asked for instruction. The boy 'declared he would prefer being an engraver—a profession that would bring bread at least, and through which he would be connected with painting'.

These accounts no doubt simplify the facts of a long struggle in which William was aided by mother in his wish to be some kind of artist. What is clear is his extremely obstinate and intractable, even violent, temperament, his passionate resistance to any course that did not gain his whole-hearted assent. At the age of ten he went to the art-school run by Henry Pars in Beaufort Buildings in the Strand, a preparatory art-school then in vogue. The pupils drew only from casts, and James Blake bought various casts for William to use at home. After a while the boy was given small sums to buy prints. The auctioneer Longford is said to have called him his Little Connoisseur and to have knocked down for him a cheap lot in kindly haste. Against the prevailing taste for Guido Reni and the Carracci, William is said to have preferred the clear line of artists like Raphael, Michelangelo and Dürer, earning the mockery of his fellow-students for his 'mechanical taste'. (In his later memories Blake may well have been projecting back in oversimplified form the positions he had then reached; but from the outset he clearly had an independent mind.)

About 1769 his father may have joined the Baptists of Grafton Street; the name Blake appears in the registers, but no Christian names are given. Such an act would explain why Robert was not baptised in the parish church and why James and his wife, with Robert and William of their sons, were buried in Bunhill Fields. But the Moravian connection is more likely than the Baptist. In August 1771 Swedenborg came to London, where he died in March 1772; but there is no sign of his early influencing Blake, who had now begun composing verse. Malkin must have been repeating what Blake had told him when later he said that *How sweet I roamed* was written before he was fourteen. The poem seems remarkably mature for such an age; Blake may have been exaggerating, or he may have revised the poem before it got into print. In it the singer, wandering in the fields, meets Cupid, Prince of Love, who reveals his paradisiac garden. The singer, who is apparently a girl, bursts into song and is imprisoned in a cage by Love like a bird.

In the summer of 1772 Blake ended his schooling and had to decide what trade to follow. No doubt he would have liked to become a painter, but the family could only afford to have him trained as an engraver. He was first taken to Rylands, engraver to the King, who had brought in Boucher's stippling technique; but on leaving he said that he disliked the man's face. 'It looks as if he will live to be hanged.' Twelve years later Rylands was hanged for a forgery on the East India Company. Here again is a tale that must have lost nothing in being retold over the years. Rylands would probably have asked for a £100 premium, his print-selling business had gone bankrupt in December 1771 and he may have already seemed a suspect character.

William was apprenticed on Tuesday, 4 August 1772, to James Basire of Great Queen Street, Lincoln's Inn Fields, for fifty guineas, with the usual clauses binding him to good behaviour and abstention from fornication or matrimony. Basire was to impart his Art and Mystery, finding the lad 'Meat, Drink, Apparel, Lodgings, and all other Necessaries' during his indenture. Aged forty-one, Basire had worked for Hogarth in the latter's last days and was now employed by the Society of Antiquaries. A portrait done by his son preserves his honest face under a bob-wig. His style was hard, firm and correct in outline, and was liked by scholars. Softer styles such as that of Bartolozzi were coming in, but Blake till the end stayed faithful to the principles of strong outline that Basire taught. He lived in his master's house till 1779, visiting his parents on Sundays and finding time to write lyrics. The house had been built in the seventeenth century and 'refaced early in the Georgian era, the parapet then put up half-hiding the old dormor [sic] window of the third story' (Gilchrist).

Basire had two young sons at the time, and on 3 August 1773 he took in as apprentice James Parker, son of a corn-chandler, who became friendly with Blake. Many scholars would have called in at such a shop as Basire's, and Oliver Goldsmith was among them. Blake liked to recount how he 'mightily admired the great author's head, and thought to himself how much *he* should like to have such a head when he grew to be a man'.

It was in these years that he acquired a copy of Winckelmann's *Reflections on the Painting and Sculpture of the Greeks* (1765); for he added to his signature the address, Lincoln's Inn. The book exalted the naked human form, disapproved of drawing from the model, preferred general forms and ideal images, and praised drapery that brought out rather than obscured the body. It stressed 'precision of Contour, that characteristic distinction of the ancients'. These ideas sank deep into Blake's mind and for long he saw Greek art as supreme. But he was also learning to love Gothic art. Here was a union and conflict of opposites that took a long time to work out.

From 1774 he was sent regularly to sketch the tombs in Westminster Abbey. Many years later he described in a letter how one day he saw the aisles and galleries suddenly filled with a procession of monks, priests, choristers and censer-bearers, and heard the chant of plainsong and organ music that made the vaulted roof tremble. We are told that the vergers often shut him in as he worked, and 'sometimes his dreaming eye saw more palpable shapes from the past: once a vision of "Christ and the Apostles", as he used to tell.' In his last years Palmer asked how he would like to paint on glass for the Abbey's west window his sons of God shouting for joy, and after a pause he said, 'I could do it', kindling at the thought.[4]

The boys of Westminster School played in the Abbey and teased the absorbed artist. One of them climbed up on a pinnacle level with the scaffold from which he was drawing. William threw him to the ground so that he fell 'with terrific Violence', and then complained to the Dean, who withdrew the boys' privileges. As they went into the Abbey for daily services, the Dean's order must have been that they kept away from the chapels where Blake was working. Blake's furious action was in key with what we heard of his tantrums as a child, but in sad contrast with his later idealisation of the freedom of children.[5]

Malkin, drawing on what Blake had told him, stated that the work in the Abbey had a powerfully formative effect on his style and his ideas about art. Blake drew the monuments surrounding the chapel of Edward the Confessor 'in every point he could catch, frequently standing in the monument, and viewing the figures from the top. The heads he considered as portraits; and all the ornaments appeared as miracles of art'. He also drew in other churches in and around London. He so identified himself with the buildings that he 'himself almost became a Gothic monument'. Discovering Gothic as 'living form', he admired its 'firm and correct outline'. Still in his last years, says Palmer, 'everything connected with Gothic art and churches, and their builders, was a passion with him'.

He seems certainly to have been present at the opening of Edward I's tomb in May 1774; for the comments added to two pencil drawings of the event resemble in their script his earliest known manuscript. One drawing shows the body 'as it appeared on first opening the Coffin', the other 'as it appeared when some of the vestments were remov'd'. Ayloffe, who described the opening, says that Edward's head and face were covered with a wrap of crimson sarsenet that had a cobwebby feel and the look of fine lint. The body was cased in close-fitting fine linen; the face retained its exact form. Blake was to develop a system of tight garments, at times seeming to flow in a filmy way out of the limbs. It seems that he was deeply affected by the apparition of the king with the cerecloth as a sort of spirit-covering, formed to the body and drifting out from it rather than covering it. The tomb-opening may indeed well have had the effect of bringing the Gothic world to strange life, felt to unveil the reality behind the sculptures and to lead back to medieval life in all its mysterious fullness.[6]

In the winter chills, leaving the Abbey, he would have helped to engrave the drawings he had made. In 1810, discussing engraving styles and championing that of Marc Antonio and Dürer, he gives us a glimpse of his days with Basire:

What is Call'd the English Style of Engraving, such as proceeded from the Toilettes of Woolett & Strange (for theirs was Fribble's Toilettes) can never produce Character & Expression. I knew the Men intimately, from their Intimacy with Basire, my Master, & knew them both to be heavy lumps of Cunning & Ignorance . . . Woolett I know did not know how to Grind his Graver. I know this; he has often proved his Ignorance before me at Basire's by laughing at Basire's knife tools & ridiculing the Forms of Basire's other Gravers till Basire was quite dash'd & out of Conceit with what he himself knew, but his Impudence had a Contrary Effect on me.

Malkin, drawing on Blake, says that the first two years 'passed over smoothly enough, till two other apprentices were added to the establishment, who completely destroyed its harmony'. Blake 'declined to take part with his master against his fellow-apprentices', being, in Basire's words, 'too simple and they too cunning'. So he was sent to the Abbey or other churches to draw monuments for the antiquarian Gough: 'a circumstance he always mentioned with gratitude towards Basire'. The records show that there were no new apprentices; but some sort of discord must have arisen in the workshop through Blake's intransigence and quick temper. Tatham tells much the same tale as Malkin, speaking of 'frequent quarrels with his fellow apprentices, concerning matters of intellectual argument'.[7]

Blake was now trying out his own designs. In 1773 he made an engraving: 'Joseph of Arimithea among the Rocks of Albion. Michael Angelo Pinxit. Engraved by W. Blake from an old Italian Drawing.' He added an explanation: 'This is One of the Gothic Artists who Built the Cathedrals in what we call the Dark Ages, Wandering about in sheep skins & goat skins, of whom the world was not Worthy; which were the Christians in all Ages.' But the impression thus given that he had arrived at his mature ideas in 1773 is delusive. The inscription is in a style dated about 1810. In 1773 all that Blake did was to copy and engrave a large powerful figure from an old engraving. He kept a pull of the work in his portfolio and many years later wrote at the bottom: 'Engraved when I was a beginner at Basire's from a drawing by Salviati after Michael Angelo.' He may in fact have used an engraving of the figure attributed to the Frenchman Béatrizat, though the source is in any event Michelangelo's fresco of the Crucifixion of St Peter. Blake added the sea and rocks at the back. Twenty years later he took up the plate, rubbed the surface, and almost completely re-engraved it. The figure has the classical foot (second toe larger than great toe) which he used throughout his career. In 1774 he made a drawing of Moses in the same general style as his Joseph.[8]

There was nothing unusual in Blake's enthusiasm for both Gothic and Greek art. Thomas Warton in his poem on Reynolds' painted window at New College, Oxford, sees medieval art as the work of 'elfin sculptors, with fantastic clew', and sets as the ideal 'to reconcile The Willing Graces to the Gothic pile'. In his poem on Vale-Royal Abbey he writes both of 'visionary gleams' and of 'daedal forms of ancient art'. Romney in Italy in 1775 was finding out 'the great simplicity and purity of Cimabue', and so on, without feeling any conflict with his neoclassic ideas. Thus arose Romantic Neoclassicism.[9]

Blake was making prints for other books than those of the antiquarians. Of special importance for him was his work in J. Bryant's *New System, or an Analysis of Ancient Mythology*, 1774–6. This book left a lasting impress in the idea of a primeval basis common to all myths and religions; and some of its symbols continued to haunt him: an Ark shaped like a crescent moon, a line of figures with arms raised and crossed, a snake entwining the world-egg, man-headed bulls which he used long before the granite bulls of Nineveh were dug up.[10]

In 1776 came the Declaration of Independence by the American colonists, which gained much support from London's strong radical elements. Popular cartoons had titles like *The State Blacksmiths forging fetters for the Americans*, 1776. Blake was deeply stirred. In 1800 he summed up the main influences of his life:

> Now my lot in the Heavens is this, Milton lov'd me in childhood &
>   shew'd me his face;
> Ezra came with Isaiah the Prophet, but Shakespeare in riper years gave
>   me his hand;
> Paracelsus & Behmen appear'd to me, terrors appear'd in the Heavens
>   above
> And in Hell beneath, & a mighty & awful change threatened the Earth.
> The American War began. All its dark horrors passed before my face
> Across the Atlantic to France. Then the French Revolution commenc'd
>   in thick clouds ...

He sets out four stages or groups of influences. First Milton and the Biblical Prophets; then the liberation in poetry represented by Shakespeare; then the movement into the full expansion of his ideas represented by the mystics; then the political impact of the American and French Revolutions.

His early poems gathered in *Poetical Sketches* give us the key to what he was thinking and feeling in the 1770s, though we have to rely on internal evidence for dating the nineteen poems, the dramatic fragments, and the three prose-poems. There are also two prose-poems in manuscript which seem composed before 1777. The shorter piece is doom-laden, a lament over sweet Elfrid cut off in the morning of her days. Oddly, though Blake of all our great poets was the least interested in the iambic pentameter, his inflated prose tends to fall into just that metre. The opening of this fragment can thus be set out in verse-form:

> Woe, cried the muse, tears started at the Sound.
> Grief percht upon my brow and thought Embrac'd Her.
> 'What does this mean,' I cried, 'when all around
> Summer hath spread her Plumes and tunes her Notes.

> When Buxton Joy doth fan his wings
> & Golden Pleasures beam around my head?
> Why, Grief dost thou accost me?'

The longer fragment, *Then she bore pale Desire*, needs much more consideration than has been given it. Though poor in itself, it reveals the awakening
of Blake's mind and shows in rough elementary form the method later
elaborated with vast subtlety in the prophetic books. At first glance it seems
a drawn-out tissue of personifications in conventional style. But, however
confusedly, Blake is trying to set out a scheme of man's historical
development.

First come Desire and Sloth, from whom is born Ignorance. These are
the gods derived from Fear, neither male nor female. They war with
Shame. Pride awakes, unaware that Joy is born, and herself bears Ambition.
She then 'Prophetic saw the Kingdoms of the World & all their Glory,
Giants of Mighty arm, before the Flood, Cain's city built with Murder'.
Babel rears up. Then we are shown Nineveh, Babylon, Athens with her
learning, and 'Rome, seated on seven hills, the mistress of the world,
Emblem of Pride'. Next we turn back to the east, to Constantine's great
city created by the flight of imperial power from Rome. 'Empire fled, Ere
long to bleed & die, sacrifice done by a Priestly hand'. (This is the only
reference that he makes to Christianity.) Rome revives under the papal
crown. 'Then Pride was better Pleas'd'. However, 'full to the Setting Sun,
a Sun arose out of the Sea; it rose, & shed Sweet influence o'er the Earth.
Pride feared for her City, but not long, for looking steadfastly, she saw that
Pride Reign'd here'.[11]

The new sun rising out of the sea seems to represent the American
revolution, but Blake does not develop the point. On the one side is the
new sun, on the other is the world still ruled by pride, 'here'. However, he
does launch into an account of a sort of cosmic conflict, with personifications
pullulating. There is a Fall. 'Conscience was sent, a Guard to Reason,
Reason once fairer than the light, till foul'd in Knowledge's dark Prison
house. For knowledge drove sweet Innocence away, and Reason would have
follow'd, but fate suffer'd not; then down came Conscience with his lovely
band.' We have here a crude version of the conflict of innocence and
experience. There follows the tale of Pride's revolt against her father.
'Down his white Beard the silver torrents Roll and swelling sighs burst
forth, his Children all in arms appear to tear him from his throne.' Pride

usurps the power of all the gods. Shame opposes her and she bears Rage. Then Shame bears Honour and makes league with Pride. 'Meanwhile Strife, Mighty Prince, was born', He brings forth Revenge, while Care brings forth Covet. So, amid a turmoil of uniting and dividing forces, we reach the critique of the existing system, where the City has concentrated all the divisive tendencies. 'Policy brought forth Guile & fraud; these Gods last nam'd live in the Smoke of Cities, on Dusky wing breathing forth Clamour & Destruction; alas, in Cities where's the man whose face is not a mask unto his heart?' So the chant ends with the accusation that the City destroys all natural relations. (Nature and Reason are still terms for what Blake most admires.) 'Go see the city, friends Join'd Hand in Hand. Go see the Natural tie of flesh & blood. Go see more strong the tie of marriage love—thou Scarce Shall find, but Self love Stands Between.'[12]

Blake is thus confusedly seeking to grapple with a situation dominated by emulation (competition) and self-love; and in the way he attempts to define a central force continually breaking up and regaining unity we see the rough sketch of his later forms of prophetic imagery. He is struggling to create a myth to explain why things have gone wrong. The picture of Hate, for instance, has elements that reappear in his later symbolism:

> The Gods all serve her at her will; so great her Power is, like fabled Hecate, she doth bind them to her law. Far in a Direful Cave she lives unseen, Clos'd from the Eye of Day, to the hard Rock transfixt by fate, and here she works her witcheries, that when she Groans she shakes the Solid Ground.

Though seeking the inner clue of history, he shows no respect for religion and gives no hint of Christ. His interest in the fall of the Roman Empire in the West and the shift to Constantinople suggests strongly that he had been reading Gibbon, and reading him sympathetically. At one point he intrudes on the story, linked with Envy. 'My cup is fill'd with Envy's Rankest Draughts.' He insists: ' 'tis Envy that inspires my Song; prickt by the fame of others now I mount, and my complaints are Sweeter than their Joys; but O, should I at Envy Shake my hands, my notes should Rise to meet the New born Day'.[13]

Artist and Poet, 1779–84

William was free of his indentures in August 1779. At this time about half the boys apprenticed at Stationers Hall went on to become freemen of their guild, but neither William nor Parker took the step formally needed for setting up on one's own. William applied for admission to the ten-year-old Royal Academy of the Arts. Such an applicant was required to submit a drawing, with a testimonial from a respected artist, to the Keeper. He then worked for three months as probationer in the Antique School, making an outline drawing of an anatomical figure with lists of muscles and tendons. Then he could apply to be a full student. On Friday, 8 October, Blake was admitted 'to study as an engraver'.

The Academy had had its cramped premises in Old Somerset Palace pulled down in 1775 and was awaiting a new home. The students were given to rough fun. We hear later of them 'playing at leapfrog, knocking off the hand of Michelangiolo's beautiful Fawn, spouting water, breaking the fingers of the Apollo, pelting one another with modeller's clay and crusts of bread, roasting potatoes in the stove, teizing the Keeper by imitating cats'.[1]

Over twenty years later Blake told of a conversation with the Keeper G. M. Moser, an enamel-painter and modeller of the Great Seal, a favourite of Reynolds. He was looking at prints from Raphael and Michelangelo in the Library when Moser came up to him and said, 'You should not study these old Hard Still & Dry Unfinishd Works of Art.' Instead he offered Blake works after Le Brun and Rubens. 'How I did secretly rage. I also spoke my mind . . . These things that you call Finishd are not even Begun how can they then, be Finishd? The Man who does not know The Beginning, never can know the End of Art.' Considering how highly Reynolds regarded Raphael and Michelangelo, Moser's behaviour is very odd and one wonders if Blake's memory is not oversimplifying. But certainly from very early, partly as a result of drawing from plaster casts and copying engravings with clear-cut forms, he felt put out by the richness and complexity of the living body.[2]

Two stories deal with his relations with Reynolds. The latter remarked, 'Well, Mr Blake, I hear you despise our art of oil-painting.' 'No, Sir Joshua,' said Blake, 'I don't despise it; but I like fresco better.' (What Blake always called fresco was in fact painting in tempera.) Gilchrist tells us that Reynolds advised him 'to work with less extravagance and more simplicity, and to correct his drawing. This Blake seemed to regard as an affront never to be forgiven. He was very indignant when he spoke of it.' He was indeed incapable of listening to any criticism, partly through a strong sense of insecurity, partly because of the need to protect the more original aspects of his convictions from a world unable to understand them.

He continued to do odd jobs for the booksellers Johnson and Harrison, and now and then for others. One illustration was from his own design, the frontispiece to *An Elegy Set to Music* by T. Commins, 1786. His style was being much influenced by Stothard. He later recalled the period with resentment, complaining (unfairly, it seems) 'of this mechanical employment as an engraver to a fellow designer', who borrowed from him, then set him to copy the version he had made of his work 'as to motive and composition' (Gilchrist). However his main hopes were directed towards original works in watercolour with themes from medieval history. *The Penance of Jane Shore* was probably done while he was still with Basire, in 1779. Soon after we meet the engraved *Edward* and *Eleanor*, and a watercolour sketch, *The Death of Earl Godwin*. To the same group belong such works as *The Ordeal of Queen Emma* and *The Keys of Calais*. He was trying to work out his ideas in terms of historical themes: divine vengeance on murder (Godwin choking), mercy (Calais), self-sacrificing love (Eleanor sucking poison from the wounded prince), the vicious hypocrisy of religious accusers (Emma and Jane). The effect of the Abbey carvings appears in Emma's drapery. Blake is seen to be strongly affected by the romantic neoclassic trend found in the medieval themes of Angelica Kauffmann, W. Hamilton and J. H. Mortimer (whom he greatly admired). Effects from the stage appear in the works of the school, and Blake was no doubt also moved by Shakespearean and other plays with themes that interested him. Thus the theme of Jane Shore, taken up not only by him but also by Hamilton and Edward Penny in 1776, was linked with Rowe's play about that heroine (revived with Mrs Siddons in 1782). Blake's settings were not accurate, but the atmosphere and even the costumes were more truly medieval than anything in Mortimer's works.

In the Academy exhibition of 1780, showing his *Earl Godwin*, he gave the Broad Street address. George Cumberland, painter and etcher, who worked for an insurance company and perhaps already knew him, said in the *Morning Chronicle* of 27 May that in the painting 'though there is nothing to be said of the colouring, may be discovered a good design, and much character'.[3]

In June he was suddenly involved for a moment in the history which fascinated him. The Gordon Riots broke out. Gilchrist says that he 'long remembered an involuntary participation'. On the fifth day of the riots the crowd wrecked a Catholic mass-house in Warwick Street, Golden Square. Francis Wheatley drew the tumults in Broad Street, and James Heath, who lived in the street, engraved the scene. The crowd moved from Leicester Fields (now Square), where they smashed the house of Justice Hyde, along Long Acre, past Basire's house, and down Holborn, making for Newgate. Blake was caught up, says Gilchrist, forced by the surging mass to 'witness the storm and burning of the fortress-like prison, and the release of its three hundred inmates'. But what we may be sure happened was that he joined the crowd in Broad Street and was swept along excitedly to Newgate. Significantly he made the Bastille the emblem of royal tyranny in his *French Revolution*.[4]

Stirred as he had been by the American rebellion a few years before, he must have seen the London uprising as the revolutionary upsurge invading Britain itself. An important element of the mob's driving-force was the conviction that the king wanted to use the Catholics against the Americans. People were saying that Catholic armies were being raised in Canada, Scotland and Ireland, while Catholics were slipping into many of the highest places to act as agents of tyranny. All the spring there were meetings of gentlemen agitating for reform, talking of the Rights of the People, the Majesty of the People. Some speakers insisted that Ireland had won independence by the force of sixty thousand bayonets and that if Parliament now ignored the people, the same means would be needed in England. In the Riots the populace were taking up the reform-agitation in their own way. The day that saw Blake on the streets was that when some of the 'better sort of tradesmen' dropped out, and journeymen, apprentices, servants, and even some criminals were out in strength. What Blake witnessed remained in his mind as the image of revolution: a great movement of the people, with uproar, burning houses and prisons, enormous exultation. The Riots brought to a powerful head all that he had been imagining about the American rebellion, and provided the elemental imagery of revolt and release in the prophetic books.

About the same time he read and responded to Boehme and Paracelsus. Probably our poet was the William Blake who in 1779 appears in the list of subscribers (with the engraver W. Sharp and Jacob Bryant, who are dignified as Esquires) to *Discourses on Various Subjects* by Jacob Duché, a preacher who, losing hope in the patriot cause, had come to England in 1777 and who had long been interested in 'the mysticism of Jacob Behmen and William Law'. Duché was later drawn to the visions of Swedenborg, as was Sharp, who engraved the frontispiece to the *Discourses*, and Blake himself took from Boehme the doctrine that the Eternal Man was bisexual. Boehme too may have strengthened his way of looking on the tales and characters of the Old Testament as symbolic. He told Crabb Robinson in his last years that the diagrams in Law's translation of Boehme could not have been bettered by Michelangelo: another example of his liking for schematic forms.[5]

Paracelsus gave him the important idea of the interaction of opposites to form the alchemical unity of generation. Blake studied *Three Books of Philosophy* (1657) with its concept of creation as a series of divisions inside an original unity, caused by an inferior god. The first division was fourfold, into non-material elements; the final division was to be the Last Judgement when all illusions and falsities would be destroyed and the cosmos left in its fundamental eternal form. Paracelsus held the imagination to be the central function of man, the source of all his activities. In *Paracelsus his Archidoxies*, 1661, it is stated that the imagination is the sun of man; it irradiates the earth, which is man. The whole heaven is nothing but imagination, and as man imagines himself to be, 'such he is, and he is also that which he imagines'.

Blake thus took from Boehme and Paracelsus ideas that were to be central to his thought, his art, his poetry. But apart from particular debts, at this crucial moment of growth he learned something essential to his whole creative vision. He learned to look inside the events that stirred him for their full meanings and to relate them to a concept of development which took in history, the cosmos, the desires, passions and activities of men, in a unitary perspective. The working out of the implications of this discovery was to take up the rest of his life. An important point is that the vital impact of the thinkers was inseparable from the political impact of the American Revolution and the Gordon Riots.[6]

2

He now attempted to make at least one drawing in which he might concentrate his sense of the great import of the Riots within the new philosophical perspective that had opened up: the work misnamed *Glad Day*. We know of it because about 1800 he looked at it and decided to engrave it. To keep the link with situation that had inspired it, he wrote, 'WB inv. 1780'. What he had drawn was a naked man standing in a gesture of great energy and determination on a mountain-top, his hair running into flame-points. A couplet explained that the single figure represented Mankind, following his idea that 'Multitudes of Men in Harmony' appear 'as One Man'. This idea may have clarified in his mind in 1780 during the Riots: a handbill *The Scourge* set out the need of 'persevering and being united as One Man, against the infernal designs of the Ministry'. Holcroft cited this handbill in his *Narrative of the Late Riots*, 1780, so that it may have been well known. In any event it shows the idiom of mass protests being used. Blake added to the print:

> Albion arose from where he labourd at the Mill with Slaves
> Giving himself for the Nations he danc'd the dance of Eternal
> Death.

By 1800 Albion for Blake is the Ancient or Universal Man, not a geographical term; he is the People. 'Labourd at the Mill' suggests not only the industrial wage-slave but also the hero Samson ready to sacrifice himself to ensure the salvation of his people. Further, expressing resurrection, the image is one of the triumphant Sun dispelling the creatures of night and death. (In 1796 Burke, dealing with 'the portentous crisis' brought about by the Gordon Riots, speaks of 'the death-dance of democratic revolution'; for Blake it is the life-dance.) Interestingly, in this work, the first original symbolic image in Blake's art of which we know, Blake fell back on a schematic drawing, a textbook diagram of human proportions, in Scamuzzi's treatise on Architecture, for the basic pattern.[7]

Blake was now on friendly terms with several artists. Besides Cumberland, there were Thomas Stothard, painter, already known as designer of vignettes for books with a sentimental charm, and Thomas Flaxman, a young sculptor. The latter had been discovered by the Rev. A. S. Mathew as he sat, sickly, behind the counter in his father's Strand plaster-cast shop, trying to learn Latin. Mathew lent him books, and Mrs Mathew read Homer aloud as he drew. Seeing some of Blake's work, he asked Stothard to introduce him. A precocious prize-winner, he became (in Josiah Wedgwood's phrase) 'a most supreme Coxcomb', till his failure to win an R.A. medal gave him a shock. For a livelihood he made designs and wax models for the cameo-wares of Wedgwood and Bentley. Wedgwood dubbed him the Genius of Sculpture but gave him less commissions when he raised his prices. Later he won fame as a carver of tombs, but at this time he still had to be frugal. Blake grew attached to him, indeed to some extent emotionally dependent, if we may trust his 1800 letter which thanks the 'Father of Heaven & Earth that ever I saw Flaxman's face', and declares, 'I could not subsist on the Earth, but by conjunction with Flaxman, who knows how to forgive Nervous Fear'.

Blake, Stothard, Cumberland and others went on sailing trips down the Thames. Probably in September 1780, when the country was at war with France, Blake, Stothard, and a friend (as recounted seventy years later by Stothard's daughter-in-law) went sketching up the Medway. As they were drawing on the shore, some soldiers arrested them on suspicion of being French spies. Their provisions were brought ashore, 'and a tent formed for them of their sails, suspended over the boat-hook and oars, placed as uprights in the ground. They were then detained, with a sentinel placed over them, until intelligence could be received from certain members of the Royal Academy.' Stothard made a pen-and-ink sketch of the scene. 'On their liberation they spent a merry hour with the commanding officer.'[8]

Flaxman introduced Blake to the salon that Mrs Mathew was trying to form. Stothard had met Blake through Trotter, an engraver and draughtsman of designs printed on calico, a conventional pietist like Flaxman, who resided in the Strand with the miniaturist Shelley. Flaxman, prim and prudish, tried to live by rules: hence the name that Blake gave him in his squib *An Island in the Moon* of Steelyard (weights and measures). During 1782–7, before he went to Italy, he collected the watch-rate for the parish of St Ann's; Smith noted him on the job with an ink-bottle in his buttonhole. So Steelyard is also called Lawgiver, a tax-collector who must 'stand & bear every fool's insult' and cope with any brats who answer the door, however much he'd like to 'wring off their noses'. His only oath is Poo Poo, and he is worried that Parliament will abolish his tax-collecting job. We see that Blake had no illusions about Flaxman and treats him, as Steelyard, with something like contempt. Still, for the moment he was enjoying his companionship with other artists. An obituary of Flaxman (perhaps by Cumberland) remarks that 'In early life he was in the habit of frequently passing his evenings in drawing and designing in the company of that excellent painter Mr Stothard, Mr Blake the engraver', Cumberland and Sharp.[9]

Henry Fuseli, after a visit to England as a youth, returned from his native Switzerland in 1780; but it was probably a few years before Blake came to know this artist whom he admired for his wit, daring and originality. The Irishman James Barry was no doubt already known. Blake liked his scorn both of the profitable portrait and of academic procedures. Barry aspired to grandiose history painting. Failing to get his scheme for St Paul's adopted, he went to the Society of Arts with sixteen shillings in his pockets and offered his services free. He worked on a set of vast pictures on Human Improvement (completed 1783) and wrote a pamphlet on his aims. A rapid lively sketch by Blake of his pugnacious face exists, tipped into a copy of the *Account*, and Blake records, 'Barry told me that while he Did that Work, he Lived on Bread & Apples. O Society for Encouragement of Art! O King & Nobility, of England!' Barry had known Wilkes and was friendly with many leading radicals including William Godwin. That Blake knew Barry well is unlikely, but he followed his career with passionate attention and long remembered him. At one time he wrote, or meant to write, a poem entitled *Barry*. Barry was quarrelsome, sprinkling his coarse speech with oaths, though liable to move into discourses on the meekness of Jesus. Such behaviour endeared him to Blake, who was also impressed by his readiness to write diatribes in self-defence and in attack on the establishment.[10]

With at least one member of his family Blake was now on close terms. He and his young brother Robert, says Tatham, 'sympathised in their pursuits and sentiments, like plants planted side by side, by a stream they grew together, & entwined the luxuriant Tendrils of their Expanding minds. They associated & excelled together.' Robert was 'of amiable & docile temper, & of a tender & affectionate mind'. This relationship could hardly have begun till William had left Basire, when Robert was about twelve. The latter seems certainly the Robert Blake admitted to the R.A. on 2 April 1782, to study as engraver. Of William's relations with his sister and his other brothers we know little. John was apprenticed to a gingerbread baker: at an enormous premium, we are told. But the normal charge of bakers for apprentices was small, at most about £20, and John does not appear in the apprentice lists. He did however become a baker, probably working awhile under relatives such as Robert and Peter Blake of Rupert Street, and then borrowing money (say £100) to set up for himself. In 1787–8 he paid Poor Rates on a house valued at £20 in Hog Lane, east of Soho Square.

William was now at last showing an interest in girls. In his twenty-fourth year he fell in love with a young woman, Polly Wood, who (says Tatham) 'was no trifler, he wanted to marry her but she refused, & was obstinate as she was unkind'. He kept company with her some time, suffering much jealousy. 'When he complained that the favour of her company on a stroll had been extended to another admirer, "Are you a fool?" was the brusque reply—with a scornful glance. "That cured me of jealousy," Blake used naively to relate' (Gilchrist). He fell ill and went for a change of air to Kew and lodged with a market-gardener, Boutcher.

He was relating to the daughter, a Girl named Catherine, the lamentable story of Polly Wood, his implacable Lass, upon which Catherine expressed her deep sympathy, it is supposed in such a tender & affectionate manner, that it quite won on him, he immediately said with the suddenness peculiar to him 'Do you pity me?' 'Yes, indeed I do' answered she. 'Then I love you' said he again. Such was their courtship.

Tatham must have based this account on what Catherine herself told him. She had previously declared that she had seen none 'among her acquaintances she could fancy for a husband'; but the moment she entered the room where Blake was, she instantly recognised 'her future partner, & was so near fainting that she left his presence until she had recovered'. After their meeting Blake left the house, with health and spirits recovered, determined to marry Catherine. 'He returned to his Lodgings, & worked incessantly that he might be able to accomplish this End, at the same time resolving that he would not see her until he succeeded. So they were parted for a year. Then he married her.'

This, anyway, was the romanticised version of their wooing as they told it in their last years. As the marriage took place on Tuesday, 18 August 1782, the first meeting would have occurred about July 1781. In a late drawing Catherine tried to catch the eager ardour of her young lover, giving him hair that flows like fire and thus suggests the figure of *Albion arose*. Tatham described Blake's looks at the time: 'Although not handsome he must have had a noble countenance, full of expression & animation, his hair was of a yellow brown, & curled with the utmost crispness & luxuriance. His locks instead of falling down stood up like a curling flame, and looked at a distance like radiations, which with his fiery eye & expansive forehead, his dignified & cheerful physiognomy must have made his appearance truly prepossessing.' There was no one who could have given him an account of the young Blake but Catherine.

The marriage was celebrated in the recently-rebuilt parish church of Battersea.[11] Blake was described as of the parish. (He must have resided there for at least the four previous weeks, perhaps staying with relatives. Gilchrist says that he traced relatives of Blake's father there, and certainly in the early nineteenth century many Blakes lived in Battersea, some born and dying in the workhouse.) The marriage bond calls Blake a Gentleman. Catherine made a mark and did not sign the register. The mark did not prove entire illiteracy; she may have found writing difficult, especially in the stress of the moment. The witness, James Blake, may have been either William's father or brother. The latter might have been expected to add *Jun.*, but both Gilchrist and Cunningham say the father opposed the marriage. Flaxman had been married a little earlier, on 3 June.

Catherine, born on 25 April 1762, had been christened at the church where she was married. Her parents, William and Mary, have their name spelt Burcher in the records. She was their last child, following eight girls (two of them twins) and four boys (two of them twins) born every second year for eighteen years. Fuseli in 1786 said that she had been a maid-servant. The mother may have been the Mrs Butcher, poor, buried fifteen days after the Blake marriage; the father the man buried on 16 September 1794, 'Aged 80 years Poor'. Blake used to boast what a pretty wife he had, but she soon lost her good looks. Someone, perhaps Flaxman, who was in Italy 1787–94, remarked that after a lapse of seven years he 'never saw a woman so much altered'. Privation and a hard life had coarsened her.

The young couple seem to gone to live at 23 Green Street, Leicester Fields, lodging with a T. Taylor; this is the address Blake gave in the R.A. Catalogue for 1784. In the same street lived the engraver Woollett, while round the corner was Reynolds. Leicester Fields was still a quiet open space where cocks could be heard crowing. In 1782, west of the family house in Broad Street, a School of Industry was opened where older workhouse children were given a strict training, with religious discipline. The boys were apprenticed or sent to sea, the girls put out to service. Blake must have been strengthened in his hatred of authority.

Flaxman was doing his best to find him patrons. On 18 June 1783 he told his wife Nancy that he had got John Hawkins, a Cornishman who wrote on mining, to commission a drawing from Blake. Nancy replied, 'I rejoice for Blake.' We do not know if anything came of the incident. T. H. Smith says that both Stothard and Flaxman 'were ever anxious to recommend him and his productions', but without success. Flaxman, we noted, had introduced him to Mrs Harriet Mathew, who lived in Rathbone Place; her husband presided at a chapel built for him in Charlotte Street and preached in the afternoon at St Martin's-in-the-Fields. Gilchrist exaggerated the importance of Mrs Mathew's salon and its blue-stocking frequenters, but Smith says that it was at her 'agreeable conversaziones I first met William Blake, the artist, to whom she and Mr Flaxman had been truly kind. There I have often heard him read and sing several of his poems. He was listened to by the company with profound silence, and allowed by most of the visitors to possess original and extraordinary merit.' Flaxman decorated Mrs Mathew's back parlour, used as a library, with 'models (I think they were in putty and sand) of figures in niches, in the Gothic manner', while Oram, Loutherbourg's assistant, 'painted the window in imitation of stained glass; the bookcases, tables, and chairs, were also decorated to accord with the appearance of those of antiquity'.[12]

The one important effect of the efforts to help Blake and find him patrons was the setting in type of a number of his poems, with the title *Poetical Sketches*. Flaxman and Mrs Mathew seem to have been the main movers in the project. The booklet is dated 1783, but there is no imprint and the work was certainly never published; the poet is named only as W.B. The costs would have been about £6 by the standards of the time.[13] No copies were sent for review. The Advertisement describes the poems as 'the Production of Untutored Youth', and apologises: the author 'was deprived of the leisure requisite to such a revisal of these sheets, as might have rendered them less unfit to meet the public eye'. There were 'irregularities and defects' on almost every page. The poems were all written between Blake's twelfth and twentieth year, we are told. That is, nothing had been composed since 1777. It is hard to credit this assertion, especially as three more pastoral poems were transcribed in a copy of the book which Nancy Flaxman gave someone on 15 May 1784. Further, the poems in the book show the influence of works by Chatterton which had appeared after 1777; the latter's prose-poem *Godred Covan* lies behind Blake's *Gwin*, and it was not printed till June 1778.[14]

The Flaxmans tried to push the book. On 26 April 1784 Flaxman wrote to William Hayley, the fashionable poet, a flattering letter which ended by saying he had arranged for a copy of Blake's book to be sent to Hayley's home at Eartham. 'His education will plead sufficient excuse to your Liberal mind for the defects of his work & there are few so able to distinguish & set a right value on the beauties as yourself. I have before mentioned that Mr.

Romney thinks his historical drawings rank with those of Ml.Angelo; he is at present employed as an engraver, in which his encouragement is not extraordinary.' Hawkins, his Cornish admirer, had ordered several drawings from him and was trying 'to raise a subscription to send him to finish studies in Rome, if this can be done at all it will be determined on before the 10th of May next year at which time Mr Hawkins is going out of England'.

Hawkins did not manage to raise the money to send Blake to study in Rome. If Blake had gone, it is impossible to imagine how he would have developed. About this time he must have felt much encouraged. In May 1784 he had two drawings at the R.A.: 'A breach in the city, the morning after a battle', and 'War unchained by an angel, Fire, Pestilence, and Famine following'. Still deeply concerned with the American war, in the second drawing he introduced symbolism for the first time in his exhibited works.

When we look at the poems in his book, we see that he had read Shakespeare's historical plays with close interest; that his reading had reached back to the Elizabethans, especially Spenser, and that he had been much affected by contemporary poets like Gray, Collins, Macpherson, Chatterton. He knew well the poems of Isaac Watts, and as late as 1825 we find him citing Parnell's *Hermit*. The imitation of Spenser, though immature, shows his early desire to break through the conventional standards of culture into deeper meanings. He rejects the prevailing norms, the critics ass-eared like Midas who 'judge of tinkling rhymes', and he longs to be inspired: through Apollo, Mercury (the messenger with decisions from on high), Minerva. He no doubt used Upton's edition of 1758 which drew on Spenser's own account of his poem as a continuous allegory and which pointed to the varying levels of historical allusion. 'Always we must look for more than meets the eye or ear; the words carrying one meaning with them, and the secret sense another.' But the fact that Blake's stanzas are all different and all wrong does not mean he is experimenting with the Spenserian model; he is just unable to control the form.

In the poems on *The Seasons* and on *Morning and Evening Star* he merges elements from Milton, Thomson, Collins in blank verse with fine effect. The ludicrous way in which commentators reread the later Blake back in his early work is exemplified by the effort to identify his *Spring* with Christ, because he draws on the sensuous imagery of the *Song of Songs*. In fact there is not the least touch of mysticism in the book, nothing religious apart from a few conventional phrases such as the lines about the ambitious soul ascending and 'leaving a track of light for men to wonder at'. Blake is there merely describing his own ambitions (as in the Spenserian stanzas); the passage is introduced by a statement in the key of his resentments about other artists. 'I know, That youth has need of age to point fit prey, And oft the stander-by shall steal the fruit Of th'Other's labour.'

He attempts the traditional ballad in *Gwin*, provides a gory Gothic tale in *Fair Elenor*, and adds ten lyrics in which his immediacy of emotion, his subtle singing directness, is entangled with imitative elements. One song rather crudely reveals his capacity for intense jealousy. 'O should she e'er prove false, his limbs I'd tear, And throw all pity on the burning air.' *To the Muses*, with its claim that poetry has become languid, forced, thin, is in the vein of many contemporary complaints; after Gray, Collins, Smart there was a sense of deep changes going on in sensibility, a desire to break into new adventurous ways of thought and feeling, which preluded the great final wave of Romanticism. In the pastoral songs Blake charmingly acclaims a life of simplicity which he feels has been lost and which he has never shared.

Two lyrics, however, show a more original note, based though they are in part on seventeenth-century models: *Mad Song* and *Memory*. Here we meet a rhythmic vitality that makes them unlike anything else in the period and seems in part to derive from music, from Blake's ability to sing his own poems. *Mad Song* further has an imaginative force all its own; the madman in his flight from light feels his song-notes mingled with the forces of nature. Blake is working in a tradition that goes back to *King Lear* and *From the Hag and Hungry Goblin*, which he knew at least from the mad songs in Percy's collection; but he achieves a definition truly his own. Indeed his poem leads on to the prophetic books where the conflicts of men, inner and outer alike, are merged with natural process in complex ways.[15]

The most ambitious part of *Sketches* is however the dramatic fragments dealing with Edward III, John, and Edward IV. We see how closely Blake had read Shakespeare's historical plays. Though part of his inspiration comes from the Abbey, the themes are not as remote as might appear. After the American Revolution George III commanded Benjamin West to paint scenes of Edward III's victories; and Blake with his keen interest in the gossip of the art-world would have heard of this. His main interest lies in the denunciation of war; but in the longer fragment on Edward III he tries to tackle the theme on the level of Shakespearean dramatic objectivity. He develops his point in the discussion between Dagworth and William, where the latter says of the king, 'Then if ambition is a sin, we are all guilty in coming with him, and in fighting for him,' and Dagworth replies, 'Now, William, thou dost

2*

thrust the question home.' Blake brings out what lies behind the invocation of liberty to justify wars of conquest, but then this interest goes. It is not that he cannot develop the inherent ironies; he is not really interested in a dramatic presentation and working-out of the conflicts. He wants to unveil directly the reality behind them, and his technical powers are unsure, torn between the wish to imitate admired past expressions and the need to make an immediate revelation of the struggles heaving around him, the history which he sees in the raw and violent marking: to clarify the nature of aggression in all ages. So, having made the first steps towards a Shakespearean kind of definition, he is driven to the direct denunciation of the Prologues, the fierce declaration of the War-song. 'When the souls of the oppressed Fight in the troubled air that rages, who can stand ? . . . O yet may Albion smile again, and stretch her peaceful arms.' Behind the themes of *Edward III* stands the analysis of Ambition and Pride in the earlier prose-poem.

The direct attack on kingly power comes out in *Gwin*. The risen people destroy the king and his armies. The giant Deliverer severs the king's head with one blow and the soldiers flee. In Chatterton's *Godred* the theme is the invasion of the Isle of Man by a Norse tyrant; in *Gwin* the oppressor is simply the king.

Then there are three prose-poems. *The Couch of Death* is a weakly pietistic account of a dying youth, but even here there is a linkage of war and plague (the Black Death). *Contemplation* has the same sort of sickly death-atmosphere, and contrasts contemplation in Nature's bosom with discordant urban life. Nature is still used in a positive sense as the source of happiness and health. The attack on the City is in the key of the prose-poem on Pride and helps to explain Blake's fascination with the pastoral theme. *Samson* is longer and stronger. Blake is stirred by the theme of the dedicated hero and by memories of Milton's play; he sets out to depict Samson in his unbroken strength and leads on to the moment when he is about to be betrayed by a woman, by his submission to sex. Blake feels that he can identify himself with the young hero confronting his fall, his entry into the deceitful life of society—'where's the man whose face is not a mask unto his heart?'—and feels the need (linked with his wish not to come into direct rivalry with Milton) to halt at the point beyond which lies blindness and toil at the mill with slaves, then the supreme challenge to an evil world.

The idiom of the prose-poems is conventional and hectic, with no echo of his later masteries. We cannot detect 'a new kind of metrical prose'

(Lowery) in which he suits the cadence to speech-rhythm. Rather, there is a pompous inflated blank verse breaking down towards speech-rhythms, but achieving nothing distinctive. Far more varied and vigorous are the Ossianic prose-poems in which Macpherson was thought to carry over the bardic chants of ancient Gaelic clan-life, or even the imitations of Ossianic style by Chatterton.[16]

If Blake had died in 1784 what would we make of *Poetical Sketches*? We would be puzzled by their mixture of conventional and original elements, but would never guess what he was to make of it all in another six or seven years. He was already past twenty-five, and his style and outlook were still largely unsettled. It seems there was a hard knot of fear and mistrust in him which yielded only to a powerful impact from without. Then the tensions set up between his inner life and the threatening world drove him to attempt to grasp at all costs what was at stake. He needed the shock of the American War and the Gordon Riots to bring about the first unlocking and liberation of his creative energies in any sustained way. But after he had then expressed himself, he became again insecure and uncertain, all too aware of the jeering world. The apologetic tone of the Advertisement to *Sketches* must have upset him and intensified his fears of coming forward. Already then we see strongly operative the mixture of emotions that accompanied all his writing activities till the end: a keen desire to press forward and an extreme fear of what the responses would be. He could not sustain self-confidence except in lonely communion with his own spirit. He desperately wanted to reach out, convinced that he had something to say of the utmost importance for all his fellows; and yet he was abjectly afraid of all the ordinary channels. Clearly, he never tried verse-contributions to the many magazines. For his art, when it was not bound up with poetry, he did not have the same inhibitions; his art-career was out in the open all along.

Blake, through his 'intending deportment'; says Smith, soon began to drop out of the Mathew circle. Probably he felt less and less at home there.

3

A Lull, 1784–8

Blake's father died in July 1784; on Sunday 4 July he was buried in a grave (that is, not a vault) for the regular fee of 13s. 6d. Blake no doubt inherited a modest sum, though no will was filed. Later, he underscored, with a double exclamation-mark, Lavater's aphorism: 'Say not you know another till you have divided an inheritance with him.' It looks as if he had some conflict with his elder brother James and was worsted. Whatever sum he got was probably used in setting up a print-selling shop this year with his old friend Parker and his wife at 27 Broad Street. He seems to have bought a copperplate press so that the firm could print off plates; for in 1800 he had a press that probably cost about £40. (At least by 1803 Catherine was an expert plate-printer.) Engravers did not normally own such presses. Blake engraved after Stothard the only two prints known to be issued by the firm (17 December 1784); they were aimed at a mildly erotic market. Catherine helped in the shop while William drew and engraved. Robert may have slept next door at the old family shop, but he seems to have been one of the household, with William teaching him to draw.

It is surprising to find Blake setting up as a businessman. The moment may well have been a promising one. By 1784 trade with the former American colonies was considerable. A single lucky print could make a fortune. The combination of Blake, skilled at line-engraving, and Parker, a specialist in mezzotint, was a good one. In 1800 Blake was still thinking amiably of print-shops. On his return from Sussex he found London changed into 'a City of Elegance in some degree' with its once stupid inhabitants entering 'into an Emulation of Grecian manners'.

There are now I believe, as many Booksellers as there are Butchers & as many Printshops as of any other trade. We remember when a Print shop was a rare bird in London & I myself remember when I thought my pursuits of Art a kind of criminal dissipation & neglect of the main chance, which I hid my face for not being able to abandon as a Passion which is forbidden by Law & Religion, but now it appears Law & Gospel too, at least I hear so from the few friends I have dared to visit in my stupid Melancholy.

Here he states plainly the atmosphere of philistine disapproval in which he had grown up. But in his letter of 25 October 1804, recording his sense of revelation after visiting the Truchsessian Gallery, he declares most poignantly that he had made a terrible mistake in late 1784. Suddenly, the day after the visit, 'I was again enlightened with the light I enjoyed in my youth, and which has for exactly twenty years been closed from me as by a door and by window-shutters.' Twice again he stresses that his fall occurred just twenty years before. 'Nebuchadnezzar had seven times passed over him; I have had twenty; thank God I was not altogether a beast as he was; but I was a slave bound in a mill among beasts and devils . . . I am really drunk with intellectual vision whenever I take a pencil or graver into my hand, even as I used to be in my youth, and as I have not been for twenty dark, but very profitable years.'

His meaning has baffled commentators, but is clear enough. He refers to his art, not his poetry. The bad turning in late 1784 can only be his decision to set up as print-seller, to base his career on the production of engravings for sale. Previously he had been putting his main hopes into the winning of fame through his art; but the death of his father and his effort to compete as a businessman with his brother James made him change direction. True, he did have four water-colours at the next R.A. (opening 27 April 1785), but these would have been done before he set up in business. One depicted Gray's Bard and was thus in line with the poems attacking kings and war; the other three dealt with Joseph (making himself known to his brethren, the brethren bowing to him, Simeon bound at his orders). If Blake was in conflict with his brothers over his choice of career and the money left by his father, into what character could he better project himself than Joseph?

He must have been feeling very family-conscious. He was housed next to James; Robert was more or less living with him; John had set up as baker at 29 Broad Street. The Blakes thus held nos 27, 28, 29. The Parkers may have been living with William. Parker was a plodding commercial engraver, respected 'for his amiable disposition, integrity, and good sense', said the engraver Raimbach. The right man for Blake at the outset, but liable to jar as a daily companion.

Luckily we know a great deal of Blake's state of mind in late 1784, for it was then that he wrote the lively conglomeration of satire, fun, and poetry that has been called *An Island in the Moon*. His own title, if it existed, is lost. He takes as the object of his wit anything that struck him as odd or amusing in the accepted world of culture. References to Balloon bonnets and Werter hats give us the date of the work. We can identify many of the characters. Quid is a joking self-portrait, with Suction as Robert. Suction ardently hopes to become an artist and wants to work according to Reynolds' advice to 'go to work, willing or unwilling, morning, noon and night'. Steelyard, we saw, is Flaxman. Mr Jacko is Richard Cosway, miniaturist and dandy with mulberry silk coats, called Little Jack-a-Dango after the monkey Jack at Astley's Amphitheatre in summer 1784. Intimate with Blake for several years, Cosway talked of ghostly visitors, including the Virgin Mary, who sat for portraits, and of his chats with God and Christ.[1]

Other identifications are not so sure. Obtuse Angle, with a study in Quid's house, may be Parker; he is the Mathematician, perhaps because he was always counting up his gains. But he wields a quadrant and seems a pedant, perhaps a schoolmaster. Sipsop, the medical student upset by the cruelties of surgery, may be the son of the Mathews or John Abernethy (recalled by Blake in an 1826 letter). Tearguts is certainly Jack Hunter, the print-collecting surgeon. Inflammable Gass may be a conflation of the chemist Joseph Priestley, George Fordyce who supplied the hydrogen or inflammable gas for Lunardi's balloon (that went up from Moorfields on 15 September 1784), Henry Cavendish who in 1784 was working on arsenic at 13 Marlborough Street (not far from Broad Street), and Gustavus Katterfelto who gave lectures with experiments in Piccadilly, 1782–4. Katterfelto's effects included pseudo-balloon ascensions, a Solar Microscope proving that 'a man is a lump of corruption', all his food and drink abounding 'with insects', and an air pump 'so capable of refining the quality of air, as to kill with its salubrity'. When drunks or jokers in the audience interfered with his apparatus he was liable to lose his temper in 'a paroxysm of rage'.

The scene is set in Quid's house, with some slight use of the houses of Steelyard and Inflammable Gass. Quid is shown as eaten up with envy. 'He is always envious', a deleted passage runs. He and Suction exchange boasts of their literary and artistic hopes. 'Then said Quid I think that Homer is bombast & Shakespeare is too wild & Milton has no feelings, they might easily be outdone. Chatterton never writ those poems!' He prophesies his own triumph over engraving rivals, 'lumps of Cunning & Ignorance'. Before ten years are out, 'How I will work those poor milk sop devils, an ignorant pack of wretches'. He cries, 'Plutarch was a nasty ignorant puppy. I hate your sneaking rascals.' His Song runs: 'Honour & Genius is all I ask, And I ask the Gods no more.' We must give Blake the credit for thus mocking at what he sees as his weak side; but we must not forget that it is indeed his weak side.

He had in mind the sort of wild satirical play, largely impromptu, that Foote had launched at the Haymarket in 1747, usually with the title *Tea at the Haymarket*. Foote died in 1777, but Blake in his youth would certainly have seen him perform. A magnificent mime, he employed in *Tea* some dozen actors, plus singers, dancers, musicians. *Tea* in fact was not a play but an occasion exploding on the stage and mixing grotesqueries with recognisable people or events. Blake uses Foote's formulaic jokes. Thus his Antiquary (perhaps Brand) talks of 'virtuous cats': according to Foote the main concern of antiquaries was the nature of Dick Whittington's Cat.

Blake also has much in mind the Handel Festival of 1784. Scopprell's son satirises the performers for making so much profit. Blake has been listening to Barry who complained that the Festival drew people away from his murals. The latter were neglected for 'an empty hubbub of fiddles and drums which was dissipated in the air as soon as performed'. Quid cries, 'Hang Italian songs! Let's have English'. After Scopprell sings, the Lawgiver comments, 'Funny enough! Let's have Handel's water piece.' Quid's call for Honour and Genius is a parody of a song from *Daphnis and Amyrillis* by James Harris, where the music is mainly from Handel with words adapted from Milton, though in this case the words are Harris's own.

An Island then shows Blake much interested in music. The part-song 'Want matches' belongs to the tradition set by Foote's pupil Edward Shuter, whose *Cries of London* was highly popular in mid-century. Together with Smith's testimony as to Blake's own singing, the songs of *An Island* bring out the importance of music in helping him to his original departures in metric and finally to the system and structure of the *Prophetic Books*. In reading his *Holy Thursday* (its first draft is in *An Island*) with its account of the mighty wind of song and the harmonious thunderings, we must not forget that Handel gave his Messiah to the Foundlings and that their chapel was the only place where his oratorios could be given in his lifetime. The singing spread to Magdalen Hospital and other institutions for orphaned or abandoned children, till there grew up the custom of uniting them all once a year at St Paul's.[2]

An Island is a slight work given importance by the way it lets us into

Blake's mind at this phase, and by the songs, which represent a halfway house between *Poetical Sketches* and *Songs of Innocence*. We see already the mixture of lyric affirmation and irony or ambiguity that was soon to grow stronger; but we must not overestimate the result. Here is a medley, a wide range, of verse-forms, nursery or folk poems, street-songs, scatological or bawdy songs, echoes of Mrs Barbauld's *Hymns in Prose*, traditional ballad-forms, stage-songs. We see how deep Blake's roots are in popular or semi-popular forms: here lies his primary strength. He is English Blake in a very definite sense. As Quid says, 'English Genius ever'.

How far do later ideas appear? There is no note whatever of mysticism or religion. Blake laughs at scientists and scholars, but then he is ready to jeer at any aspect of the social scene that comes up. The Antiquarian says, 'Voltaire was immersed in matter, & seems to have understood very little but what he saw before his eyes', but at the same time Obtuse Angle accuses him of not understanding mathematics. There are jokes about Newton and Locke, but the song merely makes the point that active benevolence is not to be despised as inferior to philosophic or theological theorising. The mockery of science may seem more serious. When a bottle of wind breaks, Inflammable Gass cries, 'This will spread a plague all through the Island'. But Blake is only repeating familiar jokes about chemistry as 'stinks'. Priestley in his *Experiments* tells of strange things happening when a bottle of wind broke; he thought he had found the principle of fire, which was commonly considered the bearer of pestilence.

Yet in some note he wrote into his copy of Reynolds' *Discourses* perhaps about 1808, Blake claimed:

I read Burke's Treatises when very Young: at the same time I read Locke on Human Understanding & Bacon's Advancement of Learning; on Every one of these Books I wrote my Opinions, & on looking them over find that my Notes on Reynolds in this Book are exactly Similar. I felt the Same Contempt & Abhorrence then that I do now. They mock Inspiration & Vision. Inspiration & Vision was then, & now is, & I hope will always Remain, my Element, my Eternal Dwelling place; can I then hear it Contemned without returning Scorn for Scorn?

Yet we find him as late as August 1799 citing Bacon's *Advancement* in a letter with approval on this very question of Inspiration. 'Consider what Lord Bacon says: "Sense sends over to Imagination before Reason has judged, & Reason sends over to Imagination before the Decree can be acted." ' And to show his close acquaintance with the text, he cites 'Part 2, p. 47 of first

Edition.' Certainly there is no note of abhorrence for Locke, Bacon and Reynolds in *An Island*.

We cannot then claim that in 1784, as far as *An Island* shows what he was thinking, he had reached any of his later philosophic positions. What the squib does possess is a riproaring joy in life, a disregard of ideas, which must represent the high hopes and feckless spirit in which he entered the new phase of his life as a tradesman; as if he were merrily announcing that there was after all nothing to worry about and that contemporary culture was largely made up of nonsense and pretence.

One other matter, however, comes up in *An Island* which was to be of great importance in his life. Unfortunately a leaf or more has been lost and we do not know how the subject was introduced. We come straight on to a discussion between Quid and his wife, in which the theme of Envy again obtrudes.

'—thus Illuminating the Manuscript.'

'Ay,' said she, 'that would be excellent.'

'Then,' said he, 'I would have all the writing Engraved instead of printed, & at every other leaf a high finish'd print—all in three Volumes folio—& sell them a hundred pounds apiece. They would print off two thousand.'

'Then,' said she, 'whoever will not have them will be ignorant fools & will not deserve to live.'

'Do you think I have something of the Goat's face?' says he.

'Very like a Goat's face,' she answer'd.

'I think your face,' said he, 'is like that noble beast the Tyger. Oh, I was at Mrs Sickancker's, & I was speaking of my abilities, but their nasty hearts, poor devils, are eat up with envy. They envy me my abilities, & all the women envy your abilities.'

'My dear, they hate people who are of higher abilities than their nasty, filthy selves. But do you outface them, & then strangers will see you have an opinion.'

In the 1780s there was much interest in stereographic printing in France and Britain. George Cumberland was involved and no doubt brought the matter to Blake's attention. He told his brother, on 10 November 1784, 'I have sent my mode of Printing to M—'s last Review & they have copied it into all the Papers, but not quite correct'. The account appeared in *A New Review with Literary Curiosities and Literary Intelligence*, edited by Henry Maty. Blake's procedures were a kind of relief-etching. The system was well known and had been set out in the first chapter of *Valuable Secrets concerning Arts and Trades*, 1758, with six more editions by 1810. What Blake seems to have added was an ink unaffected by acid, which he used to write on the copper. With his fervid mind he attached symbolic meanings to the method. The account he told, recorded by Gilchrist, made his discovery the result of long thought by day and dreams by night in 1787 after Robert's death. The image of Robert 'at last blended with it'. Robert appeared and revealed the secret. Next morning Catherine went out with half a crown, all the money they had, and spent 1s. 10d. on the necessary materials. Another story told how Joseph, Mary's husband, appeared in a vision and instructed Blake how to grind and mix his watercolours on a piece of marble with common carpenter's glue. Gilchrist adds that the vision of Robert started him off on 'what was to prove a principal means of support' through his life. In fact in some thirty-eight years of printing the illuminated books he merely made about £600.

The excited hopes of making a fortune set out in the passage from *An Island* were not just a self-critical jest. They reappear in fully serious form in his letter to his brother James in 1803. 'I now have it in my power to commence publication with many formidable works, which I have finish'd & ready. A book price half a guinea may be got out at the expence of Ten Pounds & its almost certain profits are 500 G.' The hopes here were quite baseless and he did not make any effort to carry out his scheme.[3]

But to return to the time when he was still Parker's partner and Robert was still alive. One day he watched Catherine and Robert in a heated argument till she used words that he thought unwarrantable. Up to that point he had said nothing. Now he rose and said to his wife, 'Kneel down and beg Robert's pardon directly, or you never see my face again!' His tones convinced her that he meant what he said, and she 'thought it hard,' as she used to comment, considering that 'she was not in fault'. But she knelt down and meekly murmured, 'Robert, I beg your pardon, I am in the wrong.' Robert retorted, 'Young woman, you lie! *I* am in the wrong.'

The story brings out how Blake looked on his wife as someone who must in the last resort totally obey him. Catherine was his 'Sweet Shadow of Delight', not a woman in her own right. In annotations to Lavater (*c.* 1788) he wrote, 'Let men do their duty & the women will be such wonders; the female life lives from the light of the male: see a man's female dependents, you know the man.' In his later thought the Eternal Man is the supreme figure and the women are emanations of the male. Yet in many ways he champions women's right to a free, unfettered existence. The contradictions here are never brought out and resolved.[4]

It was not to be expected that a couple like the Blakes would be able to work long with the Parkers. Smith says that Mrs Mathew—perhaps meaning Jane Matthews, aunt of Flaxman, who with her husband sold books and prints in the Strand—helped the firm. But by Christmas 1785 the Blakes had moved to 25 Poland Street, which linked Broad and Oxford Streets, while Parker carried on at 27 Broad Street till 1794. The high hopes of the print-shop had ended. Blake lived in Poland Street till 1790; an engraving of that year has the address on 28 July. The house was narrow, with a timber-yard behind the back garden. A near public house was the meeting-place of the Ancient Order of Druids when revived on 28 November 1781.

William had begun teaching Robert to draw in 1777, as a folio sketchbook records. He drew a whole figure or a part of one, and Robert made a copy alongside. Starting with lips and noses, he reached the complete figure. At the end are coloured drawings of birds and animals, several dated 1778. Blake kept some of Robert's later drawings. Gilchrist described them as 'naif and archaic-looking', but owning a 'Blake-like feeling and invention', with subjects taken from Homer and the Poets. One, now in the British Museum, shows a group of people awestruck by some nearing catastrophe. William used the design in what seems his earliest experiment in relief-etching, and this fact may lie behind the fantasies of Robert inspiring the relief-method. Another drawing, sepia wash and pen, depicts a huddled group cowering before an ancient man with upraised arms; a third shows a druidic grove with groups of males and females in long robes between two rows of trees with branches roofing over their heads. The figures are painted with bright watercolour washes. The notebook once owned by Rossetti had sketches by Robert at the front, some in pencil, two in watercolours. A knight in armour rushes from beneath a Gothic cloister, a woman in a long dress flees through a forest of slender tree-trunks. Two crowned fairies lie in a rose-like flower; over them hang two bell-shaped flowers, with a circle of little figures dancing under one of them. This latter drawing was long taken to be William's work. It still has Robert's angular figures but owns much poetic charm. Robert had freed his art imaginatively before William did, and his work must have provided a great stimulus for the elder brother, setting him a new criterion.[5]

It was probably in 1785 that Blake first took up the Job-theme. He drew Job seated between his wife and friends in an arrangement not unlike that in the plate he engraved thirty-five years later, though the technique is primitive, showing some affinities with Robert's work. The conflicts of

Robert and Catherine, and the sense of loss, even desolation, after the collapse of the print-shop and the move from Broad Street, may well have made him turn to Job, as he henceforth did at intervals throughout his life. His sense of loss was sharply increased when Robert died in February 1767, in his nineteenth year.

Blake affectionately tended him in his illness, and during the last fortnight of it watched continuously day and night by his bedside, without sleep. When all claim had ceased with that brother's last breath, his own exhaustion showed itself in an unbroken sleep of three days' and nights' duration... At the last solemn moment, the visionary eyes beheld the released spirit ascend heavenward, through the matter-of-fact ceiling, 'clapping its hands for joy'. (Gilchrist)

Robert was buried on 11 February at Bunhill Fields, but William may well have been too tired to attend. Robert was the only person with whom he was ever fully at home. For all his sense of difference, Blake was one of a closely-knit family; with Robert the deeply-felt family bond had been lifted to a new level of spiritual comradeship. After Robert's death he felt more than ever that he must carry on in an uncompromising way of which Robert would have approved.

During this troubled period he came to know Thomas Taylor and his ideas. Taylor, born in May 1758, son of a dissenting minister in London, began with scientific beliefs. Finding Newton 'a great mathematician, but no philosopher', he turned to Aristotle, then to Plato and the Neoplatonists. He lived awhile in the same house with Mary Wollstonecraft, and when she moved he continued to visit her. No later than by 1788 he was friendly with T. B. Hollis, antiquarian, who was to be an active member of the Revolutionary Society. His first project was a perpetual lamp; and after experiments with oil, salt, and phosphorus, he gave an exhibition at the Free Mason's Tavern, which he set on fire. Next he gave twelve lectures on Platonic philosophy in Flaxman's house. From 1787 to 1834 he published translations of Plato and the Neoplatonists, the Hymns of Orpheus and a Dissertation on the Eleusinian and Bacchic Mysteries.[6]

Blake became familiar with Taylor, as is shown by a story that a later friend of Taylor records:

T. Taylor gave Blake, the artist, some lessons in mathematics & got as far as the 5th proposition which proves why two angles at the base of an isosceles triangle must be equal. Taylor was going through the demonstration, but was interrupted by Blake exclaiming 'ah never mind that—what's the use of going to prove it. Why

I see with my eyes that it is so, & do not require any proof to make it clearer.'
(Commonplace Book of W. Meredith)

Taylor made accessible to Blake the Platonic and Neoplatonist universes, and the great enthusiasm shown by Blake till 1803 for the Greeks was in part the result of Taylor's impact on him. Most importantly he drew from Taylor an understanding of the symbolic significance of the ancient religious Mysteries, which supplied him with a mythical structure for his ideas and emotions as Boehme and Paracelsus could not. The Mysteries provided schemes of fall, death, resurrection, rebirth. They gave him dramatic patterns which he could use to express his deep sense of crisis, of the need to die at one level and move into a fuller humanity at another. They revivified the elements of mystery-initiation embedded in Christian myth and ritual, enabling him to discard the limiting and confusing elements added as Christianity became an established religion. Hence the enthusiasm with which in 1799 he declared his alliance with Cumberland 'to renew the lost Art of the Greeks'. Cumberland too had been attracted by Taylor's lectures.

Blake no doubt also knew about the Mysteries through Warburton's *Divine Legation of Moses*, which argued that Virgil's account of Aeneas' descent into the lower regions was an allegory of the ritual experiences of the Eleusinian Mysteries. There seems little question that it was Warburton who sent Blake to Ovid. He argued that the *Metamorphoses* told the story of the Earth from the time of Chaos to that of Julius Ceasar, 'a sublime and regular plan . . . a popular history of Providence . . . from the Creation to his own time, through the Egyptian, Phoenician, Greek and Roman histories'. On the Ovidian basis Blake developed his system of symbolic metamorphoses, which provided both a universal history and a picture of what was happening to mankind at the moment of composition. Bryant, Taylor and Warburton all gave him valuable guidelines.*

In his new questing mood Blake came on the Swedenborgians. He bought copies of two of the master's works and was drawn in the winter of 1788–9

---

* The idea of a common basis for all religions was linked with the idea of common ancestors for the great family of nations, thus explaining the interrelations of ancient cultures. Blake used a tradition that went back to the work of seventeenth-century scholars like C. J. Vossius, Huet, Bochart, who tried to bring together Biblical figures and figures of pagan myth. Mallet in *Northern Antiquities* sought for the common principles of all European religions. 'The further back we ascend to the era of the creation, the more plainly we discover traces of this conformity among the several nations of the earth.' Parsons combined Biblical and Irish myths; Audigier identified Gallus, ancestor of the French, with Noah.

to the New Jerusalem Church. Many of Swedenborg's ideas attracted him. 'In all the Heavens there is no other Idea of God than that of a Man.' Blake annotated: 'Man can have no idea of anything greater than Man.' When Swedenborg insisted on the unity of love and wisdom, Blake went further: 'Thought without affection makes a distinction between Love & Wisdom, as it does between body & Spirit.' But despite his interest in contraries, Swedenborg did not work out anything like a dialectic or link the action of contraries with his concept of progression. Blake was finally so annoyed by his many complacent and conventional positions that he turned him upside-down and parodied him in *Marriage of Heaven and Hell*. But in his critical struggle with Swedenborgian ideas Blake deepened his own grasp on the dialectic of contraries and learned how to translate his positions into accounts of visionary experiences.[7]

There was trouble too in the New Jerusalem Church. In December 1788 a circular letter was sent out by the dissidents; they wanted a new Church which would fully embrace 'the Heavenly Doctrines of the New Jerusalem'. A conference met on 13 April 1789 at a public house. Those attending signed a paper saying that they accepted Swedenborg's writings as genuine revelations. Blake and Catherine were there and signed. Thirty-two resolutions, unanimously adopted, set out what was seen as the master's Truths. The Old Church was dead; it believed in three gods; it believed that Nature was God or that there was no God. Heaven could not come to men while it existed. 'Any worship not addressed to the Divine Humanity, Jesus Christ, is lamentable.' The Second Coming, already begun, involved the destruction of the Old Church and the formation of the New. The Blakes subscribed to these views, which Blake continued to hold all his life, though he increasingly gave his own meaning to the terms used. He must have been deeply stimulated by finding himself a member of a group with whom he could generally sympathise, even though the membership did not continue.

Entertaining as well as stimulating would have been the conflict that promptly broke out in the group on the question of sexual love, on the interpretation of the master's *Chaste Delights of Conjugal Love: after which follow the Pleasures of Insanity & Scortatory Love*. The inborn *amor sexus* was taken by some disciples as an uncontrollable force; a few went on to accept fornication and concubinage, and were expelled. (Someone tore out the pages of the minute-book from May 1789 to April 1790, so details of the conflict are lost.) The expelled six serialised *Chaste Delights* in a magazine. One dissident argued that unmarried members had the right to take mistresses, and that members whose marriages were 'disharmonuous' might reject wives who rejected the new doctrine, and take concubines. Such men may be 'driven so strongly by the inborn *amor sexus* that they cannot contain themselves'.

Meanwhile Blake had made an important new acquaintance. 'When Flaxman was taken to Italy, Fuseli was given to me for season'. Flaxman had gone in 1787 and Blake grew fairly intimate with Fuseli, a friend of Johnson, for whom Blake had done some engraving. In 1788 he engraved a plate after Fuseli for the latter's version of Lavater's *Aphorisms*, published by Johnson. Fuseli had a wide-ranging medley of ideas. He translated Winckelmann's *Reflections*, a copy of which Blake owned in his early days; he wrote a defence of Rousseau in London in the 1760s; he preached the absolute preeminence of Greek art and held that art degenerated after Michelangelo; he declared that 'Modern Art, reared by superstition in Italy, taught to dance in France, plumped up to unwieldliness in Flanders, reduced to "chronicle small beer" in Holland, became a rich old woman by "suckling fools" in England.' But he praised Reynolds' *Discourses* and saw Dürer's forms, so admired by Blake, as 'blasphemies on Nature'. However, it was not so much any particular idea of his that made him congenial to Blake; it was rather the vehemence and the fantastic element in his thought and art, his passionate language. He occasionally made a remark in Blakean vein as when, after visiting Liverpool, he said that he had smelt the blood of slaves everywhere, and when he described London smoke to Haydon as 'de smoke of the Israelites making bricks'. Cunningham records him as saying, 'I see the vision of all I paint— and I wish to Heaven I could paint up to what I see'. He laid all stress on expression, which 'alone can invest beauty with supreme and lasting command over the eye': a doctrine that led in directions Blake would have approved: 'To make a face speak clearly and with propriety, it must not only be well constructed, but have its own exclusive character'.[8] Though his imaginative range was limited and tended to morbidity in comparison with Blake's, he felt an affinity with the latter's art. Both men liked emphatic talk. 'Flaxman had complained of Fuseli's foul language and asked what Blake did when Fuseli swore. "What do I do?" asked Blake. "Why, I swear again, and he says astonished, "Vy, Blake, you are swearing!" but he leaves off himself.'*

* Blake was considered fair game for exaggerated anecdotes. He was said to tell Fuseli the Virgin Mary appeared to him and told him that one of his works was very fine, 'What can you say to that?' 'Say?' exclaimed Fuseli, 'why nothing—only her ladyship has not immaculate taste', (Cunningham). He was said to have bowed to St Paul in Cheapside, but the same story was told of Swedenborg.

Fuseli's remark about Blake being good to steal from is often cited, but it would be hard to point to anything he took from Blake, who was sixteen years his junior. On the contrary we can see that Blake took from Fuseli and was influenced by him. Thus, his image of a figure with widely outstretched wings he got from the Fuseli drawing that he engraved for Erasmus Darwin's *Botanic Garden*. More important was the generally liberating influence that Fuseli's forms exerted on him from 1789. Fuseli used proportions in his figures that had little basis in real forms, repetition of attitudes and patterns, linear rhythms and undefined space, swirling movements; and Blake took over much of such systems, sometimes carrying them to excess, as in certain symmetries. Fuseli himself criticised him for that excess: 'Fancy is the end and not the means in his designs. He does not employ it to give novelty and decoration to regular conceptions, but the whole of his aim is to produce singular shapes and odd combinations.' On the other hand Stothard said that many artists blamed Fuseli's influence for what they considered Blake's abberrations. Still, other elements in Blake's art remained close to his origins in English Romantic Neoclassicism, so that Romney and Lawrence admired his designs and West praised his illustrations to Young's *Night Thoughts*.[9]

But in the years 1785–8 Blake made little headway. He had given up his efforts to win fame through watercolours in the R.A. He was badly impeded by his inability to handle oils: a failure which he rationalised by condemning oils as an inferior medium. He could not achieve plasticity and modelling in his forms except in stereotyped ways. He struggled to find alternative methods than would produce stronger effects than watercolour without the disciplines required by oil-painting. What he developed emerged from his brooding over relief-etching, but was in fact a kind of monotype. He drew outlines in black on a piece of millboard, probably with some internal modelling and other details, all in the same colour. He printed this design under low pressures on a sheet of paper. Then he coloured the millboard to complete the design and again printed what he had done on top of the black outline. He thus got a richly mottled effect, more complex in colour and form than he could get from copper plates. He touched the result up with water-colour, though not as strongly as in his printed books.[10]

During these years he kept himself by doing hack-work, doing satirical prints for *Wit's Magazine* or reproducing paintings by Hogarth, Morland, Cosway, Fuseli. By 1788–9 he braced himself to make his first tentative attempts to use his new printing methods. The notes in his copy of Lavater show his ideas maturing. 'Active Evil is better than Passive Good'. Hell is to be 'shut up in the possession of corporeal desires which shortly weary the man, *for* ALL LIFE IS HOLY.' He speaks of 'A vision of the Eternal Now.' His Christ still has nothing theological. He is the man who is 'free from all trifling accidental helps', and sees 'objects through one grand immutable medium, always at hand'.

Blake had been born and brought up in a social level where, apart from some surviving folk-elements, the cultural idiom was almost wholly Biblical. As he grew older he found that the moral, social and philosophic themes of the day were mainly treated in religious terms. He accepted this system, but not the meaning and morals conventionally attached to it. In effect he says: All right, we must argue these matters out in a Biblical idiom; but if the Bible really corresponds to life, then it cannot have the meanings you impose on it or the morals you draw from it. Christ is the perfect man, you say. Then I'll tell you what Christ is, and don't complain that what I say has no connection with the pack of lies and nonsense you have compiled over the ages. For him, then, the Bible is wholly a quarry of symbols. He does not accept it as fact, as history. There is literally no Hell. Still, it is a useful concept to explain certain things in life. And so on. Blake also derived pleasure from using conventional religious terms while turning them topsy-turvy; the shock induced by such revaluations was more likely to make people think.

His annotations in Swedenborg's *Wisdom of Angels* again stress the unity of the life-process, that 'God is a man', that 'The whole of the New Church is in the Active Life & not in Ceremonies at all'. Love and Imagination are in effect identified. The Poetic Genius is the Lord. He is denying the old dualities, which split and fragment life, dividing man into body and soul or cutting heaven and hell away from immediate earthly experience. But he also brings in an idealist element which defeats his struggle to see life always as a living whole. In his Lavater comments he says, 'Every thing is its own cause'. What he wants to do is to get away from mechanist concepts of cause and effect, and to vindicate the wholeness of the organism; but by making the latter its own cause he cuts it away from living process and makes it an isolated thing, unrelated to other organisms—indeed into the very opposite of what he intends. This sort of conflict between the unitary and materialist aspects of Blake's thought, and a tendency to idealist abstraction, carries on from first to last, and always has the same cause: the wish to deny mechanistic reductions. To keep consistently making that denial he feels that he must assert the self-creative energy of spirit. His dialectic thus has many affinities with that of Hegel, though he keeps going beyond Hegel in his stress on sensuous experience and the unity of body and mind, thus approximating to the positions of Marx.

By 1790 Blake declared that any mechanical mind could have produced Swedenborg's writings 'from the writings of Paracelsus or Jacob Behman'. That is, Swedenborg lacked a dialectical sense of the transformations of the life-process, the leap from one level to a higher one in which new qualities emerged. So his system of levels (natural, spiritual, celestial) could not involve such leaps of transformation; the stages were all on the same level, 'by Continuity according to the Sciences'. The three degrees or levels do not open into one another, and their relation to one another can be grasped only 'by correspondence, which has nothing to do with demonstration'. Science, Blake is saying, can deal only with the continuous, with things all on the same level; and from now on he uses the term Nature to represent the level defined and explored by mechanistic science (with Newton and Locke its prophets). Several important correlations follow. Persons who think of man as 'only conversant with natural Substances' do so because they are 'mercenary and worldly & have no idea of anything but worldly gain'. Nature becomes the term for the given world in all its limitations, a world ruled by money and the forces of alienation which transform men into things, a world ruled by endless inner and outer divisions. The Natural Man for Blake is the man who accepts without question this world of division in which the rule of money and the forces of the market are an aspect of a science which ignores all qualitative differences and reduces phenomena to a purely quantitative level. 'Heaven would upon this plan be but a Clock.' Heaven is the cosmos in its living totality of dialectical transformations; but in the flatly reductive Newtonian system it turns into a clock-mechanism most obviously revealed in the stars.*

Blake made his first considered statement of the issues in what seems the first use of his new printing methods for a booklet. Ten plates were used. *All Religions are One* sets out that all religions express in one way or another the

---

* Blake was correct in attributing to Newtonian science the need to see things as based in continuous motion, mathematically definable. Newton hoped for a 'perfect mechanic', which involved the hope of exact measurements in absolutely homogeneous isotropic space. Behind this attitude lay the belief that it should then be possible to render perceptual relations as purely exact and as definite as mathematical ones. Newton bases exactness in continuous motion, whose 'Geneses really take Place in the Nature of Things', so that inexactness derived from discontinuity. But though Blake is tackling with much precision the Newtonian universe, the essence of his argument applies to all purely quantitative science, however refined by Einstein and quantum mechanics, etc.[11]

imaginative insights that he groups under the heading of the Poetic Genius. All men share in that genius and religions differ only through the varying circumstances in which the nations received them. The genius is the true man, and 'the body or outward form of Man is derived from the Poetic Genius'. The terms there are idealist, but what Blake is trying to say is that the source of development lies, not in Newton's continuous motion, but in a dialectical principle of transformation which the Poetic Genius alone can grasp and express. In saying that all poetry is prophecy, the vital element in religion, he is also saying that religion has truth and value only in so far as it is poetry and truly interprets the nature of the life-process.

The tract's subtitle is 'The Voice of one crying in the Wilderness'. The first plate shows a youthful John the Baptist (Blake himself as the forerunner of the new dispensation). The fluidity of his imagery is brought out by Plate 4 where (to illustrate the Poetic Genius and the derivation of all things from that Genius, 'which by the Ancients was call'd an Angel & Spirit & Demon') he draws a bearded man with arms outstretched across the clouds in which he sits as if they were rocks. He is the human form of the cloud; but soon, in *Marriage*, he begins to be abstracted from the world and in *America* he becomes the arch-tyrant Urizen, the diametric opposite of the Poetic Genius.

Blake followed his first tract with another, *There is NO Natural Religion*. There are two versions, but each makes the same main points. Science, when purely quantitative, is a closed and static system, which he calls the Ratio or Reasoning Power. By it man can 'only compare & judge of what he has already perceiv'd'. But the poetic faculty can break through the Ratio and grasp the life-process at a new qualitative level. 'If it were not for the Poetic or Prophetic character the Philosophic & Experimental would soon be at the ratio of all things, & stand still, unable to do other than repeat the same dull round over again.' Reason, or the ratio of all that is already known, is not, he says, the same as it will be when we know more. He uses God as emblem of the life-process in its totality. 'God becomes as we are, that we may be as he is.' There is a ceaseless unbalance between what exists and what is potential in existence, an active drive to new levels. The more we become ourselves (develop), the more of the living cosmos we take into ourselves. The designs in both tracts tend to stress the closed cycle or ratio, one of them showing Nebuchadnezzar as emblem of the worst fall into 'nature'. The second version brings in imagery of resurrection to express the breakthrough, the movement beyond the ratio: Jesus as the Poetic Genius calls on

Lazarus. In the variety of the forms we see how Blake's artistic powers have gained a new release, which at last brings them into harmony with his poetry.

To understand Blake's hatred of the term Reason we must grasp how it was used in the apologetics for the existing system of society. The combination of ideas that Blake most detested can be seen clearly asserted by the philosopher Hobbes, for whom the new sciences were inseparable from a philosophic and political system that justified the exercise of power and aggression as based in natural law and self-preservation. Science and philosophy combined to provide the rationale for the class-state and the rule of the market. The astronomer Kepler had already declared that the mind could know the world only by quantity, not at all by quality. Locke asserted that the primary qualities of a body produce in the mind corresponding ideas of solidity, extension, shape, motion (or rest), number. Secondary qualities existed in objects only as powers 'to produce certain sensations in us by their primary qualities'. The mind, blank at birth, was then written on by the outer world. Adam Smith stated that the Newtonian system demonstrated the world to be an immense machine, which God contrived and conducted to produce at all times the greatest possible quantity of happiness: the religious position Blake called Deism.[12]

Along such lines not only was the world of division and exploitation proved to be natural and divinely ordained, but all the specifically human qualities, all the elements that enter into our experiences (apart from those mathematically graspable as quantities) were seen to be subjective, ghostly, not truly real. Reality was the mathematical world, the power-world, the cash-nexus and the laws of the market. This is the system that Blake groups under the heading of Reason or Abstract Demonstration, and attacks from every angle. Since the system was also held to be that of Nature, he included Nature in his attack, ignoring the fact that in the romantic counter-attack Nature was invoked to cover the impulses of revolt, of sex, and so on.*

Though he paid rates in Westminster in 1788 and 1790, he never voted

---

* Not that Blake was rigid in his terms. When Swedenborg says that the grandest and purest Truths of Heaven must needs seem obscure and perplexing to the natural man at first View, he commented, 'Lies & Priestcraft. Truth is Nature'. And at the end of the first book of *Milton* Nature appears as 'a Vision of the Science of the Elohim'. The Elohim come with the Flood and shape the world rising out of it, so their science is to reconstruct the world, life, after breakdown—which is just what Blake-Los keeps doing through the 3,000 years after the Fall. Here Nature represents the best that creative struggle can produce in a still-divided world.

there; he seems to have had no faith or interest in the existing political system. But in 1789 came the great event which released his prophetic powers, the French Revolution. Much social stress, we must remember, had also been building up in England. There were food-riots, demonstrations against food-prices. Thus at Nottingham in 1788 the doors and shutters of the shambles were torn down and burned, with the butchers' account-books. But in France a severe financial crisis had been growing. The King, faced with trouble from the aristocracy, was driven to call the Estates General, in which nobles, clergy, and commoners were represented. In the resulting conflicts the Third Estate, the commoners, dominated and the King had to command all three estates to meet as a single body. The Third Estate, with the aid of the lesser clergy and liberal nobles, took control, and by July the Revolution was under way; national sovereignty was substituted for royal absolutism. On 14 July came the storming of the Bastille; the revolt spread to the towns and countryside. In August came the Declaration of Rights. Blake was following these events with eager interest. As poet and prophet he felt that here at last were all the signs of a new dispensation on earth, and that he was called on to express and interpret the great change, the resurrection of man into freedom and brotherhood.[13]

4

Breakthrough, 1789

Blake had known for some time the radical bookseller and publisher, Joseph
Johnson, and in 1789 he became a member of the group gathered round him
at 72 St Paul's Churchyard. In 1790 Johnson planned to publish Cowper's
edition of Milton with engravings after Fuseli. Blake was to do one plate, but
the scheme failed through Cowper's illness. We are told that at Johnson's
Blake met regularly a remarkable coterie, including William Godwin,
Thomas Paine, Mary Wollstonecraft, Dr Priestley, Dr Price and Thomas
Holcroft. Johnson gave 'plain but hospitable weekly dinners' in a little
quaintly shaped upstairs room, with walls not at right angles, where his
guests must have been somewhat straitened for space (Gilchrist). But Blake's
place at the dinners has certainly been exaggerated. For instance, Godwin's
diary does not mention him. But probably he was invited now and then, and
was on nodding terms with the notable characters. His nervous withdrawn
nature, and his relative unimportance among the others, would have ensured
that he played a modest role; he was liable to speak out only under extreme
provocation or when he felt happily at home. To the other guests he would
have appeared a minor artist under the aegis of Fuseli; but with his quick
response to ideas he must have been deeply stimulated by contact with the
assured and prominent characters. More, this stimulation came just at the
right time, as he was starting on his prophetic career and seeking to grasp in
its fullness the emerging revolutionary situation. Mary Wollstonecraft he
certainly met, since he did engravings of his own designs for her work and
she was at one time a close friend of Fuseli.[1]

What we know of Blake at this time comes from the tales he told the
young artists who admired him in his last years, which Gilchrist repeated.
He 'was an ardent member of the New School, a vehement republican and
sympathiser with the Revolution, hater and contemner of kings and king-
craft'. To his latest days he 'always avowed himself a "Liberty Boy", a faithful "Son of Liberty"'; and would jokingly urge in self-defence that the shape

of his forehead made him a republican. "I can't help being one," he would assure Tory friends "any more than you can help being a Tory: your forehead is larger above; mine, on the contrary, over the eyes." ' Further, 'He courageously donned the famous symbol of liberty and equality—the bonnet rouge—in open day, and philosophically walked the streets with the same on his head. He is said to have been the only one of the set who had the courage to make that public profession of faith.' But when he heard of the September massacres in Paris, 'he tore off his white cockade, and assuredly never wore the red cap again'. But nobody could have worn the cap of liberty with impunity in the London streets from 1789 to 1792, and Blake did not feel repelled by the Terror in France. (The white cockade was in fact royalist, though radicals like Thelwell did wear a white hat. Cumberland in 1820 spoke of the days when he 'wore the white hat' of liberty.) Samuel Palmer carried the whitewashing of Blake further by declaring that he 'rebuked the profanity of Paine, and was no disciple of Priestley'.[2]

Blake had kept on writing songs over the years and in 1789 he collected many of them to make an illuminated book as *Songs of Innocence.* Childhood had come to mean for him a symbolic state as well as a phase of growth. He saw it, not as a period of immaturity through which we pass on the way to adulthood, but as one in which the life-force is contained in great purity and with its own deep potentiality. With puberty come all sorts of divisions: the psychological conflicts reflect the acceptance of a world broken up into endless divisions and oppressions, and the impulses of sex are entangled with all sorts of fears, hatreds, rivalries, suspicions, power-urges. The state of innocence found in childhood, however, maintains a joyous communion with the whole cosmos, with fellow beings, with all the manifestations of the life-process. To regain the state of innocence, after one has 'fallen' into division, is to rediscover paradise. So Blake said that in innocence one became divine: that is, achieved the inner and outer conditions of liberty, love, peace. He called this condition spiritual as opposed to the entry into division, which was natural. Socially, innocence meant the creation of the 'foundations of an imaginatively organised and truly happy prosperity' (Erdman).

Blake is not yet concerned with the process by which the sources of division are defeated. Innocence is assumed to come about by a spontaneous and all-pervasive act of faith. The imagery used is that of the pastoral given a symbolic idiom which goes back to Spenser. The use of the Lamb helps to suggest an actual pastoral scene, with Jesus brought in as a sort of benedictory overtone. As there is no suggestion that the state has been attained by struggle of any kind, there is a feeling of some kindly guardian force. Earth is not contrasted with heaven; it is itself heaven. The pastoral genre holds a memory of pre-urban stages (ultimately the stage of tribal life before classes were born).* Here in its link with such religious images as Jesus the Lamb it suggests a future in which all people will live harmoniously. Blake gives the whole tradition a new force by his passionate hatred of all divisive forces, his belief that pastoral concord will some day assert itself as the one way of life, and by linking that way with childhood—thus introducing a more precise psychological and social set of references.[3]

Not that he ignores the plight of real children. The schoolboy is jailed away from the sunlight 'in sighing and dismay'. The little boy is lost, the chimney-sweeper has been sold and damned to cruel labour, the little black boy is not loved by the English boy, and so on. But somehow the spirit of innocence saves them from complicity in the workings of evil, and somehow things will come right. The lost will be found, the lion will change his wrath to pity. The inadequacy of the concept of redemption through innocence alone, however, becomes even more apparent when the themes are transposed into adult life. Thus, in the first design for *The Little Girl Lost*, Lyca's sleep is shown as the embrace of a full-grown woman with her lover.

Not that the situation is as simple as might appear; it never is, with Blake. There are elements of irony and satire. He was early concerned with the problem of how one returned to a previous state after learning its vulnerable weaknesses; how one revived what was good in the earlier state at a new level, where the inter-relations could not but be very different. Indeed till the end he found a problem in the relation of spontaneous liberation and organised knowledge and action.

There is another important point in connection with Blake's use of pastoral. City-bred as he was, his vision of the redeemed earth is one of a free and happy city, Jerusalem. Yet it is in the green and pleasant land, glimpsed during his early walks as a different world, and in the labour put into that land, that he sees the source of all value. The peasant proprietor, he felt, was the solid basis of society, with the other classes living off him.

* At the root of the whole pastoral genre is a utopian element, which in the medieval world was linked with the Pleasant Place, the Garden, and so with Paradise. The very word *Paradeisos* reached Greece from ancient Persia where it signified the parkland that the nobles kept free from all 'civilising' elements and used for hunting, so that it represented an earlier phase of their society, before the inequalities and oppressions of settled existence came about.

Blake at Hampstead 1825,
pencil drawing by John Linnell

'Blake in his fiery youth'
as recalled by Catherine in his last years

Catherine Blake, drawn by Blake on the back of a leaf of Hayley's Ballads, about 1802

Flaxman modelling a bust of Hayley; painted by George Romney

Fuseli, self-portrait,
black and white chalk, 1780–90

Samuel Palmer,
self-portrait; about 1826

Blake and Varley;
pencil drawing by Linnell

Title page to *Europe*
with the prophetic serpent,
its mouth a trumpet

Jerusalem, frontispiece

The Human Abstract
from *Songs of Experience*
(plate 47)

Oberon and Titania, ink and wash drawing by Robert Blake

Man in a state of agricultural and pastoral equality he later personifies in Urthona (Earth-owner). The fall came when the earth ceased to be held in common ownership, and behind his call for a liberated earth lay some sort of dream of peasant ownership, such as we find in Thomas Jefferson, Mary Wollstonecraft, Thomas Spence. Here Blake was close to an important strand of radical revolt. Mary Wollstonecraft in her first *Vindication* declared that with the ending of economic domination (the existing system of economic power) England would turn an Eden with 'springs of joy' on every side, each man 'contented to be the friend of man'. Spence had a wide following with his call for a return of the land to common ownership as in the Biblical Jubilee. His call had its pastoral and millenary colouration. The gift of the earth to man was set out in Genesis and Psalms, the promise of its return in the Old Testament and in Revelation. Justice would walk forth from her temple in a New Jerusalem where swords had been beaten into ploughshares, every man dwelt beneath his vine and under his fig tree, the wolf fed with the lamb, the earth yielded its increase, and man neither laboured in vain nor brought forth in trouble. This is precisely also Blake's vision of a free society.

When we look at the *Songs* we see that much of their strong emotional impact lies in the metrical form and the idiom, which build a rich magical effect, as of a charm conjuring into being the desired world. There are strong accentual rhythms, with much alliteration and assonance, the use of monosyllabic feet, especially at the start of a line, and of short sentences, which at times make a line self-contained: 'I have no name'. Pauses often increase the effect of symmetry, and yet there is much metrical variety inside the compact stanzaic structure. Many of Blake's effects, imagery, and ideas appear in the Methodist hymns of the day. 'Bid the fallen race arise, And turn our earth to Paradise'. 'So blooms the human face divine'. 'The buckler bring, the bow extend; Grasp in the hand the spear'. 'I will as in a moment's Space, The Doom of Sin, and Satan's seal, And all their last Remains erase'. 'This ancient well (no glass so true) Britannia's image shows; Now Jesus travels Britain through—but who the stranger knows?' 'The life divine, the little leaven, My precious pearl, my present heaven'. We thus meet the sense of immediacy, of the transformation of earth, the call to arms. At times these hymns speak as if the struggle were against the mighty of the earth. 'On earth the usurpers reign, Exert their baneful power; O'er the poor fallen sons of men They tyrannise their hour'.[4]

The designs for the *Songs* show a change from the methods used to

3

reproduce the smooth decorously charming drawings of Stothard. Blake adds sharper contours and stronger linear rhythms, makes the clothes reveal forms, sets decorative elements floating in the empty spaces, and entangles the text itself with patterns of flames or vine-branches. Here is paradise regained, with no hint of themes of sin and salvation except as something evil. The state of Innocence presupposes the total rejection of such matters.

Blake thus belongs to the tradition of the Antinomians or Ranters who were vigorously vocal during the Cromwellian revolution. The moral law was repudiated root and branch, and from the repudiation was felt to come the achievement of liberty under love. In 1646 Thomas Edwards, attacking the sects, grouped the Antinomians under the name Seekers and thought they were absorbing the other groups, so that 'all will end in a looseness and licentiousness of living'. Blake cannot be understood unless there is seen in him the re-emergence of the submerged revolutionary traditions that had carried on mainly among the craftsmen and small tradesmen of the towns. Enriched, the Ranter tradition burst out to meet the new situation in which total revolutionary change seemed at last again possible. Behind these traditions lay the simple anarchist emotion: Why, with such possibilities of happiness, sensuous and intellectual fulfilment, and fraternity, must men bedevil themselves with ambitions, greeds, egoisms, divisions, which merely beget frustration and misery?[5]

The Antinomian sects, though small in their numbers, survived: Muggletonians, Ranters, Traskites. The Bolton society from which the Shakers came was presided over by Mother Jane Eardley, who declaimed: 'The new heaven and new earth prophesied of old is about to come', so that priests and the Church would be swept away. The Muggletonians still preached in the fields and parks of London. They had been founded by L. Muggleton, a journeyman tailor, and William Reeves, a cobbler, both of Rosemary Lane, who claimed to be the Two Witnesses of Revelation coming before the end of the world, and who were whipped through the streets. William Hurd tells us in 1811:

Their followers of the present age, still retain that notion (that the Witnesses will return); and they believe that these two apostles, or witnesses, will meet them when they are assembled together. They meet in the evenings of Sundays, at obscure public houses in the out parts of London, and converse about those of their sect who have gone before them. They have very little serious discourse, but are extremely free, sometimes going home drunk . . . There must still be a considerable number of these people in different parts of England; for only a few years ago a new edition in three volumes quarto was printed, of the rhapsodies of Muggleton and Reeves, and had there not been people to purchase them they would not have been printed.

They carried on the tradition from Joachim of Flore that there had been three ages, which they defined as those of Moses, Jesus, and Muggleton: the ages of Water, Blood, and Spirit. Swedenborg had announced the advent of the Third Age in 1757, the year of Blake's birth. Blake referred ironically to this statement in *Marriage.*[6]

Robert Hindmarsh, an organiser of the Swedenborgian Church, met a man from Shoreditch who told him that 'there was no God in the universe but man'; that there was a society, of which he was a member, 'of such as professed themselves to be God', and that he himself was a God. Such groups held that as all our sins had been taken away by Christ the moral law had no force or meaning. Hurd thought they had dwindled by 1811 to two or three groups meeting in public houses. In Blake's song the Little Vagabond sees the church cold and the alehouse healthy and pleasant and warm: with the moral that churches should be cheerful with drink and song. Hurd tells us of the Antinomian groups:

As morality is an unnecessary thing, and as holiness, say they, can be no evidence of faith, so some of them meet in a room in a public house every Sunday evening, having before them that much despised book the Bible. Each member pays for a pot of beer, which is drunk by the company in a social manner. Then a text of the sacred scripture is read, and every one in his turn is called to deliver his opinion concerning it. A great deal of jargon with no meaning ensues, and every thing is said that can be possible be thought of against holiness or good works. The sacred scriptures are debased to the worst of purposes, namely, to set open the flood-gates of profaneness; and youth are corrupted under the prostituted name of religion.

This testimony to the existence of open Antinomian groups in Blake's world is of high importance; and we can hardly doubt that Blake had attended such meetings or talked with some of their members. Antinomians certainly increased under the stimulus of the French Revolution. W. Reid, an ex-radical, in 1800 denounced his old allies: 'Mystics, Muggletonians, Millenaries, and a variety of eccentric characters of different denominations.'[7]

There was affinity in idiom and imagery as well as in ideas between Blake and the Cromwellian Ranters. Thus he later wrote: 'Each man is in his

Spectre's power Untill the arrival of that hour when his humanity awake
And cast his own Spectre into the Lake'. The Ranter Coope had
written: 'Kisses are numbered among transgressors—base things—well, by
base hellish swearing and cursing . . . and by base impudent kisses, my
plaguey holiness hath been confounded, and thrown into the lake of
brimstone'.*

Responding passionately to the French Revolution, Blake felt the need to
express himself in large forms that would embody the fullness of the issues at
stake. To write songs of spontaneously redeeming Innocence was not
enough. He needed a myth able to embody the essence of the historical
events. It was not enough to try to infuse new meanings into old myths, as
Dante, Spenser, Milton had each done in his own way. In the contemporary
world there was one poet who had used a mythic idiom unrelated to any
of the prevailing systems, Christian or pagan. This was Macpherson with his
attempt to recreate Celtic myth and legend in his Ossianic prose-poems—
though Gray in a smaller way had struck out new lines in his Norse poems.
In *Poetical Sketches* Blake had shown interest in Ossian, but it was largely
mediated through Chatterton. Since 1783 he had certainly read and reread
the Ossianic poems, and they had provided him with the basis for a new
start in building large-scale myths in loose rhythms, which would be quite
new and yet adequate to the issues of his world.[8]

The two works in which he thus broke through into a new poetic universe
were *Thel* and *Tiriel*. It is hard to prove which came first; but it is best to
start with *Thel*, since it springs in part from Blake's own critique of the
Songs of Innocence. Its title-page has the date 1789; but such a date merely
refers to the time he started engraving. The motto and the conclusion
(plate 6) vary in tone and style from plates 1–5 and are etched in a slightly
different script: they seem to represent changes or additions made in 1791.
Thel defines the throes of the individual seeking to advance from the stage
of Innocence; it thus has particular reference to puberty, but cannot be
limited to that moment of change.

Thel (her name derived from Greek *thelein*, to wish or want) is first heard
lamenting; she cries out against the transience of life and the certainty of
death. She is answered by four creatures: a lily, a cloud, a worm, a clod of
clay. The Lily tells her that however slight and brief is a lily's life she is
'visited from heaven'; she partakes of the blessed energies that pervade all
things. And she has her uses, helping cow, lamb, bees. The Cloud, carrying

* See Appendices on Antinomians, also on Moravrians.

out its role in the cycles of nature, sees the fulfilment of function in the delights of sexual union, and tells Thel that when she passes away, 'it is to tenfold life, to love, to peace, and raptures holy'. She is part of the changing ever-renewed world. Thel replies that she herself is outside that world. Is she to live only to feed the worm at the end? The Cloud replies that even that is to be of use, to be blest. 'Every thing that lives Lives not alone nor for itself.' He then calls the Worm, which *Thel* sees as a helpless baby. The Clod pities the Worm and bows over it maternally. She repeats the Cloud's lesson in stronger terms. 'I ponder, and I cannot ponder yet I live and love.'

Here is the experience that Thel must accept if she is to develop, to become truly human. She obeys the Clod's request to enter her house. But, once inside, she sees 'the secrets of the land unknown . . . the couches of the dead, & where the fibrous roots Of every heart on earth infixes deep its restless twists'. She cannot accept the world of birth, death, rebirth, the endless intertwining of all the forms of life in ceaseless process; she cannot accept the limitations thus imposed on her senses, with all their conflicts and snares. 'Why a little curtain of flesh on the bed of our desire?' She gives a shriek (of fear or anger) and flees back to the Vale of Har, the pastoral paradise.

Depicted as the virgin of Romantic Neoclassicism (as in Flaxman's art), she is in one sense the girl on the edge of puberty, shrinking, afraid of bearing a child. Lying in her own grave (the initiation-passage into a new life), she hears her future self crying out against the fall into the rule of tyrannical law in existent society (nature), so that the senses grow deceitful lures to destruction. The ambiguity comes out in the cry about the little curtain of flesh: the senses which are the sources of satisfaction and fulfilment have become cut off and alienated; they become barriers, prison-walls.

Possibly the first version ended with her acceptance of her destiny as a woman. But as Blake brooded over the theme, he felt that such a solution was all too easy in our world. Thel cannot carry her innocence directly into her maturing life; the earthly paradise cannot merge into our tormented world. She realises that to go further into life is to face the challenge of a divided self, a divided society (the world defined in *Tiriel*). But perhaps we can say that in returning to the Vale of Har, she does not merely express defeat; she returns to the pastoral values to gain strength for tackling the dangerous world of experience. In the final design children ride a bridled snake; innocence after all can control the released energies of life in its fullness. If the snake is phallic, Blake says that innocence can enter the sphere of sexual experience without loss. If we link the snake with that in *America* (plate 11) where Boston's Angel (perhaps Samuel Adams) denounces the tyranny of George III (Tiriel) in the name of pity, generosity, peace, the reference is much wider.

The later motto seems to sum up the moral. 'Does the eagle know what is in the pit Or wilt thou go ask the mole? Can wisdom be put in a silver rod, Or love in a golden bowl?' Love and wisdom must be united; they cannot be limited by the sceptre of power or the chalice of any ritual. Each creature has its own way of dealing with the issue of death, the moment of deep change, the awareness of the world's limiting pressures.

Was the poem suggested by a miscarriage of Catherine's? Was Thel the child that feared to be born? Some such event may have given the first impulse to the poem; but an interpretation which sees only a Neoplatonic myth of the soul afraid to enter the corrupt world of matter hopelessly distorts the scope of the poem. Blake's originality lies precisely in his power to take such themes and give them a new force by seeing them in terms of human experience. In a sense he himself is Thel as he faces the problem of understanding and defining the passage into a new level of experience when the state of innocence is left.

Many elements have gone to build the poem. Blake recalls from Young's *Night Thoughts* the phrase 'close twisted with the Fibres of the heart'. (Young's poem represents the conventional death-meditation that he is transforming.) Also he recalls Voltaire's irony, in the poem on the Lisbon earthquake, about the comfort of being consumed by worms; he shows that a fuller acceptance can eliminate the irony. More importantly, he is rewriting in his own terms Milton's *Comus* with its theme of a girl submitted to the shock of sex and a luring perilous world. What Milton saw as temptation is for him a sphere that must be accepted and entered. He has also been affected by Darwin's *Loves of the Plants*, 1789. Darwin in conventional couplets and diction gives a lively account of the sexual organs of plants in mythological terms. Thus he describes the sylphs: 'Quivering in air their painted plumes expand, And colour'd shadows dance upon the land.' (He uses the same system of myth to define scientific processes and industrial mechanisms.) Blake was impressed by Darwin's imagery of ceaseless sexual encounters among flowers and the aggressive actions of the males. Some of his flowers, given human form, seem to come out of Darwin's verses, notes, and illustrations. Thus, both his text and design recall fair Tulipa who in autumn flees 'the loud alarms, And folds the infant closer in her arms'.*

With *Tiriel*, which also has the Vale of Har in the background, we move into the full social and political scene. Tiriel is both George III and any individual who has succumbed to the power-ethic. The theme is his discovery that the society he has created and dominated is a dead and deadly thing. He has enslaved one brother, Zazel, while another, Ijim, lives fiercely alone in the wilderness. Tiriel stands, old and blind, before his beautiful palace, rejected by his children and by his wife Myratana, a name taken by Blake from Bryant's Myrina, Queen of Amazons in the West of Africa. Tiriel curses his sons, then tries vainly to find refuge with his senile parents Har and Heva. Ijim, honest and grim, does not recognise him and takes him scornfully back to the palace. There Tiriel again curses his children and compels one of his daughters, Hela, to lead him to Har. On the way they pass Zazel and his sons, who insult him. Come before Har, he gives a long speech on the cruelties, deceits, miseries, of a divided world. Here the text comes close to the final speech of Thel, bringing out the link between the two poems.[9]

The mythic element is slighter than in *Thel*. Blake wants to write a more or less straight poem, of the Gothic type, which sets out the impasse of despotism. It seems certain that he at first hoped to publish in a normal way. The manuscript is filed in a cover marked 'Tiriel/MS by Mr. Blake' as if he had submitted it to a publisher, no doubt Johnson. More, the illustrations do not resemble his illuminated designs, but would have suited the kind of copper-engravings used in ordinary books.

As with *Thel*, Blake rewrote the ending in an effort to deepen the work's meaning. Tiriel belatedly recognises the evils he has fostered, a world in which man regresses to a reptilian state. 'And now my paradise is fallen.' No explanation is given for the fall, and we do not know what his sons mean to do with the world they have taken over. They merely say that he enslaved them, so they rebelled. Tiriel's 'blessing was a cruel curse. His curse may be a blessing'. However, the drawings show the sons as representing three different phases of historical development. The first, with vines in his hair,

* He may have been drawn to flower-symbolism also by Boehme, who predicted the coming Age of the Lily: its bloom would soon burst out, especially in the North where lilies were rare. The Nettle stood for the stern dispensation of the Law; the blood-red Rose the dispensation of the Son. The Coming of the Lily meant the Birth of the Life and Love and Joy of God in the lives of men. Blake links rose and lily twice in *Songs of Experience* and they appear together in the Prophetic Books.

represents an early Bacchic culture; the second has the laurel wreath of an heroic age; the third has the spiked crown of cruel kingship that he will inherit.*

Blake makes clear that Tiriel is George III and that the direct theme is the breakdown of George in 1788. George did not go blind, but the Queen said that at times his eyes were 'nothing but black currant jelly'. The distracted king insisted that all marriages were annulled and violently desired the lady of his wife's bedchamber. He had recently signed a Proclamation against Vice and Immorality, but three of his sons rebelled against the moral code; they were publicly drunk, took up with prostitutes, and started their own gambling club. Tiriel curses his five daughters (his senses) except the youngest, Hela (emblem of loose love, named after the goddess of death in Gray's *Descent of Odin*). She recognises that he merely wants to exploit her and calls him an accursed man of sin, who scoffs at love. George was hysterically unbalanced with his daughters, screamed when unable to reach them, and was calmed only by the youngest, Amelia, aged five. After a fit, finding his four girls waiting to receive him, he cried, 'I return to you a poor old man, weak in mind and body.' Blake's stress on Kingdoms of the West suggests the relation of the action to America.[10]

In *Thel* the Vale of Har is the closed paradise of childhood, of pastoral innocence. In *Tiriel* Har and Heva are shown as if aged babies. Blake thus stresses that there is no solution in clinging passively to childhood's values. Har and Heva also represent an etiolated feeble art such as that ruling in Blake's world: pastoral or sensuous elements made sentimental or debased as in the art of Blake's friends Stothard and Flaxman. The Vale of Har is opposed to the oppressively enclosed system of Tiriel's kingdom (gigantic columns, doors, pyramids), yet offers no true alternative. Throughout there is stress on failure of vision. Tiriel is blind. Har and Heva are so absorbed in one another that they cannot take in anything else, Mnetha (Athena, Mnemysyne), guardian of the Vale, stares blankly into space, apparently representing Memory and Nature.

* The sources are much more complex than in *Thel* : *King Lear* and the Bible, Ossian and Sophocles' *Oedipus*, Bryant and the Book of Enoch, Mallet's *Northern Antiquities* and Edward Davies, whose *Celtic Researches* appeared some fifteen years later. The name Tiriel is from Cornelius Agrippa, associated with the planet Mercury and the element Sulphur. Mercury is god of commercial transactions, causing prosperity or poverty; changing reports of George's health did affect trade and stocks. Blake could have got many of his names from popular sources. *The Conjurer's Magazine*, October 1771, had a table with magic names including Tiriel, Zazel, Adonai, Bne Seraphim.

In *Thel* Blake decisively develops his illustrative system. The text is linked dynamically with the decorations, whether they are a mere tendril or a fully worked-out scene. When we see Thel in her tall nakedness (with impossibly long legs) confronting the babe-worm and the cloud-youth, the poem gains a new fullness. Decorations like that of the snake of the end suggest a new dimension of meanings extended ever more subtly so that finally poem and design become an indissoluble whole.

Blake was now at last launched as a prophetic poet. The American Revolution had stirred his first deep questionings as to the nature of his world. Now his need to understand and express what was happening in the French Revolution was one with his need to tell his fellow-men what he had discovered. But the problem of how to reach out and gain an audience was insoluble for him. He was both in the central storm of change and yet cut off from all communication with those he so passionately wanted to address. Herein lay a tragic conflict and at the same time a driving-force that would not let him rest: as if he had only to struggle on and reach some point of final illumination that would restore his contact with the masses to whom all the while he felt an active relation. The situation was one without parallel and its contradictions played their part in determining the form and direction of his work. No poet had ever felt himself so deeply inside the forces of history; no poet with something importance to say had ever been more cut off from any significant audience.

5

Marriage of Heaven and Hell, 1789–93

The crucial years 1789–90 saw more than *Thel* and *Tiriel*. Blake felt the need to make a more directly personal statement of his position, which he did in *The Marriage of Heaven and Hell*, and also to relate his symbolism directly to the events of the French Revolution. It was probably in the spring of 1790 that he embarked on what was to be a long poem describing the Revolution and bringing out its full meaning. Again he made tentative efforts to publish in a normal way and then drew back. The first book of his *French Revolution* got into proofs, but that was all. The publisher would certainly have been Johnson, and we can only surmise that once again Blake's nerve deserted him. It is more than unlikely that Johnson became afraid to issue the poem. True, in February 1791, after publishing the first volume of Paine's *Rights of Man*, he grew afraid and Paine had to find another publisher. But Johnson put out an abridged edition of Paine's book in August 1791 and in 1792 he published strongly radical works by Barlow. It was round this time that the political scene much worsened. Cumberland wrote in a letter of 1792–3: 'It would be safer to write one's sentiments in Turkey or Venice than in this unfortunate island—where the inhabitants are running blindfold to total ruin—and lick the hand just raised to shed their blood.' But in 1790–1 a poem such as Blake's could not possibly have provoked prosecution.[1]

An Advertisement in the proofs states: 'The remaining Books of this Poem are finished, and will be published in their order.' The title-page is dated 1791. Whether Blake had actually written more or had merely resolved to do so, we cannot tell. What we have covers the early stages of the Revolution, before the attack on the Bastille; the theme is the challenge to king and nobility by the Third Estate. There are shortcomings. Blake does not seem to know the difference between army and militia, and makes the Assembly more effective than it was. He sets the scene, not in Versailles, but in Paris. All his characters are symbolic. He invented a Duke of Burgundy to represent

56

the hostile nobility while using the Duke of Orleans to represent the liberal section; the Abbé Sièyes represents the people while the Archbishop represents the Church, the Accuser. The events of June and July are drawn together in a sort of Last Judgement. The king, sick on his couch, is a Tiriel who has lost his nerve. The events and characters dissolve and assume new contours in a dynamic clash of the elements. 'O princes of fire, whose flames are for growth, and consuming,' cries Orleans. 'Fear not dreams, fear not visions . . . Can the fires of nobility ever be quenched, or the stars by a stormy night?' From now on the stars are Blake's symbol for power, for military might.*

Blake merges his persons with natural forces such as fire, wind, cloud, water, light. Man's relation to nature is also his relation to his fellows and to himself. Hunger and filth are 'pestilent fogs round cities of men'. The spectres of religious men are driven out of the abbeys 'by the fiery cloud of Voltaire, and thundrous rocks of Rousseau'. (These thinkers are thus seen in positive terms, as forces breaking down an evil society.) Clouds play a large role in the symbolism. They represent power, they are high and immaterial, emblems of transcendence. But they are also the source and site of storm and darkness. Shadowing the earth, they are the barrier of the brooding dead that obscures the sight of the living. Yet as they ascend and grow luminous, fading into the sun, they represent true vision. Thus they can stand for the imposed unity of obscurantist authority and the free unity of brotherhood. In their conflicts of darkness and light, gloom and ruddy glow, the human struggle is reflected and given deeper meanings. The convening Commons are spirits of fire in the porches of the sun, bringing a new dawn to the anxious city.

The movement up and down of wind and cloud reflects the stage of the struggle and the values of the social situation. As the king symbolically comes down from sky to earth, the nobles are 'shady mountains . . . each conversing

---

* They belong both to Newton and tyrant Urizen. 'What dread night when Urizen called the stars round his feet' (cancelled plate in *America*). When in the French Revolution the king invokes the scorn of his ancestors on the rebels, 'his bosom Expanded like starry heaven.' In *The Four Zoas* (V) the stars, the counter-revolutionary armies of Yorktown and Valmy, are called on by Urizen's council to deny God, but are overcome. 'The stars threw down their spears & fled naked away.' In *A Song of Liberty* the gloomy king leads his 'starry hosts through the waste wilderness', where 'he promulgates his ten commands'. Stars casting down their spears are soldiers dropping their arms. Stars were ancient emblems of power through astrologic ideas of their control of human destinies. Paul defied the astral powers; the Gnostics held that Jesus had broken the power of the stars. Paracelsus wrote of the Peasant Revolt, 'The peasants have submitted to the stars and have been beaten by them. Whoever trusts the stars, trusts a traitor.'

with woes in the infinite shadow of his soul'. They gather like clouds and further obscure the king's light; their fearful thunder is taken in and softened, 'embosomed', by the woods of France, and echoed by the higher 'clouds of wisdom prophetic' rolling over the palace roof. The scene is now set for the struggle between the higher clouds, the people, and the lower clouds, the nobles, while the clouds of prophetic truth dominate the situation.

We next go deeper, down to hell, the dens of the Bastille, and the theme becomes a harrying of hell. (Blake also calls hell the sulphur heaven: power based on war-destructiveness.) Next we ascend to the Commons, who have taken over the realm of light, and then make a different descent, in the darkness of the Louvre where the nobles deludedly think they are still aloft. (Here we are close to the scene of the fallen angels in Milton.) The archbishop's vision draws on Revelation in a sort of parody: the heavenly court descends to earth in glory and the snow-white aged God is the counterpart of the king, his heaven that of the French court.

With the Abbé Sièyes we return to the Commons, and there is danger of thunder, fire, plague, as the Commons reject the horse of war, the pale horse of famine and pestilence, and initiate an apocalypse of peaceful fraternity and equality. Now comes the working-out of the Revolution. Lafayette descends as a new Lucifer to take the army away from the Satanic king. A final great upward movement opens the bottoms of the world, brings the enormous dead to life as pale fires, and leaves the king and nobles powerless, while 'the Senate sat in peace, sat beneath the morning's beam'. All mankind, the whole universe, is carried into a new age.

There is continual reference to, and transformation of, the themes of *Paradise Lost* and Revelation. There are seven scenes in a symmetrical pattern: Louvre, Bastille, Commons, Louvre, Commons, Army, Louvre. The Louvre, seat of kingly power, is at the start, middle, and end, but hemmed in by the Commons, with the Bastille balancing the Army. This construction looks to Revelation with its three sets of seven events, each seventh event issuing in a world-shaking storm. At the same time Blake is reversing the narrative of *Paradise Lost*, showing how men rise from the depths to turn earth back into paradise. He moves to and fro in time to reveal the wrongs that have led to the Revolution, till at last the prisoners look up and laugh at the jailer's light. A power is rising up from the deprived and oppressed which will destroy the king in the hell he has built.[2]

Blake's own conditions were bettering. His brother James was also doing well. In August 1790 he applied to the Commissioner for Paving and was given permission 'to take up the paving to erect Stone Columns' in place of the wooden ones before his house. He was probably building a more imposing ornamental portico. In the autumn of that year Blake moved to 13 Hercules Buildings, Lambeth, across Westminster Bridge. The buildings, running diagonally between Kennington Road and Lambeth Palace, consisted of disparate houses, one to three stories high, each with a small front garden. Lambeth was still not much more than sets of houses along roads and lanes driven through meadows and marshes. No. 13 (with eight or ten rooms, says Tatham) was one of the biggest of the twenty-six attached houses in the Buildings; in the garden of no. 15 was a house owned by Philip Astley, proprietor of the circus about three streets away. Between no. 13 and the Palace on the south and Blackfriars Bridge on the north were mostly open fields. Blake enjoyed the setting and wrote in his notebook: 'At Lambeth, beneath the poplar trees'. In his garden was a big-leafed vine, which he could not bear to prune, and several fruit-trees. From 1791 to 1800 (5 June) he paid annual rates here, at an average of 17*s*. 1½*d*. That decade was his most prosperous, and during it he produced a large number of poetic works. For a while Catherine had a servant, until she decided that she preferred to do the housework herself.

Blake was busy engraving in 1790–1, mainly for Johnson, who in a letter to Darwin on 23 July 1791, about the engraving of Wedgwood's Portland Vase, remarked that 'Blake is certainly capable of making an exact copy of the vase, I believe more than Mr B[artolozzi].' Blake did five plates for Darwin's poem, was mentioned in the prospectus for Fuseli's Milton works, and in October 1791 was asked to do engravings for the third volume of Stuart and Revett's *Antiquities of Athens*. He replied, 'Tho' full of work he is glad to embrace the offer of engraving such beautiful things and will do what he can by the end of January.' (In fact he completed the work on 3 April 1792.) He also engraved six drawings which he himself made for Mary Wollstonecraft's *Original Stories from Real Life*.[3]

He felt the need to add a direct statement of his principles to the mythic definitions he had begun with *Thel*, *Tiriel*, and *The French Revolution*. So he wrote and printed *The Marriage of Heaven and Hell*, which from one angle was a satirical parody of Swedenborg and from another an attempt to show his version of true visionary experiences. He linked the work with Swedenborg by the half-jesting remark, 'As a new heaven is begun, and it is now thirty-three years since its advent, the Eternal Hell revives. And lo!

Swedenborg is the angel sitting at the tomb; his writings are the linen clothes folded up.' The new heaven had begun with Blake's birth in 1757; the Eternal Hell had revived in 1790 with the French Revolution—not at all the kind of thing Swedenborg wanted or foresaw.

The work carried on with a reversal of all accepted values and set out the dialectic of the union of opposites:

Without Contraries is no progression. Attraction and Repulsion, Reason and Energy, Love and Hate, are necessary to Human existence. From these contraries spring what the religious call Good & Evil. Good is the passive that obeys Reason. Evil is the active springing from Energy. Good is heaven, Evil is Hell.

To the definition made by the 'religious' he opposes the Voice of the Devil denying the duality of body and soul and the evil nature of Energy:

Man has no Body distinct from his soul; for that call'd Body is a portion of the Soul discern'd by the five Senses, the chief inlets of Soul in this age. Energy is the only life, and is from the Body; and Reason is the bound or outward circumference of Energy. Energy is Eternal Delight.

These statements are crucial for the understanding of Blake at all his phases. He goes on to transvalue all the accepted moral positions. In *Paradise Lost* the Governor or Reason is called Messiah, but in the *Book of Job* Milton's Messiah is called Satan, and so on. The creed of Energy is set out in the vigorous Proverbs of Hell. Blake again denies any gap between God and Man. 'God only Acts & Is, in existing beings or men. And Man only exists in and through the Body.' Proclaiming the end of all divisions, the reversal of the Fall, Blake declares that with 'the return of Adam into Paradise' the whole creation appears 'infinite and holy, whereas it now appears finite and corrupt. This will come to pass by an improvement of sensual enjoyment.'*

Since all significant acts have their relation to the fall or the liberation of man, he claims that the ending of the delusion that man has a body distinct

* In saying that Milton was of the Devil's Party without knowing it, Blake picks up a term from the Cromwellian period where first the Royalists were called the Devil's Party, then after 1660 they themselves used the term of the revolutionists. Salmasius, attacking Milton, had seen him as of the Diabolical Party, and by 1764 the Whigs or Republicans were often called 'the party of the devils'. In 1780 Charles Dibdin issued a weekly, *The Devil*, asking, 'Can the Devil speak truth?' English Jacobins called the Devil the first Jacobin and Adam and Eve Sans-Culottes, as also were Moses and Aaron as 'abolishers' of the slave-trade.[4]

from his soul is expressed and brought about by his printing methods using corrosives 'which in Hell are salutary and medicinal, melting apparent surfaces away and describing the infinite which is hid'. In one of his *Fancies* he links the six stages in his printing system with the six days of creation. So every print of his is a recreation of the world, a moment in the reachievement of paradise. Then in the last *Fancy* he sets out the Antinomian concept of Jesus as the condemner of the ten commandments and the law. 'Jesus was all virtue, and acted from impulse, not from rules.'

In the 1790s the term Energy was far from having the mechanical relations that were soon to come with Carnot and Joule. The Cambridge-Platonist Henry More had defined Energy as Operation, Efflux, Activity, giving as examples 'the light of the Sun, the phantasmes of the soul'. Citing Plotinus, he ended, 'I cannot better explain this Platonick term, Energie, then by calling it the rayes of an essence, or the beams of a vitall Centre'. Thomas Taylor carried on this usage and was fond of the terms energy and energising, often using them when there was nothing of the sort in the Greek text of Plato's *Timaeus* which he was translating. Scientists used energy in a very general sense: 'Nature unquestionably abounds with numberless unthought-of energies', we read in an Essay on Sun-Spots in the *Philosophical Transactions* for 1783. Energy and its fettering by oppressive social forces became a key-theme in progressive works of the 1790s. A parody of the way in which it was exalted occurs in Elizabeth Hamilton's anti-Godwinian *Memoirs of a Modern Philosopher* (1800):

Besides, in a corrupt state of society, where many people believe in a God, the existence of laws and government generates weaknesses which no one can entirely escape; the energies cannot arrive at that state of perfection to which they will be found to approximate, as soon as these existing causes of depravity have been entirely removed.

'All removed among the Hottentots!' cried Glib. 'No obstacles to perfectibility among the Conoguais. No priests! No physicians; All exert their energies.'

Though the author could not have heard of Blake, she could not have more aptly satirised his concept of energy. We see certain links of his ideas with those of Godwin in his anarchism and Hartley with his faith in Human Perfectibility. But Blake worked out his positions in terms of a dialectical concept of development (as we saw in the quotations given above from *The Marriage*) as the others did not.

The writers to whom Blake is close are the late Gothic novelists. Thus *Zofloya or the Moor*, 1806, by 'Rosa Dacre better known as Rosa Matilda', tells at length of 'enslaved energies', of 'dreams of mysterious tendency flitting about the disordered eye of sleep', and of 'images presenting themselves to mental vision', of 'boldly organised minds'. The key of such works is set by the phrase Enslaved Energies. (*Zofloya* strongly influenced young Shelley.) Blake states that 'war is energy enslaved'.[5]

That the Blakes read Gothic novels and were moved by them is shown by the tempera on canvas, inscribed: 'Agnes, From the novel of The Monk. Designed and painted by Catherine Blake, and presented by her in Gratitude and Friendship to Mrs. Butts'. And as late as 1800 Blake told Crabb Robinson of La Motte Fouqué's *Sintram*, 'This is better than my things'.

Two more points from *The Marriage* must be noted. We find that Blake knew of initiation-ritual, with its tests and ordeals, among tribal peoples, and that he saw the prophet's ordeals, exemplifying the pangs of growth and renewal in all men, as carrying on the initiation-pattern. He asks Ezekiel 'why he ate dung, & lay so long on his right & left side', and the prophet answers, 'The desire of raising other men into a perception of the infinite: this the North American tribes practise'. Secondly, using his own terms, he divides men into two classes, the producers and the exploiters. The Prolific are preyed on by the Devourers. To the latter 'it seems as if the producer is in his chains; but it is not so, he only takes portions of Existence and fancies that the whole'. The Devourers or Masters cannot realise the element of freedom that lives on in the producers, who in fact are creating life and all its potentialities. Blake adds, 'Whoever tries to reconcile them seeks to destroy existence. Religion is an endeavour to reconcile the two.' So Religion seeks to destroy existence. (He thus formulates the need of class-struggle in a divided society; his formulation has links both with the Hegelian concept of Master and Servant, and with Marx's discussion of alienation.)

Blake speaks of redemption brought about by an improvement of sensual enjoyment. Improvement was a key-term of the period, applied especially to advances in agricultural technique, but invading all spheres of thought and helping to develop the idea of Progress. By the end of the century improvement was the test of value. Thus, the *General Biography* says in the preface to its first volume, 1799: 'the circumstances which appear most worthy of guiding the decision [of selection] are those of invention and improvement'. Edward Young writes, 'How changed the face of Nature? how improved?' The evangelists even improved the Bible. *The Evangelical Magazine* in 1794 wrote of one of them, 'He attempted in 1753 to expound and improve some portion of the Sacred Scriptures.' The same magazine dealt with the 'progressive knowledge of glorified saints', and declared that 'if there is no increase of knowledge after the first moment of the saint's entrance into the upper world, then one great end of society is destroyed, which is improvement'. Blake transfers the idea from the mind to the senses. In this he had some support in Methodist hymns. Here is one chosen by Wesley for his Collection: 'Earth then a scale to heaven shall be, Earth shall point out the road; The creatures all shall lead to thee, And all we taste be God.'[6]

Blake was dilatory in answering letters. On 21 November 1791 Nancy Flaxman wrote to her sister-in-law in London, 'Pray call on Mr. Blake & beg of him to answer your brother's letter directly.' One of the jobs he was doing for Johnson was the engravings for *Narrative, of a five years' expedition, against the Revolted Negroes of Surinam, in Guiana*, by Captain John Gabriel Stedman. On 1 December Stedman wrote in his journal that he had got 'about 40 Engravings from London. Some well Some ill . . . I wrote to the Engraver Blake to thank him twice for his excellent work but never received any answer.' Since 1789 there had been much debate in Parliament and the press on the Slave Trade, but the bill for the abolition was defeated in 1793 through anti-Jacobin attacks. Blake wrote his *Little Black Boy* in the early days of the agitation.[7]

Stedman was an interesting character. Son of an officer in the Scots Brigade in Holland and an aristocratic Dutchwoman, he had leanings to art but entered the brigade. He described himself as bold, stirring and quarrelsome, at times taken to be mad through his 'studying to be singular'. After some riotous years he went on the expedition to Guiana. There he fell in love with a mulatto slave-girl, Joanna, who nursed him through a bad illness. He married her and she bore him a son John; but he left her in Guiana through lack of money to buy her freedom. The Dutch in 1775 favoured the American colonists and interned the brigade; in 1782 Stedman had to choose between Dutch nationality and dismissal without compensation. Joanna died, apparently poisoned. Stedman, now married to a Dutchwoman, was joined by John, who entered the navy and was drowned at the age of seventeen. Stedman, in poor health, retired to Tiverton, Devon, where he fathered four children, farmed in a small way, and wrote his *Memoirs* and *Narrative*. Drawings he had made in Surinam (now lost) were used in his book, where he records his horror at the brutal treatment of the slaves. Blake did sixteen of the eighty engravings. In his journal Stedman does not record anything of Blake's talk. He was patriotic and anti-radical as well as explosive in temperament; and it is certain that Blake disclosed nothing of his views during their meetings, though they would have agreed on the question of slavery. Stedman knew Blake only as an engraver. His attitude to prophetic matters is shown by his reference to the millenarian Brothers as 'a mad Prophet'. The first record of captain and artist meeting is on 21 June 1794, though they must have met often before than.

During 1791 Blake, we saw, met Mary Wollstonecraft. Her *Vindication of the Rights of Women* must have deeply moved him, even if he disagreed with the feminist approach in itself. Mary's main interest however was in Fuseli, with whom she was in love in 1792.

Though averse from any direct involvement, Blake could not but have closely followed political developments in London. The Society for Constitutional Information was revived early in 1791 by Horne Tooke, Hollis, and William Sharp among others, mainly in support of Paine's *Rights of Man*. One attender of meetings was John Richter, whose brother, Henry, an engraver, knew Blake. Early in 1792 Paine issued the second part of his book, and county and corporation addresses were got up in protest against seditious publications. Pitt had a proclamation made against such works and began a libel action against Paine, which was to be heard in September.

A story about Blake warning Paine has been uncritically repeated. The latter, at Johnson's, was telling how he had delivered a fiery speech to the Friends of Liberty, when Blake laid his hands on his shoulders, saying, 'You must not go home, or you are a dead man!' So he hurried him off to France, where he had been elected as a deputy in the Assembly. The customs officials turned over his baggage with 'extra malice', but he got aboard his ship. Too late 'an order was received from the Home Office to detain him'. The facts were that the government and its spies knew all about Paine's movements. He was shadowed all the while, but the last thing that Pitt wanted was to arrest him and hold a political trial that would have had enormous repercussions. Spies trailed him all the way to Dover, and the government must have been greatly relieved when they reported his departure to France.*

Blake, romanticising the past, must have told the story of his warning Paine to the young artists about him in his later years. No doubt he had met Paine at Johnson's a few times. A person he certainly did know well was the engraver Sharp, a perfervid character, ready to acclaim any man or movement that might possibly herald the overthrow of the existing system. A Jacobin, he joined the main radical organisations and was on the committee of the Society for Constitutional Information, which in May 1792 was instructed to inquire into the rumours of Paine's prosecution and which reported in June that information had been laid against him. Sharp may well have told Blake of these events. Godwin met him continually among those talking of 'ideas and revolutions' at Horne Tooke's; and his evidence helped the acquittal of the S.C.I. leaders when they were arrested. He became an ardent follower of Brothers and of Joanna Southcott.[8]

Blake was far too cautious to attend any meetings of the S.C.I. His name does not appear in the very detailed records of the sedition trials of 1794. In his own Lambeth there was a resolute group called the Loyal Lambeth Association, which had its own uniform with cockades in the cocked hat, and officers ranging from captain to three corporals, as well as two drummers and fifers. They held military exercises, a witness stated, with muskets. Again his name does not appear in the records.[9]

In January 1792 the print-dealer Bowyer announced an edition of Hume's *History* in five volumes; Blake and Sharp were to be among the engravers. But Blake's name does not appear on any of the 195 plates. He must have been dropped; for in December 1806 he wrote that the dealers Boydell, Macklin, Bowyer looked on him 'as Incapable of Employment'. He and Sharp were also to do work for Fuseli's *Milton*, but Boydell dropped the project, afraid that it would harm his own edition of Milton. About 7 September 1792 Blake's mother died. On Sunday the 9th she was buried in Bunhill Fields, 'nine feet deep', for a fee of 19s.

---

* Behind Blake's story may lie the fact of Paine's arrest on a trumped-up charge of debt (£200) at a dinner of the Society of Friends of the People on 11 April 1792. Johnson and another bookseller followed and paid the money. It is barely possible that Blake was at some discussion about the matter held at Johnson's place. Paine clearly refused to leave England until in September he heard of his election to the French National Assembly. There were no Friends of Liberty; but there were Friends of the Liberty of the Press, who, on 15 June 1792, held a dinner to celebrate Fox's Libel Bill.

Blake had been writing short poems in which he added a concentrated social protest to direct lyric statement. Outstanding is *The Tyger*. There he confronts a universe in which gentleness and ferocity exist side by side, and asks how they can be balanced, united in the meaning of the whole. The 'fearful symmetry' lives in the Tyger itself, expressed in its powerfully organised form and achieving its own kind of beauty; it also appears in a universe which can contain both Tyger and Lamb. The Tyger is both symmetry and energy. The energy threatens to drive the symmetry beyond the bounds of its living structure, to upset its organic balances. If the bounds are transgressed, the Tyger becomes terrible and destructive. The Creator, daring to frame the Tyger, is the imaginative artist, Blake, who is one with the revolutionary people. That people can be terrible and destructive, though they hold also all the promises of redemption. Blake, the Poetic Genius, alone realises in fullness the marriage of contraries, the fearful symmetry, the ceaseless struggle between destruction and creation. So he both blesses and fears the tyger-form. 'The tygers of wrath are wiser than the horses of instruction,' said the *Proverbs of Hell*. The fiery creature in *The Marriage*, appearing 'to the east, about three degrees', the distance of Paris from London, is the force of the Revolution; the angel with his distorted vision sees it as Leviathan. It has a tiger's forehead.*

The Tyger then is, above all, the energy in people which can break beyond its normal bounds, but without which the necessary transformations cannot come about. The French people have destroyed the power-system that had held them in subjection. This point is made clear by the lines, 'when the stars threw down their spears, And water'd heaven with their tears'. We saw earlier that this image meant for Blake the collapse of military power, of despotic authority in all matters. He asks if the violences in France are necessary and acceptable, or to be rejected and denounced. He decides that we must accept the fearful symmetry of life (symmetry breaking down into asymmetry and then regaining its inner and outer balances on a new level). The Terror in France is unavoidable. It is part of a dialectic moving towards a fuller humanity, a broader and more secure symmetry of relationships between men and men, men and nature.

If the fearful symmetry is quite lost, the Tyger becomes a mere beast of

---

* Symmetry for Blake has two meanings: the inner coherence and dynamic balance of form which gives that form true identity and functional force (its fourfold existence), and the dead mechanistic equipoises of the Newtonian world where action and reaction are equal and opposite. In *The Marriage* Blake is thinking of the beast from the sea in *Revelation*, cxiii, 2.

prey, of indefensible violence. In *The Four Zoas* (IV), men 'dishumaniz'd' by war take on the 'forms of tygers & of Lions'. In Blake's Notebook, three pages after the Tyger, we meet the Sun rising 'clad in robes of blood & gold . . . Crownd with warlike fires and raging desires'. The Sun, emblem of innocent energy in *Songs of Innocence*, takes on tigerish qualities in its resistance to tyranny. In a later poem the passage to the future has been cleared and violence is no longer needed: we go through the Gates of Wrath to the break of day where the war of 'swords & Spears Melted by dewy tears Exhales on high'. The tears of defeat shed by the oppressors have turned into fertilising dawn-dew that ushers in the new day.*

Drafts show that Blake found it hard to shape the *Tyger* so that it effectively expressed his meaning. The date seems that of the September Massacres, 1792, which were followed fast by the defeat of the Austrians at Valmy, the formation of the National Convention, and the declaration of the Republic.[10]

The lyric *London*, which tells of Blake's roaming in the streets, can be dated 1792–3. He wrote, 'The german-forged links I meet', then changed the line: 'The mind-forged manacles I meet'. The first version states that he sees everywhere signs of the State, the German monarchy, fettering people. Much indignation among democrats had been caused by English collaborations with the counter-revolutionary forces. A letter which the London Corresponding Society proposed should be sent to France in October 1792 read:

Let German despots act as they please, we shall rejoice at their fall . . . with unconcern then we view the Elector of Hanover join his troops to traitors and robbers; but the King of Great Britain will do well to remember, that this country is not Hanover. Should he forget this distinction, we will not.

Things grew worse when German troops landed in England. The reports of the 1794 treason trials repeat the phrase: 'It was just at the time the Hessian troops were landed without the consent of Parliament'. The accused Hardy was cited as saying: 'Hessians and Austrians are already among us, and if we tamely submit a cloud of these armed barbarians may shortly be poured in

---

* The lying-down of lion and lamb, which is for Blake the resolution of the conflicts of the Tyger, meant for anti-Jacobins the confounding of all order. Lord Abingdon, 1792, in the slavery-debates, said the Levellers were prophesying that 'all being equal, blacks and whites, French and English, wolves and lambs, all, "merry companions every one", promiscuously pig together; engendering . . . a new species of man as the product of this new philosophy.'

among us.' (Note the Blakean use of the term cloud.) In April 1795 a resolution thanked Earl Stanhope and the patriotic associations whose protests have had 'the salutary effect of chasing the Hessian and Hanoverian Mercenaries from our Coasts: who, but for these exertions, might have been marched, ere this, into the very heart of the country'. In Blake's changing of his line we see his fear of a too-direct political allusion. He drops the plain accusation of the state and speaks instead of the inner enslavement which power brings about.[11]

Originally the adjective for street and Thames was 'dirty', but when Blake printed the poem in *Songs of Experience* he substituted 'charter'd'. He refers, not to the City's Charter, but to the chartered companies, the big money-powers, which he sees as owning the city and its people. The social content is deepened. (Perhaps there is an ironic touch. Despite the old charters of liberty, the city is enslaved by the new commercial charters.) Blake is building on Isaac Watts' *Song IV* in *Divine Songs for Children*: 'Whene'er I take my walks abroad, How many poor I see . . . How many children in the street, half naked I behold.' When he made a design for his poem, he depicted an old man with crutches being led by a boy along the street past a closed door, while another vagabond boy warms his hands at a street fire. (In *Jerusalem* he reused the design, but now the old man, named London, is being led to an open door. He is not closed out, there is mercy.) The wanderer is also Ezekiel, the man with the writer's inkhorn at his side, to whom the Lord said: 'Go through the midst of the city, through the midst of Jerusalem, and set a mark upon the foreheads of the men that sigh and that cry for all the abominations that be done in the midst thereof'. Finally, we may note that the first version of the poem ended with the third stanza and its attack on church and state; Blake then added the stanza dealing with the lot of women: the repressive attitudes embodied in marriage create prostitution, which in turn poisons the marriage-bed with disease as well as making it a mockery. The afterthought may well have come through a memory of Mary Wollstonecraft and her writings.

It was probably in 1793 that he wrote the ballad usually called *Fayette*. Its importance lies in showing how he followed the events in France and remained fully in sympathy with the Revolution during the Jacobin period. His many changes and deletions no doubt came from the difficulty in clarifying the situation as reports came in; but what he is seeking to do is to trace the decline of the hero into the traitor, the fears and corruptions that eat into many persons who begin by supporting social changes. He ends by asking who will side with the forces of war and destruction, and abandon the newborn society.[12]

An event of 1793 much disturbed Blake. In the first two quarters of the year his brother John the baker failed to meet the Poor Rate for his house in Broad Street; after that the house was empty as the occupant had 'run away'. John 'lived a few reckless days. Enlisted as a Soldier & Died' (Tatham). He became for Blake the Evil One. He had chosen to fight in the wars on the side that Blake abhorred. The latter attached to *Marriage* an Argument and *a Song of Liberty*. The first deals with the meek and humble driven to wrath; the second acclaims the new Republic in France. There is something of a transition to the sort of symbolic figures Blake was to use systematically in the coming *Prophetic Books*. *A Song* is a prose-chant hailing the birth of the new revolutionary force (soon to be personified as Orc). The jealous king (George III and God) is dismayed, leading his starry hosts through the waste wilderness where, like Moses, 'he promulgates his ten commands', and stares across the Channel. But reaction gathers in vain. 'Empire is no more! And now the Lion and Wolf shall cease.' The solution emerging from the Tyger's fearful symmetry is at hand. For 'every thing that lives is holy'.

The mingled influences of Mary Wollstonecraft and Stedman made Blake want to invent a myth that would deal with both the lot of the woman and the lot of the slave. Since women were enslaved in the marriage-system they could be correlated with the Negro slaves of the plantations. Thus was born his poem *The Visions of the Daughters of Albion*. The title-page has the date 1793, but lacks the address Lambeth which he began to put on his books with *America*. Here at last he draws together the various elements to be found in *Thel*, *Tiriel*, and *The French Revolution*, and develops his mature kind of myth. The theme is closely connected with Macpherson's Ossianic prose-poem on Oi-thona, the Virgin of the Waves. She has married the hero Gaul, who is called away, and she is left at the family-seat, Dunlatmon. Dubrommath, King of Uthal (taken to be one of the Orkneys) carries her off by force to a desert island, Tromathon, where he hides her in a cave. Gaul arrives and finds her disconsolate, resolved not to survive the loss of her honour. Disguising herself as a warrior, she is killed in the ensuing battle. Blake takes this situation, but changes the emotions, the problems, the whole moral outlook. His poem consists of three parts: the narrative, three speeches, then a long outpouring by the heroine, Oothoon.

Her name seems that of the Ossianic girl with the Os drawn out as in African words cited by Stedman, e.g. *ooroocoocoo*, snake. Her lover is Theotormon, his name suggested by Macpherson's Tonthormod as modified by Stedman's *toremon* (a shiny black bird, the name meaning tale-bearer or spy) and by the wish to make it sound like God-tormented. The ravager's name is Bromion: in Greek Bromios means noisy, roaring. Oothoon wanders like Thel but dares to accept the love of a flower that wants to be plucked. She puts it between her breasts and its love enters her heart. She hastens to her lover, but Bromion rapes her and brags of his deed to Theotormon, who jealously rejects her as defiled. He ties her and Bromion back to back, so that they are turned away from life and love. Oothoon justifies herself at length, and Theotormon's jealousy appears as something more evil than Bromion's violence. She tries to convey to him the vision of delight she saw in the flower; but he is too dominated by fear and property-sense to accept her vision. Bromion ends by claiming that there is one law for lion and ox, and calling for fire and chains to 'bind the phantoms of existence from eternal life'.[13]

He represents the slaver, owning slaves in both Americas, 'stampt with my signet . . . the swarthy children of the sun'. Thus the question of woman's place in society merges with that of the slave in the commercial and productive spheres. Oothoon's revolt against an oppressive sexual morality merges with the revolts of the slaves against exploitation. 'Bromion rent her with his thunders.' Theotormon, to whom she went winging over the Atlantic in 'exulting swift delight', proves to be as bad in his own way as Bromion, who at least makes no pretences. He stands for the liars and sentimentalists who talk of love but think in property-terms, the reformers afraid to follow out their principles to the logical conclusions and who, for example, talk against the slave-trade but shrink from attacking slavery through fear of being called Jacobins, knowing what big profits are being made out of slave-labour; men who may even attack slavery in the Americas while exploiting sweated labour at home.*

Visions thus becomes a call for entire honesty and thoroughness in democratic principles and their application, a demand that every individual, including women and slaves, should have complete right to self-fulfilment.

---

* The Abolition Society in February 1792 declared it did not want the freeing of existent slaves. Wilberforce, its champion, was afraid of being accused of 'democratical principles', and in his campaign against immorality, for which he got a Royal Proclamation, was organising what became known as the Vice Society.

Sexual repression is equated with the greeds and violences linked with property, and the demand for freedom from political and economic oppression is linked with the demand for sexual freedom, for the ending of all the concepts of sin that bedevil men and women. Once more the moral is that all that lives is holy. Though Blake had learned much from Stedman of the horrors of slavery, he is in part condemning him as a Theotormon. Stedman had failed to redeem his Joanna, whose crime was to refuse 'to submit to the loathsome embraces of her detestable executioner'. He was afraid of 'sudden emancipation' of people who were 'perfectly savage' in Africa.

Blake, whose position in all matters was based on the unity of theory and practice, was not the man to set out an ethic of free love and not to believe wholeheartedly that he had the right to act on it. But just as he was afraid to come forward with his writings, he was the last person who would in fact put such a system into practice. It would have shattered the strict discipline by which he kept going. But we can be sure he set out his creed of free love to Catherine and that she stoutly resisted. In 1826 Crabb Robinson recorded in his diary: 'he had learned from the Bible that wives should be in common. And when I objected that marriage was a Divine Institution he referred to the Bible "that from the beginning it was not so"—He affirmed that he had committed many murders, And repeated his doctrine, that reason is the only Sin And that careless gay people are better than those that think &c &c'. As usual Blake refused to draw a line between emotion or impulse and action. Swinburne relates that he once proposed to bring in a concubine, but Catherine cried and he gave up the idea. The tale probably reflects the arguments that the pair were having about this time. The poems *William Bond* and *My Pretty Rose Tree* probably show his attitudes in this matter, though we need not take them to refer to actual incidents. It seems clear that in early years he had difficulty in breaking down Catherine's conventional ideas on sex and making her accept that women too should enjoy 'the lineaments of gratified desire'. We see something of the situation in a quite late story, suggesting that the arguments went on till the end.

'Do you think,' he said once in familiar conversation, and in the spirit of controversy, 'if I came home, and discovered my wife to be unfaithful, I should be so foolish as to take it ill?' Mrs. Blake was a most exemplary wife, yet was so much in the habit of echoing and thinking right what he said that, had she been present, adds my informant, he is sure she would have innocently responded, '*Of course not!*' 'But,' continues Blake's friend, 'I am inclined to think that (despite the philosophic boast) it would have gone ill with the offenders.' (Gilchrist)

Indeed, one way or another sexual conflicts, direct or indirect, clearly attended the pair continually and provided a great deal of the material in the prophetic books, where the male forms and their emanations ceaselessly break away from one another, attack one another in jealous and suspicious terms, and come together in amity again. The experiences thus defined are almost wholly derived from Blake's life with Catherine, the only person with whom he was on close terms after Robert's death, though the interpretation and the application cover all aspects of life, personal and social. Even with an artist like Flaxman he remained on the periphery, amiable, but unable to break through into truly intimate intercourse. He might exchange comments-in-character pleasantly with Fuseli, but was never friendly with him in an uninhibited way. With men like Butts, Cumberland, Hayley, he could express only a small part of himself. The young men who admired him in later years he treated with a sort of avuncular affection; but though at times he was now garrulous, with them or with Crabb Robinson, there was no real contact. He enjoyed talking of certain aspects of his past, which were romanticised in the telling, certain aspects of his thought, which were mostly interpreted in conventional mystical terms. The only person with whom he was always able to discuss things was Catherine. She was no fool, a strong-minded and warm-hearted woman, but she quite lacked the capacity to grasp the real bearing of his ideas. Her sustaining love kept him alive, but every now and then she must have infuriated him by her shallowness, the literal superficiality of her acceptances. He was probably saved by their childlessness. Had there been children, Catherine could not have given him her total absorption; the problems of feeding and bringing up a family would have crushed him. Any kind of adaptation to such a situation would have resulted in the breakdown of the Blake we know.[14]

The positive side of his relationship with Catherine is well expressed in a *Milton* plate where a man and woman lie on a shelf of rock above the sea of space and time; the man's eyes are fixed on the eagle of inspiration hovering above. Blake 'was very much accustomed to get out of his bed in the night to write for hours, and return to bed for the rest of the night' (Tatham). Catherine rose also at such times. 'She had to sit motionless and silent; only to stay near him mentally, without moving hand or foot; this for hours, and night after night' (Gilchrist). The support she gave him cannot be overestimated.

Gilchrist tells a story which he says Butts was fond of narrating. 'At the end of the little garden in Hercules Buildings there was a summer-house.

Mr. Butts calling one day found Mr. and Mrs. Blake sitting in this summer-house, freed from "those troublesome disguises" which have prevailed since the Fall. "Come in!" cried Blake; "it's only Adam and Eve, you know." Husband and wife had been reciting passages from *Paradise Lost*, in character, and the garden of Hercules Buildings had to represent the Garden of Eden: a little to the scandal of wondering neighbours, on more than one occasion.'* Such nakedness was at the heart of the Antinomian tradition. The Ranter Coope was accused of preaching 'stark naked many blasphemies and unheard of villainies in the daytime, and in the night' lying with a wench 'that had also been his hearer stark naked'. Though he denied the charge, nakedness was certainly used symbolically in sects such as his, as among the Pre-Adamites. The Ranters called themselves the Third Adam, Adam in a state of regained innocence. Costumes coming out of the French Revolution stressed the body under clothes, so that the dramatist F. Reynolds jestingly remarks in his *Life and Times* of the years 1796–8 that they saw 'the reign of NUDITY AND NATURE', or 'the Grecian costume', as the absence of all clothes was called. Nakedness even became a revolutionary symbol. J. Bowles, in his *Thoughts on the late General Election*, 1802, says that a Jacobinical mob at Nottingham paraded with a Tree of Liberty, the song *Millions be free*, and 'a female, representing the Goddess of Reason, in a state of ENTIRE NUDITY'.[15]

A note made by Blake on a Sunday in August 1807 gives his ideal picture of Catherine and himself. 'My Wife was told by a Spirit to look for her fortune by opening by chance a book which she had in her hand; it was Bysshe's Art of Poetry.' She opened at a poem by Aphra Behn describing two lovers in copulation. 'He growing more fierce & she less coy . . . Her new desire she could not hide.' Their raptures are vast and luxuriant, 'such

---

* Oddly, this tale, revised in the second edition, caused panic among Blake's Victorian admirers, Linnell, Palmer, Ellis, even Swinburne. Ellis lyingly stated that Linnell asked Butts if it were true and Butts replied, 'Of course not.' Linnell's notes however said that he thought Butts would have told him of the episode if it had happened. Even Bentley in 1969 declares that the tale was finally discredited when 'the late Captain Butts said that he distinctly remembers his grandfather declare that there was no truth in it.' But even if we did not have the tale, we could be sure that Blake would have enjoyed such nudity. Nakedness was favoured also in advanced radical thought. Franklin startled a servant with a letter by coming naked to meet her in a garden. Mrs Newton, Shelley's friend, let her children run naked through the house, though she kept her own nudity for her private room. Holcroft hoped to prolong life by standing naked for an hour or so, night and morning. Barry in his *Inquiry* declared that lewdness could be depicted in terms of clothes, while 'a great mind can raise virtuous thoughts, though he shews all the parts of the body in their natural way'.

as prove The immortality of love'. They mingle and melt their souls: 'Now
like the Phoenix both expire, While from the ashes of their fire Spring up a
new & soft desire.' Blake adds, 'I was so well pleased with her Luck that I
thought I would try my own', and he turned up a passage about the storm-
winds failing to uproot the Mountain Oak (from Dryden's *Virgil*).

· With *Visions* Blake fully formed the new kind of metric he was seeking.
The lyric form was admirably adapted to his more gnomic and compressed
utterances, but did not serve for prolonged and complex definitions. Ever
since the later seventeenth century there had been a quest for freer forms in
which a sustained statement might be achieved. Hence the advent of the
Pindaric Ode. Milton's blank verse also explored more free and varied
systems than were possible in the heroic couplet or stanzaic forms. Hence
the way in which he dominated the poetry of the century after the 1720s,
both in the mechanics of blank verse and the fashion for religious epics.
Such epics were felt as the only form that could adequately define the throes
of change in society and find symbolic terms to give them meaning. But for
a world where 'Energy is Eternal Delight', Blake could not accept even the
Miltonic fetters. He turned rather to the prose-poem and sought to find, by
studying the work of Chatterton and Macpherson, how an extended system
of rhythms could be devised that would give as much freedom as possible
without losing the verse-basis, with definite patterns and recognisable
music.

At first he experimented with the line of fourteen syllables, familiar in
Methodist hymn and popular ballad. But he realised that if he were to avoid
monotony he must not only vary the stresses within the fourteener, but must
also use lines both longer and more varied in rhythm. How close his long
lines are to Ossianic prose is obvious if we print some of the latter, broken
up according to its punctuation:

As the dark shades of autumns fly over hills of grass;
So gloomy, dark, successive came the chiefs of Lochlin's echoing woods.
Tall as the stag of Morven, moved stately before them the king.
His shining shield is on his side, like a flame on the hearth at night;
When the world is silent and dark, and the traveller sees some ghost sport-
    ing in his beam.
Dimly gleam the hills around, and show indistinctly their oaks.
A blast from the troubled ocean removed the settled mist.
The sons of Eron appeared like a ridge of rocks on the coast;
When the mariners on shores unknown are trembling at veering winds.

Here are the sort of metrical variations Blake used in his fourteener. At times a lengthening movement, with eight beats to a line; at times a falling back, with six beats, and all the while a shifting skein of tensions so that we are not too aware of the main basis.*

But Blake's debt to the Ossianic prose-poems is not merely metrical. He learned also how to merge his figures with elemental or cosmic forces. Macpherson's system is relatively simple. The heroes detach themselves, then return to the womb of nature, to mist, cloud, wind, snow, fire, darkness: above all, to mist and cloud.

The awful face of other times looked from the clouds of Croma . . . She turned her blue eyes towards the field of his promise. Where art thou, O Fingal? The night is gathering round . . . Was he white as the snow of Ardvan? Blooming as the bow of the shower? Was his hair like the mist of the hill, soft and curling in the day of the sun? . . . He came to his place in his terrors and shook his dusky spear . . . Darkness gathered on Utha's soul . . . Autumn is dark on the mountains; grey mist rests on the hills. The hero moved on before his host, like a cloud before a ridge of green fire . . . The white mist rose slowly from the lake. It came in the figure of an aged man, along the silent plain . . . Who pours from the eastern hills like a stream of darkness? . . . Open your airy halls, O fathers of Toscar of shields. Unfold the gates of your clouds; the steps of Malvia are near.

At times Macpherson uses the idiom with great power. 'Her eyes are wandering fires, amidst disordered locks. Her high-heaving breast is seen, white as foamy waves that rise, by turns, amidst rocks. They are beautiful, but terrible, and mariners call the winds.' 'Thought on thought rolled over his soul, As waves on a secret mountain-lake, each with its back of foam.' 'I was a lovely tree in thy presence, Oscar, with all my branches round me.' 'Their joyful faces bend, inequal, forward, in the light of the oak.'[16]

In both Blake and Macpherson there is a heroic note. In the latter we look backward into a vanishing world; the loss of clan-brotherhood and heroism is expressed by the way the figures merge into cloud, mist, shadow.

---

* We can trace the birth of *vers libre*, free verse, out of the impact of Ossian on the political sphere. The club of Fox's followers, Esto Perpetua, made satirical attacks on Pitt in the 1780s, especially in the *Rolliad, Political Eclogues and Probationary Odes*. One Ode runs: 'A song shall rise/Every one shall depart at the sound!!!/The wither'd thistle shall crown my head!!!/I behold thee, O King!/I behold thee sitting in mist . . ./Thy form is like a watery cloud,/Singing in the deep like an oyster . . .' The imagery is Ossianic. The rhapsodic state is expressed by the exclamation-marks; The Pindaric Ode has become free verse.

In the former we are looking into the present and the future; the dynamic relation to nature expresses a different kind of loss (that of alienation) or suggests the unions of a world-brotherhood without the flaws that broke up the ancient Gaelic clans and divide men today. We see then that it was no accident that Blake turned to Macpherson for the systems he needed if he were to break up the existing forms of metre and imagery, and to create a new kind of sensibility, a new relation of poet and people.

6

Political Prophecy, 1794–5

Blake now decided to return to the direct theme of revolution, using the matured technique of *Visions* and inventing symbolic figures to represent the main elements of conflict in a situation. He turned to the American rebellion, partly because *Visions* had made him think afresh of the Americas and partly because that rebellion had been the first stage in the revolutionary situation which was maturing in France. So he composed his *America*. The Prophecy begins with the defiance of Washington. Then comes a verbal conflict defining what is at stake, followed by a battle between Orc, the figure devised to represent the spirit of defiant freedom, who is supported by the guardian Angels of the thirteen colonies, and Britain's spirit, Albion's Angel. The latter threatens Washington; but Orc rises out of the Atlantic to defend him. A revolutionary spirit is aroused in the colonists, with a suggestion of a return to a lost Atlantean world. (The dividing Ocean has replaced the Hills of Atlantis that once united the two lands, with access to the paradisiac Golden World.) After the colony-spirits refuse to obey Albion's Angel, war rages in the heavens, casting its malign influences on all below. Albion's Angel uses pestilence; Orc, fire. As Orc drives the pestilence back into Britain, a tyrant-god Urizen intervenes to freeze and arrest the whole action. The poem ends with a promise that Orc's fires in time will melt Urizen's frost; the revolutionary struggle will revive.[1]

Blake seems to have written the Preludium last. Here he lifts the issues to a yet more purely symbolic level. We are told of the meeting of the daughter of Urthona (Orc's jailer) with Orc. (The jailer's daughter who falls in love with the imprisoned hero is a common folktale motive.) Orc breaks out and ravishes her, to her delight. She cries that she will not let him go, for he is the 'image of God who dwells in the darkness of Africa', come down to give her life in regions of dark death. She is the passive earth-mother spirit (as Urthona is a grim earth-spirit who in the early prophecies is allied with Urizen). She represents the incomplete elements of the American revolt.

77

She feels the stirrings of renewed struggle, not in the United States, but in Canada, Mexico, Peru, the South Seas. (Blake uses a sort of totemic animal to represent the tribal societies.) All the oppressed peoples are awakening.

But this optimistic statement is followed by four lines engraved in the design that shows Orc, with the sun behind his head, climbing out of a rock. The lines run across the rock and are found only in the earliest and the two latest copies. They reveal Blake in dire despair:

> The stern bard ceas'd, asham'd of his own song; enrag'd he swung
> His harp aloft sounding, then dashed its shining frame against
> A ruin'd pillar in glittring fragments: silent he turned away,
> And wander'd down the vales of Kent in sick & drear Lamentings.

Why was he so ashamed? Because he had nothing to offer the gigantic conflicts except some poems he was afraid even to try to publish? Because he saw round him a rising tide of reaction in England and the persecution of radicals who protested? However, he grew ashamed in turn of his shame; he masked or erased (once) the lines in most printings. That he was much afraid is shown by his cancellation of two plates that dealt directly with George III in council. That he was suffering much at this phase is shown by his Notebook: 'I say I shan't live five years. And if I live one it will be a Wonder June 1795.' The strong revulsion he was feeling from orthodox positions is expressed in an entry at the end of the Notebook attacking the Bible. 'The Hebrew Nation did not write it. Avarice and Chastity did shite it.'

The designs for *America* are large and vigorous. In two plates Blake draws on his 1784 watercolour, *A Breach in a City*. We see Orc chained in the breach, head sunk on knees, a disconsolate woman with two children at his side; but when he rises out of the rock, when the rock becomes Orc, the breach will be closed. In the text Urizen appears in action for the first time. He holds things up for twelve years, after which France receives 'the demon's light' and struggle begins afresh. In the lull the rulers of France, Spain, Italy, do their utmost to hold subjects down. The political repression is at the same time an alienation of man from his body, from sensuous fulfilment. Privation mildews the food and the senses of taste and smell, and so on.[2]

Interest in prophecy was very deep and widespread. There was a strong feeling that the political upheavals portended some millenary event. The Rev. R. Beere, rector of Sudbrooke in Lincolnshire, in a *Dissertation on*

Daniel, 1790, proved that the restoration of the Jews to Palestine would start in 1791. From late 1792, as Pitt prepared for war, there was a search for old prophecies that could be used against the Revolution in newspaper or pamphlet. Efforts were above all made to identify the French Republic with the Beast of Revelation, dropping the traditional link with the Papacy. England was thronged with refugee priests and the government was in effect leagued with the Catholic powers against democracy. Mrs Piozzi, much interested in such matters, noted the 'odd idea now that the Beast of the Revelation is this French Democracy'. Much attention was directed to the prophecies of Fleming in 1701, which were first reprinted in the *Whitehall Evening Post*, January 1793—though he had been concerned with the French Catholic monarchy of his day, holding that the last vial of God's wrath would end with the destruction of that monarchy in 1794. A pamphlet, *Antichrist in the French Convention*, tried to extend Fleming's work; and in 1793 came an anti-French collection, *Prophetic Conjectures on the French Revolution*. New works were A. Pirie's *The French Revolution exhibited in the Light of the Sacred Oracles*, 1795, and James Bicheno's *A Word in Season; or a Call to the Inhabitants of Great Britain, to Stand Prepared for the Consequences of the Present War*, 1795. Bicheno saw the vial, poured out on the sea, as affecting maritime powers; Joanna Southcott in 1794 saw the vials, poured out of the Sun, as producing extreme heat, consuming the Corn, and bringing about poor harvests and high prices.[3]

Blake was alone in giving the prophecies a Jacobin coloration. Perhaps his depression recorded at the end of *America*'s Preludium was helped by his finding so many 'false' prophecies broadcast, while nobody heard his voice. This conjecture is supported by the fact that he now made, or prepared to make, an effort to reach the general public. He drew up a Prospectus, dated 10 October 1793, briefly describing his new printing methods, 'which combines the Painter and the Poet', and claiming that he had regularly brought before the public works 'of equal magnitude and consequence with the production of an age or country'. He meant to engrave a series of subjects from the Bible and English history, and argued that by printing his own works he overcame a problem that had always attended poets.

The Labours of the Artist, the Poet, the Musician, have been proverbially attended by poverty and obscurity; this was never the fault of the Public, but was owing to a neglect of means to propagate such works as have wholly absorbed the Man of Genius. Even Milton and Shakespeare could not publish their own works
[4]

He asks for no subscriptions and offers ten works for sale: two engravings (*Job*, 12s., and *Edward and Elinor*, 10s. 6d.), six illustrated books (*America*, 10s. 6d., *Visions*, 7s. 6d., *Thel*, 3s., *Marriage*, 7s. 6d., *Songs of Innocence*, 5s., *Songs of Experience*, 5s.) and two small books of engravings: *The History of England* and *The Gates of Paradise*, each 3s. Probably need of money was part of the driving-force of the project. But again his fears proved too strong. There is no sign whatever that he did anything about the Prospectus.

He mentions *Songs of Experience*, but the title-page is dated 1794. Though he went on printing *Songs of Innocence* by itself, he issued *Songs of Experience* only with the former book. Its poems came from the realisation, set down in *Thel* and *Tiriel*, that the state of innocence, with its pastoral world, could not itself solve the problems of an alienated society. A sub-title states: 'Showing the Two Contrary States of the Human Soul'. He was working out the dialectical logic expounded in *Marriage*: Innocence, Fall, Redemption or Renewal of Innocence on a new level. He had in mind what the Methodists called books of experience. Priestley in his *Memoirs* tells how as a sickly child he read 'books of Experience', and fell into a great distress, to which he always looked back with horror. Such books told of the fall from innocence into sin and the redemption by Christ. The pattern was thus the same as in Blake, but he releases the terms from their narrow religious application.[4]

Each poem in *Songs of Experience* has a poem in *Songs of Innocence* to which it is related. At times the connection is close; at times there is little more than the title that links. The themes of Experience are lack of freedom and openness in love, enslavement (especially of children) by deceit or force, the tyrannies exerted by law, state, and church. The Introduction sets the scene. 'Hear the voice of the bard', Blake. He has heard all the deadly words uttered by the Biblical God, who holds that men have fallen through sin, whereas what has broken them is the acceptance of law, authority, abstract reason, inner and outer division. The bard knows better. Awaiting a different dispensation, he calls on Earth to return. Till that dawn there is only 'the starry shore' of Urizen-Jehovah and 'the watery shore', the indefinite world of the Fall. Earth, replying, attacks God, 'Selfish Father of men! Cruel jealous selfish fear', and demands love and work in the open day, with the breaking of the bonds imposed on love, which by its nature is free. Linked with this poem we may take the colour-print of 1793, *God creating Adam*. Such creation is in fact anti-creation; it marks the advent of the fall, which is symbolised by the serpent wound round Adam's leg. With this print Blake makes an important advance in his art.

As example of the contraries in the two books we may take *The Blossom* where a happy flower watches a sparrow and robin: a praise of the direct release of emotion (with its sexual aspect)—against which is set *The Sick Rose*, where the worm of repression destroys life in dark secrecy. In *The Divine Image* mercy, pity, peace, and love are simply seen as essential aspects of a true humanity; but *The Human Abstract* mocks that position, for pity and mercy now need poverty and misery if they are to be stimulated. 'And mutual fears bring peace, Till the selfish loves increase', and there is born the Tree of Mystery (religion, law, oppression). The abstraction of man is the opposite of the concrete reality. *Holy Thursday* depicts the moving sight of the massed charity-children singing in St Paul's; *Songs of Experience* points to the facts behind that scene: 'Babes reduced to misery, Fed with cold and usurous hand'.

Blake's Notebook has a list of themes from English history, which look back on his early drawings. They begin with the early Giants and the landing of the legendary Brutus, and move on to Jane Shore. Then as Blake nears the present his fears intrude and he deletes the execution of Charles I as well as the last word of 'The Cruelties of Kings and Priests'. He ends with 'A prospect of Liberty' and 'A Cloud': one of his favourite symbolic objects. What he was going to do with it here we do not know. Nothing came of the project.*

He did however execute the booklet *The Gates of Paradise* based on the popular emblem-books and described as 'For Children'. In intention he aims at a wide audience. We see the birth of man as a chrysalis, as a mandrake dragged from the earth under a tree, then his passage through the four elements. As a lad he seeks vainly to catch a fairy in his hat; a little older, he shakes a spear at an aged man. Then he sets a ladder against the moon. 'I

---

* Blake's full list runs: 1. Giants ancient inhabitants of England. 2. The Landing of Brutus. 3. Corineus throws Gogmagog the Giant into the sea. 4. King Lear. 5. The Ancient Britons according to Caesar. 6. The Druids. 7. The Landing of Julius Caesar. 8. Boadicea inspiring the Britons against the Romans. The Britons' distress & depopulation. Women fleeing from War. Women in a Siege. 9. Alfred in the countryman's house. 10. Edwin & Morcar stirring up the Londoners to resist W. the Conqr. 11. W. the Conq. Crown'd. 12. King John & Mag. Charta. A Famine occasion'd by the Popish interdict. 13. Edward at Calais. 14. Edward the Black Prince brings his Captives to his father. 15. The Penance of Jane Shore. 19. The Plague. (17. The Reformation of H. VIII—*del.*) 20. The fire of London. (18. Ch. I beheaded—*del.*) 16. The Cruelties used by Kings & Priests (*word del.*) 21. A prospect of Liberty. 22. A Cloud.'[5]

want! I want!' But he falls drowning in the seas. Next, Aged Ignorance cuts the wings of a youth rushing to the sunrise; an old man swings up resurrected from a corpse; a traveller hastens in the evening; an old man enters death's massive door; a dead man sits in a shroud, still holding his travelling-staff erect among tree-roots in a grave, with a worm around him.

But the dead man is alive with intent and searching eyes in some kind of rebirth, a moment of intense prophetic vision. Some twenty-five years later Blake reprinted the plates with an explanatory poem; but in 1793 the little book seems a mixture of conventional moralisings and deeper private interpretations. Thus plate 13 with the corpse and the resurrection has the text, 'Hope and Fear are—Vision'. The Notebook adds, 'What we Hope we see'. Plate 9 attacks Gillray's satire on radicals such as Charles Fox, where the ladder is too short to reach the moon-utopia of Libertas. Blake is saying that we must keep on hoping, struggling, whatever the setbacks; and that what we hope has a true basis, which will be realised some day. The four elements confine, crush, condition the youth to a limited existence. Air submits him to the rule of the Stars (Urizen, Newton, the State); but out of Fire he rises unsteady, rebellious, with a touch of Orc—the Notebook identifies him with Satan rising in Pandemonium against God. The title page has the imprint of J. Johnson, showing that Blake intended to sell the book normally; but once again he drew back.

Europe is dated 1794 on the title-page, but the text seems to have been begun in 1793. Blake did a plate, dated 5 June 1793 and captioned 'Our End is Come'; it shows the king aghast between two warriors (one of whom seems to be Pitt) inside a flame-wrapt doorway. The drawing is on a sheet with two others which depict famine and sacked villages. The set is best dated soon after the outbreak of war with France and suggests that Blake was already at work on *Europe*. He rewrote the caption in June 1793, fearing that the attack on George III was too obvious, and watered it down by citing from his Prologue for *Edward the Fourth* lines about the soul 'driven to Madness'.

Europe is linked with *America*, using the episode of Albion's Angel (in the deleted passages) smitten with his own plague as it blows back from America. The reference to the guardian of the secret code being driven from his mansion by the fires of Orc comes from the dismissal of Lord Thurlow as Lord Chancellor on 15 June 1792. Thurlow was in fact dropped on Pitt's advice, but Blake sees any such fall of the mighty as the result of the revolutionary forces. The poem, carrying on from the *Song of Liberty*, prophesies the disastrous effects of Britain's entry into the war against France, with ruin for Pitt (Rintrah) and Parliament (Palambron). Ally of the counter-revolutionary lion and wolf of the continent, Pitt tries to rouse Armageddon; he lifts the Trumpet of the last doom, blows thrice—and fails to produce a sound.[6]

Blake stresses the way in which the war was used to rivet oppression on the British people themselves. They are bound in leaden gyves; every house is a den with Fear over the chimneys and 'Thou shalt not' written over the doors. The king's proclamation on 21 May 1792 against 'divers wicked and seditious writings' is represented by Urizen unclasping his Book. We see the Angel reading the proclamation to a reluctant muster of young militia. From May to August regiment on regiment of the called-up youth marched through London to camp on the heath west of the city. Pitt, without reference to Parliament, began building barracks in the industrial centres. On 1 December the proclamation was repeated and directly linked with the call-out of the militia. Orc rejoices at the upheaval in Europe, and the poem ends with him fierily spreading the revolutionary spirit there, while Los (here the poet-prophet Blake) comes to his aid, calling 'all his sons to strife of blood'. Tigers symbolise the rebellious energies: they 'couch upon the prey and suck the ruddy tide'.[7]

In the middle is inset the dream of Enitharmon (Los's wife and emanation) which seeks to go deeper into the meaning of the situation. It gives an account of her woman's world with its religion of vengeance, violence, repression, chastity. This world is in fact the Christianity of the last 1,800 years, which is called a female dream. European history has been the dream of Enitharmon, which from another angle is the work of Jehovah-Urizen. Yet the Hebrew world of aggressive male morality, strongly based in war, was in no sense the work of Enitharmon. Rather, she relates to earlier cults of the earth-mother which, with their fertility-rituals, Jehovah's devotees set out to exterminate at all costs. But from now on Blake holds fast to his condemnation of the female. After the Flood man's relation to nature is hidden within her; she symbolises the fallen life of the passively receptive senses. In the next period man tries to dominate with his will the 'hidden mystery' of the natural environment defined as 'the Female hidden within a Male'. In *Jerusalem* Los bids Paul look back into the church's origins: 'Three women around the Cross! O Albion, why didst thou a Female Will Create?'

Enitharmon's name seems to be derived from the Greek *anarithmon*, (countless), or from (z)enith plus (h)armon(y). It also contains the letters of

Catherine. The names of her parents, Enion and Tharmas, are enclosed in it: Eni-tharm-on. Tharmas represents the Body; Enion, his emanation, represents lust or the generative impulse. Later we find that Enitharmon, unlike the other three emanations of the Zoas, is not evanescent, but is a vegetated mortal wife of Los. Los, when she is a quiescent part of him, is the Zoa Urthona; but in his struggles he gives form to Urizen and the resulting convulsions and divisions cut him off from his emanation-wife. The poetic impulse derives from this division, which shows up in the sexual difficulties of puberty: 'Two Wills they had, Two Intellects, & not as in times of old'. Enitharmon, given her name, announces her independence and declares that the world is woman's world, with the sexes in conflict. She decides to create secret places. 'A triple Female Tabernacle for Moral Law I weave, that he who loves Jesus may loathe, terrified, Female Love, till God himself becomes a Male subservient to the Female.' The marriage of Los and Enitharmon takes place 'in discontent & scorn', and the demons sing the nuptial song of war. (War is thus seen as born out of sexual division and conflict between man and woman.)*

As Los is Blake, so Enitharmon is Catherine. In November 1802 he wrote to Butts from Felpham, where they moved, 'Here is Enitharmon's Bower.' The conflict of the male and the female emanation, especially that of Los and Enitharmon, in the prophecies is largely worked out in terms of his relations with Catherine. Since the love between them was the great stabilising force in his life, so all discords or misunderstandings between them rocked him to the depths and reflected for him all the outer discords of history. Enitharmon was thus seen as responsible for all that had gone wrong in the world, war and property-lust. Blake sees the male as the prime reality, with an emanation that reflects one side of his bisexuality and which becomes the

* In Neoplatonism we meet the idea of the world as coming about through a series of Emanations from Deity. Blake would have known this from Taylor, but he drew rather in the Kabbalistic notion of the exile of the female part of the divine (The Shekkinah) from its male partner. Other ideas he learned from the Kabbala were those of a pre-Adamic Fall, of the necessity of Evil for the emergence of Good, and of the way in which the adept repairs the breaches in the universe, though he saw the reconstruction as done by inspired art and poetry, not by rituals and prayers. Adam Kadmon, the primordial Adam of Jewish mysticism, who contains all things, helped him to form his final notion of the Giant Albion. There was also the contemporary use of the term emanation. Robert South in a 1692 sermon had said, 'This Emanation of Gifts from the Spirit, assures us that Knowledge and Learning, are by no means opposite to Grace.' Robespierre on 5 February 1794 defended the Terror as prompt, severe, inflexible Justice. 'It is then an emanation of Virtue'.[8]

female. In a divided world the emanation torments the male. In eternity
there is no division, no marrying, no sexual separateness. The emanation is
absorbed back and becomes an active harmonious ingredient in a united
personality. 'There is no such thing in Eternity as a Female Will.'

The male, cut off from his emanation, tends to wither into a being who
seeks abstract and tyrannic power. He is then a dark spectre or in his spectre's
control. Spectres, however, in the mythic system, unlike the emanations, are
given no names. A man is saved from his spectre if his wife knows her place,
comforts and supports him, and becomes his 'concentring vision'. However,
the moment she separates herself, she stirs 'the torments of love & jealousy'.
Los has incessant marital troubles with Enitharmon, who, jealous of male
activities, drives all other females away, devises the system of sin and guilt
that poisons life, and murders all the male's innocent pleasures, ignoring that
they come from her. She denies herself to him and avoids his embraces. She
is even jealous of his work, which takes his attention from her, and she does
her best to stop him working. He is thus compelled to be a selfish and
demanding spectre, abandoned to the abstract reasoning power and letting
off his suppressed energies in war. (All living things, including nations,
have emanations. Thus Blake says that when Britannia at last awakes, she
sees how she had been disastrously behaving as 'the Jealous Wife'.)[9]

From one angle then Blake is saying that in a divided world the female
tends to take on the possessive elements of the emanation, the man to take
on the aggressive aspects of the spectre. In eternity (the stage where the
present conflicts are overcome in a new unity) there is then neither female
will nor male dominance. There is no marrying in the old sense; there is
only free union. Sexual division in the old sense disappears. We could then
say that when Blake blames the female, it is the spectre in him speaking.
Eternity thus is an ambiguous term. It is the moment when the female is
absorbed back into the male; it is the moment when both female and male
cease to make false and destructive demands on one another. It is a condition
of being beyond our present level of existence; it is the moment when present
conflicts are resolved and men move on to a higher level of earthly existence.
Elements of conventional meaning cling to the terms that Blake uses; but
everything that is creative and original in him discards that meaning and uses
the terms always to define phases of earthly struggle, with precise references
to history and to particular stages of division and unity. Thus, the waking
into God's bosom, which seems to link Blake's system with that of conventional religion, is seen to signify the going-forth and returning of man in an

endless movement of loss and fulfilment, a continual recreation of humanity and its modes of life, with one great moment—that of total revolution (the ending of alienation), luminous in the future and determining the present forms and directions of struggle. To clarify this point here, as we need to do if we are to find our way through the rich mazes of Blake's *Prophetic Books*, we must glance forward at the last sections of *Jerusalem*, in which he concludes and sums up his views of human development. There we find eternity used to express the moment of full revolutionary resolution of all the conflicts and contradictions previously examined in the fallen world. The emphasis is throughout on the elimination of all that makes for war, and the restoration of complete (fourfold) creativeness to men.

I am not claiming that Blake thought things out in the terms I have been using. Part of him certainly believed in spirits as existing outside our dimension of time and space, and saw eternity as a condition he would inhabit after death. But such positions were in direct conflict with all that was most creative and original in his expression. Deepest of all his concepts was his grasp of the unity of the life-process and his grasp of the dialectical forms of development inside that process. Body and spirit were one; all life in the last resort was one, interrelated and following the same dialectical laws, but not mechanistically reducible to the flat basis of a single level. Eternity stood for the liberating arrival at this understanding. Truth then ceased to be an abstract or static thing; it involved an active movement of comprehension, which united the thinker dynamically with the world he explored. Action and thought were then only different aspects of the same moment of realisation. Eternity was both the richly developing cosmos in its totality, which included human society, and the act by which a human being grasps the living unity of the processes of development and thus achieves a new relation to himself, his fellows, nature, the universe. Blake needed the term Eternity so that he could oppose the concept of dialectical unity to Nature or Ulro, as he came to call it—the existent human world with all its distorting divisions and alienations—and Reason, the rationalisation of Ulro and its delusions.

Eternity then stands for imaginative activity and the grasp of the dialectical principles of development; and because in it thought cannot be abstracted from activity, it involves the struggle for brotherhood, for Eden. At the start of the *Four Zoas* Blake writes: 'Four mighty ones are in every man; a perfect unity Cannot Exist, but from the universal brotherhood of Eden,

The universal Man, to whom be glory for ever.' To realise the unity of the self is to realise the self in all its fraternal relations, the Eternal Great Humanity. Near the end of *Jerusalem* Jesus says that his death is life for Albion, for he will rise again. 'This is friendship and brotherhood; without it man is not . . . Thus do men in Eternity, One for another to put off by forgiveness every sin.' Such forgiveness is Blake's term for the actualisation of brotherhood. Albion declares that he cannot exist 'but by brotherhood', by eternally dying for his fellow and thus being reborn into a fuller life. Eternity is then both every affirmation of human solidarity in the existent world and the stable condition which is the ultimate aim of such affirmations. So far from there being an absence of conflict, of the clash of contraries, in eternity, in the myth it is precisely Urizen's attempt to bring about that absence which precipates his fall, the advent of a divided world. He wants to build a society governed by unchanging power and a mechanistic system of ideas. 'I have sought for joy without pain, For a solid without fluctuation.' Such an aim wrecks eternity, which has then to be regained by social and intellectual struggle.[10]

Eden is another term for eternity in *Milton*. Eden is not represented as perfect; it includes elements of both truth and error, integration and failure. In the *Four Zoas* there seem to be both Albion who falls and other eternals, who are disturbed but do not fall. No such are mentioned in *Milton*, and Albion seems to include the whole of human reality. The Divine Family (united humanity) has been broken up. In a similar way, throughout the epics, the fall of Luvah, Prince of Love, sums up the disunity of the Zoas. (The Four Zoas, Tharmas, Urizen, Luvah, Urthona, represent the four fundamental aspects of Man: his body, his reason, his emotions, his imagination. Both Orc and Jesus are defined as forms of Luvah.) Eden or eternity is not then a fixed condition or level of being; it weakens as Albion breaks up. The forces that preserve the hope and possibility of reunion or redemption lie in Jesus with his unconditional forgiveness and in Los with his ceaseless struggle of reconstruction. Eden, threatened, survives. However evil society grows with greeds and aggressions, and however confused history appears, there are always forces and forms expressing brotherhood, always a struggle towards the truth in its fullness. Imagination is human existence itself, and so the forces making for Eden in men can only be destroyed by the destruction of mankind. That destruction is possible. At least Los feels that it is near (*Milton*, 23–4) when he calls on his four remaining sons to stay with him in Golgonooza and not become vegetated like their

4*

twelve brothers. Blake has come to feel that with the Napoleonic perversion of the revolution the situation is grave indeed. (Urthona-Los has as his domain Earth, 'the auricular nerve of human hope which is the earth of Eden'.)

As we are here considering Blake's spiritual geography, we need to look also at Beulah, which in *Thel* appears as a purely female sphere but which grows ever more complex as Blake develops his ideas. It is the emanation of Eden, a place of recuperation for those temporarily exhausted in the struggle. It reveals the way in which the inhabitants of Eden are vulnerable to error, but also the merciful wisdom of the Eternal Great Humanity. More, it is the source of poetic inspiration and dreams; in it 'Contraries are equally True'. And so in it there is also sexual happiness. It keeps alive the hope of freedom when outwardly all is lost. In Blake's dialectical system Beulah is thus the place of momentary or passing resolutions of conflict, without which life on earth would be intolerably and ceaselessly torn by discord. But the experience-levels it represents need to be carried further from threefold to fourfold vision or realisation, before a comprehensive and stable resolution (Eden) is possible.

In all these formulations we need to note that Blake's idiom at certain points is idealist, failing to distinguish between a thing and the ideas held about it. Eden, Beulah, Generation, Ulro, and all the other spiritual sites or states are aspects of our earth, our cosmos, our society. But the level at which quantitative or reduction science, for instance, operates is different from the level of our total sensibility; and Blake defines these different levels as different worlds, not different views of, or responses to, the one and only world which other aspects of his thought postulate. In his treatment, however, he himself continually breaks down the idealist gap.* Golgonooza, the sphere of creative activity, is bounded by Bowlahoola and Allamanda, which may be defined as the bowels and the alimentary canal, the bodily processes

---

* Take the symbolism of the sandals in *Milton*. 'Blake's tying on of the sandal is his acceptance of the generative world as his means of entering into eternity . . . The seventh day is about to end; the eighth dawn is apocalypse.' Both his sandals are bound on. 'The poet's stride is now unbroken. Inspiration is no longer lame, but strong and firm; Los-Blake-Milton strides towards Golgonooza' (Fox). Thus the levels are virtually integrated. In *A Vision of the Last Judgment* Blake says, 'Eternity exists and all things in Eternity.' That is, Eternity has nothing otherworldly about it; it is simply the creative life of humanity. Note however again the idealist touch: because without imaginative creative effort there would be no humanity, all things 'exist in' the imagination; in his fuller definitions Blake argues that human process cannot function without imaginative creative insights which unite men afresh with their fellows and with nature.

in their assimilative aspects. They are thus also the productive processes by which the crude materials of nature are taken over, transformed, adapted to human life, distributed. Art is dynamically linked with the bodily and productive processes. In such ways Blake continually inverts his idealist positions and sets out a materialist dialectic.[11]

We might say then that Blake, like Hegel, took over the idealist position that spirit was the sole source of activity in order to get away from all reductive mechanistic standpoints. But he was not an intellectual philosopher concentrating on the working out of a system of dialectical logic. In *Marriage* he set out the necessary basic ideas, and then proceeded to express his sense of the complex interrelations of the factors in human development through imagery, symbols, myths. The ambiguities and contraditions in his positions, exemplified above, were the price he paid for the vast unprecedented scope and subtlety of his vision of life, his ability to decontaminate that vision from all the 'rational' systems of his world. The concrete force of his poetic realisations continually brought what was abstract in his formulations down to earth, down to the reality of human experience in its fullness. He thus, as was noted earlier, drove beyond the Hegelian idealist element into the sort of realisations that we find in the young Marx.* One quotation from the 1844 *Manuscripts* of the latter will bring out the kinship between the two thinkers. Marx is seeking to define the active and creative element in man which he wants to see fully liberated by a society without divisions. 'Only here has his *natural* existence become his *human* existence and nature become man for him. *Society* is therefore the perfected unity in essence of man with nature, the true resurrection of nature, the realised naturalism of man and the realised humanism of nature.'[12]

One aspect of Blake's concrete down-to-earth element appears in his close relation to history, to the social forces and formations of his day. He felt a complete solidarity with all revolutionary impulses and movements, together with a deep rejection of all bourgeois ways of thought and feeling. Yet he had no conception as to how the final revolution he desired was to come about except by some spontaneous uprising of all peoples. He was a craftsman working on his own, helped only by his wife, and he had no idea or experience of working-class organisation. That the movement into the sort of

---

* Hegel was like Blake a direct product of the French Revolution, which 'provided a specific concrete case which precipitated and governed the structure of his philosophy' (Spragens); 'the impact of the Revolution was indeed the experience that fundamentally formed Hegel's existence' (Vogelin).

changed society he wanted would be possible only after long working-class organisation and struggle was something he could not have comprehended; it simply did not come within the range of his mind, his experience. (Here lie the roots of the idealist element we have noted as accompanying his most down-to-earth realisations.) His fears, his withdrawals, which indeed were necessary if he were to survive to carry out his prophetic function in such a situation, prevented him from even taking part in such bodies as the Lambeth Loyal Association or the London Corresponding Society, and thus enjoying the comradeship of men who shared at least some of his ideals. Thus there was a sharp contrast between his dreams of universal brotherhood and his isolated existence. He avoided being another Paine or a mere mystical dreamer of apocalypses by his close relationship with Catherine, in which he dramatised all his hopes of union and all his fears of division. The revolution became the liberation of Blake as Albion, but at the same time the liberation of Blake reflected all the harmonies and conflicts which would have to be objectified in history if the revolution was to come about in its completeness.

We see how Blake turns his private conflicts into a reflection of the struggles going in history if we consider how he depicts the female will at work in corrupting the revolution. In his ballad on Lafayette he depicted Marie Antoinette as an Enitharmon luring and destroying that hero. The English Queen Charlotte is made Marie's sister in crime. Not that he invents the characterisation; he is in fact echoing what was being commonly said. 'Observe,' wrote Governor Morris to Washington in September 1790, 'that he [Pitt] is rather the Queen's man than the King's, and that since his Majesty's illness she has been of great consequence'; the May proclamation against seditious writings had come from 'the Queen's House'. The cartoonist Gillray showed her as Sin protecting Pitt (Death) against the Chancellor Thurlow (Satan): a snaky Sin with the keys of the backstairs. She controls the gates of hell, just as Enitharmon in 'woman's triumph' has made an accursed jail of all the peoples.[13]

In his Notebook Blake describes her as a dead upas-tree, England. In *Europe* (plate V) Rintrah in scaly armour stands between two queens whom he defends so that 'woman, lovely woman, may have dominion'. The queens Leutha and Elynittria may thus be taken to stand for Marie and Charlotte. Plate XI shows two queens paying obeisance to a spectre bat with papal crown. The text describes the spectre as Albion's Angel with a paper copy on his knees of Urizen's brazen book which 'Kings & Priests had copied on

Earth', and which he expounded from North to South as Empire extended. Thus the demoralising Female Will is linked with the Male Spectre, who represents all that hardens, deadens, limits. Urizen, though not called a spectre, in fact sums up all the dehumanising elements which characterise the spectres. *Europe*'s Frontispiece shows him with his compass, alone in the universe, inside a disc, himself a sort of figure-diagram. The disc is a sun or a shield covering the sun, with clouds rolling round; it encloses him save for one arm reaching down and out to create the universe. (He is both Newton and Jehovah, Moses and Locke.) Blake recalls Milton: the Almighty taking 'the golden Compass' to circumscribe the universe; 'one foot he centred, and the other turn'd'. He is subduing the stormclouds with his rigid law.*

Meanwhile Blake was carrying on with his daily tasks. His last ten plates for Stedman's book are dated 2 December 1793. On Saturday 21 June 1794 Stedman recorded, 'Call on Mr. Johnson & Blake.' In October and November he wrote letters to Blake. Flaxman was back from Italy with crammed portfolios that showed his increasingly classical taste; he had made designs from Homer, Aeschylus, and Dante that soon were to spread his fame through Europe. He was at once elected a member of the R.A. and set up his studio in Buckingham Street, Fitzroy Square, which then lay open to the hills of Hampstead and Highgate. In Fitzroy Square, the fashionable part, also resided Thomas Butts, a jovial and kindly pietist (probably not a Swedenborgian), whom Blake came to know about this time. For some thirty years Butts bought, at moderate prices, drawings and temperas from Blake, and was thus by far his most important patron. At this time, too, Blake made two books of designs, one large, one small, for the miniaturist Ozias Humphry, combining the methods of the printed books and the monotypes. He used plates from the *Prophecies* on which was no text, and applied colouring, with a rich mottled effect, all over.[15]

---

* The importance of this image for Blake is shown by the episode on his deathbed. He had coloured for Tatham the print of the Ancient of Days striking the first Circle of the Earth; he laid it aside, saying, 'There I have done all I can! It is the best I have ever finished'. J. T. Smith says the design was based on a figure that Blake saw hovering over his head at the top of the staircase at Lambeth. 'He has frequently been heard to say, that it made a more powerful impression upon his mind than all he had ever been visited by. The subject was such a favourite with him, that he always bestowed more time and enjoyed greater pleasure when colouring the print, than on any thing he ever produced.' Yet the image represented all that he considered most evil in life.[14]

Blake must have been much interested and disturbed by a book, *A Revealed Knowledge of the Prophecies and Times*, published in 1794 by Richard Brothers. Brothers, born on Christmas Day in the same year as Blake, had entered the navy at fourteen and had seen war service off the African coast and against the American rebels. In 1783, promoted to lieutenant, he was discharged on half pay and travelled in Europe but was back in England in 1786. He married, but seems to have lived with his wife only two months. In September, in London, he was attending a Baptist chapel. In 1790 he felt scruples at having to take a 'voluntary oath' to get his pay. So his pay was stopped and in August 1791 he was put in a workhouse. He had broken his sword and began seeing visions, in one of which he was told that London would be destroyed. By lying on his face three days and nights, fasting, he saved the city. In January 1791 he had a warning in the loudest thunder-crack since man's creation, which was the voice of the Angel of Revelation proclaiming the fall of Babylon. His guardian angel explained that Babylon was London. Brothers had a vision of Satan walking towards London (satirised by Coleridge and Southey in *The Devil's Thoughts*, 1799).

In the workhouse Brothers lived in expectation of a lady descending from the clouds, a vast shower of money, and the end of the war with peace, love, and happiness for all mankind. In February 1782, discharged, he drew large crowds to visit him, partly through giving small sums to those whose eyes he touched. He turned to politics and wrote letters to the king and to Pitt and other ministers, declaring that 'the Revolution in France proceeded from the judgement of God. Therefore all attempts to preserve the monarchy there would be opposing God'. On 17 March he went to tell the Commons that they would fall into the jaws of the earth through an earthquake if they persisted in hostility to the Revolution. Refusing to pay rent, he was shut in Newgate for eight weeks till he signed a power of attorney for the collection of his pay, striking out the description of the king as 'our sovereign lord' as blasphemy.[16]

Then came in 1794 the book describing his visions, which declared that the king and his empire would soon end for the crimes of sin and corruption. Growing more political, in 1792 Brothers announced the triumph of the French armies. After leaving Newgate he saw himself as destined to gather the Jews (including the hidden ones such as himself) and to lead them to Palestine where he would rule over them till the Second Coming. An army captain supported him and got his books printed. Among the artists drawn in were Sharp and Loutherbourg.* Sharp tried to convert Holcroft to Brothers and to get Flaxman to act as Architect of the Promised Land; in April 1795 he issued his portrait-print of Brothers as Prince of the Hebrews. He would have canvassed Blake on Brothers' behalf, as later he did with Joanna Southcott. Blake would not have listened. 'Blake himself a seer of visions and a dreamer of dreams,' remarked Crabb Robinson after talking with him, 'would not do homage to a rival claimant of the privilege of prophecy.' He found him guilty of excessive pride; Sharp was of 'a quieter and more amiable turn of mind'.

Brothers' supporters published many old prophecies that could be taken as pointing to their hero as prophet. Brothers' own book had an immense success: four editions in London and one in Dublin, 1795; eighteen in the United States, including one in German; a French version in Paris, 1795. In England a wide discussion about him raged in pamphlets and periodicals, with leading magazines devoting a section to prophecies. Brothers was largely a pacifist; he had resigned his commission as he 'could not conscientiously receive the wages of Plunder, Bloodshed, and Murder!' Thus, though no revolutionary, he opposed the war against France. Blake found a prophet on his side, a prophet who had evoked a vast agitated response, and who had gained wide support among the craftsmen and merchants of towns like Leeds and Hull. He could not but have been deeply affected. He set his face against showing any sympathy for Brothers; but he felt himself driven more deeply back in on himself, with important effect on his work and attitudes in the years 1795–7.

Meanwhile, however, he was at work on prophecies which carried directly

---

* The Rev. Beere prophesied the return of the Jews in 1791. John Foxe in his *Book of Martyrs* had taught the English they were the Chosen People picked by God to fight the Catholic Antichrist. In the Cromwellian period the Ranter John Robins and a goldsmith, T. Tany, proposed to lead the Jews home. Tany, circumcised, obeyed a vision that told him to kill all MPs and attacked Parliament with a rusty sword. When released from jail he built a boat and went to gather the Jews of Holland, but disappeared in Amsterdam. C. Smart in his (unpublished) *Jubilate Agno* called the English Abraham's Seed and himself a descendant of David, who would be a Prince when Christ came in 1760 to build the New Jerusalem in England. Explorers of the century in Asia, Africa and America hoped to find the Lost Tribes. The painter Loutherborg turned from alchemy to revivalist preaching, then to Swedenborg; he was a founder of the Theosophical Society with two more painters and two engravers. Later he took up spiritual healing; he and his wife are said to have treated 3,000 people a day, free, at their Hammersmith house, which in 1789 was attacked by a crowd of disappointed patients.

on from *America* and *Europe*. The date 1794 on the title-page of *The First Book of Urizen* no doubt refers to the time when he began etching the book. Seven copies are known, of which six were printed before 1800. There is no record of a Second Book. Here Blake sets out to give a full account of the Urizenic distortion of life. The work is a compact and sustained attack on authoritative concepts in all spheres of life. Blake rejects the narrative of Genesis as a mere rationalisation made by a divided society to justify itself; and he attempts to devise a counter-myth of creation that will really explain how and why men have become divided spiritually and socially. The act or process of division, as we have seen, he calls the Fall. Urizen, archetypal character of oppressive authority, falls by devising an abstract method for dealing with reality: a method that takes one aspect in isolation and treats it as a thing-in-itself. Linked with such a method is an inturned self-sufficient individualism in people. The result is the reduction of men to things and the construction of systems destructive of free expression, love, individuality.[17]

From one angle Blake is describing the invention and working out of systems of purely quantitative science, which reflect a divided society, its cash nexus and war-needs. But with his mythopoeic imagination he sees the advent of such a science as the actual reduction of the cosmos to the elements which have been taken as solely real. However, if that were all, we should have only a dead scurry of abstract forms. So Blake brings in Los, who, though frightened, sets to work struggling against the Urizenic reductions (Blake calls them petrifactions). Urizen fails to arrest process and turn the universe into a system of dead units. Los cannot restore the systems of Eternity, but he can use his organising art-powers to stop the deadening process to some extent and even to reverse it. Urizen in turn struggles, going through change after alienating change in an attempt to break down Los's resistances. But each time Los regathers his forces, takes on a new form, and gives that form a definite and vital organisation.

The conflict is continuous and terrible. Los cannot, under the strain, maintain the fullness and clarity of form he desires; he loses his direct contact with the sources of life, but preserves the memory of them and the need to seek ceaselessly for what has been lost. He is himself divided through the sense of loss, which Blake calls pity. His emanation is the first female; the Eternals call her Pity and flee. She is Enitharmon. Los embraces her and she bears Orc. Los is now indeed cut off from Eternity, the fullness of reality. He and his wife take Orc to a mountain-top and chain him jealously 'beneath

Urizen's deathful shadow'. Orc's cries begin to stir all things. Urizen in reply develops his science of quantitative measurement. The four elements appear —Tiriel, air; Utha, water; Grodna, earth; Fuzon, fire. Life begins. Urizen curses his progeny, 'for he saw That no flesh nor spirit could keep His iron laws for one moment. For he saw that life lived upon death.' He wanders weeping and devises the Net of Religion, tormented as he is at the insoluble contradiction of trying to make life function according to the laws of death. Mankind appears (in a fall that parodies the six days of Genesis) and Fuzon calls together the few sons who retain a desire for true life. He leads them out of the Bondage of Egypt, the fleshpots of the cities, into the desert. (We see how arbitrarily Blake takes bits from the Bible for his symbols. Here Fuzon is Moses as a redeemer, though earlier in the same poem Moses–Urizen, law-giver, appears as the most disastrously evil of characters.)[18]

For his account of Creation in this poem Blake draws strongly on recent biological work in which were being formulated the first stages of a theory of evolution. Precursors of Darwinian theory were Buffon in France, John Hunter in England and K. Kielmeyer in Germany, who developed theories of embryogenesis. Kielmeyer published his Biogenetic Law in 1793, just about the time Blake was at work on *Urizen*; but Blake's source was certainly John Hunter, whom he most probably met at Basire's and whom he depicted as Jack Tearguts in *An Island*. Blake goes further than Hunter in dividing the foetal processes into definite stages. He writes of Seven Ages, thinking of the Seven Days of Genesis, but giving them an evolutionary basis. He is drawing also on William Harvey, whom Hunter much admired, especially his *De Generatione* with its seven-staged account of embryogenesis. From Harvey too Blake took the globe of blood out of which comes Enitharmon. For Harvey considers blood the 'primary, generative principle', and describes globes of blood as pulsating or palpitating. Blake writes: 'The globe of blood trembled . . . A female form trembling and pale.' We may then say that Urizen is born through an evolutionary process of embryogenesis, while Enitharmon emerges from a primitive level of organic life (symbolised as the blood). Orc too is born through an evolutionary process, beginning as a worm—though Blake may be using the worm to signify the moment when life is regenerated out of death. The idea of organic evolution is indeed reflected in the whole structure of *Urizen*. The movement is not through the setting-out of philosophic positions which logically expand. Rather, the symbols grow and extend in a kind of organic development. For the full picture Blake is not content with schemes of embryogenesis alone; he brings in the creative human aspect through imagery of fire and the forge. Here is where Los desperately intrudes.*

Blake then does not take a simple denunciatory attitude to contemporary science. The account of evolutionary ascent is used to describe the descent of Urizen from his role in the unitary process of cosmos and humanity. What Blake is concerned with is the way in which the analytic method breaks up the unitary process and so can be used to express or symbolise the actual breaking up of that process. On the other hand, from the perspective of Eternity (the unitary grasp) the material would appear quite differently. The movement of life from the globe of blood to Enitharmon, or from the worm to Orc, would then take on a positive significance and would express the transformation of life into ever higher forms of organisation. Blake was fully aware of this point. At the end of *Jerusalem* all the creative forms that Blake loves are united with the systems he detests in a new unity. Quantitative science then has a valuable and necessary contribution to make to knowledge.

> The druid spectre was annihilate—loud thundering, rejoicing, terrific
>   vanishing,
> Fourfold annihilation: And at the clangour of the arrows of intellect
> The innumerable chariots of the Almighty appeared in Heaven:
> And Bacon & Newton & Locke, & Milton & Shakespeare & Chaucer,
> A man of blood-red wrath surrounding Heaven on all sides around,
> Glorious, incomprehensible by mortal man; & each chariot was sexual
>   threefold.
> And every man stood fourfold.

Urizen becomes what he originally was: the first born Son of Light, a naked bright-beaming youth, throned on mountains of silver (love), amid the sweet fields of bliss 'where liberty was justice & eternal science was mercy', where everything has its rightful place.

---

* Both John Hunter and his brother William were interested in art and employed Basire to engrave book-illustrations. Blake may well have visited the surgical theatre, Great Windmill Street, and the museum and laboratory at Hunter's house, Earls Court. (Artists often went to see dissections or to dissect corpses, as did Fuseli in Rome. Blake's vivid account of the operating table in *An Island* is in the vein of Hogarth's print showing the surgeons, and suggests personal experience.) Hunter was, in the words of his editor R. Owen, the first scientist to enunciate 'the resemblance of the phases of embryonic life to the series of inferior forms of animal species.' In his museum he had many sketches of the stages of development of various animals, using as illustration the heart, the brain, spine, and so on.[19]

Blake next wrote two shorter prophecies, *The Book of Ahania* and *The Book of Los*, which completed the first arc of his symbolic world-picture. Both are dated 1795 and engraved in the ordinary way, as if he wanted to get them off his hands quickly. Only one copy exists of either work: which again makes it seem that he wasn't much interested in them. *Ahania* takes up the story of Fuzon's revolt. He begins rather like the Orc of *America*, but fails. He strikes at Urizen, thinks that he has killed him, and exults at becoming God. His blow has set free Urizen's emanation Ahania, and Urizen at once lusts after her. He has knocked Fuzon down with a rock that falls on Mt Sinai (becomes the tablet of the Law). Fuzon himself he takes and nails on the accursed Tree of Mystery (Religion) as a 'pale living corse' (Jesus) around whom pestilence breeds. The Tree still grows over the void, 'enrooting itself all around, an endless labyrinth of woe'. Jesus is thus seen as a defeated revolutionary who has tried to kill his father and who merely succeeds in poisoning life, serving the tyrant whom he meant to supplant. Ahania laments round the Tree, crying over the days when 'I found babes of bliss on my beds, and bosoms of milk in my chambers'. Now cruel jealousy and selfish fear have wrought her desolation. (Her name is the Ossianic *Annia* plus *Ah*; she represents earth or nature in the era before property.) Through her again Blake declares that science need not be merely mechanistic. Before the advent of division Urizen had hands full of generous fire and a lap full of seed which he cast on the virgins of springing joy. 'In the human soul to cast The Seed of eternal science', that is, science with a unitary and dialectical basis.

The fate of Fuzon reflects what had been happening to the French Revolution; he stands for Robespierre who has failed to find the way forward into the promised brotherhood. Though he denounces Urizen, he succumbs to him. Blake seems to have seen as anti-Urizenic the ceremony in June 1794 in the Champs de Mars, which deposed the Goddess of Reason and set up the worship of the Supreme Being—though later, in the *Four Zoas* (111), he felt that there was not much difference between Reason and Robespierre's Supreme Being.

Blake's names often enclose much ingenious thought. Urizen seems to combine *Your Horizon* (*Yours* in a limited sense) and Greek *ourizein*, to limit. Los may well represent *Sol* (the sun as light) reversed, but his name is also meant to convey the sound of *Loss*. As the creative imagination, in his forge he makes the material sun while his planet is the spiritual sun (the totality of solar energies which are linked dynamically with human energy). *The Book* *of Los* deals with the counter-attack of the Poet, who represents all the forces of transformative energy in men that resist the fettering limits imposed by Urizen (State, religion, all divisive ideologies). The poem opens with the lament of Eno, a shadowy figure, over the advent of property (covetousness). Then Los fights against the flames that threaten to consume all life. He stamps them out till he gains a cleared space; but in so doing he has hardened everything into rock, which holds him fast, 'a vast solid without fluctuation'. Such a space was what Urizen sought. Fluctuation is connected, for Blake, with Newton's fluxions and his reduction of the motion of water-waves to the periodic oscillatory laws of pendulums. By contrasting fluctuation with solidity he points to the inability of Newtonian mathematics to deal simultaneously with the continuous and the discrete; he rejects the idea that quantities are generated by the 'fluxions' of points while the quantities generated in physical space are atomic and discontinuous. Later he develops a theory of pulsational Moments, rhythmic and concrete, as against Newton's indefinite and infinitely divisible flowing 'moments' of the fluxional calculus.*

Los has then the problem of breaking up the Newtonian abstraction and bringing 'life back again'. He now makes the contrary error and falls into 'horrid vacuity bottomless': the void which is another aspect of Newton's atoms, atoms and void combining to make up the 'identity' of his real world. But at last Los has some success. His attempts at imaginative (unitary and dialectical) organisation turn the void into the elements. Here at least is the simplest basis out of which a stable world may be constructed. Los struggles with the waters till at last light begins. But what he sees is Urizen's backbone twisting like a serpent or a flailing chain. He sets to work, forms an anvil and hammer of adamant, and works to bind Urizen. He hammers a globe into shape. Urizen becomes our world: the world of divided or fallen man. 'A form was completed, a Human illusion. In darkness and deep clouds involved.' The problem of breaking the illusion and creating (realising) what reality is in its fullness is still to be solved.[20]

There remains *The Song of Los*, dated 1795, which completes the Lambeth prophecies. The year was one of famine and bread-riots, and the scale of the

---

* The last three prophecies were written in a quite different metre than that in *Visions*, *America*, *Europe*. The basic line is one of three beats. Blake wanted a quick, hammering, relentless beat. 'Sundering, darkening, thundering/Rent away with a terrible crash,/Eternity rolled wide apart,/Wide asunder rolling/Mountainous, all around/Departing, departing, departing/Leaving ruinous fragments of life.' Having used this effect in books describing the immediate results of Urizen's self-dividing, he did not return to the metre.

war was bringing about an increase in taxes. Discontent broadened. The London Corresponding Society could draw some fifty thousand to its outdoor rallies, and the anti-war crowd in the street at the assembling of Parliament in October was unprecedented. 'Lecturers and pamphleteers such as Thelwall in London and Coleridge in Bristol linked the war and the famine in earnest invective, and the number of "lectural and political" gatherings increased beyond all former periods' (Erdman). *The Song of Los* might have been written any time after *Europe*, but its rather pessimistic mood fits in with 1795. In it Blake turns from the description of the Urizenic universe to complete the world-picture of *America* and *Europe*. Los's song is sung to four harps and presupposes the insertion of the two earlier books between the sections here named *Africa* and *Asia*. Blake makes the link clear by re-using *America*'s first line as the last line of *Africa*. So *Africa* ends in 1775, and *Asia* begins with Louis XIV's execution in January 1793 or any other event of the Revolution that would make kings howl.

The poem takes up the story of the fettering of men by religious abstractions, their destruction by anti-sensuous anti-sexual creeds. Orc is chained on Atlas with the Chain of Jealousy. 'Then Oothoon hovered over Judah and Jerusalem, And Jesus heard her voice (a man of sorrows); he received A gospel from wretched Theotormon. The human race began to wither.' Thus Jesus is seen as one of the betrayers of love. In his world only the diseased propagated, while the worlds of Mohammed and Odin flourished with a code of war. 'There were the churches, hospitals, castles, palaces, Like nets and gins and traps to catch the joys of Eternity.' Rousseau and Voltaire are now linked with the destructive forces, of which Urizen has made Newton and Locke the guardians. The phrase 'Urizen wept' links his act of betrayal with that of Jesus. Los is here an indefinite, ineffective character, Enitharmon's husband. His sons fade out as the picture of Urizen is elaborated. *Asia* continues with the account of Urizen's domination, but stresses the outbreak of Orc, which brings a new life to the deadened earth.

The two new sections are brief, to match the contraction of an oppressed world. 'Noah shrunk beneath the waters.' Har and Heva 'shrunk into two narrow doleful forms'. 'The sullen earth Shrunk.' In a powerful passage Blake attacks all the ruling principles of the bourgeois world.

> Shall not the king call for famine from the heath,
> Nor the priest for pestilence from the fen?
> To restrain, to dismay, to thin

> The inhabitants of mountain and plain—
> In the day of full-feeding prosperity
> And the night of delicious songs?
> Shall not the counsellor throw his curb
> Of poverty on the laborious
> To fix the price of labour,
> To invent allegoric riches?...

Blake there in his own way states what Marx has to say of the difference between abstract and concrete labour, of the contradictions between the great powers evoked in production and the alienating effects.

The full-page plates, at the start and end of the book, summarise the themes, the distances traversed in the working out. Urizen kneels to worship a sun darkened with runes of mystery (the commands of the Law). Los leans in dire exhaustion over the sun, resting on his hammer; he has cleansed the sun of the Urizenic runes, though some slight clouds yet linger. An epoch has ended and a new one has begun, with new forms of struggle. The strained intense look on Los's face suggests that he is not quite sure what will emerge or just how the fiery impact of Orc will work out. In fact, Blake had reached a difficult point. He had expounded his Urizenic myth, and, looking round at the world outside him, with militarisation and oppression worsening in England and with the French Revolution coming up against unexpected obstructions and difficulties, he feels driven further back into himself, sure that his deepest convictions are true, but unsure as to the way things are going to work out. Well might he feel that he needed to rest and seek a new start. His prophecies had gone through three stages. First, the experimental works that come to a head with *Visions*, where his method matures. Secondly, the works in which he applies his method directly to the revolutionary situation and seeks to grasp the fundamental patterns of history. Thirdly, the works in which he explores the Urizenic world of false consciousness, of alienation. The idealist element appears in the way in which he defines the birth of bourgeois science through a creation-myth: as if the ideas actually created a universe corresponding to their preconceptions instead of reflecting certain abstracted aspects of the real universe. But this method has the virtue of giving an immense urgency and power to his exposition of the alienating distortions inherent in the ideologies of a divided world.

Blake hated the industrial system as incarnating the Urizenic science that saw the universe as a vast machine and the machine itself as a reflection of that universe in the productive sphere. He hated it for cruelly torturing and malforming the men, women, and children caught in its toils. One aspect involved the other. But he knew little about the advanced technology of his day. The mill and the wheel became his main symbols for the system. There was an Albion Mill, the first London workshop to use steam-power, in Black-friars; but it was burned down in 1791 and he does not refer to it. He had read in Darwin's *Botanic Garden* about Savery's use of steam-power to raise water, a method developed by Watt and Boulton to drain mines: the simple water-wheel giving way to complicated machinery. In *Jerusalem* he tells of 'intricate wheels invented, wheel within wheel, To perplex youth in their outgoings & to bind to labours in Albion'. The wheel symbolised the whole imprisoning system, found in the clock-wheel of dead time and the revolving heavens of Newton. He knew also of weaving and spinning processes, of brick-making, of printing presses, of the forge. But even with the forge he did not seem to be thinking of the new ironworks, but to look back to days when the Surrey woodlands provided charcoal for smelting. 'Loud groans Thames beneath the iron Forge', and 'the Surrey hills glow like the clinkers in the furnace', in his vision of the forging of instruments to bring about a bloody harvest of men. The dark Satanic mills and the furnaces were for him very much a part of the war-industry he found so busy on his return to London in 1803. Albion's children seemed terribly unaware that they were living in 'gore'.[21]

The term Irritability was applied to Blake's behaviour and reactions by his acquaintances such as Flaxman and Hayley, and it is worth while to look at the contemporary use of the term, which is linked with the prevailing ideas of nervous fibre and of madness. The nervous system was thought to have as its functions sensibility and irritability, sensation and movement. The fibre connected all the organs and made communication possible between them, however distant or physiologically dissimilar they were. Diseases of the nerves were seen as diseases of sympathy. The female body in particular was riddled with obscure and strangely direct paths of sympathy; from one extremity of its organic space to the other it enclosed a perpetual possibility of hysteria. (We may compare the way in which Blake's female emanations break off into unstable states of emotion or sensibility.) Nervous sufferers were most irritable, owning too strong a sympathy for what was happening around them. Thus emerged the disorders or unbalances that brought about the first stage of madness, in which was seen a continuity between disposition (irritability) and pathological event (irritation).

Blake himself was much interested in the idea of nervous fibres, which appear in his evolutionary depictions. In *The Book of Los* they are used to define Los's fall, his breakdown or disintegration into an 'immense fibrous Form, stretching out Thro' the bottoms of immensity raging'. When he sees Urizen's threshing backbone he reacts by 'unfolding his Fibres together to a Form of impregnable strength'.*

How the irritability of nervous fibre was thought to operate can be seen by looking at *Passages from the Diary of a Late Physician* (1832–7) by Samuel Warren. This is a fictional work, but Warren had studied medicine at Edinburgh before he turned to law. Later, 1859–77, he was a Master in Lunacy. *Passages*, which first appeared in *Blackwood's Magazine*, attracted much attention and was often reprinted and translated; he had spared no pains in making its medical aspects correct and acceptable. He links irritability with mental instability and a proneness to seeing visions or spectres. Thus in Chapter X of his book he remarks that nowadays 'these mysterious visitants are to be resolved into optical delusions, acting in an excitable fancy—an irritable nervous temperament'. He cites a correspondent of December 1830: 'Such spectra are by no means rare among studious men, if of an irritable temperament, and an imaginative turn. I know a learned baronet who has his study sometimes crowded with them; and he never feels so much at home as when surrounded by these airy spirits'.

In Chapter XVII, writing of spectral transformations, Warren cites a patient: 'Once I saw him' (the spectre) 'leading an army of huge speckled and crested serpents against me; and when they came upon me, I suddenly found myself in the midst of a pool of stagnant water, alive with slimy reptiles; and while endeavouring to make my way out, *he* rose to the surface, his face hissing in the water, and blazing bright as ever. Again, I thought I saw him in combat by the gates of Eden, with Satan—and the air thronged with swart faces looking on!' These visions were the confused recollection of Milton readings, in the earlier part of the sufferer's breakdown. 'Again, I thought I was in the act of opening my snuff-box, when he issued from it, swelling soon into gigantic proportions, and his fiery features diffusing a light and heat around, that scorched and blasted! At another time I thought

* A theorist like S. A. Tissot saw a complex pattern of movement when nervous fibre simultaneously transmitted the stimulus of a vibratory movement and the impression left on an organ. This twofold function combined an undulatory movement for the stimulus and a corpuscular movement for the sensation. Alterations of tension and relaxation were important in nervous disease. See Foucault with references to the theoreticians Tissot, T. Sydenham, R. Whytt, etc.

I was gazing upwards on a summer sky; and in the midst of a luminous fissure in it, made by the lightning, I distinguished *his* accursed figure, with his glowing features wearing an expression of horror, and his limbs out-stretched, as if he had been hurled from some height, and was falling through the sky towards me. He came—flung himself in my recoiling arms —and clung to me—burning, scorching, withering my soul within me! I thought I was all the while the subject of strange, paradoxical, contradictory feelings towards him—that I, at one and the same time, loved and loathed, feared and despised him!'

Warren says that this man was obsessed by making himself a 'sacrifice' of some sort, 'goaded on to do so by the spectre, by the most dazzling tempta-tions, and under the most appalling threats'. We have here an internalised version of the situation of Jesus in *Paradise Regained*. There is a close relation to the way in which Blake projected his fantasy-experiences in the prophetic books.

To illustrate the colloquial use of the term I give some more examples, drawn from Shelley and his circle. Maria Gisborne says of Mrs Godwin, after Mary had gone off with Shelley, that Godwin 'described her as being of the most irritable disposition possible, and therefore suffering the keenest anguish on account of this misfortune, of which Mary is the sole cause, as she pretends; she regards Mary as the greatest enemy she has in the world.' Here the term denotes an extreme sensitivity to any form of outrage or attack, and is linked with an element of paranoia. In 1811 Shelley wrote to Godwin: 'My feelings at intervals are of a deadly & torpid kind, or awakened to a state of such unnatural & keen excitement that only to instance the organ of sight, I find the very blades of grass & the boughs of distant trees present themselves to me with microscopical distinctness. Towards evening I sink into a state of lethargy & inanimation, & often remain on the sofa between sleep & waking a prey to the most painful irritability of thought.' Here again there is the excessive response to stimuli from outside or to anxieties from within, linked with abnormal sensory conditions.

In 1823 Shelley wrote to Claire Clairmont, 'If you would take my advice you would give up this idle pursuit after shadows, & temper yourself to the season; seek in the daily and affectionate intercourse of friends a respite from these perpetual and irritating projects.' Here the term means upsetting or disturbing, and is linked with the 'pursuit after shadows' in contrast to the acceptance of normal existence. (Clair and Shelley, it must be remembered, shared various visionary experiences.) Again, in 1821 he wrote to her: 'As to pain, I care little for it; but the nervous irritability which it leaves is a great and serious evil to me, and which, if not incessantly combated by myself and soothed by others, would leave me nothing but torment in life.' Here the term again signifies a deep inner disturbance which prevents one from living a normal life; it suggests Blake's 'nervous fear'. In 1815, again writing to Claire, Shelley spoke of her bad and good sides. The first side 'I should call irritable if it were not for the nervous disorder, the effects of which you still retain; the nervous Claire is reserved and melancholy and more sarcastic than violent . . .' Here he tries to distinguish between a settled irritability and a nervous state induced by illness, but the general associations are the same as in the other examples. To be irritable is to be unbalanced, extremely vulnerable and open to a sense of attack, easily disturbed, and driven into an unstable inner world.

7

Night Thoughts, 1795–8

Richard Brothers still excited much interest. In February 1795 he declared that when he, Brothers, was revealed, George would yield up his throne. God had ordered Brothers to leave for Constantinople in July, about which time London and much of the world would be destroyed by earthquake. N. B. Halhed, MP for Lymington, who had been an official of the East India Company and translated both Latin verse and Hindu Laws, published a *Testimony* in which he cited the Old and the New Testimony to prove Brothers' claims. (In it he defined the Hindu triad of Brahma, Vishnu, Shiva, as personifying Matter, Space, and Time.) Other supporters included a rich Hull Merchant, Coggan, and William Bryant, a London engraver, who had left wife and family in 1789 and gone with a friend to visit a society of Illuminati at Avignon 'favoured with divine revelation'. On 4 March *The Times* printed an ironically hostile account of Brothers, and that day he was arrested. The *European Magazine* said that the messengers had to face 'the fury of the multitude'. He was taken before the Privy Council and declared insane on 27 March. The doctors said it was a criminal act to have fallen in love with the Princess Royal; he replied that God had commanded him to acknowledge her as wife and queen. Halhed defended him in the House and for months there was a flood of pamphlets for and against him, with a series of testimonies of visions, dreams, and omens in his support.* The Royal Circus in St George's Fields put on a pantomime, *The Prophecy; or, Mountains in Labour* . . . On 4 June there was much fear of the prophesied

* There were many women visionaries. One of Brothers' landladies had visions and was asked by a heavenly voice, 'How do you know but he is John the Baptist?' Mother Ann Lee had been declared the Christ by her Shaker followers; Sarah Flaxmer saw herself since 1779 as the one chosen by God 'to reveal Satan'. She had visions and dreams from God, who directed her in a loud voice. Mrs S. Eyre of Cecil Street was a rival of Brothers. In a series of letters in the *Oracle* she denounced France as the Beast and held that Brothers' call for peace would bring destruction on England. Soon Joanna Southcott was to appear on the national scene.

earthquake. Stedman noted next day, 'London disloyal, superstitious, villainous, and infamous. An earthquake prophesied by Brothers. Many leave town.' On the 4th Gillray had published his cartoon, *Pressages of the Millennium, with the Destruction of the Faithful, Revealed to R. Brothers.* That night there was a bad storm. John Binns, radical printer and leader of the London Corresponding Society, took shelter in a bar-room and found fifty to sixty men and women there with their children; they had been alarmed by the prophecy.

Stedman, having trouble with Johnson, had come to London to see his book through the press, and on 2 June he called on Blake, from whom he wanted help. On 5 June he forced Bartolozzi to return the plates he had, and repaired them. A few days later he gave 'a blue sugar cup to Mrs. Blake', and dined with Blake, Johnson, Bartolozzi, and the artist Rigaud, who, like Blake, had subscribed to his book. On 24 June he got his first volume and thought it marred, 'oaths and Sermons inserted &c.' He cancelled half the volume. Apparently a few days later, he 'gave an oil portrait to Mr. Blake', and dined with him and Catherine. Then, it seems in August, 'I visit Mr. Blake for three days who undertakes to do business for me when I am not in London— I leave him all my papers.' The character of the man comes out in his rapid jottings:

The King's coach insulted. Damn Bartolozzi. He goes away. Was at Greenwich to dinner. I was also at Lambeth Gardens, Johnson uncivil all along. Fire at Jamaica & Constantinople . . . Famine in all Europe. Send Moverd [friend in Holland], and Johnson. St. Paul's. My brother's family rebels . . . Met 300 whores in the Strand. French prisoners come home. Abershaw &c. hang'd 8. Saw a mermaid. Meat and bread abused. Russian fleet down. Two days at Blake's. Quiberon expedition fail'd. 199 emigrants executed.

Finally in September: 'all knaves and fools—cruel to the excess—Blake was mob'd and robbd.' This tantalisingly brief reference cannot mean that Blake suffered a political attack; otherwise Stedman would have elaborated. He may be referring to an event recorded by Tatham (no doubt told to him by Catherine) that one day when the Blakes were out on a visit, thieves entered the house and stole plate to the value of £60 and clothes to the value of £40. Some people may say, he adds, 'Had poor half starved Blake ever a suit of clothes beyond the tatters on his back?' Yes, in his earlier days he enjoyed 'not only comforts but necessaries' (*sic*). Catherine must have told Tatham also about Blake lending £40 to a man whose pretty wife came next day to ask Catherine's opinion of 'a very gorgeous dress'. The man had told Blake that his children lacked food. He was, according to Tatham, 'a certain free thinking Speculator, the Author of many very elaborate philosophical treatises'. Tatham has worked the tale up to attack Godwin; but there is clearly no basis in his identification.[1]

Catherine must have kept rosy memories in her old age of the Lambeth days. Tatham must again be blowing up her reminiscences in his statement that Blake now had pupils of high rank. After he had given the drawing lessons, the latter found him 'so entertaining & pleasant, possessing such novel thoughts & such eccentric notions, together with such jocose hilarity & amiable demeanour, that he frequently found himself asked to stay dinner' and spend the evening in entertaining them. Finally he was recommended as drawing-master to the royal family. He was aghast, not on account of his 'republican humours, not from any disaffection to his superiors, but because he would have been drawn into a class of Society, superior to his previous pursuits & habits; he would have been expected to have lived in comparative respectability, not to say splendour, a mode of life, as he thought, derogatory to the simplicity of his designs & deportment.' What slight element of fact lies behind this story, we cannot say. Perhaps Blake did indeed give some drawing-lessons and found that they used up too much of his time; but the grand setting conjured up by Tatham can be dismissed. Tatham's aim was to prove that Blake was a perfectly conventional character, who sometimes, when provoked, talked in a wild extravagant way. 'Unalloyed & unencumbered by opposition, he was in all essential points orthodox in his belief, but he put forth ramifications of doubt, that by his vigorous & creative mind, were watered into the empty enormities of Extravagant & rebellious thoughts.'

Another tale from Tatham may well have some better basis in fact and belong to the Lambeth years. A young man with a portfolio used to pass the house, looking 'interesting & eager, but sickly'. Blake sent Catherine to call him in, took an interest in him, and 'gave him every instruction possible'. But the youth fell ill. The Blakes visited him daily and tended him till he died. Perhaps he reminded Blake of Robert.

In December Stedman noted: 'Send a goose to Johnson and one to Blake.' For all his eccentricity he was extremely patriotic. 'All Scots officers here, literally mad, and several painters addendum . . . Of Oxford militia, two men shot at Brighton, and 2 hang'd at . . . in mutiny. A riot at Birmingham . . . The Bill passes against seditious meetings . . . Plague and famine is expected.' We may recall Blake's use of the plague motive in connection with war. 'The nobility all marry old women. I kick the landlady at the *Saracen's Head*. Damn'd cold . . . The inn is full of whores & rascals. The dragoons all home from the continent.' Next he mentions his three-day visit to Blake. If Blake had then or any other time hinted at his political ideas and his visions, Stedman would have noted it explosively and would have lost his faith in Blake as a capable level-headed man who could handle the muddle-headed Johnson.

Now at last we have one of Blake's own letters, written on 6 December 1795 to Cumberland with information about preparing an etching plate. Cumberland wanted to engrave his own designs for his book, *Thoughts on Outline*. Blake thinks of him secluded in Windsor Park and hopes that his drawings will show the world how 'Peace & Plenty & Domestic Happiness is the Source of Sublime Art, & prove to the Abstract Philosophers that Enjoyment & not Abstinence is the food of intellect'. He cites Locke with approbation. 'Locke says it [is the] same faculty that Invents Judges, & I say he who [can] Invent can Execute.' On the 27th Cosway wrote to Cumberland, praising one of his outlines. 'Why do you not get Blake to make an engraving of it? I should think he would be delighted to undertake such a work, & it wou'd certainly *pay him very well* for whatever time & pains he might bestow.' But nothing came of the suggestion.[2]

This year Blake made good use of his monotype technique, producing a set of works that seem to be planned as a series. He began with *God Creating Adam* (already mentioned). Then came the Fall and its effects: *Satan Exulting over Eve*, *God Judging Adam* (lost), *Lamech and his Two Wives*, *The Lazar House*. Then a triad dealing with the growth of false consciousness: *The Triple Hecate*, representing necromancy and the deliberate distortion of human energy, *Newton* immersed in matter and representing the Urizen-trend with the compasses of quantitative science, and *Nebuchadnezzar*, representing the complete alienation of the human senses. Next, two works on the female principle, *Pity* and *Ruth*. Finally two works dealing with the curse of the law: *Adam cast out by God*, and *Good and Evil Angels* showing fettered energy.[3]

These works reveal a big advance in his art, the result of the loosening up of his rhythmic sense through the designs for his books and the general imaginative stimulus that the books had given. They own much power in their massive simplification of form and of the systems holding the elements of the design together, e.g. in the horizontals of *Satan Exulting* and *Pity*. There is a strong use of symmetry without mechanical balance. More, the rich texture that the method of printing imparts helps to get rid of any feeling of emptiness in the spaces. In many respects these works are the finest pictures he ever achieved.[4]

In 1795 he was commissioned by R. Edwards, bookseller of Pall Mall, to illustrate Young's *Night Thoughts*. The book was published in 1797 and Edwards later said that Blake had been 'employed for more than two years' upon it. His reputation must have risen for such a commission to come his way; probably Fuseli had put in a word for him. On 19 February 1796 Joseph Farington noted: 'West, Cosway & Humphry spoke warmly in favour of the designs of Blake the Engraver, as works of extraordinary genius and imagination.—Smirke differed in opinion, from what he had seen, so do I.'[5]

We get a glimpse of what Blake was feeling about his surroundings in Lambeth these years from a passage in *Milton*. Los calls to his Fellow-Labourers of the Vintage and bids them go forth from what he considers the world-centre: 'Jerusalem's Inner Court, Lambeth, ruin'd and given to the detestable gods of Priam, to Apollo, and at the Asylum Given to Hercules, who labour in Tirzah's looms for bread.' At the crossing where Hercules Road ran into New Road and York Place, on the north side were three Pleasure Gardens of Flora and Apollo. These had grown up in the early days of the French Revolution and were now in decay or being put down as disorderly houses to which resorted 'democratic shopmen . . . railing against King and Church'. To the south was the Royal Asylum for Female Orphans along the New Road, where once stood the Hercules Tavern, and, more to the west, Blake's row of houses and the Charity School.

The Hercules of whom Blake is thinking is the hero enslaved to Omphale and forced to spin among the women. (Jacob Duché was secretary and chaplain to the Asylum, where he 'warmly welcomed' to the chapel persons interested in Swedenborg, 1779 to 1792.) The fettered hero Blake–Hercules must have felt his kinship with the children at asylum and school who had to labour at Tirzah's looms for bread. (Tirzah, prudish daughter of Rahab the whore, represents the false idea of women and so is 'Mother of my Mortal part', weaving the body of the fall.) In *Jerusalem* Blake sets out at length his sympathy for the women toiling at loom and spinning-wheel. 'Terrible their distress . . . Endless their labour, with bitter food, void of sleep. Though hungry they labour. They rouse themselves anxious, Hour after hour labouring at the whirling wheel—Many wheels, & as many lovely daughters sit weeping.' Yet their only joy in life is their work. They expect no pity. 'For they labour for life & love, regardless of anyone But the poor spectres that they work for, always, incessantly.' Here the spectre becomes the employer of sweated labour.[6]

In January and February 1796 Stedman wrote three times to both Johnson and Blake. This year saw a savage advance of reaction, and Blake seems to have grown ever more afraid. Perhaps now he wrote the depressed quatrain over the picture of Orc rising from the earth: he shattered his harp on a ruin'd pillar (broken freedom) and 'wander'd down the vales of Kent in sick & drear lamentings': he walked along the Old Kent Road, trying to throw off his dismay. How radicals were feeling can be read in a letter of 25 March from Cumberland, of whom Blake was seeing a lot, to his brother: 'I know no news, but that *Great* Britain is hanging the Irish, hunting the Maroons [in Jamaica], feeding the Vendée [French counter-revolutionaries], and establishing the human-flesh trade—as to our war of Religion, virtue in humanity, its success seems to equal its pretensions.' (This year Wordsworth turned from politics to 'the open fields'.) In May Stedman noted that he had written twelve letters to Blake, and cursed Johnson as a demon of hell who tormented him by altering the dedication to the Prince of Wales, &c., 'he being a damn'd eternal Jacobin scoundrel'. Clearly he had no idea of Blake's Jacobinism.

On 18 June Thomas, sixteen-year-old illegitimate son of the poet William Hayley, who had been apprenticed as sculptor to Flaxman, wrote to his father in terms that suggest the latter was already well acquainted with Blake and his work. 'I have not yet seen anything of Blake or his drawings. I have written this on Saturday eve that I may if possible take a walk to his house tomorrow morning. Till then adieu I will add a line to tell you how I succeed . . . Monday morning. I have not been able to call on Blake yesterday as I intended but I will lay hold on the first opportunity. You know it is a great distance from us. Nevertheless I hope to be able to see him very soon.'

On 24 June Farington recorded a talk with Fuseli about Blake, 'whose genius & invention have been much spoken of'. Fuseli made his comment about fancy being his end, not his means, and gave details of the Young commission. Edwards 'has had the letter press of each page laid down on a large sheet of paper. There are abt. 900 pages—Blake asked 100 guineas for the whole. Edwards said he could not afford to give more than 20 guineas for which Blake agreed.—Fuseli understands that Edwards proposes to select abt. 200 from the whole and to have that number engraved as decorations for a new edition.—Fuseli says, Blake has something of madness abt. him. He acknowledges the superiority of Fuseli: but thinks himself more able than Stothard'. The details of the transaction are hard to make out. If only £21 were to be paid for the 537 finished watercolours, each 16 × 12 inches, Blake got only 9½*d*. each. Smith says he was paid a 'despicably low' sum; Gilchrist, probably guessing, makes it a guinea a plate.

In July Stedman wrote twice to Blake. In early August Cumberland's book appeared, with a third of the twenty-four plates engraved by Blake. Cumberland in an appendix thanked him for instruction and encouragement, and called him a man of extraordinary genius. Blake was sent a copy; but with his usual difficulty in answering letters, he did not reply for some five months, till 23 December. He apologised for holding six plates that Cumberland had asked him to get done. Asking him to call, he uses the term 'nature' in a strongly positive sense. 'Such works as yours Nature & Providence, the Eternal Parents, demand from their children; how few produce them in such perfection: how Nature smiles on them: how Providence rewards them.'

A book with translations of Burger's *Leonora* had appeared with a frontispiece by Blake. In September the *British Critic* remarked on the designs 'distorted, absurd, and impossible monsters', and went on to attack the 'detestable taste, founded on the depraved fancy of one man of genius [Fuseli], which substitutes deformity and extravagance for force and expression, and draws men and women without skins, with their joints all dislocated; or imaginary beings, which neither can nor ought to exist'. In November the *Analytical Review* said that Blake tried to express 'the wild conceptions of the poet, but with so little success, as to produce an effect perfectly ludicrous, instead of terrific'. Blake in fact drew a rigid rocking-horse with incredibly long legs. On 22 December Edwards composed an Advertisement for *Night Thoughts*; at the end he merely stated that 'the original conceptions, and the bold and masterly execution' of Blake cannot pass unnoticed or unadmired.

During the Lambeth days occurred an episode told by Tatham. Looking from his window into the garden of the circus-owner Astley, Blake saw a boy hobbling along with a log tied to his foot such as was used to stop a horse straying. 'Blake's blood boiled.' He rushed out and had the boy freed. Astley, learning what had happened, came to Blake's house and asked 'by what authority he dare come athwart his method of jurisdiction'. They almost came to blows, but Astley calmed down after a while.

We know little of Blake's life in 1797. On 12 January a committee of the R.A. (Farington, Hoppner, Stothard, Rigaud, Opie) met at a coffee-house to discuss a manuscript supposed to contain Titian's colour-secrets. They 'supped together and had laughable conversation. Blake's eccentric designs were mentioned. Stothard supported his claims to Genius, but allowed he had been misled to extravagance in his art, & he knew by whom.' Clearly he meant Fuseli. 'Hoppner ridiculed the absurdity of his designs, and said nothing could be more easy than to produce such. They were like the conceits of a drunken fellow or a madman. "Represent a man sitting on the moon, and pissing the Sun out—that would be a whim of much merit."—Stothard was angry mistaking the laughter caused by Hoppner's description.'[7]

In the spring Blake was one of nineteen engravers signing a testimonial for a device that prevented the forging of banknotes; and there appeared the prospectus for *Night Thoughts* with 'forty [actually forty-three] very spirited engravings from original drawings by Blake. These engravings are in a perfectly new style of decorations surrounding the text which they are designed to elucidate.' The book was to be the first of four parts with 150 engravings in all, the set costing five guineas, with prices higher for non-subscribers. The moment was an unfortunate one; there had been a banking crash and the arts were suffering. The book, coming out in June, sold badly; Edwards dropped the idea of three more volumes. Blake must have been deeply disappointed. The project, which for the one and only time made him the subject of much discussion in the art-world, seemed at last to provide him with a chance of breaking through into the ranks of esteemed artists. The system of drawings around the text was a tamer version of the combination of art and verse in the Prophecies; and in general the designs were weaker versions of the sort of thing he had been doing there. In such works the weaknesses of his draughtsmanship were liable to come to the fore, since he could not trust boldly to his impulses. But, when the worst is said, the book stood out among other contemporary attempts at ambitiously illustrated poems for its force and originality. Its failure was decisive in destroying Blake's hopes of anything like normal success.

Though Stedman had drawn Blake on to his side in the disputes with Johnson and the latter's *Review* had ridiculed the *Leonora* illustration, Johnson still gave Blake odd jobs. Godwin in his diary for 4 April 1797 mentions a dinner at the bookseller's where he, Fuseli, Blake, Grignion (engraver), Dr John Anderson and Arthur Aikin (nephew of Mrs Barbauld) were present. At about this time Blake made 116 designs for Gray's poems; perhaps he hoped to use them in a book to follow his Young. He was attracted by the poems against tyrants like *The Bard* and *Fatal Sisters*. His old villain,

Edward III, was shown soaring like Urizen over villages as the 'scourge of France'. The *Ode to Adversity* with its personifications of Poverty, Disease and Despair, and with a king chained in his own dungeon, suited the emotions stirred by the famine-year of 1795–6. In lighter mood Blake played with the overtones of the *Ode on the Death of a Favourite Cat*, developing subtly the relations of Cat, Fish, and their spirit-forms.[8]

Commentators have quite failed to realise what Blake found in Young. What he found in *Night Thoughts* were many elements akin to his own outlook, though set out in the conventional Miltonic diction of the day. Far back, with the first impacts of Newtonian thought, there had begun what we may call a counter-movement which sought to break down abstract infinite space in terms of human needs. The despised poet Blackmore began this work, merging natural and industrial processes in order to 'humanise' space. His imagery seemed nonsense to the Augustan wits, who pilloried him.* Young in a more grandiloquent way used the same sort of method. Already in his *Last Day* he packed his sense of the world's unexplained wrong and his conviction that immensity must be brought down to manageable proportions by relating abstract space to human needs or activities. 'One nail supports Our falling universe: that gone, we drop.' 'Already has the fatal train took fire; A moment, and the World's blown up to thee, The Sun is darkness and the Stars are dust.' Man is set at the heart of things. 'Man the sole cause Of this surrounding storm! and yet he sleeps As the Storm rocked to rest.' 'O Thou! whose Word from solid Darkness struck That Spark the Sun: strike Wisdom from my soul.'

This sense of a threatening immediacy of fusion between individual existence and world-patterns appears also in the Evangelist area and might be much illustrated from Methodist hymns; what Young adds is intellectual breadth in his space-time concepts. His formulations bring out strongly how the union of man and nature, involving both the struggle of knowledge and the extension of industrial techniques, was bound up with the problems of a society in the throes of dissolution and renewal. His style, with all its elegance and pomp, has links with the proverbs in its concision and often homely contrasts, as these random lines show: 'For ever on the brink of being born

* Thus he writes: 'Who the rich metal beats, and then, with care, Unfolds the golden leaves, to gild the fields of air?' 'Th' Almighty Chemist does his work prepare, Pours down his waters on the thirsty plain, Digests his lightning, and distils his rain.' 'Canst thou set forth the ethereal mines on high, Which the refulgent ore of light supply? Is the celestial furnace to be known, In which I melt the golden metal down?'[9]

... A Sun extinguished, a just opening Grave ... Look Nature through, 'tis
Revolution all ... The world of Matter, with its various forms, All dies into
new life ... Nature thy daughter, ever-changing Birth Of thee the great
Immutable ... Man's heart eats all things and is hungry still ... Heart-
buried in the rubbish of the world ... The Man emerges, mounts above the
wreck, As towering flame from Nature's funeral pyre ... Nature revolves,
but Man advances ...'

We see that Young has something of Blake's sense of what the improvement of the senses implies, of what true progression means:

> How changed the Face of Nature? How improved?
> What seemed a Chaos, shines a glorious World,
> Or, what a World, an Eden, heightened all!
> Is it another Scene! another Self!
> And that a Self far more illustrious still.
> Beyond long Ages, yet rolled up in Shades,
> Unpierced by bold Conjecture's keenest Ray,
>   What Evolutions of surprising Fate?
> How Nature opens, and receives my Soul
> In boundless Walks of raptured Thought? where Gods
> Encounter and embrace me! What new Births
> Of strange Adventure ...

We understand then why Blake was interested in Young, and why, having
set himself to brood on the poem and produce over 500 illustrations to it, his
next work was profoundly influenced by *Night Thoughts*.* It is as though he
said: 'Young has projected the incoherent and often uncertain material of a
new universe of thought, now I shall reveal the structure of experience which
such a universe involves, and show what the new births of strange adventure
in it are like.' He divided his new work, *Vala or the Four Zoas*, into Nine
Nights like Young's poem, and he wrote it out mainly on proof-sheets of the
Young engravings. It exists only in manuscript. The title-page gives the date
1797, which may indicate the time when he first got to grips with the work.
The text seems mainly of 1797–1800, with most changes completed by 1804
and only a few passages added later, though he may have worked on it till

---

* Translated as a prose-poem into most languages of Europe (including Hungarian,
Swedish, Portugese) *Night Thoughts* played an essential part with Ossian, in stimulating
the full romantic movement. It was especially popular in France, and Robespierre slept
with it under his pillow.

1810. The textual problems are acute, and it is impossible to regain the original form. Blake made many deletions, transposed passages, inserted revisions without clear indication where they went, and left gaps when removing lines. And all the while he was deepening and extending his vision. The thing got out of control, but he kept on seeking new ways to bring the elements together in an interlinked whole. What he learned in this struggle he applied in *Milton* and *Jerusalem*.

After the Urizenic poems he had found himself at a difficult point of development. He could not continue with the method of *Europe* and *The Book of Los* because the check to the revolution in France had produced a new set of problems. The savage increase of repression in England intensified his fears; and the appearance of Brothers in his open defiance of the king and Pitt made him question afresh just what his prophetic function was. In his period of uncertainty and search he went on concentrating on Young as an artist. The result was *Vala or the Four Zoas.**

The problem was to move from myth more or less directly related to history into the definition of the complex inner struggles decomposing and reconstructing the individual psyche while at the same time seeking a revelation of history and human purpose on a new level. The theme is the Eternal or Universal Man. The whole Cosmos makes up One Man. His elements (reason, passions, and so on) can take on human forms of a lesser kind; in turn they may have children. A child of any figure is someone who follows the pattern of thought and action that the latter sets. Urizen and his Sons turn Sons of Los when Los draws them into his influence. All things from stars to trees are part of the One Man, and in Eternity the gigantic whole or the interrelated parts can be viewed at will. The Man falls sick. That means an endless inner division. The parts separate and fight, and are themselves again divided.[10]

The concept of the One Man had a wide currency in the romantic era. While Blake was working on *Jerusalem*, Fabre d'Olivet in France was obsessed by 'the Collective Man, the Man formed abstractly by the assemblage of all men', or, 'Man in general, Universal Man'. The mystic of Lyons, philosopher and social reformer, Pierre-Simon Ballanche, said the basic

---

* At different times he gave four titles to the poem (1) 'The Bible of Hell, in Nocturnal Visions collected Vol. I Lambeth' (on the back of a Young drawing) (2) 'The Book of Vala' (on an early rubbed-out version) (3) 'Vala Or The Death and Judgment of the Ancient Man a Dream in Nine Nights' (1797 title-page) (4) 'The Four Zoas The Torments of Love & Jealousy in the Death and Judgment of Albion the Ancient Man' (? as late as 1807). He added sketches to the MS and ended each Night with a full-page drawing.

concept in his *Palingénésie sociale* was 'Universal Man . . . General Man, that is to say Man taken in the totality of his generations . . . Cosmogonic Man'.*
But Blake's One Man, from one angle, reveals a vast solipsism, an egocentric fantasy, an idealist abstraction. However, as usual, he finds ways of turning the idealist entity into its opposite, bringing it down into the real world and its relationships. He is always aware that his One is also the Many, and the unity he seeks to define is at once physical, spiritual, social. In 1810 he wrote, 'These various States I have seen in my Imagination; when distant they appear as One Man, but as you approach they appear Multitudes of Nations . . . I have seen, when at a distance Multitudes of Men in Harmony appear like a single Infant, sometimes in the Arms of a Female; this represented the Church.' It is all then a matter of the way the problem is approached.

We must also recall Spenser's influence on the young Blake. In *The Faery Queen* Arthur, gathering in himself all social and personal virtues, is not directly defined but is shown through the various heroes who embody some aspect of his totality. Take the First Book. The Red Crosse Knight, separated from Una (principle of unity), is fragmented, as is symbolised by Duessa. His struggle is to regain unity with his emanation, which he does in his marriage with Una. The same pattern—the defeat of the spectre and the resulting union with the emanation—is used throughout the poem, unifying its method and world-view. Spenser of course does not use Blake's terms, but the relations he sets out have the same general significance, at a more simply allegorical level. In Blake the final form of his system comes in *Jerusalem*'s climactic phase, where the various nations are united in One Nation, after Los has formed and driven out his spectre. All the emanations unite in Jerusalem; all the forms in Jesus. Then the One Nation (England) enters Albion's bosom; the Zoas unite in Albion; Albion joins with Jerusalem. The marriage of Arthur and Gloriana (not presented in the poem) expresses the same sort of ultimate harmony and unity: England as One People—though on a cruder and lower level than Blake's vision of world-harmony in freedom and brotherhood. Spenser's ideal leads to the Absolute Monarchy of the sixteenth century, with all its unresolved conflicts, whereas

* Lammenais, Christian democrat, said the individual was a fragment. 'The true being is the collective being, Humanity.' Balzac marvelled at 'this great being called humanity. . . humanity all together animating itself as a single being, reasoning like a single spirit and proceeding, like a single arm, to the accomplishment of its action.' Victor Hugo's *Légende des Siècles* was inspired by 'this great single and multiple figure'. Blake's own sources were, we saw, in Jewish mysticism. Boehme too had his androgynous Primal Man or Adam. 'Man is, as it were, a community in miniature.'

Blake's looks to a world where the sources of division have been truly eliminated. (We must recall also the part played by Ovid's *Metamorphoses* in begetting the idea of an epic at once cosmic and human, and based on concepts and images of mythic transformation. Spenser, Ossian, Ovid merge to give him much of his new perspective.)[11]

We have already glanced at the Four Zoas: Urizen, Luvah, Urthona, Tharmas: Reason, Passion, Imagination, Compassion. Blake treats the plural of the Greek *zoön*, living creature, as a feminine singular, but does not use the word in the poem. Each Zoa has his emanation: Ahania, Vala, Enitharmon, Enion. After the fall Urthona appears as Los and Luvah as Orc. While the Man is asleep, Urizen and Luvah struggle to dominate him; Urizen wins and the other three Zoas split off. The sickening Man gives in to masterful Urizen and falls into a coma. Urizen strives to dragoon all life into rigidly settled forms, afraid of any indefiniteness and of Luvah's sleep. But Luvah has been divided into Orc and Vala, who appear in earthly forms as Los and Enitharmon. Urizen can deal with rebellious Orc, but his world of delimited elements succumbs to the secret tricky female will. Ultimately in Night IX, on the edge of total break-up, the Man reasserts himself and reconstitutes his unity. His faculties work in harmony, the pastoral world of happiness returns.

'The war of swords is departed now. The dark religions are departed, & sweet science reigns.' In the picture of universal release from oppressive toil, 'the slave grinding at the mill', there may be an acclamation of the abolition of the slave-trade in 1807. 'All the slaves from every earth in the wide universe Sing a new song . . . Composed by an African black.' But there are wider implications. The rejoicing vintage and the golden feast look to Revelation (xiv) and the vision is of universal brotherhood. How the reversal of the dividing trends has come about is, however, not defined.

Each Zoa has a complex set of correlations. Urthona–Los has his emanation, his imaginative and wrathful nature, his work as blacksmith, creative shaper and prophet, his element of earth, his seat in the body (heart and ear), and his cosmic point (north). Luvah–Orc has his emanation, his passionate desiring nature, his work as wine-grower and prince of love, his element of fire, his place in the loins and nose, his point in the east. Urizen has his emanation, his abstract reasoning and ambitious nature, his work as farmer and prince of light, his place in the brain and eyes, his point in the south. Tharmas has his emanation, his element of water, his place in the bowels and tongue, his point in the west. A set of correlations of this kind is very like the sets linking man and nature in tribal cultures, from the Australian totemic levels to the relatively sophisticated stages of the Amerindians.

In his symbolic universe Blake attempts a synthesis of all the elements of conflict, change, balance and unbalance in his age: elements social, political, economic, psychological, scientific, aesthetic, moral. Herein lies his great achievement, which we continue to analyse. But there is also an archaic element which, as noted, has close parallels with tribal cultures where all the forces of the universe, inner and outer, are linked in an explanatory system. One example will suffice. The Panare Indians of Venezuela have sets of correspondences and contraries which make up the living cosmos. Thus, they link the rainbow with the wet season and the Milky Way with the dry— and so on till the whole structure of their world is covered and everything is interlinked. They think in terms of four different living spaces. These they make use of according to a daily and seasonal rhythm by means of which they symbolically understand, manipulate, and control their world. Their analysis of the structure of space (seen as a cultural entity) involves reference to both time and the sensuous categories of experience. Time is seen as both a natural and a supernatural element: the seasonal cycle marked by the movements of celestial bodies, which in turn have a sexual connotation and express a reversed or discordant sexuality and a well-tempered one that reflects the life-cycle of birth and death, marriage and solitude. Thus conceptually the year-cycle is equated with the life-cycle, repetitive time with accumulative time (quantitative with qualitative). So the Panare feel that they control time by the 'ideological manipulation of space-categories, such as the presence, movement, isolation, and so forth, of celestial bodies', and 'the sensible categories are conceptualised, in the same way as time and space are conceptualised, around the structural oppositions between a natural disorder and a supernatural disorder, that only the cultural order adequately mediates.'[12]

This is not to argue that Blake's system and that of the Panare are identical; but one cannot but be struck by a remarkable similarity in the struggle to organise a unified grasp of the life-process round certain basic categories of movement and change, time and space. It is seldom realised how the essential bases of human conciousness, the deep patterns by which men interpret their inner and outer worlds, have been created in tribal society, then extended and reapplied, often in broken-down forms, in the stages of class-society. Of special importance is the concept of development through a triadic pattern of life–death–rebirth derived from initiation rituals and experiences. Blake is the outstanding example of a creator in whom, because of his total opposition to all systems of division, there is an intuitive and large-scale rebirth of tribal systems, which are however transformed by his struggle to apply a unitary and dialectical outlook to all aspects of a culture infinitely more complex than anything in the tribal world.*

The idea of the primal man was linked with the syncretising tendency, stimulated by the discovery of Hindu culture, to find a single basis in all religions. The primal man was often seen as bisexual, as in Blake. Voltaire remarked of the seventeenth-century visionary Mme Bourignon that she 'was sure Adam was a hermaphrodite, like the divine Plato's first men'. Ballanche wanted to compose 'a cosmogony made up of all the cosmogonies, since all the transformations of one into another', and he went on to relate the division of universal man into two sexes. Woman brought will into that man; the female will had to be 'initiated' by the male. Ballanche sees everywhere the male principle imprisoning the female as the patrician imprisons the plebeian. The struggle is for unity; in the end mankind will function as a single being, with the androgyne reconstituted.[14]

To develop the theme of the one man Blake has to build an elaborate creation-myth, as if the forms of conflict inside the divided individual and his world are actually externalised in a gigantic cosmic drama of division and union. He is able to do all that through his theory of correspondences. The cosmos does in fact follow the same laws of symmetry and asymmetry, of the unity of opposites, as society in its movements or the individual in his experiences. Blake then uses the imagery of social change and personal experience to define the cosmic processes. One level shifts into the other in a ceaseless involvement and series of symbolic reflections. Unity is not regained by the lifting of the sick man into a quite different sphere of being; it comes from the resolution of a particular set of problems posited by the phase of division. Eternity is eternal only in the sense that the resolution of conflicts is an eternal aspect of process. In his creative positions Blake rejects

---

* In him as in the Amerindian systems we find emphasis on orientation, opposition of right and left, the seasons, parts of the body, levels of space. He shares with them a concept of reality as fourfold (winds, space-points, dominating powers). In the tribal systems the fourfold concept is often linked with the camp-layout, the camp being felt as a world-centre. Blake gained access to some of these ideas through the alchemists; for alchemy was a system which in many aspects carried on elements, ideological and technological, from the last stages of tribal society—though he reconstituted the ideas in a dynamic and unified way all his own. Claiming to be a possessed prophet, he revived the role of the shaman who guides his people through the mazes and dangers of the spirit-world in moments of difficult transition.[13]

5*

all transcendentalism or metaphysics. His idea of the divine is pantheistic in that he feels a living unity in the cosmos, but not in the sense of levelling all being. He sees everywhere a transformative process at work on varying levels of being, with humanity as the highest level. So the divine is the truly human; the divine humanity is humanity with a maximum consciousness of its nature and a drive to realise that nature in creative activity and love.

In such fundamental matters there is consistency in Blake; but he is not rigid in his use of terms or the angles from which he approaches problems. There is one universal man, but that is no reason for not mentioning other eternals or a council of universal men. Many changes of formulation or angle of approach occurred between *Europe* and *Vala*. He was now trying to construct a comprehensive myth in a way that had not worried him when writing his shorter prophecies. This myth had to cover all aspects of human life and history, past, present and future, not merely to present the aspects that had seemed important as he strove to interpret the American and French Revolutions up to 1795. In the new focus immediate history became both more distant and more closely impacting. One important aspect of the change in method is the new role assigned to Jesus. We meet a shift of focus, of world-view, which represents a deep rethinking of his positions in the light of the check to the French Revolution.[15]

Previously Jesus had been the lamb of the pastoral sphere, of childhood and innocence, of Eden regained on the other side of experience. He had been a pervading presence assumed as the basis of innocence and merging simply with the other symbols of uniting love. He appears without drama in Lavater's *Aphorisms*, summing up what Blake feels to be the central positions of a good life. At the end of *Marriage* Jesus is briefly described in Antinomian terms, linked with the message that energy is eternal delight, and not playing any role in the unfolding of the conflicts. On the other hand, where he does come into the world of action he is not seen as an effective fighter for liberation. Rather, he is an accomplice in the Jehovah–Urizen system or a victim of it, a wretched Theotormon unable to cast off the bonds of jealousy and moral law, or a Fuzon hung on the tree of mystery and become a source of pestilence.[16]

But to get more fully into Blake's mind at this phase we need first to look at the statements he has made in annotations to some books. First we must grasp how extreme reaction was invading all spheres of social life, even sport. The breakdown of the reform organisations, with their sympathy for the

French Revolution, had the effect of turning the apocalyptic hopes of the craftsmen into passive forms, as can be seen in the response to Joanna Southcott and the Methodist revival. The alliance between the impatient radically-minded industrial middle class and a proletariat in its first formative stages was broken almost as soon as it was formed. Wordsworth and Coleridge dropped their enthusiasm even for reformist movements, and retreated into themselves. Blake did not give up the ghost as the others did. He merely lengthened his perspective for the maturing of the changes he wanted and which he considered would have to come about unless men were to destroy themselves.

Johnson was fined and jailed for selling copies of Gilbert Wakefield's *Reply to Watson Bishop of Llandaff's Address*, though other booksellers sold the work unpunished. In prison he still gave his weekly dinners in the Marshall's house. Godwin was one of those who attended; Fuseli remained Johnson's friend. We hear nothing of Blake. Wakefield, an odd classical scholar who lived in Hackney, a friend of Charles Fox, had been outraged by the bishop's *Apology for the Bible* in letters addressed to Paine. He remarked that the labouring classes had little to lose by a French invasion. 'Within three miles of the house, where I am writing these pages, there is a much greater number of starving, miserable human beings . . . than on any equal portion of ground through the habitable globe.' Jailed, he was released from prison only to die at once.

Many other prosecutions tried to stop the circulation of anti-war literature. [17] In 1796 Kyd Wake, a Gosport bookseller, was sentenced to the pillory and five years hard labour for saying, 'No George, no war'. Prosecutions for sedition went on in Lancashire and Lincolnshire. A Somerset basketmaker was jailed for saying, 'I wish success to the French'. The Duke of Portland at the Home Office sent out instructions for the shutting down of tavern-societies and the committal to the House of Correction of children selling Spence's halfpenny sheets. In October 1797 a letter from a Leeds society with some hundred members, 'chiefly Working Mechanics', stated that over the last three years 'the arbitrary proceedings of our Justices operated in so terrifying a manner' that people had been scared and 'the Sacred Flame which had been kindled in their Breast was almost extinguished'.*

* Coleridge wrote to Wordsworth in 1799: 'I wish you would write a poem in blank verse addressed to those who in consequence of the complete failure of the French Revolution, have thrown up all hopes for the amelioration of mankind, and are sinking into an almost epicurean selfishness, disguising the same under the soft titles of domestic attachment and contempt for visionary *philosophes*'.

Paine in *Agrarian Justice* (the English edition of 1797) had been uncertain 'whether to publish it during the present war', but he had grown indignant at the title of a sermon preached by Watson: 'The Wisdom and Goodness of God, in having made both Rich and Poor'. So he issued his book in refutation of such a position. It was probably after reading Paine's preface that Blake bought Watson's book (1797 edition) and filled the margins with fierce defences of Paine. He could not accept Paine's Deism, but he hated all the things that Paine hated. 'It appears to me Now that Tom Paine is a better Christian than the Bishop', and he set out his own position:

To defend the Bible in this year 1798 would cost a man his life. The Beast & Whore rule without control. It is an easy matter for a Bishop to triumph over Paine's attack, but it is not so easy for one who loves the Bible. The perversions of Christ's words & acts are attack'd by Paine & also the perversions of the Bible; Who dare defend either the Acts of Christ or the Bible Unperverted? But to him who sees this mortal pilgrimage in the light that I see it, Duty to his country is the first consideration & safety the last. Read patiently: take not up this book in an idle hour: the consideration of these things is the whole duty of man & the affairs of life & death trifles, sports of time. But these considerations [are the] business of Eternity. I have been commanded from Hell not to print this, as it is what our Enemies wish.

Duty to his country, he insists, is the first consideration and safety the last; yet he obeys the orders from Hell not to speak out. Again in the same breath he declares his belief in the Bible and his rejection of the Jewish Scriptures, which 'were written as an Example of the possibility of Human Beastliness in all its branches'.

Christ died as an Unbeliever & if the Bishops had their will so would Paine: see page 1; but he who speaks a word against the Son of man shall be forgiven. Let the Bishop prove that he has not spoken against the Holy Ghost, who in Paine strives with Christendom as in Christ he strove with the Jews.

The rejection of the Old Testament could not be more complete, yet in these very notes Blake says that one can use David or Abraham as Examples. A good man will abhor wickedness in them, while 'if he is wicked he will make their wickedness an excuse for his & so he would do by any other book'. That is, one interprets the Biblical material entirely as it suits one. The system set out in the Old Testament, he repeats, is 'the Abomination that maketh desolate, i.e. State Religion, which is the source of all Cruelty'. Against it is set the antinomian position: 'The Gospel is Forgiveness of Sins & has No Moral Precepts'. This position is that of the Everlasting Gospel, a term he now uses for the first time. He wonders how Paine could disbelieve in miracles when he himself had worked them, overthrowing 'all the armies of Europe with a small pamphlet'. Miracles for Blake have nothing arbitrary in them; they are born of the union of prophet and people. Such a union is able to bring about developments that would have been previously impossible.

In using the term 'Everlasting Gospel' Blake again shows his link with the Cromwellian Ranters and the like. Their creed of revolutionary chiliasm went back to the book with that title published in 1254 under the name of Joachim da Fiore, though the explosive material lay rather in the Notes and Introduction to three of his works, which were written by some dissident Franciscan. The main point of these heretical expositions lay in the claim that the Christian epoch was now superseded. History was divided into three great phases: that of Jehovah the Father, represented by Judaism and the Mosaic law; that of Jesus the Son, in which appeared Grace, with crucifixion the ending of the old law; that of the Holy Ghost, beginning in 1260, which superseded the era of Jesus. In the third era came great tribulations ushering in the millennium of perfect justice, peace; the stress would be on the Holy Ghost, the community of the faithful, without churches or sacraments.*

The problem of whether or not to speak out, which agitated Blake in 1798, recurs in the prophecies. In Night I of the *Four Zoas* Tharmas as the voice of the people reminds Los that vision uncommunicated is barren. Of the Zoas, Tharmas especially represents the Body, the Senses; and since 'Energy is the only life, and is from the body', he is the parent power and the mighty father. His emanation Enion stands for the sexual urge. He is the shepherd and his metal is brass (taken as the metal of social organisation); his art is painting. His seat is in the tongue, as well as in the loins. The tongue as the means of communication among men represents the parent sense. The

---

* The Everlasting Gospel had found renewal in the German Anabaptists of the sixteenth century, influencing T. Munzer, leader of the revolting peasants. It also affected Boehme, whose works began appearing in English in the 1640s, several of them published by Giles Calvert, at first a Ranter, then a Quaker. Similar views appeared among the Familists of England and the Spirituels of Germany and Holland. E. Pagitt, attacking the Familists in 1645, stated that each of them says 'he is godded with God and co-deified with him. These horrible blasphemies with divers others does this N. H. [Henry Nicholas, their teacher] and his Familie teach to be the Everlasting Gospel.'[18]

fall of speech thus means the enslavement of self-expression by the divisive forces, with reason providing the mode of accommodation. (In such contexts reason signifies class-ideology, the forms of rationalisation by which groups of men adapt themselves to a distorted situation.) In a world where revolutionary forces are stirring, reaction has to control and censor Tharmas, who stands for the free press, free expression. In an unfallen world Tharmas and Enion (the content of expression) are in harmony; Tharmas is inspired and supplied with material by Enion. In a fallen world the pair break apart and quarrel. Their children are lost or murdered, and they themselves become harlots of reaction. Tharmas must then hide his truth in silence or in complicated allegories. Or he and Enion must leave for 'a far distant Grove', as did Priestley, Paine and others, and as Coleridge and Southey planned to do with their Pantisocracy. The third alternative is for Tharmas to prostitute himself, mating with his whore Enitharmon. Blake sees no hope for truthful expression while the war goes on. 'Return O Wanderer when the Day of Clouds is over.'

Blake thus defines his difficult situation, his sense of being gagged, in the myth of Tharmas. In the *Four Zoas* Tharmas keeps on doing his best to support Los. He confronts Urizen when he hears his driven-out children screaming, but lacks the power to deal with him. He keeps on doing what he can to help Los, and in the seven days of the Last Judgement (the successful revolution) he and Enion are gradually restored. In his conflicts with Enion Blake brings out the point that sexual harmony and free self-expression are in the last resort inseparable.[19]

He had a copy of Bacon's *Essays* printed in 1798 and round that time he annotated it. He sees Bacon as the typical rationaliser of the bourgeois scientific revolution, an apologist for the state and the money-ethic; and stresses the link between mechanist science and the cash-nexus. 'Bacon was a usurer . . . Bacon is in his Element on Usury; it is himself and his philosophy.' Blake also annotated the second edition (1798) of Reynolds's *Discourses* in pencil. One comment underlines that he had in no way lost his enthusiasm for the French Revolution. Taking up the editor Malone's reference to 'the ferocious and enslaved Republick of France', with a citation of Pope's couplet about those who lived in woods and caves, and thought that all but savages were slaves', he writes: 'When France got free, Europe 'twixt Fools & Knaves Were Savage first to France, & after—Slaves.' The counter-revolutionary wars lead only to the barbarism and enslavement of the people who accept them.

In the years 1789–95 Blake's interest lies in the incarnations of the Holy Ghost or creative imagination, especially Los and Orc. Jesus matters only as the inaugurator of the second era of the Everlasting Gospel, who denounced the rule of law. The important thing is the forms of energy now transforming history, above all Orc, the driving-force of revolution. In *America* we learn of Orc's birth as the first child of Los and Enitharmon. Out of cloudy terrors comes 'a Human fire fierce glowing', which seems a horrid spectre to George III. At puberty Orc breaks his chain and becomes the freed Orc of 1776; now comes the reunion of man and earth, and nature henceforth dies or is reborn for man's benefit. The Preludium to *Europe* asks how many Orcs are needed before the millennium. In all this there is no hint that Jesus is needed. In *America* Orc is the figure linked with resurrecting humanity, with the freed slave grinding at the mill and the man jailed by the oppressor. *Europe* starts its account with an allusion to the Nativity (an echo of Milton's *Ode*), but what is being born is the corrupted night of Enitharmon. That is, Christ's birth is ineffective and brings in a reign of evil for 1,800 years. However, a new Saviour is born, Orc, who is to achieve the delivery which Christ failed to bring about. Orc is thus linked with Christ only by way of contrast.

He expresses the rising tide of fire in the French Revolution, which promises to end the empire of lion and wolf. As Armageddon comes on, there is an increasing conviction of the millennium he heralds. But by 1799 he is dehumanised. On 9 November Napoleon overthrew the Directory and made himself Chief Consul. The constitution of the Republic was broken. 'The form of Orc was gone he reard his serpent bulk among The Stars of Urizen in Power rending the form of life Into a formless indefinite & strewing her on the Abyss.' This passage from the *Four Zoas* (VIIb) shows how the concept of Orc has changed. He disappears, then returns new-born: Luvah in his fallen state (V). Blake has not lost hope in him; in Night III he is born of the dark sea and Urizen serves him, 'With light replenishing his darkness'. But in Night V, when he fights Urizen, he seems to have no effect. Los repents that he has chained him on the mountain and decides to free him: 'Even if his own death resulted, so much pity him paind.' (This is Blake fearing a dire penalty if he publishes his work.) But Orc's young limbs have 'strucken root in the rock' and not 'all Urthona's strength, not all the power of Luvah's Bulls' can 'uproot the infernal chain'.

The poem carries on with the story of Urizen, who strives to overcome chaos with his rigid systems, but fails. He wanders till Tharmas, Orc and

Urthona's spectre oppose him. In VIIa Orc is drawn under the power of Urizen's Tree of Mystery, and, still chained to his rock, changes to a serpent. In VIIb Vala tries to seduce him; he breaks free in serpent-form and she joins Urizen. Orc attacks her. The only result is that he is destroyed except for his evil serpent-shadow. (Books VIIa and VIIb present many textual problems; I am drawing on them here only to show the sad lot of Orc in the later Nights.) In VIII comes the temporary triumph of the female principle; and now at last Jesus comes in as an active character, with Vala and Urizen as his enemies. In IX Urizen is regenerated and the Eternal Man is redeemed; Orc as a lower form of Luvah is burned away, 'in mental flames, Expending all his energy against the fuel of fire. The regenerate Man stooped his head over the universe & in His holy hands received the flaming demon & demoness of smoke.' Luvah and Vala are sent down into their place, 'the place of seed not in the brain or heart'. Everything is being integrated in its proper place.

Blake had concentrated on Orc when he felt that the spontaneous forces of the people would carry on and complete the revolution. With the check of those forces he was at a loss, unable to think how the next stages of advance could be brought about. He had no notion of the positive forces at work in the industrial system: the way in which the gathering of ever-larger masses of men and women in work would produce new forces of union and resistance, new forms of fraternal organisation. So he fell back on the need for long-suffering devotion, compassion and endurance, readiness for self-sacrifice. Jesus provided the symbol for these qualities. Blake was thus combining the role of the Holy Ghost in the Joachite scheme and that of Jesus the free spirit in the Antinomian creed: combining them with a new force and fullness.

He had further worked out his dialectical system, defined largely in terms of vision or comprehension. This is so important that we may glance at it again. Single vision saw things at their lowest mechanical level, which he called Ulro. Double vision saw the two sides or contraries in a situation. But the clash of opposites, however essential, could not by itself bring development about. So Blake works out the concepts of threefold and fourfold vision, Beulah and Eternity (Eden). Beulah lies between Eternity and Ulro, between secure resolution of the conflict-and-unity of opposites and the sphere of purely mechanical motion. (Ulro is thus the sphere of all persons who accept uncritically a divided world.) Blake feels that a simple opposition of Ulro and Eternity is too stark and simple; so he puts Beulah between them to represent the moments of resolution which prevent a ceaseless fall into division and integrate one aspect of the struggle or other, but do not lift the whole of life on to a new stable level. The active inhabitants of Beulah are its daughters. They are the Muses of inspiration, not those of memory: that is, they glimpse the fullness of process instead of drawing passively on given systems. They represent the living flow of time as opposed to time in a mechanistic system such as the Newtonian; one of them stands between each of any two moments, providing the concrete continuity. They represent each moment of achieved sexual love; and in *Jerusalem* they appear as the champions who protect liberty, ensuring that the political struggle has direction and coherence. They represent in art the vital point of contact between the mind and its material.[20] They thus provide the necessary link between the world of direct experience and eternity, the goal of secure human freedom and brotherhood.*

History, we noted, does not play so clear a part in the *Four Zoas* as in works like *America* and *Europe*. But the war between England and France is an essential part of the theme. The difficulty of comprehending what is happening is reflected in the fate of Los, who is in danger of being subdued to the material he works in. In his struggle to bind Urizen, he enters so much into the nature of Urizen that he tends to become what he sees and grapples with; he reaches the limits of opacity and contraction, Satan and Adam. He goes mad with rage and is so obsessed with cursing that he lets the anvil cool and the furnace die out. His desperate effort to reverse the course of history is expressed in the episode when he tries to free Orc, which we noted above. After the dehumanisation of Orc (Buonaparte's coup of the 18th Brumaire) there seems little to choose between the wars of Pitt and the French. Blake painfully follows the fortunes of war, seeking and finding no solution.

* The alchemic tradition, with its basis in craft-mystery (going back to tribal days), kept alive the idea of a triadic movement leading to qualitative transformation. How close the imagery could be to Blake may be seen by taking a Greek poem of the early seventh century AD by Archelaos. Chemical change is seen as a conflict of contraries, body and soul, which is resolved by a third force spirit and finally stabilised by the fourfold elements. The process is seen as a resurrection, also as a struggle with the female principle. In the end, 'These three united in a steady bond of firm affection and of constant love shall dwell together, truly unified, Body, Soul, and Spirit: not subdued by fellowship but rather beautified . . . They feel no fear, a stronghold triply fortified and stable, to one another intimately mated in fourfold manner by the elements.' In medieval alchemic systems Prima Materia appears as a dragon-woman who kills husband and offspring, then revives them with her breasts. A dragon-woman in the MS of the *Four Zoas* seems to depict this creature.[21]

Night I of the *Four Zoas* records the British triumph (probably in the eastern Mediterranean) with its spiritual reflection in the conflict of Los and Enitharmon. Night II gives the other side of the national situation in Enion's lament over the miseries brought upon the people. But a central aspect of these miseries is the big advance of industrial activity, above all in the metal-lurgical and allied fields, which Blake sees as almost a new cosmic creation. Though he is unable to grasp at all the new forms of working-class resistance that were to emerge, he does realise that the struggle for world brotherhood, for a new kind of man, is going on at the heart of the industrial processes. But in a divided and alienated world the processes are used destructively and their potentialities for union are inverted. Luvah, who is Love and Lava, Brother-hood and industrial processes of fire-transformation, dies to bring about the union of men in production; but under Urizen, the master of industry, his death is useless. Vala is charcoal or coal, the part of nature destroyed in the production of steel, which is in turn used destructively in weapons of war. So Urizen uses the opposition of Luvah and Vala, inhibiting the harmonious relation to nature, which is an aspect of brotherhood. Metallurgy, developed by war-needs, also serves commerce and so wins over the citizens who, thinking in terms of cash-nexus, support war as necessary for trade expansion and the imperial subjugation of other peoples.

Blake extends his picture with accounts of textiles and building, where work too has been perverted by the Urizenic system. In Night VIIb he stresses the alienated condition of the workers. The labouring masses are kept at trivial repetitive tasks, filing and polishing brass 'hour after hour laborious workmanship Kept ignorant of the use that they might spend the days of wisdom In sorrowful drudgery to obtain a scanty pittance of bread'. Urizen, work-master and industrialist, fancies that he can hold his place of power for ever: 'A God & not a Man . . . And all the Sons of Everlasting shall bow down at my feet.' Tyranny, furious, emerges from the conflict in Night VIIb; and there is to be yet another long Night before the final challenge comes.[22]

Beginning perhaps in 1798 and carrying on into 1800 Blake did a series of paintings for his patron Butts, using a variant of the tempera medium (with carpenter's glue instead of egg) which he himself called fresco. The subjects are very different from those of the 1795 colour-prints. They show the change in his outlook, a change that may well have been accentuated by the tastes and influence of Butts. The set seems to consist of thirty-seven works, eight dealing with the Old Testament, twenty-nine with the New, whereas in 1795 he was not interested in the New Testament at all. The Old Testament

themes include those considered to foreshadow Jesus: Moses in the bul-
rushes and the sacrifice of Isaac—or episodes raising the question of sexual
morality: Susanna, Lot and his daughters, Bathsheba, Samson and Delilah.
Nine of the New Testament set deal with Christ's childhood, others with the
miracles, the crucifixion, the four evangelists, Christ as mediator. For the
first and only time Blake uses strong passages of light against an environing
darkness, perhaps influenced by Rembrandt, even if the results suggest
rather works of early fifteenth-century Flanders. These light-passages seem
to reflect his sense of moving from one stage of life to another. In the
Lambeth prophecies Orc had been a young figure of blazing fire; now, after
feeling himself darkly imprisoned in a Urizenic world, Blake turns to Christ
as a source of consoling light. In the Nativity the Child leaps from the Virgin
in a radiation of light into the arms of another woman (St Elizabeth with
John the Baptist). Blake feels the need of someone who can symbolise his
long-drawn sufferings and his hope of final resurrection rather than his fierce
unslackening revolt.[23]

8

Pastoral Retreat, 1799–1801

1799 seems to have been rather an empty year for Blake. Times were bad.
On 18 June the mother of Robert and Leigh Hunt wrote: 'The engraving of
Pictures is at present but a dull business. The war occasions a scarcity of cash,
people in general find it difficult to obtain the necessary comforts of life, and
have not a surplus of money for elegancies.' Cumberland had recommended
Blake to the Rev. John Trusler, who lived, like him, at or near Egham,
Surrey. Trusler, author of *Hogarth Moralised* and *How to be Rich and
Respectable*, was unlikely to get on with Blake. However, he commissioned a
picture depicting Malevolence. Blake was slow with the work, but on
16 August he wrote that daily for a fortnight he had tried to follow Trusler's
'Dictate', but had been compelled by his 'Genius or Angel to follow where
he led'. His only purpose in life was, in conjunction with men like Cumberland 'to renew the lost Art of the Greeks'. He repeated that he was inspired
so that the design was not really his. He would rather paint in oils than make
drawings. 'By this means you will have a number of Cabinet pictures, which I
flatter myself will not be unworthy of a Scholar of Rembrandt & Teniers,
whom I have studied no less than Rafael & Michael Angelo.' An odd statement in view of his attacks on oil-painting and his later hatred of Rembrandt.
What he had drawn was a man saying goodbye to wife and child whom 'two
Fiends Incarnate' are preparing to murder; the style was that of the Gothic
Novel and had nothing whatever Greek about it.

Trusler was not impressed. He disliked Blake's drawings as being 'in the
other world or the World of Spirits'. His own aim was to follow the nature of
this world while living in it. Blake for once answered promptly, in a long
letter, on 23 August. He insisted that he needed no one to elucidate his ideas;
what was too explicit was not good for instruction; Moses, Aesop, Homer
and Plato agreed with him. He rejected the view that his picture showed no
motive for the attack. 'I have therefore proved your Reasonings Ill propor-

tion'd, which you can never prove my figures to be; they are those of Michael Angelo, Rafael, & the Antique, & of the best living Models. I percieve that your Eye is perverted by Caricature Prints.' In fact the figures are all out of proportion; the heads are too small, the legs unnaturally long, and the lower part of the bodies is not in the same plane as the upper. Blake takes up Trusler's use of the term Nature. 'In the Eyes of the Man of Imagination, Nature is Imagination itself . . . To me This World is One continued Vision of Fancy or Imagination.' He again turns to the ancients and insists: 'I am happy to find a Great Majority of Fellow Mortals who can Elucidate my Visions, & Particularly they have been Elucidated by Children.' Discussing prices, he asks for £30 and says that to engrave after another artist is infinitely more laborious than to engrave after one's own inventions. 'Engraving is the profession I was apprenticed to, & should never have attempted to live by any thing else.' He boasts that orders for his paintings and designs have been daily increasing.

Trusler noted on Blake's letter, 'Dimd with Superstition'. Blake, disturbed by the argument, wrote to Cumberland, 'I cannot paint Dirty rags & old shoes when I ought to place Naked Beauty or simple ornament'. He urges Cumberland to carry on. 'Do not throw aside for any long time the honour intended you by Nature to revive the Greek workmanship. I study your outlines as usual, just as if they were antiques.' He adds an account of his fortunes very different from the boast he had made three days earlier. 'I live by Miracle. I am Painting small Pictures from the Bible. For as to Engraving in which art I cannot reproach myself with any neglect, yet I am laid by in a corner as if I did not Exist, & since my Young's Night Thoughts have been publish'd, even Johnson & Fuseli have discarded my Graver.' The only orders he has are those from Butts. It was now just twenty years 'since I was upon the Ocean of business', that is, since he ended his apprenticeship with Basire.

From now on he and Fuseli drifted apart. In September 1800 he wrote: 'Fuseli was given to me for a season.' Later that year he bitterly told Butts that Fuseli's gift to him had been 'a dark black Rock and a gloomy Cave'. He saw their relationship as one in which he had been an exploited slave. In January 1802 he complained of drudgery and the efforts made to confine him to it. 'This from Johnson and Fuseli brought me down here.' In this case as in all others throughout his life Blake ended by being bitterly resentful of anyone who had tried to help him.[1]

On 7 October 1799 he inscribed a copy of *America* for C. H. Tatham, who had published *Etchings, Representing the Best Examples of Ancient Ornamental Architecture*. His acquaintance with Tatham carried on vaguely till the end of his days; we shall hear more of Tatham and his son when we come to those last years. Blake was coming closer to the poet Hayley, who wanted to complete his *Essay on Sculpture*, in a series of *Epistles to Flaxman*. He was worried about his son Tom, who was dying of a spinal disease, and he wanted two illustrations, a vignette of Tom's head and a frontispiece engraved after a drawing by Tom. Flaxman recommended Blake for the work, and in January 1800 reported on progress. By late February the frontispiece was done; and on 7 March Hayley wrote to Samuel Rose, barrister, who helped him in his projects, with the suggestion of a book on Greek and Etruscan art, with outlines done by Tom. Flaxman, the painter Howard, and 'that worthy ingenious Engraver Blake' were to be drawn in. Tom had rallied after an operation, but soon grew worse. Hayley became impatient at Blake's delay with the vignette, and Flaxman gave him Blake's address. Blake wrote a pious letter, ending, 'So prays a fellow sufferer & your humble servant'. Hayley disliked the portrait, 'a heavy sullen sulky Head', he told Flaxman. Some ten days later Blake sent a new proof and Hayley in reply said that Tom had not long to live and he wanted a good likeness. Blake was to shorten the upper lip, put a dot at the corner of the mouth, and add a darker touch at the bottom of the eye, to give 'a little gay juvenility'. He referred to Blake as 'a kind-hearted brother of Parnassus'.

Tatham tells us that Blake was possessed of a violent temper, but had a method in it. He flung a plate, on which was Lavater's portrait, across the room, infuriated at failing to get the effect he wanted. On being asked if he had injured it, he replied, 'O I took good care of that'. Tatham adds, 'he was subject often of much internal perturbation & over anxiety', for he spoilt as much work by over-labour as would take some artists a whole life of ordinary industry to accomplish. The Lavater plate is dated 1 May 1800. Next day young Tom died and by 4 a.m. Hayley had composed a sonnet on him; soon he had a volume of such sonnets. On the 6th Blake sent his condolences. 'Thirteen years ago I lost a brother & with his spirit I converse daily & hourly in the Spirit & see him in my remembrance in the regions of my Imagination. I hear his advice & even now write from his Dictate.'

He was going on Tuesday evenings to visit the Buttses. On 13 May Tommy Butts, twelve years old, recorded, 'Mr. and Mrs. Blake and Mr. T. Jones drank tea with mama'. This month at the R.A. Blake showed his picture of the Miracle of Loaves and Fishes. His reading of Bishop Watson on miracles may have suggested the theme; but at the same time he was stirred by the food shortage, bad harvests, rising prises, and growing discontent. Parliament, meeting in February, treated the hardships with contempt, discussing bread substitutes and ways of lessening consumption. In May an ex-soldier shot at the king and missed him. There were minor uprisings in the country, and in August and September the people took over some of the markets. Blake's picture showed how a more brotherly world would deal with scarcities.

On 2 July he wrote to Cumberland. News that the king and the ministry were considering plans for a National Gallery roused a wild enthusiasm. 'The immense flood of Grecian light & Glory which is coming on Europe will more than realise our warmest wishes.' He mentions that Flaxman admires the book of Outlines and is 'more and more of a Grecian'. Hayley in Notes to his Essay has mentioned Cumberland. 'Poor Fuseli, sore from the lash of Envious tongues, praises you & dispraises with the same breath; he is not naturally good natured, but he is artificially very ill natured, yet even from him I learn the Estimation you are held in among artists & connoisseurs.' He himself has been in a serious depression. 'I begin to Emerge from a Deep pit of Melancholy. Melancholy without any real reason for it, a Disease which God keep you from & all good men.' Describing the days when print-shops were few, he adds, 'at least I hear so from the few friends I have dared to visit in my stupid Melancholy'. His depression has then been of long standing, a distracted state which we would surmise from the evidence of the *Four Zoas* discussed above.[2]

Meanwhile Hayley had asked Blake to come down to Felpham, the hamlet by the sea where he lived in Sussex. He wanted to superintend his work, but he must also have taken a liking to him. On 5 July Flaxman wrote that Blake would take down a bas-relief for him and thus save packing and carriage-fees. Soon after that the Blakes left on their visit. On 16 July Hayley wrote to tell Flaxman 'the good Blake' was working hard at Tom's portrait by Romney and would give all the news on his return. On the 22nd he wrote to Lady Hesketh, Cowper's cousin, a prickly character, suggesting that Cowper's biography should be done in the form of letters to Earl Cowper. He himself was glad that now he would not need to send Romney's portrait of Tom away to be engraved. For 'a most worthy enthusiastic Engraver' has attached himself to Hayley and taken a cottage in the village. 'As he has infinite Genius with a most engaging simplicity of character I hope he will execute many admirable things in this sequestered scene, with the aid of an excellent Wife, to whom he has been married 17 years, & who shares his Labours and his Talents.'

Hayley was pleased. He was polishing a sonnet on Blake, 'laborious artist of a liberal heart', and he wrote a poem in a copy of his *Triumphs of Temper*, which he presented to Blake: 'Accept my gentle visionary, Blake'. The copy had once belonged to Tom. 'So from an angel it descends to thee.' In London Blake's friends were happy at the change. Gilchrist says that Butts 'rejoiced aloud, feeling his protégé's fortune made'. Flaxman wrote, thanking Hayley for his benevolence. He thought Blake would be able to make a living at Felpham, engraving and teaching drawing. 'But if he places any dependence on painting large pictures, for which he not qualified, either by habit or study, he will be miserably deceived.' Blake himself later, in *Jerusalem*, looked on his move to Sussex as a flight. Hayley, writing to Blake's early patron, Hawkins, called him 'that worthy Enthusiast, the ingenious Blake', and said that he 'appeared the happiest of human Beings on his prospect of inhabiting a marine Cottage in this pleasant village'. Only one circumstance, he had said, would increase his felicity. 'Are you aware, that I allude to his wish of seeing *you also* settled *in Sussex*?'[3]

Hayley, twelve years Blake's senior, was an odd mixture of the conventional and the original; at least he had a wide range and an intelligent pertinacity in his interests. Educated at Eton and Cambridge, he published in 1778 his first work, *A Poetical Epistle* to Romney. *The Triumphs of Temper* was written to help women in overcoming the effects of spleen. In 1784 came his essays *On History* and *On Epic Poetry* in verse, reissued with some plays (not then acted) in six volumes in 1788. *A Philosophical, Historical, and Moral Essay on Old Maids* in three volumes was considered to show him as 'an attentive observer of life' owning 'the talents which constitute an elegant moral painter'. He had thus hit the taste of the genteel public, 'For ever feeble and for ever tame', as Byron later wrote; and he self-consciously acted out his role as Hermit of Eartham. On the other hand he maintained friendships with Gibbon, Romney and Cowper. Cowper admired him; Wordsworth annotated his poems; Coleridge and Southey respected his *Essay on Epic Poetry*, where, as in his *Life of Milton*, he showed himself capable of genuine insights. A kindly man, ambitious and determined, he did not attend church, but held his own household services. In 1790 he refused the offer of the Laureateship. He had many works of art in his house, including portraits painted by Romney at Eartham. Blake was much taken with him and lived in intimate relations with him for some years.

After arranging to take a cottage from the landlord of the Fox Inn at a rent of £20 a year, the Blakes were back in London in early September. Tommy Butts noted on the 10th: 'Mr. and Mrs. Blake, his brother, and Mr. Birch came to tea.' It is of interest to see James Blake in such a setting; but Tommy's note is only one of several hints that Blake kept on closer terms with James and his sister Catherine than is usually thought. John Birch, surgeon of St Thomas's Hospital, was a keen advocate of the use of electricity in healing; in 1804 Mrs Blake used his treatment. Blake had been won over by his arguments.

How happy and hopeful Blake now was appears in his letter to Flaxman on the 12th. 'It is to you I owe all my present happiness. It is to you I owe perhaps the Principal Happiness of my life.' As usual he was dilatory in contacts. 'I have presum'd on your friendship in staying so long away & not calling to know of your welfare, but hope now every thing is nearly completed for our removal to Felpham, that I shall see you on Sunday, as we have appointed Sunday afternoon to call on Mrs Flaxman at Hampstead'. His high spirits burst out in the statement that 'the time is arriv'd when Men shall again converse in Heaven & walk with Angels'. He then is moved to compose the poem (cited earlier) on the stages of his development, which ends, 'My Angels have told me that seeing such visions I could not subsist on the Earth, But by my conjunction with Flaxman, who knows how to forgive Nervous Fear.'

Two days later Catherine wrote to Mrs Flaxman in the same excited tones. They were to leave on Tuesday. 'It is only Sixty Miles, & Lambeth was One Hundred, for the terrible desart of London was between . . . the Swallows call us, fleeting past our window at this moment. O how we delight in talking of the pleasure we shall have in preparing you a summer bower at Felpham.' The angels of their journey have inspired William with a song. In it he sees Felpham as the pastoral paradise of Innocence. 'For Heaven is there; The Ladder of Angels descends thro' the air . . . The Bread of sweet Thought & the Wine of Delight Feeds the Village of Felpham by day & by night,' while at his door stands the bless'd Hermit (Hayley), 'Dispensing Unceasing to all the whole Land'. (In between the two letters Tommy Butts noted, 'Mr. Blake breakfasted with Mama.')

The excitement was so extreme that Catherine exhausted herself; Blake wrote on the 16th to say they could not leave till Wednesday or Thursday. 'That Day shall be marked on my calendar with a Star of the first magnitude. Eartham shall be my first temple & altar. My wife is like a flame of many colours of precious jewels whenever she hears it named.' As for himself, 'My fingers Emit sparks of fire with Expectation of my future labours.' The same day he breakfasted with Mrs Butts.[4]

At last they got away on Thursday, 18 September, Blake's sister Catherine accompanying them. Starting between 6 and 7 a.m., they arrived at 11.30 p.m., moving themselves and their sixteen boxes and portfolios to seven different chaises during the day. The luggage included stocks of paper, copper plates and a hand press. Three days later Blake wrote to Flaxman, as exalted as ever. The cottage 'seems to be the Spontaneous effusion of Humanity, congenial to the wants of man'. Terms very suitable for the Pastoral Paradise. Hayley had received them with his usual brotherly affection. 'I have begun to work, Felpham is a sweet place for study, because it is more Spiritual than London. Heaven opens here on all sides her Golden Gates.' The two Catherines had bathed, 'courting Neptune for an embrace'. Two days later he wrote in the same tone to Butts. His sister was returning home in a week. The escape from London must have been made more dramatic by the fact that it occurred in a week of mounting social tension. On Monday the populace had stormed the Corn Market and brought down the price of bread, and for the rest of the week the agitation against hoarding and forestalling had gone on.*

Gilchrist describes the cottage as it was in Blake's day:

A long, shallow, white-faced house, one room deep, containing but six in all,— small and cosy; three on the ground floor, opening one into another, and three above. Its latticed windows looked to the front; at back the thatched roof comes sweeping down almost to the ground. A thatched wooden verandah, which runs the whole length of the house, forming a covered way paved with red brick, shelters the lower room from a southern sun; a little too much so at times . . . The entrance is at the end of this verandah, out of the narrow lane leading from the village to the sea. In front lies the slip of garden (there is none at back), inclosed by a low, flint wall. In front of that again is a private way, shaded with evergreens, to the neighbouring large red brick mansion, surrounded by ample gardens . . . Beyond, corn-fields stretch down to the sea, which is not a few furlongs distant, and almost on the same level,—the coast here being low and crumbling. To the

* The visits to the Buttses, which entailed a walk from Lambeth to Fitzroy Square, involved something of a ceremony. The family long kept a George III tea pot and stand with a George III silver mug, which Blake was said to have used. Blake's watercolour, done about this time, of Job being answered by God out of the whirlwind may have expressed his sense of deliverance in leaving London's turmoil, the scene of his defeat and melancholy.

right are scattered one or two labourers' humble cottages, with their gardens and patches of corn-field. Further seaward are two windmills standing conspicuously on a tongue of land which shuts off adjacent Bognor from sight.[5]

The upper windows had 'a glorious view of the far-stretching sea, with many a white sail gleaming at sunset in the distance . . . Often, in after years, Blake would speak with enthusiasm of the shifting lights on the sea he had watched from those windows.' A few steps up the winding lane, past the Fox Inn, brought him to the postern-like gate of Hayley's residence, a plain white house in the middle of the village, with its turret in a corner of the high-walled garden. For walks the Blakes had the sands below the shingle or lanes for some five or six miles inland through cornfields and pastures.

Butts answered Blake's letter in a few days, writing in a heavily jocose strain and much intrigued by the picture of Catherine bathing in the sea, in Neptune's embrace. But he adds a comment which shows how he had considered Blake's way of life at Lambeth unhealthily withdrawn and self-centred. 'Whether you will be a better Painter or a better Poet from your change of ways & means I know not; but this I predict; that you will be a better man—excuse me, as you have been accustomed from friendship to do, but certain opinions imbibed from reading, nourished by indulgence, and rivitted by a confined Conversation, and which have been equally prejudicial to your Interest & Happiness, will now I trust, disperse as a Day-break vapour, and you will henceforth become a member of that Community of which you are at present . . . but a Sign to mark the residence of dim incredulity, haggard suspicion, & bloated philosophy'—odd terms to use of Blake, but strong evidence that his friends considered he had been sinking into a bad state. Butts hopes that soon Blake will become 'a more valorous Champion of Revelation & Humiliation than any of those who now wield the Sword of the Spirit'. He ends with a poem of pious hopes and returns to a jest of embracing Catherine like Neptune.

In his reply Blake humbly accepts the 'reprehension of follies by me foster'd', finds Butts's poor poem a Crown of Laurels, and promises good behaviour. 'In the future I am the determined advocate of Religion and Humility, the two bands of Society'—the sort of statement which, read in Locke or Bishop Watson, would have been annotated by him as cant and humbug. He accepts Butts's evangelical idiom. He goes on, 'I have commenced a new life of industry to do credit to that new life by Improved works', then lets go in an ecstatic lyric of short two-beat lines, describing his vision of Nature transformed into humanity. He, with wife and sister, 'like Infants descend In our Shadows on Earth'. He has had a new birth into the pastoral paradise. 'I remain'd as a Child.' In a return to his early historical enthusiasms he states, 'The People are Genuine Saxons, handsomer than the people about London.'[6]

Hayley had written a sentimental ballad, *Little Tom the Sailor, drowned at sea*, to be sold to relieve Tom's mother. Blake on 5 October completed two engravings for it. In November Hayley went on a visit to London and wrote asking for copies of the ballad. Blake replied that he had been busy on the frieze of poets' heads for the study in the Turret, and had stopped printing *Little Tom* but would start again next day. At times, he said, he tried to feel miserable so as to do more work, but that was 'a foolish experiment'. Flaxman 'is the theme of my emulation in this industry, as well as in other virtues and merits . . . Happy son of the immortal Phidias'. He had dispatched more copies of the ballad, for in December Hayley sent one to Romney, remarking on the 'decorations of our good enthusiastic Blake, who is happily settled in that Cottage . . . you used to admire'.

A person of whom Blake saw a great deal was Miss Paulina (correctly Henrietta) Poole of Lavant, north of Chichester. Hayley usually rode over twice a week to breakfast with her, to gossip and to get his mail. Blake, who had taken over the dead son's pony Bruno, accompanied him and grew very fond of Paulina; he even thought later of living in Lavant. She lived in a red-brick house with terraced garden at the back overlooking Lavant Brook.

Blake was kept busy through 1801. Hayley helped him to tackle miniatures; and he and Miss Poole introduced him to members of the local gentry who gave him commissions. Among them were Lord Bathurst of Lavant and Lord Egremont of Petworth. Hayley was working on his *Life of Cowper*, with Blake engraving and printing the illustrations, only one of which was from his own design. On 25 January Lady Hesketh wanted Blake to make Romney's portrait more like Cowper. Hayley, who never lost a chance to praise Blake in his rather patronising way, wrote to Romney about him, mentioning that he had taught him to paint in miniature, and he assured Lady Hesketh that Blake, 'an excellent enthusiastic Creature', would do Cowper's head *con amore*, 'as he idolises the Poet'. He himself was at work on a long poem about missionaries, the first canto of which he read in late February to Miss Poole, and certainly to Blake as well. Blake was giving drawing-lessons to Lady Bathurst's children and she proposed to engage him as salaried painter-in-ordinary to the family. The only order he is known to have refused (a set of handscreens) seems to have been hers.

In March the Rev. Johnny Johnson came to help with the life of Cowper, of whom he was a cousin. After leaving he wrote, 'Remember me most kindly to our dear friend Blake, and the Duck to whom he is a Drake'. Blake painted a miniature of him and three panels for his chimney-piece at Taxham Rectory; and later described him as 'a happy Abstract, known to all his Friends as the Most innocent forgetter of his own interests'. Throughout these years Johnny J. in his letters makes affectionate references to Blake. Meanwhile Hayley had sent Lady Hesketh Blake's miniature of Cowper based on Romney's portrait. She found it dreadful, mocking. 'The Sight of it has in *real truth* inspired me with a degree of horror, which I shall not recover from in haste.' Apparently she disliked the hint Romney had given of Cowper's madness. Hayley replied discreetly, but was determined to use the work.[7]

In May Blake wrote to Butts, apologising for delay in answering. 'Mr. Hayley acts like a Prince, I am at complete Ease, but I wish to do my duty, especially to you, who were the precursor of my present Fortune.' He will soon send some pictures, but is taken up with work in miniature, which 'is become a Goddess in my Eyes'. Felpham is 'the sweetest spot on Earth, at least it is so to me & My Good Wife'. In May Hayley wrote to a friend about the way in which he had recently taught a worthy creature to paint miniatures.

In June life was made easier in the Turret by the installation of a new housekeeper. Hayley, though often ill, carried on with his many schemes, such as a London monument to Cowper and Milton's Latin poems in his translation. (Both projects fell through, though the Milton was done later in 1808 with illustrations not by Blake.) Blake was engraving designs by Maria Flaxman for a new edition of *The Triumphs of Temper*. John Carr, a friend of Hayley's, came to stay in the summer with his travel-sketches, which he discussed with both Hayley and Blake, whom he called the ingenious artist of Felpham. There was also a Mr Chetwynd whose drawings they looked over. Blake called Chetwynd 'a Giant in body mild & polite in Soul as I have in general found great bodies to be'.[8]

Blake, though treated as a humble and worthy servitor, was thus admitted to a considerable degree of intimacy. But his unmixed happiness with Hayley was nearing its end. His sister had visited him and was given a portrait-drawing of Butts to take to Butts himself. In his letter Blake made excuses for failing to keep his promises. At first he holds himself in. He is improving at miniatures, he says; his friends tell him so. He wants to paint another portrait of Butts, but 'I have now discover'd that without Nature before the painter's Eye, he never can produce any thing in the walks of Natural Painting'. He sends his best respects to the surgeon Birch with the news that 'Felpham men are the mildest of the human race; if it is the will of Providence, they shall be the wisest. We hope that he will, next summer, joke with us face to face.' (Blake had tried to get Flaxman and Butts also to visit him.) But at this point he cannot sustain his role of the industrious and humble artist; he breaks out in terms that show how unhappy and out-of-place a deep part of him feels:

Time flies faster (as seems to me) here than in London. I labour incessantly & accomplish not one half of what I intend, because my Abstract folly hurries me often away while I am at work, carrying me over Mountains & Valleys, which are not Real, in a Land of Abstractions where Spectres of the Dead wander. This I endeavour to prevent & with my whole might chain my feet to the world of Duty & Reality; but in vain! the faster I bind, the better is the Ballast, for I, so far from being bound down, take the world with me in my flight, & often it seems lighter than a ball of wool rolled by the wind. Bacon & Newton would prescribe ways of making the world heavier to me, & Pitt would prescribe distress for a medicinal potion; but as None on Earth can give me Mental Distress, & I know that all Distress inflicted by Heaven is a Mercy, a Fig for all Corporeal! Such Distress is My mock & scorn. Alas! wretched, happy, ineffectual labourer of time's moments that I am! who shall deliver me from this Spirit of Abstraction and Improvidence. [8]

His idiom here is odd, as if he is yielding to abstraction and spectres when he turns to his own inner world and its poetic expression, leaving the Buttsian world of duty and industry. Perhaps he has been struggling with the *Four Zoas* and losing his way. Night VIIb deals with a hopelessly distressed empire, though as the prospect of peace grew stronger he tried to bring in a milder note, replacing VIIb with VIIa and composing a gentler introduction to IX (Providence and Mercy, late intruders, appear in VI, VIIa and VIII.) But the fact that he kept both versions of Night VII suggests that he could not quite make up his mind whether to hope or to see only a darker descent into deceit. That he was doing his best to show a face of humility is testified by a letter from Carr of 15 September which remarks of Blake that his 'modesty is the Companion of much merit'. And he was working hard. On 1 October Hayley told Johnny J. 'the warm-hearted indefatigable Blake works daily at my side, on the intended decorations of our Biography.—Engraving, of all human works, appears to require the largest Portion of patience'. Blake was slow at getting what he wanted on the plates.[9]

On 7 October Flaxman excused himself from paying a visit, but offered to sell for Blake any of the drawings with which 'I know you relieve yourself from more tedious labours'. Like Hayley he had no idea that Blake might be writing poetry. Hayley seems to have been somewhat worried about Blake's behaviour. He wrote two quatrains asking his dead son to inspirit him and control 'a Failing Brother's Hand & Eyes or temper his eccentric Soul'. Note how he makes Blake into Tom's brother; all along he had seen Blake to some extent as filling Tom's place, despite the difference in age. However on 18 October he told Flaxman that Blake was growing ever more attached to Felpham, drawing from it 'a perpetual increase of improving Talents, & settled Comfort'. He and Blake hoped Flaxman would find time to design a simple marble monument for Hayley's dead wife. Writing on a page left blank by Hayley, Blake mentions a clergyman who wants to buy his designs for *Comus* when they are done; and he rapturously welcomes the peace-negotiations going on. 'The Kingdoms of this World are now become the Kingdoms of God & his Christ, & we shall reign with him for ever & ever. The Reign of Literature & the Arts Commences. Blessed are those who are found students of Literature & Humane & polite accomplishments . . . Such have their lamps burning & shall shine as the stars.' He hopes that France and England will now become one country, with united arts. Such an idealisation of the situation is ludicrous. With all his deep insights he is quite unable to make a realistic evaluation of the historical forces in his world.[10]

On 8 November Hayley sent Johnny J. a feeble epitaph he had written on Cowper's friend, Mary Unwin; it had won applause 'from the accomplish'd Lady of Lavant, from our good enthusiastic Blake', and others. He and Blake were reading the *Iliad* together every evening from a copy sent by Johnson the publisher. They hoped to carry on with the *Odyssey*. 'The good Blake still advancing happily in his engravings joins with me in fervent Benediction to you.' Blake had become thoroughly absorbed into Hayley's daily life. Hayley, writing to Johnny J., says that the latter's letter has just reached him in Paulina's apartments and delighted them all: 'by *all*, I mean Paulina, Blake & myself'. So he has seized a pen and is writing a reply while the coffee is coming to the table. He transcribes a recent epitaph on the gardener William. 'Blake & I had the mournful Gratification of attending Him (by

accident) in the last few Hours of his Life . . . Paulina & Blake send you
their kindest Remembrances & best wishes.'[11]

Blake clearly enjoyed being thus a part of the Hayley household; yet his
poetic conscience chafed all the while after the first blithe months. There is
a sense of environing evil in the later Nights of the *Four Zoas*. From VIIa
Urizen's tree of mystery grows increasingly important. Enitharmon's
shadow enters Urizen's spectral world and is seduced by Urthona's spectre
(as Eve by Satan). Blake went on struggling to resolve this situation, and
managed to reconcile Los and Enitharmon. But in the outer world the war
between England and France dragged on. Night VIII, confused by alterations, tells of the seeming victory of evil in its most cruel female form. The
Lamb of God takes the place of Luvah, who has been Urizen's chief enemy-
victim, and this directly Christian turn in the symbolism is accentuated by
later additions. The victory of Vala over the Zoas is paralleled by the victory
of Rahab, controlling the Synagogue, over Jesus.*

A key to the ending of the *Four Zoas* is Blake's letter, cited above, about
the Treaty of Amiens. We see how wildly he was excited. His isolated
brooding on the war had made him deeply uncertain as to how peace and
redemption were to come about. Must the people rise up or would the rulers
by some change of heart 'unbuckle the girdle of war?' The long-suffering of
the people convinced him that the rulers would not relent unless they were
compelled. So he makes Albion give the call. Only then does Urizen–George
repent and abandon the idea that war is justified by the trade-benefits it
brings, and that trade needs slavery. A thorough harrowing of empire results.
Urizen now appears as a worker whose energies have been misdirected. He
agrees to end oppression and censorship, and announces, 'Rage, Orc; Rage,
Tharmas! Urizen no longer curbs your rage'. So the seven-day transformation of the world begins. The rising of the dead is the liberation of all men
from their jails of oppression and privation. The Last Judgement begins, but
it is the people who judge, not King or God. As Erdman says:

Blake's Judgment gives the oppressed their opportunity for vengeance, a brief but
violent dictatorship not only of the child-bearers (proletariat) but of the children

---

* No doubt Blake was influenced by Butts around this time. After the failure of the
Young project, Butts was the sole patron who enabled him to do original work, and this
fact could not but affect him strongly. When in January 1802 he wrote to him, 'Your
approbation of my pictures is a Multitude to Me', he was paying no empty compliment;
Butts was his substitute for a mass-audience.

themselves, the child laborers of street and mill who have been compelled to take the spectre form of despair. Christ, appearing himself as a 'Cold babe . . . furious,' authorises the vengeance, for this is Blake's grim version of 'Suffer the little children to come unto me.'

The captives are freed, the broken families are reunited by the act of tearing the ruling class, 'Kings & Councellors & Giant warriors', limb from limb. The judges are judged by those they sentenced. There begins the apocalypse of harvest and vintage, the realisation of brotherhood in work, which entails a harmonious relation to nature: Luvah joins happily with Vala, Tharmas with Enion. Urizen, redeemed, stabilises the situation. Tharmas does the final winnowing of wheat from chaff. 'The good of all the Land is before you for Mystery is no more.' The new song is 'Composed by an African Black', and sung by 'All the Slaves from every Earth in the wide universe. Bread and Wine are made ready for the Golden Feast'. What had been the screws and racks of oppression now function to produce the new wine of freedom. 'The evil is all consumd.'

That Blake should be stimulated to such a vision by the temporary lull in warfare through the Peace of Amiens brings out the way in which he over-values the immediate events while at the same time he is symbolically distancing himself more than ever from them. This unbalanced relation-ship was now to continue, for his isolation from the world around him was to keep on increasing. It did not matter so much in *Milton*, where the theme was largely personal, but it was to leave its mark deeply on *Jerusalem*. More and more his confusion as to the working out of the historical process centred on the symbolic role of Jesus. Was Jesus the meek counsellor of total sub-mission to evil or was he the liberator who comes with a sword?*

Blake weakens now in such positions as that any belief in an external providence was a pernicious illusion. The Saviour tends to become a *deus ex machina*. Erdman rightly points out:

---

* Blake's hopes for peace were echoed by other millenarians in their own terms. In February 1799 Holcroft called on Sharp, who told him that his print, *The Sortie of Gibraltar*, would be the last ever on a war-theme. 'The tongue of wisdom was now subdued, meaning Egypt, which was not only a slip of land resembling a tongue, but the place in which the learning of the world originated. Thus, by the help of a pun and a metaphor, he had double proof . . . Syria, Palestine, and all these countries are soon to be revolution-ised; and those who do not take up arms against their fellow men, are to meet at the Grand Millennium.' Note how Sharp's argument helps us to understand Blake's construc-tion of symbolic names.[12]

6

In this view, the French Revolution appears to have been a predestined pageant rather than a drama of human conflict. 'Even Jesus who is the Divine Vision Permitted all lest Man should fall into Eternal Death.' Christ formed a part of the French Terror and 'himself put on the robes of blood' to preserve France and Fraternity from extinction—'Lest the state called Luvah should cease.' The coming of peace demonstrates that Christ lives; the war must have been 'permitted' in order to make that demonstration.

Blake himself describes the moment of crucial change in his ideas. The new principle is that 'thou . . . of thyself Art nothing being Created Continually by Mercy & Love divine'. When Los hears this statement he is struck with 'irresistible conviction', so that he trembles at himself and all his former life. Here was the revelation and humility which Butts had wanted Blake to accept: a creed which he could share with Hayley. Oddly the spirit that thus converts Los–Blake is a spectre; Los calls him 'spectre horrible'. We are reminded of the conflict described in the letter to Butts between duty and hurrying abstractions. The submissiveness demanded of Los–Blake is just the sort of humble gratitude he keeps pouring out to Hayley. In his letters Blake indeed almost wallows in abject statements, yet he cannot fully give in to the horrible spectre. Therein lies the conflict that now dogs him.[13]

The concept of struggle on all fronts, on all levels of being, had been Blake's essential creed. Now with the contradiction between the ideas of total submission and of all-out liberation of energy as eternal delight, Blake cannot successfully complete his epic. He inserted a passage of eighty-eight lines at the start of Night IX, which robs Albion of any effective role. The Last Judgement comes about simply because the resurrected Jesus appears to Los and Enitharmon as they weep over the sepulchre and the crucified body. The role of the poet–prophet is denied any real efficacy. Los–Blake loses his contact with the people, who are 'sunk down in a deadly sleep'. He turns from building Jerusalem, from playing his active part in the struggle for a redeemed earth, and concerns himself with Golgonooza, the City of Art. Dominated by pity, he wants only to give eternal life to 'those piteous victims of battle' who need a refuge in Enitharmon's bosom. To cite Erdman again, 'Now personal salvation, even a sort of spiritual opportunism, is the theme, and the emphasis becomes strongly domestic, pointing to the happy collaboration of William and Catherine Blake, he engraving and etching, she tinting.' Here we have the idealisation of their daily life under Hayley. Golgonooza is conceived in terms of Chichester with its cathedral, and Blake is convinced that he has a great future as a painter of history. The spectre in Night VIIa tells him in effect that he must subordinate prophet to artist and admit that he is Blake's 'real Self'. Here is outlined the programme that Blake was to attempt to carry out until 1809, a programme emerging from the pietistic quietism and hopes of worldly success that we can trace amid the welter of conflicting changes recorded in *The Four Zoas*.[14]

9

Felpham Crisis, 1802–3

On 10 January 1802 Blake wrote a long letter to Butts in which he at last confessed his divided state. He apologises for delay in writing. He has been ill, and Catherine has been suffering from ague and rheumatism, which have afflicted her ever since they arrived. He is not so sanguine as he was at first: 'because I was ignorant of many things which have since occurred, & chiefly the unhealthiness of the place'. But he does not repent; he is sure that Hayley will ultimately lift him out of his difficulties. He then adds a comment with a touch of paranoia. 'But this is no easy matter to a man who, having Spiritual Enemies of such formidable magnitude, cannot expect to want naturally hidden ones.' He refuses Butts's offer of money, and tries to console himself with thoughts of future greatness. 'When it is proper, my Talents shall be properly exercised in Public, as I hope they are now in private; for, till then, I leave no stone unturn'd & no path unexplor'd that tends to improvement in my beloved Arts.' He claims that he has resumed his 'primitive & original ways of Execution in both painting & engraving, which in the confusion of London' had been lost and obliterated from his mind.

He refers to the series of watercolours he began at Felpham and continued in the years immediately after his return to London. Here he used his earlier tempera method, though on a larger scale. In the end he turned out more than eighty works, all related to the Bible. The twenty-seven Old Testament subjects mainly deal with the victory of good over evil and the foreshadowings of Christ, but they also treat the tyranny of the law, the defeats of the Jews, the question of sexual freedom. (The four that deal with the Creation are conventional, unlike the 1795 monotypes, where the Creator is seen as Urizen.) In the New Testament series Blake at times intrudes his own symbolism: Christ in the carpenter's shop holds a pair of dividers to show that under the new dispensation science will lose its Urizenic elements. Technically Blake tries to simplify forms and compositions at times achieving a rich rhythmic quality, at times falling back on an inert symmetry. Despite his theoretical stress on light as a living force, he gives up trying to use it in organising his pictures, and soon rationalises his weakness here by violent attacks on Rembrandt.[1]

To return to his letter to Butts: 'My unhappiness has arisen from a source which, if explor'd too narrowly, might hurt my pecuniary circumstances.' That is, he is revolting against Hayley's supervision. 'I find on all hands great objections to my doing any thing but the meer drudgery of business, & intimations that if I do not confine myself to this, I shall not live.' He adds that this kind of subjection has always been his fate, under Fuseli and Johnson. Their treatment drove him to Felpham, '& this from Mr H. will bring me back again'. He is cut off from his true work.

It gives me the greatest of torments. I am not ashamed, afraid, or averse to tell you what Ought to be Told: That I am under the direction of Messengers from Heaven, Daily & Nightly; but the nature of such things is not, as some suppose, without trouble or care. Temptations are on the right hand & left; behind, the sea of time & space roars & follows swiftly; he who keeps not right onward is lost, & if our footsteps slide in clay, how can we do otherwise than fear & tremble?

To refuse the call is to earn the name of Judas. 'But I am no longer in that State, and now go on again with my Task, Fearless.' He has decided to return to London before the winter comes on.[2]

But however fearless he was, he had not brought himself to tell Hayley of his intentions. Late in 1801 the latter had written several weak ballads on animals, which he decided to print 'for the emolument of the interesting artist who had settled in a Cottage, as the Poet's Neighbour,' as he wrote later in his autobiography, not naming Blake. But for the moment he was taken up with the engravings for the Cowper *Life* and a design he had made for a Cowper monument: the Bible supporting the poet's *Task*, plus palm and laurel-wreath. In January and February 1802 he was writing much about it and the *Life* to Flaxman, Lady Hesketh and Johnny J. 'Blake at my side unites in Benediction . . .' Flaxman in a letter called Blake the New Grecian. Hayley sent Lady Hesketh a neat copy of his plan for the monument 'from the kind Hand of the friendly Zealous Engraver, who daily works by my side, & who flatters me so far as to say, that he never saw any monumental design more modestly appropriate to the honoured dead'. Whether Blake was being honest or merely polite, his comment hardly earns our respect. Flaxman wanted to put a lyre in the monument, to Hayley's displeasure. As Lady Hesketh had not replied, Hayley sent her another copy by 'the neat pencil of that friendly & zealous artist, who labours every day in my presence, with admirable industry'. Soon afterwards he wrote again, enclosing a poem written to encourage Blake, 'Good Angels guide the Graver's Hand'. His design was finally adopted, but with the *Task* now propping the Bible.[3]

On 16 May Hayley wrote that both the good Blakes had been in bed for a week with a severe fever, but were now better. Blake was at his side, engraving the frontispiece for the ballads. Each ballad was to have three designs drawn and engraved by Blake. Hayley had taken up with a Chichester printer, Seagrave, who stammered and whose compositors were often drunk. Despite Johnson's opposition he decided to give him the Cowper *Life* to print. Hayley, who was also working on a Memoir of his dead son, wrote a preface to the ballads in which he said that he had wanted to divert and cheer Blake, since engraving was slow and often irksome to 'a person of varied talents, and of a creative imagination'. The ballads had 'succeeded perfectly as an amusement to my Friend'. The scheme had been devised to give Blake a chance to show his 'diversified talent' for design and delicate engraving: 'Since friendship induced this meritorious Artist to leave London (the great lucrative theatre of talents!) for the sake of settling near me.' Hayley may well have felt something of Blake's restiveness and hoped that the scheme would please him; also no doubt he did want to help him. But it would hardly have been possible to devise a project less suited to Blake's talents.[4]

Hayley did his best to enlist the aid of friends for selling the ballads. In June publication began, and since there was a grateful elephant in the first ballad, Hayley wrote playfully: 'A score of Elephants will begin their March to you tomorrow.' 'Metamorphose this Tribe of animals into Half Crowns for our Benevolent Artist.' 'He & his excellent Wife (a true Helpmate!) pass the plates thro' a rolling press in their own cottage together.' 'The good Blake & his elephants are in triumphant activity.' The themes included a devoted dog jumping into a crocodile's jaws to warn his master, a baby carried to an eagle's nest, and an elephant lifting up a vegetable-monger to an upper window away from a tiger (not shown).

Hawkins took two copies and sold two more. Lady Hesketh said Bath was deserted and by July she had sold not more than half a dozen ballads. Worse, persons claiming taste criticised the drawings and she cited at length the objections of two persons (apparently the Bishop of Worcester and Princess

Elizabeth). Blake would have been furious. Later he wrote that the question was not whether a man was talented, but whether he was obedient 'to Noblemen's Opinions in Art & Science. If he is; he is a Good Man: If Not he must be Starved.' A woman visitor to Felpham asked if Blake would engrave a drawing that a gentleman had made of a prize bull. (He was William Meyer, a miniaturist's son, who, with his mother and sister, often came to Felpham and who became acquainted with the Blakes.)

·Blake was still falling ill. Writing to Lady Hesketh from Levant, Hayley said that Blake usually accompanied him, 'yet today sickness detained Him in bed —But I trust He will speedily revive under the care of perhaps the very best Wife that ever mortal possessed'. When he had leisure he would write at length on the Blakes. He was having trouble about paper for his Cowper, but Blake had got paper for the ballads from his own stationer in London. Then in reply to more criticisms of Blake's designs from Lady H. he wrote to her an account which shows much genuine understanding of Blake as well as affection.

Whatever the Merits or the Failings of my diligent & grateful artist may be, I know I shall interest your Heart & Soul in *his Favour*, when I tell you, that he resembles our beloved Bard [Cowper] in the Tenderness of his Heart, & in the perilous powers of an Imagination utterly unfit to take care of Himself.—with admirable Faculties, his sensibility is so *dangerously acute*, that the common rough Treatment which true genius often receives from *ordinary Minds* in the commerce of the World, might not only wound him *more than it should do*, but really reduce Him to the Incapacity of an Ideout without the consolatory support of a considerable Friend. From these excesses of Feeling, & of irregular Health (forever connected with such excess) His productions must ever perhaps be unequal, but in all he does, however wild or hasty, a penetrating eye will discover true Genius, & if it were possible to Keep his too apprehensive Spirit for a Length of Time unruffled, He would produce Works of the pencil, almost as excellent & original, as those works of the pen, which flowed from the dear poet, of whom he often reminds me by little Touches of nervous Infirmity, when his mind is darkend with any unpleasant apprehension.—He reminds me of him also by being a most fervent admirer of the Bible, & intimately acquainted with all its Beauties.[5]

We see that Blake had still not shown Hayley anything of his prophetic poetry or set out any of his Antinomian views. Hayley adds:

They have no servant:—the good woman not only does all the work of the House, but she even makes the greatest part of her Husbands dress, & assists him in his art—she draws, she engraves, & sings delightfully & is so truly the Half of her good Man, that they seem animated by one Soul, & that a soul of indefatigable Industry & Benevolence—it sometimes hurries them both to labour rather too much, & I had some time ago the pain of seeing both confined to their Bed.

In describing Catherine as one half of William, Hayley comes close to Blake's picture of her as his emanation. However, his comparison of Blake and Cowper annoyed Lady Hesketh. A few days later he again expressed alarm for Blake's health, but said he was now reviving.*

On 22 November Blake sent two letters to Butts, letting himself go to the one person with whom he could unbosom himself. James Blake had been with him. 'My Brother tells me that he fears you are offended with me. I fear so too.' Probably as usual he had been dilatory with letters. He explains that for two years he has been making 'an intense study of those parts of the art which relate to light & shade & colour'. He praises his own work for Butts as 'equal in every Part of the Art, & superior in One, to any thing that has been done since the age of Raphael', and approvingly cites Reynolds in the argument that Venetian finesse cannot be 'united with the Majesty of Colouring necessary to Historical beauty'. His own works are equal to those of the Carachi or Raphael, 'or Else I am Blind, Stupid, Ignorant and Incapable in two years' Study to understand those things that a Boarding School Miss can comprehend in a fortnight.' He means now to 'Go on with the Vigour I was in my Childhood famous for.' His works may have some faults, but so have the works of all the great masters. Further, each artist makes his own specific contribution. We cannot compare Carachi with Correggio, or Correggio with Raphael. He apologises for not having done Mrs Butts' miniature, and says such works need the original to hand.

It is hard to see how he had been studying light, shade and colour in art. But he has not yet closed his mind. He does not denounce the Venetians and Correggio; he is ready to consider the contributions of the most varied artists to the tradition. His thinking on art, however, is strictly limited to Renaissance categories as redefined in the eighteenth century; he stands opposed to the trends making for modern art, which begin decisively with Hogarth, find new strength in the period of the French Revolution (Goya and David), and in Géricault and Courbet transform the category of

* The ballads were not doing well. Samuel Greatheed at Newport Pagnell reported that he had shown copies to many gentlemen and ladies, but sold none. On 15 November Romney died. Hayley composed an epitaph 'before the break of day', and thought of yet another biography in which Blake was to help.[6]

history into that of realism. The long struggle had been to absorb the imaginative element into the depiction of everyday life, not to separate it out as the property of gods, heroes, kings, as in history painting. Blake accepted the split in life and art represented by history, unable to grasp that the struggle for democratic revolutionary positions was working out as the absorption of history into the present with all its deep conflicts. He himself broke down the old categories in that he wanted history to symbolise the contemporary struggle, but he could not conceive of the imagination as a transformative element in close relation to people, to events, to life-as-lived, lifting Nature to a new level of integration (as in Turner) and grappling realistically and directly with the full material of experience.

In his letter he goes on to say that he has been very unhappy and has burned many letters to Butts. Then he gives a hyperbolic account of his breakthrough; its intensity gives us some idea of the anxieties with which he has been wrestling. 'I am again Emerged into the light of day; I still & shall to Eternity, Embrace Christianity and adore him who is the Express image of God; but I have travel'd thro' Perils & Darkness not unlike a Champion. I have Conquer'd, and shall still Go on Conquering. Nothing can withstand the fury of my Course among the Stars of God & in the Abysses of the Accuser, My Enthusiam is still what it was, only Enlarged and confirm'd.' He sends two pictures and an account of moneys received and work done.[7]

He was so agitated that no sooner had he finished this long letter than he began another one. 'Tell me in a letter of forgiveness if you were offended.' He discusses further work and says that his wife has asked him to copy out a poem composed about a year before while walking to Lavant to meet his sister. This poem, in octosyllabic couplets loose in rhythm, gives an ecstatic account of his summer walk. He feels deeply a living relationship with everything in Nature; and this sense of union, as is usual with him, makes him feel the human presence in nature and vice versa. At the same time, the fact that he is going to meet his sister conjures up family-images, his Father hovering in the wind, with his brother Robert just behind, 'and my Brother John, the evil one'. His anxiety grows and his fears that he will be forced back to London, to the old exploitations by Johnson and Fuseli. Why is he torn between contending friends and relations? If he gives Hayley due respect, 'must Flaxman look upon me as wild, And all my friends be with doubts beguil'd?' Why does he have to suffer, again torn, as his wife and his sister quarrel? All that threatens him in life seems concentrated in a

6*

thistle that suggests a grey old man. He strikes down the thistle and finds that he has to contend with Los (coming down out of the Sun). He defies Los (his own prophetic self, his poetic destiny), rebelling against the need to suffer, to drudge away day and night, and yet never find any peace. He defies the aghast universe, feeling secure in his fourfold vision, his grasp of the full dialectics of life and art. (After citing the poem he tamely mentions that he encloses some copies of the ballads and a letter to be given to his brother.)

Blake was fiercely trying to nerve himself for the break with Hayley and the latter must have felt something wrong, for he gave up mentioning Blake in his letters. Johnny J. wrote on 3 December, 'By the bye is our dear Blake *dead*? You are silent about him as the *grave*!' When the Flaxmans returned from a visit to Paris, Nancy asked Hayley to 'give our love to the good Cottagers', Hayley wrote on the 16th to say that Catherine had been suffering severely from rheumatism but was recovering. On 20 December he wrote to Lady Hesketh about the delayed Cowper *Life* and mentioned his good zealous Coadjutor.

My Friend, the anxious, enthusiastic Engraver says, that all the Demons, who tormented our dear Cowper when living, are now labouring to impede the publication of his Life.—To which I reply that it may be so, but if it is, I am confident my two dear Angels the Bard & the Sculptor [Cowper and Flaxman] will assist us in *our Conflict* with *the powers* of *darkness*, & enable us to triumph over all *their Machinations*.[8]

A few days later Lady Hesketh, to the relief of Blake and Hayley, wrote that she liked the engraving of Cowper's head.

On 30 January 1803 Blake wrote a letter to his brother James which further reveals his feelings at this juncture. Butts, he says, was wrong in saying he had an ague; it was a cold. But Catherine has had agues and rheumatism almost ever since they arrived. He mentions the illnesses only because of 'a determination which we have lately made, namely to leave this Place'. Then he comes out with the paranoiac suspicions that always afflicted him after someone had tried to help him. 'I am now certain of what I have long doubted. Viz that H. is jealous as Stothard was & will be no further My friend than he is compell'd by circumstance. The truth is, As a Poet he is frighten'd at me & as Painter his views & mine are opposite; he thinks to turn me into a Portrait Painter as he did Poor Romney, but this he nor all the devils in hell will never do. I must own that seeing H. like S[tothard],

Envious (& that he is I am now certain) made me very uneasy, but it is over now & I now defy the worst & fear not while I am true to myself which I will be.' Blake's accusation that Hayley tried to turn Romney into a portrait-painter could not be more untrue. After Romney won fame with his portraits, Hayley at Eartham kept pressing him to turn to history and suggested subject after subject. And we have seen from Farington's diary how Stothard in January 1797 was the one artist who defended Blake and Flaxman.[9]

Blake now reveals his dream of making a fortune, and asks James to pass the news on their sister. 'I am fully Employ'd & Well Paid. I have made it so much H.'s interest to employ me that he can no longer treat me with indifference.' He, Blake, can stay or go because he is 'getting before hand in money matters'. Watching Hayley at his publishing transaction, he has decided that 'the Profits arising from Publication are immense, & I now have it in my power to commence publication with many very formidable works, which I have finish'd & read'. He boasts of the work he is doing, and the money he will make through having 'known H. and his connexions & his method of managing'. Returning to London in the spring, he will start publishing; but he also speaks of taking a house further from the sea, probably at Lavant, on or near the London road. For the moment all is well. 'We are very Happy sitting at tea by a wood fire in our Cottage, the wind singing above our roof & the sea roaring at a distance, but if sickness comes all is unpleasant.' He adds, 'I go on Merrily with my Greek & Latin; am very sorry that I did not begin to learn languages early in life as I find it very easy; am now learning my Hebrew. I read Greek as fluently as an Oxford scholar.' He mentions that Seagrave owes Catherine twenty guineas. 'This is a small specimen of how we go on: then fear nothing & let my Sister fear nothing because it appears to me that I am now too old & have had too much experience to be any longer imposed upon.' He wants badly to convince James, and perhaps himself as well, that at last he is going to be be rich.*

* Even with Hayley's name to them the ballads were doing badly. On 3 April 1803 Hayley wrote to the bookseller Evans of Pall Mall who was handling London sales. Blake had prepared designs for more ballads, but had already spent £30 on paper (and the copies sold in the country had not met half that sum). 'I am very desirous of not leading him into an unprofitable adventure ... What Cash have you for him?—He is an excellent creature, but not very fit to manage pecuniary Concerns.' Hayley proposed a book of the ballads with one plate per animal. (A small book was done in 1805, with plates not by Blake.) Hayley speaks of Blake as 'Devoted to a life of Industry & Retirement'. He has no idea of Blake's plans or of illuminated books. In December 1805 Blake still owed Seagrave money.

On 23 April Blake, after a pressing letter from James, wrote to Butts with apologies for delays. He hadn't quite finished a picture, but he sent ballads to be given to Birch. He says disingenuously, 'The Reasons the Ballads have been suspended is the pressure of other business, but they will go on again soon'. (There were to be no more.) Blake then declares that only in London can he carry on his visionary studies 'unannoy'd'.

What is very pleasant, Every one who hears of my going to London again Applauds it as the only course for the interest of all concern'd in My works, Observing that I ought not to be away from the opportunities London affords of seeing fine Pictures, and the various improvements in works of Art going on in London.

But none can know the Spiritual Acts of my three years' Slumber on the banks of the Ocean, unless he has seen them in the Spirit, or unless he should read My long Poem descriptive of those Acts; for I have in these three years composed an immense number of verses on One Grand Theme. Similar to Homer's Iliad or Milton's Paradise Lost, the Persons & Machinery intirely new to the Inhabitants of Earth (some of the Persons excepted). I have written this Poem from immediate Dictation, twelve or sometimes twenty or thirty lines at a time, without Premeditation & even against my Will; the Time it has taken in writing was thus render'd Non Existent, & an immense Poem Exists which seems to be the Labour of a long Life, all produc'd without Labour or Study. I mention this to shew you what I think the Grand Reason of my being brought down here.

The poem to which he refers may be the *Four Zoas*. *Milton*, which is a little over 1,600 lines, is hardly immense, though he probably conceived it in his last days of Felpham and may even have written some of it there. It is just possible however we have lost the work and that it was part of the MSS destroyed by Tatham after Blake's death.

On the same day as Blake wrote this letter Hayley wrote to Lady Hesketh. He had mentioned earlier an artist who wanted to paint her; and she, sure that the man must be Blake, refused, but offered £5 as a gift; now Hayley replied that he had wanted the portrait for himself. He would tell Blake of her offer in a way that would not hurt his honest pride. During the spring he asked the Duchess of Portarlington if Blake could call on her with some designs; he recommended him strongly and called Catherine 'a virtuous, & singularly amiable woman'. The Blakes had passed their lives on an income so scanty 'as scarcely to have afforded them the means of subsistence'.

By May Blake had finished the plates for the *Triumph of Temper* enough to date them. On 6 July he wrote to Butts, sending one picture and mention-

ing seven more on the stocks; he still hoped to paint Mrs Butts. 'I ought
to tell you that Mr H. is quite agreeable to our return, & that there is all
the appearance in the world of being fully employ'd in Engraving for his
projected Works, particularly Cowper's Milton.' (The work was not issued
till 1808, and then with two plates engraved by Raimbach after Flaxman.)
Blake now calls his epic a Sublime Allegory. 'I May praise it, since I dare
not pretend to be any other than the Secretary; the Authors are in Eternity.
I consider it as the Grandest Poem that the World Contains.' In speaking
of his poems as dictated he must have meant that he wrote under an extreme
excitement which gave him a sense of composing without any conscious
control. The fact that he made many alterations, corrections, deletions, inser-
tions, proves that there was not in any sense a form of automatic writing;
he was in full conscious and critical control. His sense of inspiration was no
doubt linked with his eidetic power of projecting images so strongly that
they seemed visions coming from outside. (We have all known the hypnog-
ogic images that can float up and be held on the edge of sleep, at times with
extraordinary sharpness of form.) In Blake's case there was no doubt a
greater gap between conscious thought and the act of projecting an image on
to paper or canvas, which gave the creative act a special sense of autonomy.
It was in the nature of Blake's whole outlook and sensibility that he fused
the two elements in a metaphor with special force. Say that Los is the Sun
and the Sun is Los, then when he is excited he feels a living identity of Sun
and Los. The seeing of visions, apart from this creative sense of union with
its powers of momentary projection, was probably rare and sporadic in his
earlier years, but grew commoner after 1808, when the sense of failure and
isolation worsened. At least then he seemed to have talked more of visions
as a kind of compensation for his neglect by the world.[10]

In the letter to Butts he goes on about his epic. He can talk bravely
about giving it to the public when the decision is still far off; when the time
comes, he retreats as usual in fear.

This Poem shall, by Divine Assistance, be progressively Printed & Ornamented
with Prints & given to the Public. But of this work I take care to say little to Mr H.,
since he is as much averse to my poetry as he is to a chapter in the Bible. He knows
that I have writ it, for I have shewn it to him, & he has read Part by his own
desire & has looked with sufficient contempt to inhance my opinion of it . . .
Mr H approves of My Designs as little as he does of my Poems, and I have
been forced to insist on his leaving me in both to my own Self Will; for I am
determin'd to be no longer Pester'd with his Genteel Ignorance & Polite Disappro-

bation. I know myself both Poet and Painter, & it is not his affected Contempt that can move me to any thing but a more assiduous pursuit of both Arts. Indeed, by my late Firmness I have brought down his affected Loftiness, & he begins to think I have some Genius; as if Genius & Assurance were the same thing! but his imbecile attempts to depress me only deserve laughter . . .

I shall leave every one in This Country astonish'd at my Patience & Forbearance of Injuries upon Injuries; & I do assure you that, if I could have return'd to London a Month after my arrival here, I should have done so, but I was commanded by my Spiritual friends to bear all, to be silent, & to go thro' all without murmuring, &, in fine, hope, till my three years should be almost accomplish'd; at which time I was set at liberty to remonstrate against former conduct & to demand Justice & Truth; which I have done in so effectual a manner that my antagonist is silenc'd completely, &, I have compell'd what should have been of freedom— My Just Rights as an Artist & as a Man . . .

So Blake had at last nerved himself to show Hayley some of his poetry. What it was, we do not know, but his terms suggest it was the epic on which he worked. Hayley no doubt was dumbfounded, since the poem would not have fitted into any category known to him; he probably fobbed Blake off with some vague noncommittal comments. His letters prove that he looked on Blake entirely as an artist; the poem that Blake showed him must have seemed the wild and peripheral work of an enthusiast, of no importance. Whatever he said had a shattering effect on Blake; the man that Blake had hailed in September 1800 as the Leader of his Angels now seemed a vile and obtuse enemy. His deep hurt shows in every word of his letter, for instance in his accusation that Hayley despised his designs, which is completely untrue. Hayley had written to the Countess of Portarlington that Blake was unequalled among British artists, owning 'great original powers and of uncommon Merit in his Inventions'. The hurt appears too in Blake's claim that he had wanted to leave as soon as he arrived in Felpham, when we have his letters expressing the immense joy he found in his new home.

But luckily we have a letter from Hayley to Flaxman on 7 August which tells us just what happened in the scene when Blake demanded his Just Rights and completely silenced his antagonist. Hayley starts by saying that the ladies have been finding fault with the engravings for *The Triumphs of Temper*, and it is a lady's book. 'Our poor industrious Blake has received sixty Guineas for them from my Bookseller & I believe that both the artist & the paymaster are dissatisfied.' Then comes the account of Blake's great revolt, which in fact was merely a demand for better prices.

Blake has made two excellent drawings of Romney one from his own large picture the other from our dear disciples Medallion—I thought of having both engraved for a single quarto volume of his life—but Blake surprised me a little in saying (after we had settled the price of 30 Guineas for the first the price which He had for the Cowper) that Romneys head would require much Labor & he must have 40 for it—startled as I was I replied I will not stint you in behalf of Romney— you shall have 40—but soon after while we were looking at the smaller & slighter drawing of the Medallion He astonished me by saying I must have 30 G for this —I then replied—of this point I must consider because you will observe Romneys Life can hardly circulate like Cowpers & I shall perhaps print it entirely at my own risk—So the matter rests between us at present.

Blake in fact engraved only one plate for the Romney.

But a few days later, on Friday 12 August, he was involved in troubles that made his argument with Hayley seem a trivial matter. On the 16th he wrote a full account to Butts. His first paragraph deals with seven pictures he is sending, then he plunges into the story of his catastrophe.

I am at Present in a Bustle to defend myself against a very unwarrantable Warrant from a Justice of Peace in Chichester, which was taken out against me by a Private in Captn Leather's troop of 1st or Royal Dragoons, for an assault & Seditious words. The wretched Man has terribly Perjur'd himself, as has his Comrade; for, as to Sedition, not one word relating to the King or Government was spoken by either him or me. His Enmity arises from my having turned him out of my Garden, into which he was invited as an assistant by a Gardener at work therein, without my knowledge that he was so invited. I desired him, as politely as was possible, to go out of the Garden; he made an impertinent answer. I insisted on his leaving the Garden; he refused. I still persisted in desiring his departure; he then threatened to knock out my Eyes, with many abominable imprecations & with some contempt for my Person; it affronted my foolish Pride.

I therefore took him by the Elbows & pushed him before me till I had got him out; there I intended to have left him, but he, turning about, put himself in a Posture of Defiance, threatening & swearing at me. I, perhaps foolishly, perhaps not, stepped out at the Gate, &, putting aside his blows, took him again by the Elbows, &, keeping his back to me, pushed him forwards down the road about fifty yards—he all the while endeavouring to turn round & strike me, & raging & cursing, which drew out several neighbours; at length, when I had got him to where he was Quarter'd, which was very quickly done, we were met at the Gate by the Master of the house, The Fox Inn (who is the proprietor of my Cottage), & his wife & Daughter & the Man's Comrade & several other people. My Landlord compell'd the Soldiers to go in doors, after many abusive threats against me & my wife from the two Soldiers; but not one word of threat on account of Sedition was utter'd at that time. This method of Revenge was plann'd between them after they had got together into the Stable. This is the whole outline . . .

I have been before a Bench of Justices at Chichester this morning; but they, as the Lawyer, who wrote down the Accusation told me in private, are compell'd by the Military to suffer a prosecution to be entr'd into: altho' they must know, & it is manifest, that the whole is a Fabricated Perjury. I have been forced to find Bail.[11]

Hayley stood bail for £50, Seagrave for £50, while Blake himself was bound over in £100 for his appearance at the Quarter Sessions. (Blake states that Hayley's bond was £100; perhaps Hayley had lent him £50.) Near the end of his letter Blake bursts into verse: 'O why was I born with a different face?'

> Then my verse I dishonour, My pictures despise,
> My person degrade & my temper chastise;
> And the pen is my terror, the pencil my shame;
> All my Talents I bury, and dead is my Fame.

The soldier was John Scolfield (Schofield, Scofield), his friend Trooper John Cock.*

The noise of the affray brought out many villagers. Those at the inn were Grinder, the landlord, his wife and daughter, Mrs Haynes, wife of the miller's servant, who had a garden next to the Blakes, and her daughter, Hayley's gardener (probably Hosier who was ready next day to testify as to what Scolfield said), Cosens, mill-owner, William who was inn-hostler and Blake's gardener, and an old man who stayed in the taproom. The strength of Blake's defence lay in the fact that nobody had overheard what occurred between him and the soldier in the garden, and the witnesses by the inn had heard no accusations of sedition.

Scolfield in his deposition of 15 August stated:

One Blake a Miniature painter . . . did utter the following seditious expressions vizt. That we (meaning the people of England) were like a parcel of Children, that they wod. play with themselves 'till they wod. get scalded and burnt, that the French knew our strength very well and if Buonapart shod. come he wod. be master of Europe

---

* Scolfield, born in Manchester, had been a fustian cutter; he enlisted in the Dragoons on 19 March 1793 at Sarum, was promoted to corporal, then sergeant in September 1797, but was reduced to the ranks, 30 December 1798. He may have hoped to regain his promotion by nosing out a traitor. Trooper John Cock (Cox) had joined in March 1800 after serving in the Berkshire Fencibles (militia); he had been in 1803 with Scolfield in Truro. The Company had then marched to Dorchester, Dorset, and on to Chichester where it stayed June to February 1804.

in an hour's time, that England might depend upon it that when he set his Foot on English Ground that every Englishman wod. be put to his choice whether to have his throat cut or to join the French & that he was a strong Man and wod. certainly begin to cut throats and the strongest Man must conquer—that he Damned the King of England—his Country and his Subjects—that his soldiers were all bound for Slaves & all the poor people in general—that his Wife then came up & said to him this is nothing to you at present but that the King of England wod. run himself so far into the fire that he might [?not] get himself out again & altho she was but a Woman she wod. fight as long as she had a Drop of Blood in her—to which the said Blake said, my Dear you wod. not fight against France —she replied, no, I wod. fight for Buonaparte as long as I am able—that the said Blake then addressing himself to this Informant, said, tho' you are one of the King's Subjects I have told what I have said before greater people than you . . . that his wife then told her said Husband to turn this Informant out of the Garden— that this Informant thereupon turned round to go peacefully when the said Blake pushed this Informant out of the Garden into the Road, down which he followed this Informant & twice took this Informant by the Collar without this Informant's making any resistance and at the same time this Blake *damned the King & said the* ——*Soldiers were all Slaves*—(this can be proved by another Soldier).

Much of this language could not have been used by Blake, but the general anti-war tone was not far from his sentiments. Perhaps he or Catherine, who was capable of imprudence, had said similar things in milder terms to neighbours or in the inn, and the soldiers had heard of them. Scolfield was doing no harm in the garden; he had been invited to work there. Blake made no effort to hear what he had to say; the mere sight of a soldier on his grounds set him off in a violent rage, in which he may well have said things about soldiers which he later could not recollect. Catherine's irruption, apart from the bloody tone of the remarks, is what we would expect of her. She, it seems, pushed Blake into violence, though he does not mention her in his own account. The local folk may well have been sympathetic to Blake and his anti-war position. It is noteworthy that while many folksongs support Napoleon, none of them praise Wellington or the war.*

* In *Boney's Lamentation* Napoleon looks back on his Russian campaign; in *A Dream of Napoleon* his ghost cries: 'On the plains of Marengo I tyranny hurled, and wherever my Banners the Eagles unfurled, 'twas the standard of Freedom all over the world'. On his side is *The Bonny Bunch of Roses, Oh!*, apparently an adapted Jacobite song; also the sea-chanty, *Boney was a Warrior*. The authorities were aware of the sympathy for him. The Mayor of Leicester wrote to the Home Office, warning that any failure in the bread-supply would draw a fourth of the people to 'join the French Standards if they had an opportunity'.[12]

The magistrate was John Quantock. Each soldier had to put up £50, as also the officer responsible for preferring the charge, Lieut. George Hulton. Blake's memorandum, drawn up with legal advice, ably picked out the inconsistencies in the charge. Thus, Scolfield repeated that he did not know how the quarrel started; Mrs Haynes heard no sedition; the people at the stable-door did not corroborate the soldiers' charge that Blake damned the king; Mrs Haynes said that Scolfield made no charge of sedition at the time, and so on. The only proved fact was that Blake ordered Scolfield out of the garden. Scolfield had told Grinder that Blake's house should be searched, 'as I might have plans of the Country,' said Blake, 'which I intended to Send to the Enemy; he called me a Military Painter; I suppose mistaking the Words Miniature Painter, which he might have heard me called. I think this proves his having gone into the Garden, with some bad Intention, or at least with a prejudiced mind.' Scolfield had threatened to knock out the hostler's eyes, as he had threatened Blake and his wife, because the hostler refused to go with him to Chichester and swear against Blake. Hayley's gardener, passing, had thought him drunk. Blake summed up: 'If such a Perjury as this can take effect, any Villain in future may come & drag me and my Wife out of our Home, & beat us in the Garden, or use us as he pleases, or is able, & afterwards go and Swear our Lives away'.

Blake's comment on Scolfield's description of him as Military Painter brings out how quick he was to detect environing conspiracies. Even more revealing is Scolfield's statement, which bears every mark of truth: 'Blake, then addressing himself to this Informant, said, tho' you are one of the King's Subjects, I have told what I said before greater People than you, and that this Informant was sent by his Captain or Esquire Hayley to hear what he had to say, and then go and tell them'. Blake jumped to the conclusions that Hayley was betraying him for his request for higher fees, and that he had sent the soldier to draw him into some compromising remark. As time went on, he grew ever more convinced that the whole thing was a government trap and that Hayley was involved in it. In his later years he used to assert that 'the Government, or some high person knowing him to have been one of the Paine set, "sent the soldier to entrap him" '. Certainly, in the period between the scuffle and the trial, he must have been very afraid that his early proclaimed republicanism would be brought up. The fact that it was not mentioned at the trial proves that there was no plot of the kind he described.

On 24 August Flaxman, knowing nothing of Scolfield, wrote to commiserate with Hayley about 'Blake's irritability, & your consequent trouble'. It may well have been the tension Blake felt after asking for higher fees, an episode which for him was a bold defiance of the powers of evil, that led to his uncontrollable burst of rage against the soldier. There could hardly have been a worse moment to become entangled in a sedition charge in Sussex. The war, resumed in May, had aroused acute fears of invasion. In August there were rumours of French transports having sailed, and 'all women etc' were ordered away from the south coast. Soldiers would be on the lookout for French agents or sympathisers. The gentry would be prejudiced against anyone charged with sedition.[13]

In September the Blakes moved back to London. The last lines of *Milton* seem to echo the relief that Blake then felt. There, in a sort of Last Judgement, Jesus walks out of Felpham's Vale to enter Albion's bosom. Blake watches in Felpham and his soul returns to 'Resurrection & Judgment in the Vegetable Body', with Catherine, his sweet shadow of delight, trembling at his side. The lark mounts from the vale and the scene changes to Wimbledon's green empurpled hills. Los and Enitharmon (William & Catherine) go over the hills of Surrey towards London. 'Soft Oothoon pants in the Vale of Lambeth, weeping o'er her Human Harvest.' That is, the Lambeth visions have ended in a yet more enslaved condition of mankind. 'Los listens to the Cry of the Poor Man, his Cloud over London in volume terrific bended in anger.' Los–Blake found a city being fortified to meet invasion, with small arms manufactured day and night in the Tower and various workshops, and with captured French ships crowding the Thames. Muskets were needed for the 400,000 volunteers. On 19 October a General Fast was held.

The struggle between wrath at iniquity and fear of expressing it (rationalised as the need of long-suffering meekness) was to rend Blake till the end of his days. His inner debate is set out in *Jerusalem* (7) where his spectre is full of rage and horror at the shadowy generation of Englishmen caught up in 'webs of war & of Religion'. The spectre objects to his 'friendship to Albion' and tries to arouse him to 'murderous thoughts against Albion', to fierce struggle against the complicity of people in evil. 'I saw it indignant, & thou art not moved!' But the poet refuses to be moved into expressing his anger, satisfied with looking ahead to the future day when somehow Albion will be resurrected in peace, freedom, brotherhood.[14]

10

Return to London, 1804

Blake now had to wait till January for the trial to open. The intervening months must have been a time of intense anxiety, with suspicion of plots and treacheries. The Blakes were now living at 17 South Molton Street, not far from the old Tyburn gallows, where they stayed till 1821, renting a few rooms. Cumberland often visited Blake there, finding him in quarters far inferior to anything he had previously had. When Linnell met him he had the first floor, and the landlord was Mark Martin. On 18 September Blake wrote to Hayley, praising Flaxman and telling of the work he himself had in hand; but we have only a summary of the letter. On 4 October the Michaelmas Quarter Sessions were held at Petworth before the Duke of Richmond, the Earl of Egremont, a baronet, a lieutenant-general, and several JPs. Blake's case was presented to the jury, who found true bills on charges of sedition and assault: which meant that the case would go to trial. Blake entered into a recognisance for £1,000, with two sureties in the like sum. (After Blake's case the jury found a true bill against the men of Littlehampton for rioting and rescuing a man from a press-gang.)[1]

On 7 October Blake wrote in very friendly terms to Hayley. 'Your generous & tender solicitude about your devoted rebel makes it absolutely necessary that he should trouble you with an account of his safe arrival'—back from the Sessions at Petworth, which he had attended. Catherine was in poor health. Art was flourishing in London and engravers in particular were in demand; but no one gave Blake any jobs. 'I suppose I must go a Courting, which I shall do awkwardly; in the meantime I lose no moment to complete Romney to satisfaction.' He, a practised and studious lover of art, now fifty years old (actually forty-six), is ignored while young untried craftsmen are sought out.

Yet I laugh and sing, for if on Earth neglected I am in heaven a Prince among Princes, & even on Earth beloved by the Good as a Good Man; this I should be perfectly contented with, but at certain periods a blaze of reputation arises around me in which I am consider'd as one distinguish'd by some mental perfection, but the flame soon dies again & I am left stupefied and astonish'd. O that I could live as others do in a regular succession of Employment, this wish I fear is not to be accomplish'd to me.

What were the high moments of reputation it is hard to make out. For a while there was discussion about him when he got the Young commission, and there must have been moments when Fuseli or Flaxman praised him; but that was all. The wild hopes, expressed in the letter to his brother about the huge fortune he will make, have now quite faded out.

On 26 October he again wrote to Hayley about his quest for some Romney paintings. He has been asked to do two engravings to Shakespeare, and Johnson has said there was no lack of work. But Evans had given him 'small hopes of the ballads'. Catherine was still in poor health. In late November Lady Hesketh, who had never liked him or his work, wrote to Hayley that she had reason to believe that he was 'more *Seriously* to blame than you were at all aware of' in the Scolfield affair. Meanwhile Flaxman had got him an odd job, and on 13 December he wrote to Hayley more about his quest for Romney works. 'My wife is better; we are very anxious about Miss Poole's health.' On the same day R. Dally, a Chichester solicitor, working on Blake's case, wrote to the Clerk of Peace for a copy of the indictment.[2]

On the first day of 1804 Hayley wrote to Johnny Johnson, hoping that he would arrive to hear the barrister Rose 'eloquently & successfully defend our interesting artist'. Next day he added the news that 'a new stout & tall Horse fell suddenly in his Canter & had I not luckily had on a new strong Hat my skull would have been smashed by a Flint—as it is I have a little Cut in the Forehead'. That day Flaxman wrote to him that he felt sure the Bill against Blake would be thrown out, but his 'irritability as well as the Association & arrangement of his ideas do not seem likely to be soothed or more advantageously disposed by any power inferior to That by which man is originally endowed with his faculties'. He thinks that Romney's cartoon should be etched in a bold manner 'which I think Blake is likely to do with great success & perhaps at an expense that will not be burthensome—but at any rate give him one to do first for a tryal'. He is amiably trying to help Blake and lessen the effect of his demand for higher prices, and sees him as affected by irritability.[3]

Blake no doubt went to Felpham a few days before the trial. As gifts he took Hayley an essay by Flaxman on bas-reliefs and his own Fuseli engraving for the Shakespeare book. On 11 January the trial took place in the Chichester

Guildhall, which had been the choir of a monastery church, before the Duke of Richmond and six magistrates. One of the latter, Poyntz, may have been well disposed, as in 1802 there had been a proposal for Blake to engrave a drawing for him. Two others Blake used in *Jerusalem*: Peachey and Quantock (spelt in the poem Gwantock, Hwantoke, Guantock, Kwantok). We have a transcript of Rose's speech for the defence, which was said to be taken down in shorthand. It praised Blake's patriotism and saw the charge as one of most extraordinary malignity. Lauding Blake and Hayley, it stressed Scolfield's reduction to the ranks for drunkenness, and argued that he had accused Blake of bursting into sedition before any words were exchanged; that the man working in the garden not more than ten square yards away had not heard him; that the soldiers contradicted one another—Scolfield saying that the seditions were all spoken in the garden, and Cock that they were spoken before the inn, where Mrs Grinder would have heard them. 'I will call these witnesses and you shall hear their account—you will then agree with me that they totally overthrow the testimony of these Soldiers.'

At this point Rose seems to have broken down. Hayley says, 'In the midst of his defence a sudden illness seiz'd Him, & altho' he maintained his station, He ended his Speech with apparent Infirmity—but he had gained his Cause. —The verdict of the Jury was in favour of his calumniated client.' The exultation of Hayley was great; and the greater because he had observed, with concern & indignation, that the chairman of the Sessions, the old Duke of Richmond, was bitterly prejudiced against Blake and had made some unwarrantable observations in the course of the trial that might have excited prejudice in the jury. As soon as their verdict was given, Hayley approached the duke and said: 'I congratulate your Grace, that after having been wearied with the condemnation of sorry vagrants, you have at last had the gratification of seeing an honest man honourably delivered from an infamous persecution. Mr Blake is a pacific, industrious, & deserving artist.' The Duke replied, rather impolitely, 'I know nothing of him.' 'True, my Lord,' rejoined Hayley. 'Your grace can know nothing of him; and I have therefore given you this information. I wish your Grace good night.'

It was late in the evening; and as Miss Poole, anxious and ill, had not been able to attend, the others went to sup with her at Lavant. At the trial the soldiers had not stood up well to cross-examination, while Hayley and others testified to Blake's gentle disposition. Under the rules neither Blake nor his wife could be called to testify, but Blake volunteered. A young man then present declared in later years that the only thing he remembered was Blake's flashing eye. Catherine was not there, but she used to tell 'how, in the middle of the trial, when the soldier invented something to support his case, her husband called out "False!" with characteristic vehemence, and in a tone which electrified the whole court and carried conviction with it'. Even though his radical past was not raised, he would probably have been found guilty under a chairman like the duke but for the support of men like Hayley and Rose. The *Sussex Weekly Advertiser* of 16 January reported that 'after a very long and patient hearing' Blake was acquitted by the jury, 'which so gratified the auditory, that the court was, in defiance of all decency, thrown into an uproar by the noisy exultations'. The cold that attacked Rose supplied the basis, says Hayley, for the rheumatic fever that killed him before the year was out.

Immediately on his arrival back in London Blake wrote to Hayley with prayers for Mrs Poole's health. As for Hayley: 'Gratitude is Heaven itself; there could be no heaven without Gratitude. I feel it & I know it. I thank God & Man for it & above all You, My dear friend & benefactor in the Lord.' (Yet he could later write that Hayley hired a Villain, that is, Scolfield, to bereave his life.) He begs him not mount again the horse that threw him, citing the remarks made by an old soldier in the coach, that not even the most expert rider should attempt a trooper's horse, 'they are taught so many tricks'. He has already seen Flaxman and is to see Johnson in the afternoon. 'My poor wife has been near the Gate of Death as was supposed by our kind & attentive fellow inhabitant, the young & very amiable Mrs Enoch, who gave my wife all the attention that a daughter could pay to a mother, but my arrival has dispell'd the formidable malady & my dear & good woman again begins to resume her health & strength.' On the 18th Hayley wrote to Johnny Johnson that Blake's letter had been 'so full of the most cordial Gratitude & Felicity on his safe return to his anxious Wife, that no feeling Mortal could read it without Tears'.

The quest for Romneys went on. On the 27th Blake wrote that he been confined to his room for a week with a bad cold.* In his search for Romneys

---

* The same day Johnny Johnson sent Hayley 'a thousand thanks and huzzas, for yr. letter, about poor dear Blake'. Greatheed wrote: 'Gratitude and my deference for Genius in every situation' had stirred him on reading a brief newspaper report of Blake's trial. 'I knew our friend's eccentricity, and understood that, during the crisis of the French Revolution, he had been one of its earnest partisans; but of everything else I remain ignorant.' He recalled Blake's concern when the horse he had been riding at Feltham came home riderless. About this time Cowper wrote to Lady Hesketh of his Cowper monument. Blake had told him that the plaster model in Flaxman's studio was 'universally admired for its elegant simplicity'.

he was trying to locate Lady Hamilton, and was in high spirits. He had taken a present from Hayley to Rose, no doubt a cheque, with a laudatory sonnet that he had copied out in his best copperplate hand.

My Wife gets better every Day: hope earnestly that you have entirely escaped the brush of my Evil Star, which I believe is now for ever fallen into the Abyss—God bless & preserve You and our Good Lady Paulina with the Good things both of this life & of eternity & with you my much admired & respected Edward the Bard of Oxford [apparently Edward March of Oriel College] whose verses still sound upon my Ear like the distant approach of things mighty and magnificent; like the sound of harps which I hear before the Sun's rising, like the remembrance of Felpham's waves & the Glorious & far beaming Turret, like the Villa of Lavant, blessed & blessing.[4]

On 23 February Blake had still not finished the Cowper plates and was chasing after collectors with Romney works. One man had shown him the 'very fine portrait of Mrs Siddons as the Tragic Muse' and assured him that he 'knew immediately my Portrait of Romney'. (Blake does not seem to have known that the Mrs Siddons was by the detested Reynolds.) Rose was too ill to be seen. As for Flaxman, 'he has never yet, since my return to London, had the time or grace to call on me'. On 12 March the plates were almost done. (The Blakes, as always, asked after Miss Poole.) On the 16th proofs were at last sent, but without the final touches. Blake was still running around. He had called on Flaxman and the painter Prince Hoare, but neither was at home. Rose was said to be getting better.[5]

On 21 March Blake was still on his Romney quest. He sent two proofs of each of the two plates, but lacked paper for the dozen required; also he still wanted to work further on the plates. Hayley grew worried as he had promised copies of his book to friends. He begged for the prints by the 27th. On Saturday the 31st Blake still had not sent them, but promised they would go on the Tuesday coach. On Sunday Hayley, before getting Blake's letter, wrote to Rose that he and Seagrave were in extreme consternation at Blake's remissness; he feared that a fire reported in the papers as destroying many of Sharp's plates might have done the same to Blake's, for the latter had said he was having the plates printed at the workshop in question. 'Perhaps his little parcel is only loitering in the Coach office in London—I am weary of conjectures.' Then he added the news that Blake's letter had come and all was well. Blake did send off the prints on the 2nd, but twelve and not fifteen copies, pleading lack of paper. He was to do two plates for Flaxman's Homer and was worried about £15 he had sent to Dally the solicitor about a fortnight back. 'Money in these times is not to be trifled with.' He asked about Miss Poole, 'as you are silent on that most alarming and interesting topic'.

The details about the prints may seem trifling; but this is the only period in which we have anything like a day-to-day record of Blake's doings. Unless we had this precise information about his slowness and unreliability as a craftsman, we should have to take at their face value his own remarks about his unremitting industry. But a new project came up, and on the 7th he wrote to Hayley about it: a new kind of periodical to be issued by Richard Phillips, who owned the *Monthly Magazine* and had been jailed in 1793 for selling Paine's works. Blake, though unclear as to the project, was very keen about it and tried to flatter Hayley into taking the editorship. 'You can have no idea, unless you are in London as I am, how much your Name is lov'd & respected.' He adds 'Literature is your Child', and tries to explain the project or what he hoped it would turn into. 'Knowing your aversion to Reviews & Reviewing I consider this present proposal as peculiarly adapted to your Ideas; it may be call'd a Defence of Literature against those pests of the Press & a Bulwark for Genius, which shall with your good assistance disperse these Rebellious Spirits of Envy & Malignity.' Phillips too wrote to Hayley, who rejected the proposal. Blake however wrote again in a vain attempt to win him over. He also asked for an early notice of what was to be engraved for the Romney, as 'endless work is the true title of engraving'. He was happy that Miss Poole was 'again in such health as when she first mounted me on my beloved Bruno', the pony.*

On 1 May Flaxman, receiving his Cowper copy, thanked Hayley for helping Blake at the trial. He tries to be tactful about Blake and his prices. The latter is to get five or six guineas for each Homer design; but Flaxman says that he is not sure what should be the payment for more finished plates. He suggests for the Romney book two or three 'bold etchings shadowed on a small scale, in which Blake has succeeded admirably sometimes', plus outline designs for head and tail pieces. On the 4th Blake told Hayley he was still running about on Romney errands, talking to a collector and the old print-seller Boydell. 'You would have been pleas'd to see his eyes light up at the mention of your name.' Blake thanked Hayley for the *Shipwreck* of Falconer, 'an admirable poet, and the admirable prints to it by Fitler', from which he

---

* Blake's private opinion of Phillips appears in the epigram where he says that Phillips loved his friends only so that he might use them 'to serve his Ends'. He loved Blake 'for no Gain at all But to rejoice & triumph in my fall'.

could get some 'excellent hints'. Rose was not well, but looked 'tolerably, considering the terrible storm he has been thro' '. He, Blake, was getting five guineas each for the Homer designs. 'Mr. Flaxman agrees with me that some-what more than an outline is necessary for the execution of Romney's designs, because his merit is eminent in the art of massing his lights and shadows.' (Later Blake was to attack chiaroscuro.) He does his best to be ingratiating and conventionally patriotic in praising Hayley for his 'very beautiful little poem on the King's recovery; it is one of the prettiest things I ever read, and I hope the king will live to fulfill the prophecy and die at peace; but, at present, poor man, I understand he is poorly indeed, and times threaten worse than ever'. Sad stuff indeed for the author of *Tiriel*, *Europe*, and the *Four Zoas* to write; but he is determined to prove how unseditious he is. Catherine, he adds, is still stiff-knee'd, but well in other respects'.[6]

On the 5th Rose wrote to his father-in-law that he had been 'magnificently remunerated by Hayley' for his work at the trial. On the 28th Blake made more reports to Hayley on his Romney quest and tried to revive the project of the periodical, which he had discussed with Carr. Much of the letter was taken in describing Johnson's efforts to get the printing and publishing of Hayley's books away from Seagrave. He sums up: 'I will venture to give it as my settled opinion that if you suffer yourself to be persuaded to print in London you will be cheated every way.' In London every calumny and false-hood uttered against another of the same trade is thought fair play. 'Engravers, Painters, Statuaries, Printers, Poets, we are not in a field of battle, but in a City of Assassinations. That makes your lot truly enviable, and the country is not only more beautiful on account of its expanded Meadows, but also on account of its benevolent minds.'

Commenting on a Life of Washington, he says, 'As the French now adore Buonaparte and the English our poor George; so the Americans will consider Washington as their god. This is only Grecian, or rather Trojan, worship, and perhaps will be revised [?] in an age or two. In the meantime I have the happiness of seeing the Divine countenance in such men as Cowper and Milton more distinctly than in any prince or hero.' Here for the first time he turns on the Greeks whom he begins to see, like Romans, as based in war.[7]

Hayley had understandably come to feel that Blake could not be relied on to do work on time. He now asked Flaxman to find other engravers for the Romney *Life*. On 8 June Flaxman replied that he had thought of Caroline Watson, but felt it advisable to consult a leading engraver. He was told that she engraved 'in the dotted manner only, which is not fit for the decoration of

Books', and her lowest price would be 35 guineas. Hayley felt uncomfortable about telling Blake of his decision, and the latter reported on 22 June that he had located three more Romneys. He repeated that finished engravings, not outlines, were needed; and remarked that his old partner Parker had just turned down the offer of 400 guineas for a plate; other good engravers were all so busy they would be 'hardly prevail'd upon to undertake more than One of the plates on so short a notice'. After thus having tried to create an atmosphere of high prices, with no one except himself available for the work, he agreed to accept Hayley's prices. 'My wife continues to get better, & joins me in my warmest love & acknowledgments to you, as do my Brother & Sister.' Clearly the latter pair had been more often at Felpham than we know.

But meanwhile Hayley was discussing his plans with Flaxman. Flaxman reported that he had seen two miserably executed heads by Miss Watson, and wanted Hayley himself to carry on any further negotiations. Obviously he did not want to act behind Blake's back. Hayley at once replied, using a semi-literate amenuensis. (He was probably not well; Blake had acted as amenuensis for him at Felpham when he was ill.) Hayley cited Blake on London as a City of Assassinations, and said he would rely on Flaxman's judgment. He was ready to use the engraver Cromek at a fee of 25 guineas; but the picture to be done was one of three in Blake's possession and he would be sorry to risk 'wounding the Feelings of our quick-spirited Friend' by asking him to send it to some other engraver.[8]

We have only summaries of Blake's next two letters. He praised the *Letters* of the wife of the German poet Klopstock and said that the novelist Samuel Richardson had won his heart. Flaxman wrote to Hayley that Cromek was busy and much sought after. In the end Miss Watson engraved seven plates while Blake did only one, the 'Shipwreck'. He told Hayley that only the best artists should be used for Romney and added, 'Money flies from me. Profit never ventures upon my Threshold, tho' every other man's doorstone is worn down into the very Earth by the footsteps of the fiends of commerce.' He sent Hayley some books and proof of the 'Shipwreck'. In the Strand he had met Spilsbury (probably Jonathan, brother of the engraver John) who said he had given up painting as a profession but would practice it for himself. Blake applauded him for turning from 'the drudgery of fashionable daubing'. He asked Hayley for £10 to carry him through the 'Shipwreck' and the head of Romney, 'for which I am already paid'. Chetwynd of Felpham days had called on him with his brother. Another acquaintance that Blake had made was B. H. Malkin, a London schoolmaster and enthusiast for the picturesque. Malkin was a radical, for Godwin met him dining at Horne Tooke's in 1796–7 and at Fuseli's Milton Gallery on 17 May 1800 with Fuseli, Johnson, Flaxman and Smith.

Blake at his lodgings in South Molton Street had at once noted the ominous fact that the street ran into Tyburn Road (Oxford Street) and thus led to 'Tyburn's fatal tree' and the park of military reviews. On a plate interposed near the beginning of *Milton* he wrote: 'Between South Molton Street & Stratford Place, Calvary's foot, Where the victims were preparing for sacrifice'. He thus saw himself on a spot symbolically representing the Cross and the Tree of State-Murder. In *Jerusalem* he describes nights of anguished fear, with his wife listening to his self-communings. 'He hid her from the spectre, in shame & confusion of face. In terrors & pains of Hell & Eternal Death, the Trembling Globe shot forth Self-living & Los howld over it.' The Globe is Catherine–Enitharmon separating herself from him. 'And the Spectrous Darkness from his back divided in temptations, And in grinding agonies in threats . . .' And so on in endless despair. He cannot forget Scolfield. 'Go thou to Skofield . . . Tell him to be no more dubious: demand explicit words.' Scolfield, he cries, is his (Blake's) minister of evil to those he hates. 'For I can hate as well as they.'

Here is the sort of thing that was seething in his mind as he sought to play a rational role with Hayley or Flaxman. The watch-fiends are all round him, trying to catch him out. He is tormented by the need to hide from them what he thinks and writes. Once he uses reversed script that has to be read in a mirror; but what he has written is: 'Contraries are Positives. A Negation is not a Contrary'. After all their prying the watch-fiends (the informers, the police) will only read that they are a negation, a non-existence. In more mirror-writing he draws attention to a page where, he says, the watch-fiends will never be able to find out his meaning. 'There is a grain of sand in Lambeth that Satan cannot find Nor his watch-fiends find it.' Lambeth seems here to refer, not to the Lambeth prophecies, but to its vale as a centre of inspiration. The right kind of reader, Blake goes on, will however find his way of entering into freedom (Oothoon's palace), into redeemed earth and heaven (Vala and Jerusalem). Watch-fiends will only call it sin and 'lay its Heaven in blood of punishment'. In such a nerve-wracked state he was keyed up to look for a sign from outside pointing in a new direction and giving him the conviction of a new birth, a secure liberation. It was soon to come.

On 23 October he wrote to Hayley that he was happy to hear of Miss Poole's bettered condition. 'My wife returns her heartfelt thanks for your kind inquiry concerning her health. She is surprisingly recovered.' She had taken Birch's electrical treatment. 'Electricity is the wonderful cause; the swelling of her legs and knees is entirely reduced.' He hopes to see Hawkins, who is in town. Then comes his outburst, his account of the revelation which he believes has restored him to his original purposes and enabled him to defeat the attacking spectre. He first sees the experience as breaking down the division between him and his Emanation–Catherine. The wrong kind of art is seen as linked with the gods of the Greeks, who represent tyranny and war, and who prevent harmony in married life. 'For now! O Glory! and O Delight! I have entirely reduced that spectrous Fiend to his last station, whose annoyance has been the ruin of my labours for the last passed twenty years of my life. He is the enemy of conjugal love and is the Jupiter of the Greeks, an iron-hearted tyrant, the ruiner of ancient Greece. I speak with perfect confidence and certainty of the fact which has passed upon me.'

Then he explains what the experience in fact has been. He has visited the Truchsessian Gallery and seen the pictures owned by Count Truchsess, who claimed to have lost a large fortune in the French Revolution and who tried to set up a company to buy his pictures as the basis of a permanent exhibition. The count had opened his show in August 1803. Passavant in his *Tour of a German Artist in England* says, 'It included a copy of Van Eyck's Ghent altarpiece, Petrus Christus' *Virgin and Child with Saints*, as well as works attributed to Memling, Antonina de Messina, Schöngauer.' Looking at these works, Blake was suddenly convinced that he had taken the wrong turn just twenty years before, when he opened his print-shop with Parker in 1784. 'Every one of my friends was astonished at my faults, and could not assign a reason; they knew my industry and abstinence from every pleasure for the sake of study, and yet—and yet—and yet there wanted the proof of industry in my works. I thank God with entire confidence that it shall be so no longer —he is become my servant who domineered over me, he is even as a brother who was my enemy. Dear Sir, excuse my enthusiasm or rather madness, for I am really drunk with intellectual vision whenever I take a pencil or graver into my hand, as I used to be in my youth . . .'

The pictures in the Gallery were by no means what the Count claimed them to be. Farington on 21 August 1803 records:

Lawrence has been this morning to see the exhibition of Count Truchesis [*sic*] pictures near the New Road, Marybone. He gave a most unfavourable account of them—saying there was scarcely an original picture of a Great Master among them . . . There are 1,000 pictures & Lawrence does not think the whole lot worth £2,000. The Count values them at £60,000.

The fact that they were copies, even inferior ones, would not have bothered Blake, who was not interested in the handling of pigment, in painterly qualities. What mattered for him was the idea and the general approach to form. The pictures helped him to get back to the strong medieval elements which had been one component of his early art-outlook, and to give up any ideas of trying to master texture, colour, chiaroscuro in the tradition of oil-painting. At the same time they helped him to complete his revolt against the Greeks and Romans. Logically he should now have scorned the works which a few years back he had told Butts were great masterpieces, and should have made a radically new start. That however was not what occurred. His experience did have a powerful effect upon him, but in complex and devious ways. In estimating the strains he went through in 1803–4 we must take into account Catherine's bad health. If she had died, it is hard to see how he could have carried on.[9]

In a letter of 4 December to Hayley, after praising 'our noble Flaxman', he again expressed his sense of new birth. 'I have indeed fought thro' a Hell of terrors and horrors (which none could know but myself) in a divided existence; now no longer divided nor at war with myself, I shall travel on the strength of the Lord God, as Poor Pilgrim says'—his first known reference to Bunyan's work. Such statements of his are not mere rhetoric; he had to fight through ceaseless nervous fear to survive and to carry on.*

On 18 December Blake wrote about the proofs of his two plates, stressing the approval of the Flaxmans for the 'Shipwreck' and the need to do yet more work on the portrait. 'I must solicit for a supply of money and hope you will be convinced that the labour I have used on the two plates has left me without any resource but that of applying to you. I am again in want of ten pounds.' He remarks that Johnson pays 25 guineas for each plate in Fuseli's Shakespeare, the concluding numbers of which he sends so that the plates may be compared with his 'Shipwreck'. 'Your beautiful and elegant daughter Venesea' (Hayley's poem *Venusia* published by Seagrave) 'grows

---

* Hayley was having some qualms about Blake and the fees he paid to engravers. He asked Flaxman about the possibility of using Sharp. Flaxman wrote, 'You can have little need to dwell on your friend's [Rose's] illness as an apology for not having been liberal to the artists employed in Romney's life.' Sharp was a difficult man. Parker was capable, also the engravers in Bowyer's *History of England*. Flaxman did not know what they charged.

in our estimation on a second and third perusal.' He seems to have a genuine nostalgia for his Sussex days.

My wife joins me in wishing you a merry Christmas. Remembering our happy Christmas at lovely Felpham, our spirits seem still to hover round our sweet cottage and round the beautiful Turret. I have said *seem*, but am persuaded that distance is nothing but a phantasy. We are often sitting by our cottage fire, and often we think we hear your voice calling at the gate. Surely these things are real and eternal in our eternal mind and can never pass away. My wife continues well, thanks to Mr. Birch's Electrical Magic, which she has discontinued these three months.

On 28 December he writes about Rose's death, adding much grateful praise of him and thanking Hayley for ten pounds. On checking his accounts, he finds that Hayley was right in saying that the full sum had already been paid. So now he owes Hayley twelve guineas. He discourses at length about some Romney drawings and the portrait on which he is still working.

It is hard to allot any poems definitely to the Felpham years, but it seems likely that especially in the last year or so he regained his lyric powers, now with a much more complex content. On the other hand we have simple country-ballads, such as *Mary*, in which occurs the line, 'O why was I born with a different face?' When he used that line in the letter to Butts he was no doubt recalling the poem. There is also the bawdy *Long John Brown & Little Mary Bell*, where fairy and devil appear without any abstruse meanings. Felpham probably started him off on his *Auguries of Innocence*, behind the aphoristic couplets of which we feel folk-rhymes such as the Cornish: 'Hurt a robin or a wran, Never prosper, boy or man'. By its nature, however, this is a poem to which couplets could be added at any time, though there is a climax in the glorification of the principle of energy in the human form. The whore and the gambler may have intruded after the return to London.[10]

I saw a Monk may have come from broodings on his trial and the resumption of war. It tells of the tortured defender of peace who will not surrender or recant; the Chichester trial is defined as a martyrdom. At times the style is close to that of *Auguries*. The hero now is not the fiery Orc but the passive resister. 'The hermit's prayer and the widow's tear Alone can free the world from fear . . . A tear is an intellectual thing, And a sigh is the sword of an Angel King.' Charlemagne is used as a type of the martial king, and Gibbon, Voltaire, Rousseau are seen as the rationalising defenders of power. A passage in *Jerusalem* (52) explains: Deists 'charge the poor Monks & Religious with being the causes of war: while they acquit & flatter the Alexanders & Caesars, the Lewis's & Fredericks: who alone are its causes & its actors'. They praised the mighty of the state, Gibbon as historian of the Roman Empire and Voltaire as friend of Frederick the Great. Though they attacked the superstitions that buttress tyrannies, the mystery they knocked down arose up afresh in their own abstractions. (Similarly, in the *Four Zoas*, dealing with Robespierre's religious projects, Blake says that the only result was that Satan divided against Satan.) His personal fears appear in the way he changed 'Seditious Monk' to 'Thou lazy Monk' when he used the poem in *Jerusalem*.

The Mental Traveller probably also comes from this period; it is the one lyric in which is compressed a set of ideas analogous to those in a Prophetic Book. It deals with the disastrous effect of the female principle on the individual, on society, on history: depicting its action as a cyclic movement which yet spirals into change. At that principle's core lies the possessiveness that exploits and destroys. It is linked with gold: the mother numbers the child's nerves as a miser his gold, and gems and gold are meat and drink to the corrupted man. The ghastly possessive relationship is repeated in mother and child, in the lovers who try to start a new life. Despite the pretence of romance the lovers fall back into the old pattern of parasitism. As usual Blake fuses inner and outer effects, the social and the spiritual. Out of the struggles of man and woman preying on one another, history moves forward. Another civilisation is created, but, betrayed at every point, it loses its human value. Yet every birth holds the potentiality of revolutionary change; each babe is both Orc and Christ. But at once the old woman, the female principle as jealousy and possessiveness, sets to work to break down that potentiality. The cottage-setting suggests Felpham.[11]

One moment of the cycle is defined in *The Crystal Cabinet*. Here the ardours of love seem to transform the world, making it in fact Beulah, the moment when the dialectical resolution of conflict seems achieved, but is in fact unstable, partly subjective. A life based solely on personal love must founder. Its enclosed nature ensures that, whatever the romantic pretences, the parasitic element will reassert itself: which for Blake means the dominance of the female will. Behind the poem may well lie his hopes and disappointments on returning to London. He and Catherine have come from the wilds of Sussex in the hope of finding another Lambeth, 'another pleasant Surrey bower', but the dream of inner and outer harmony breaks down. The

'Weeping Woman pale reclind' is then Catherine still sick and depressed; under her discontents he cannot sustain his hopes, which anyway had no real basis. He cannot remain in his private dream, his crystal cabinet. The other side of his divided being appears: 'My Spectre around me night & day Like a Wild beast guards my way. My Emanation far within weeps incessantly for my Sin'. He still sees the solution in turning from female love. Till that is done, 'I shall never worthy be To step into Eternity', where is only forgiveness. Forgiveness for Blake is an active or transformative process, bringing about a state of being that transcends what is forgiven. So to turn from female love in eternity means the achievement of a new kind of love, a love that has gone beyond the situation where forgiveness was required.

The poem is tense with a sense of pity for Catherine, of bitter conflict with her. She argues: 'What transgressions I commit Are for thy transgressions fit; They thy harlots, thou their slave, And my bed becomes their grave'. He replies: 'Poor pale pitiable form That I follow in a storm, Iron tears and groans of lead Bind around my aching head'. The woman must submit. 'The woman that does not love your frowns will never endure your smiles.' Blake found it hard to grapple with the poem's material; the many deletions and additions show his difficulty in objectifying his torment. The reference to downs suggests that he was writing at Felpham. (We have already noted that the casting out of the spirit of self-righteousness is expressed in terms similar to those used by the Ranter Coppe.)

We now come to the epical poem *Milton*. Whether or not Blake began it in his last days at Felpham we cannot determine; what is important is that the Felpham period supplies its material and the poem is an attempt to sum up all that he had then learned and put it in a prophetic focus. There had been a sense in which all along his own experiences underlay the prophecies; but here there is a far more direct relation. Blake explores Milton's expression, which represents the highest level of consciousness generated by the Cromwellian revolution as his own prophecies represent the highest level generated by the French Revolution, Blake is thus himself Milton, but Milton operating at a more advanced stage of history, poetry, prophecy. A key-character is Ololon, who stands for the unity of Milton's sixfold emanations, the reality underlying his erroneous ideas about women. He comes down from heaven to earth to recover her. (To get the right ideas about women also means to get the right ideas about revolution, history, human development.) Ololon has not yet a definite form, and she and Milton go through many states, with

7

the climax when she meets the twenty-eighth lark as she descends into Blake's Felpham garden. She looks like a virgin of twelve years just become nubile as she enters the Polypus (society in a fallen state). The moon-number of twenty-eight may mean that she now menstruates, has become a full woman. Blake explains that Los, when joining him, whirled him up from Lambeth and set him down at Felpham, where he 'prepar'd a beautiful Cottage for me, that in three years time I might write all these Visions To display Nature's cruel holiness, the deceits of Natural Religion. Walking in my Cottage Garden, sudden I beheld the Virgin Ololon & address'd her as a Daughter of Beulah'. Asking her into the cottage, he inquired what her message was. 'What am I to do now? Is it again to plunge into deeper affliction? behold me Ready to obey, but pity thou my Shadow of Delight: Enter my Cottage, comfort her, for she is sick with fatigue.' Blake thus dates the inspiration of *Milton* to his last days at Felpham. The design shows him walking in the garden as Ololon comes down.*

The book's title-page, like that of *Jerusalem*, has the date 1804, which suggests that the two works were planned together, though not finished in their extant form for many years. The advent of Ololon, in a moment of lark-inspiration, is linked with Catherine's illness; the resolution of Milton's problems, objectified in Ololon, is linked with the resolution of Blake's own sexual, poetic and political problems.[12]

An important aspect of Milton's impact on the eighteenth century had been the feeling that epic poetry should somehow be revived in order to express a world-view capable of reasserting human significance in face of the advance of mechanistic science. So we find the Newtonian system intruding in all the more serious poetic systems of the century, from Thomson's *Seasons* to Young's *Night Thoughts* or Darwin's poems. Such works attempted a new synthesis of science and human purpose. Blake more consciously than these other poets recognised that the challenge of Milton was inseparable from the challenge of Newton. The call for a new kind of epic was in turn linked with the sapping of Christian dogma by Biblical

---

* Blake links *Milton* with his Lambeth days when describing how Los bound his sandals on in Udan-Adan (sphere of formlessness, with Los's Golgonooza of art-construction on its verge and with the mills of Satan and Beelzebub on its islands and margins, round the roots of Urizen's Tree). 'Trembling I stood Exceedingly, with fear and terror, standing in the vale of Lambeth.' Blake defines a moment of deep choice and decision. Los has left Golgonooza to find Milton; with his descent Milton's spirit has entered into him. So he appears to Blake, Milton's counterpart in the world of the French Revolution. Lambeth is simply used as the symbolic site of the inspiration.

criticism, especially German, and with the attempt to give the Bible a new life by harmonising it with other mythologies, especially the Eastern ones that became more and more known with the expansion of trade. Robert Lowth's *Lectures on the Sacred Poetry of the Hebrews* (in Latin, 1794–50), which for the first time considered the Old Testament simply as literature, as Oriental literature, had a profound effect and ultimately underlay such efforts as those of Blake to treat the Bible as a source of poetic symbolism. The Unitarian movement had a special liking for Biblical criticism; its middle-class sections responded to the Germans, e.g. T. Belsham, who founded the Unitarian Book Society in 1791—though German influences went much further back, e.g. in N. Lardner, who died in 1768 and whom Coleridge read. Among the worker radicals the response was rather to the French: de la Metrie, Voltaire, Volney.

Many of the advanced ideas of the period were set out in Hayley's *Life of Milton*, 1796, and his *Essay on Epic Poetry*, 1782. Hayley tried to rescue Milton from such prevailing poetic canons as those laid down by Dr Johnson; he saw Milton as 'a poet of the most powerful, and, perhaps, the most independent mind that was ever given to a mere mortal'. Milton differed from Homer in that his two epics showed 'an abhorrence for the atrocious absurdity of ordinary war'; they thus revealed a purer religion and a 'greater force of imagination'. He spoke of Milton returning to earth: 'I am persuaded his attachment to truth was as sincere and fervent as that of honest Montaigne, who says: "I would come again with all my heart from the other world to give any one the lie, who should report me other than I was, though he did it to honour me". '

Milton, adorned with every graceful endowment, highly and holily accomplished as he was, appears, in the dark colouring of Johnson a most amiable character; but could he revisit earth in his mortal character, with a wish to retaliate, what a picture might be drawn, by that sublime and offended genius, of the great moralist, who has treated him with such asperity.

These passages may well have started Blake off thinking of a poem in which Milton returned to vindicate himself, to discover his own full purpose. Hayley's comment on Homer may also have started Blake off on his criticism of the Greeks and Romans as based in war.

In the Monk poem he wrote: 'A Grecian Scoff is a wracking wheel. The Roman pride is a sword of steel. Glory and Victory a phallic whip'. And he set out his revulsion in the *Milton* Prefaces. 'We do not want either Greek or Roman models . . . The Daughters of Memory shall become the Daughters of Inspiration'. In thus rejecting the Greek myth of Mnemosyne as mother of the Muses, he may be drawing on the distinction made by Milton in his *Reason of Church-Government*.

Despite the conventional diction and metre of Hayley's *Essay on Epic Poetry*, Blake would have found many congenial comments. Poetry, 'endu'd with energy sublime, Unquestion'd arbiter of space and time! Canst join the distant, the unknown create', pouring myriads of forms on the astonished mind. Hayley insists on new unrealised possibilities in epic. Critics may think that Heaven and Hell can yield the form nothing more, 'Yet may she dive to many a secret source And copious springs of visionary force: India yet holds a Mythologic mine, Her strength may open, and her art refine.' Hayley suggests that the future of the epic lies in England, where the poets 'steer by Freedom's star to Glory's port'. While, led by Fancy, 'Our steps advance around her epic plain . . . And every confine of the realm explore, See Liberty, array'd in light serene, Pours her rich lustre o'er th' expanding scene!' There is a claim that the poet should free himself from 'oppressive awe' of rules and 'spurn faint allegory's feeble aid'.

Blake may then have found the *Essay* stimulating. Not that he owed anything important to it except that, when he read it at Felpham, it may have done much to direct his thoughts to Milton and then to the difference between Milton and himself, Milton and Hayley. In *Milton* the opening song of the Bard remodels the myth of the Fall of Satan to define Hayley's relations with Blake. Satan's error has been to take on activities that are not truly his. Arrogance and self-righteousness then shut him out from heaven: deny him full consciousness of reality. The connection with Milton is established by making him realise, as he hears the Bard, that he too went wrong on the lines of Satan–Hayley. 'I in my Selfhood am that Satan; I am that evil one; He is my Spectre.' Milton then has to go through the experience of realising himself as Hayley in order to escape from his Satanhood and become a fully liberated prophet: that is, Blake: Blake as he has developed through his resolution of the conflict that Milton historically could not resolve. In one sense this means the representation of the conflict between Hayley and Blake as a conflict between their concepts of Milton. In the working-out, however, Blake cannot resist giving his Satan some minor characteristics that belong to Hayley alone. He says 'unkind things in kindness' and does 'the most irritating things in the midst of tears & love'. Also, Blake unfairly blames Hayley as being responsible for all evil: 'Glorying to involve Albions Body in fires of eternal War'.[13]

Blake begins his poem by defining three classes of men: the Elect, the Redeemed, the Reprobate. He inverts the usual meaning of the terms in an Antinomian way. The Elect are the self-righteous, sure that they incarnate the Law. The Redeemed are those saved by Jesus, the Reprobate are the transgressors of the Law; these two are linked as contraries and act creatively, obeying impulse and inspiration. Jesus is the typical Reprobate, never losing faith for a moment, while the Redeemed are perpetually tormented by the Elect. Satan–Hayley is a pure example of the Elect. 'With incomparable mildness, his primitive tyrannical attempts on Los, with most endearing love He soft intreated Los to give him Palambron's Station.' Palambron like Satan–Hayley is a son of Los; here he stands for Blake. Palambron–Blake is a hard worker, coming home 'with labour wearied every evening'. At last Los hands over to Satan 'the harrow of the Almighty'. Satan harrows all day (a thousand years), and next morning Palambron finds the horses maddened, and the Gnomes, servants of the harrow, accuse Satan. Palambron denounces Satan–Hayley:

> You know Satan's mildness and his self-imposition.
> Seeming a brother, being a tyrant, even thinking himself a
>   brother
> While he is murdering the just: prophetic I behold
> His future course thro' darkness and despair to eternal death.
> But we must not be tyrants also: he hath assumed my place
> For one whole day under pretence of pity and love to me.
> My horses he hath madden'd and my fellow servants injur'd,
> How should he, he, know the duties of another?[14]

Satan replies; 'mildly cursing Palambron, him accused of crimes Himself had wrought'. Believing his own words, he almost wins Los over. Los falls back on the order that everyone must stay in his own station and not act 'in pity false' or 'in officious brotherhood'. But Satan still accuses his brother. Finding his own neglected mills in a bad way, he returns to Los with fresh charges. Los takes the blame on himself. (The harrow here stands for an engraving tool; the mills are Hayley's manufacturing system for churning out verses and art, though they have the wider link with the Satanic mills that exploit the masses. But as usual with Blake there is not only one level of interpretation. He also surrounds Milton–Hayley with themes from the

Cromwellian revolution, the impasse of which is linked with Milton's abstract side as a poet. Satan appears as Cromwell taking over Parliament and diverting the harrow from its function of revolutionary harrowing, and so on.)

The conflict extends. Palambron calls a great solemn assembly in eternity. The political aspects take over. Satan draws out 'his infernal scroll of Moral laws & cruel punishments upon the clouds of Jehovah'. The abyss opening into the state of Satan is Ulro, sheer abstraction and mechanism. Los and then Enitharmon realise that Satan is Urizen. The political aspects expand into social and cultural ones. The moral law and the State, with all their ideological extensions, again dominate. Leutha (emanation of Bromion) intrudes, representing love in a divided world, love as sin. She takes all the blame on herself. Intending to help Palambron, she 'stupefied [Satan's] masculine perceptions and kept only the feminine awake'. Thus she brings about his 'soft Delusory love to Palambron, admiration join'd with envy'. She tries to usurp the place of Palambron's wife, but cannot control his horses, which break their traces, with disastrous effects for England, for the cosmos. And so on, the relations of Hayley and Blake and those of Milton and the Revolution being merged, and Hayley's interference with Blake's marital relations being sharply attacked. As Leutha and Satan together constitute the spectre of Luvah (France), the situation is also linked with that of the French Revolution, and Leutha takes on some of the characteristics of Marie Antoinette.[15]

The Bard, at the end of his song, 'terrify'd took refuge in Milton's bosom'. Milton, hearing the song, understands that Satan's errors are his own. He leaves heaven to return to earth. His new prophetic insights enable him to correct old religious errors, and he struggles with Urizen. All the time he is moving into the present, coming to Blake and inspiring him. He is also walking, though darkened, in heaven, attended by the seven Angels of the Presence, till they are all driven out to join the watchers in Ulro. There is thus a complex narrative movement of successive actions that are also simultaneous and occur on different levels. The heavenly tribe of Ololon, who have driven Milton out, follow and meet him in Blake's cottage-garden. Here occurs the manifestation of Ololon already discussed. Milton is reunited with his emanation in true harmony and prophecy is one with history: men understand the processes that form them. The distorting veil has been rejected, but not annihilated. The poem ends with the promise of new inspirations from the regenerated spirit of Milton: through Blake's poetry and the rebirth of the revolutionary movement in all its purified vigour.

The construction of the epic reveals a series of symmetries. First, the two books balance one another, dealing with the making of the poet, then the making of the poem. Inspiration stirs the imagination and becomes the poem; the poem in the last resort is not to be distinguished from the poet. There is the song of the Bard setting out the three classes of men; the song of Beulah with its account of Contraries—each song providing the basis which the book expounds and develops. Each song is the prelude of a descent, first Milton's, then Ololon's. Each book has a vision as its climax: the first, that of the time-world, the second, that of eternity, the world of unity. There are three divisions (16 plates, 16 plates, 18 plates), each starting with a descent and ending with a union. First, the Daughters of Beulah are called on to descend the nerves of the arm into the brain, with the union of Bard and Milton. Secondly comes the descent of Milton into his own self, with the union of Milton and Blake, Los and Blake. Thirdly comes the descent of Ololon, her union with Milton. Time appears as both succession and simultaneity. The sons of Los are at work constructing history and making the earth man's home, but this extended work depends in the last resort on the creative imagination. The sons build 'Moments & Minutes & Hours And Days & Months & Years & Ages & Periods, wondrous buildings', but the act of inspiration occurs in a flash, achieving a new unity of relationships: in 'a Moment, a Pulsation of the Artery'. For in this Period 'the Poet's Work is Done, and all the Great Events of Time start forth & are conceiv'd in such a Period'. Space too has this dual aspect. The vegetable earth is but a shadow of eternity in the sense that mechanistic systems are mere flat patterns of the moment of living wholes.[16]

Book II starts with the poet and the poem symbolised by nightingale and lark. The nightingale is Milton since in *Paradise Lost* (III) he compared himself to the bird that 'sings darkling'. The lark recalls *L'Allegro*, and has here become an emblem of liberated song. At the end the poet is merged with his song, his prophetic act, and there is only the lark. Personal sufferings are lost in the rapture of creation, which makes the sufferer one with all the movements of life. The lark appears thrice: at the descent of Ololon, at her advent in the garden, and at the poet's awakening, his acceptance of his task (Blake's return to London). It is linked with wild Thyme. Lark and flower represent time and space; and on account of its name the plant has been taken to represent time: time in its wild or free creative sense as opposed to clock time.

But a case can be made for the lark as such time and the stationary plant as space. Perhaps Blake intended the ambiguity, to suggest a unity of time and space at a level incomprehensible to quantitative science.

Another point of symmetry appears in the introduction of Blake's brother Robert in the designs at the crucial moment of Milton's entry into the poet. Blake uses a mirror-image of the design that shows the star entering his own left foot. In Robert's case it enters the right foot. (The star thus enters both the lucky and the unlucky foot.) Behind William are three steps of ascent; behind Robert are four. That is, William still inhabits threefold Beulah but Robert is in fourfold eternity. In a small design we again see the star entering William's foot; further on is the stony altar of sacrifice and Catherine turning away. She has been striding towards William, but now she turns with her right arm hiding her face. Is she driven back by William's wrath just before the star-advent, or did that advent scare her? Blake uses the term 'tarsus' for the point of the star's entry, suggesting an analogy with the convulsive moment of conversion experienced by Paul of Tarsus. He probably means that the star-entry saved him from some act of persecuting wrath against his wife: a point brought out also by the stone altar between them.

The themes of perfect unity with Robert (Blake's own self in eternity) and of disunity with Hayley (the false brother) are reflected in other designs. The true brothers Palambron and Rintrah (William and Robert) turn from the treacherous Satan–Hayley. The primal break comes with the murder of Abel by Cain. The redemption of Milton makes him William's brother or other-self. The theme of *Milton* is thus from one aspect the failure or achievement of the brotherly bond. Poetic liberation is bound up with the struggle for revolutionary fraternity.[17]

At each stage in his development of prophetic poetry Blake finds himself facing an enormously extended problem of unifying his material. At each moment of advance or decline in human struggle he grows aware of an increasing variety of levels that need to be taken into consideration. Sometimes the conflicts on the different levels converge or reveal their inter-connections; at other times they obstinately carry on in their own corner of the self, society, cosmos. So we are presented with a series of more or less parallel or simultaneous movements, which come together or separate. The moment of change can be viewed from a large number of angles or per-spectives; its inner tensions can be defined in various ways. Each set of tensions, each particular focus, can yield a different picture, even if all the pictures become part of a single scene in the fullness of the dialectical moment.

Clearly such a method needs a remarkable degree of concentration and breadth of vision if the poet is not to fly off in apparently unrelated directions and lose all significant structure. In all the prophetic books, but above all in the three big ones, Blake has to struggle hard to control his material, every now and then defeated by its weight and complexity, then reasserting his mastery. Two crucial questions arise. There must in the last resort be some hierarchical system or it would be impossible to tell the central struggles from the peripheral ones; and there must be a specific cause underlying the moment of what Blake calls fourfold vision or eternity, the moment of decisive resolution of struggles that threaten to tear individual and society to pieces. For Blake the goal is the whole man, the fully harmonious society, so that he has a criterion by which to judge each moment of the struggle: to what extent does it extend and deepen joy, freedom, brotherhood? But he does not find an easy answer to the question: how does one bring about the resolving moment in a world of endless discord? He insists that the artist or poet with imaginative vision plays a necessary part in bringing about the release, and so does every pair of lovers who break down all divisions of fear between them, who reject all property-sense in love. But just how imaginative activity and happiness in love come together to create the spontaneity of mass-revolt symbolised in Orc is not so easily answered. After the check to the French Revolution Blake turned from Orc to Jesus; but, as we saw with regard to the latter parts of the *Four Zoas*, he found it more than difficult to explain why some future moment of crucifixion was going to create a world of brotherhood when the past crucifixions had failed to do it.

In *Milton* he had a more limited task than in the *Four Zoas* or *Jerusalem*. The theme is the regeneration of poetry; the pattern keeps in the main to the relations of Milton and Blake; and the conclusion, in which Blake takes over Milton's revolutionary task on a new level, is logical enough. The Bard's Song tells us much of the way in which things have gone wrong; and the account of the works of Los brings out much of the significance of the struggles of the truly imaginative artist. In a sense everything in the poem happens in a single moment, expressive of Blake's matured creativity and revolutionary understanding—though here again Jesus intrudes to weaken and render passive the relation of the prophetic struggle to history, to people.

The title-page seems originally to have read 'in 12 Books'. The poem perhaps did have, or was meant to have this number, the missing books

7*

covering the social and political struggles of both Milton's and Blake's periods. The correlations are present to some extent in the books we have, but not in a clarified way. Interpolations from the lost or partially written books seem to be present in what remains, dealing mainly with the shifts and corruptions by which men carry on during the Napoleonic Wars while they await the Last Judgement, and with the revision of Milton–Blake's ideas to meet that situation of long delay. The lesson has to be driven home that we must not change one tyranny for another. As a reward for his readiness to wait without wrath Blake is granted a certain mental release that will enable him to return to London and listen to the endless cry of human misery. At the same time Milton has to learn the lesson so that he can unite with Ololon as History-as-it-should-have-been: which in turn means that he unites with Jesus and Blake can return to his vegetable body in the Felpham cottage, badly shaken but prepared for the Great Harvest.

The original draft of *Milton* seems to be represented in some extra pages that Blake printed in the last two known copies of the poem. Here he seems to take the English Civil War as the basis of his exposition, with the conflict of Satan and Palambron symbolising the conflict of Cromwell and Parliament. Cromwell would then have been shown as following a course parallel to that of Napoleon. Perhaps Blake gave up trying to depict this situation at length, or, having done so, gave up trying to engrave it, feeling unable to impose on all the material the moral that the guilty must be forgiven. He does however provide two visions of the Judgement of the Beast Satan and the repentance of the Whore (Leutha seen as Milton's Sin). Milton has to face the fact that he bears what Erdman calls bardic responsibility for the failure of the Cromwellian Revolution and so in turn for the wars and corruptions still dogging the revolutionary process in Blake's day. Logically then Blake would have to face his own bardic responsibility for Robespierre and Napoleon, for Pitt and Nelson.

In telling how Milton learns of the poverty and suffering of the people, Blake uses imagery from the textile industry, partly because he wants to define the revolution as the rending of the veils, the garments of oppression, and partly to bring out the links of the oppressive conditions with the manufacturing system. To change the world men must assume 'a garment of Pity & Compassion'. So far all revolutions have been premature. Blake cites 'an old Prophecy' about Milton's Orc-liberating powers, his capacity to precipitate a revolution by his wrathful indictments; but he does so in order to change the moral and stress the virtue of long-suffering patience. Voltaire and Rousseau were wrong to let loose the forces that led to 1789 and 1793; Calvin and Luther were wrong to stir up conflicts that led to the Peasant Revolts and the English Revolution. Blake himself was wrong to summon up Orc in the early 1790s. He implies that Milton was also wrong in dropping poetry and turning to polemical prose—though he himself owed a considerable debt to the *Areopagitica*. The key-problem lies in timing, as is stressed again and again through Los. Jesus as the seventh wheel comes at the right time and stops the wheel of misery from turning. But what that right time is, there is no clear indication. Meanwhile, however, war crushes Human Thought 'beneath the iron hand of Power'. The poet-prophet cannot and must not speak out; but in secret, secure from the watch-fiends, he continues to bear witness.[18]

But in fact Blake found it very hard to subdue wrath. The Sons of Los noted his struggle. 'They saw that wrath now swayd and now pity absorbed him.' The Divine mercy may have replaced the human wonder; Jesus may have replaced Orc; but Blake still feels in his bones that the task is to destroy 'the destroyers of Jerusalem'. Orc once stamped the stony law to dust. Now Milton shakes down Satan's Synagogue 'as webs'. Milton–Blake tells Satan: 'I know my power to annihilate And be a greater in thy place', but he controls his power to dispense destruction since his aim is now to teach men to despise death. And yet all the while he longs to crush every hireling writer, every submissive artist, 'who creates under State Government'.

But now yet another prophet has come up as a national figure. It was probably in 1804 that Blake wrote his satirical quatrain on the virginity of the Virgin Mary and Joanna Southcott. Joanna, a chubby Devon servant-girl, had for some time been proclaiming herself a prophetess. From 1792, at the age of forty-two, she corresponded with interested persons throughout England, and a delegation of seven of these, some of whom had been followers of Richard Brothers, called to see her at Exeter and were won over. Sharp, one of them, had a big box made to hold the prophecies she was heaping up. In May 1802 she came to London, lived in Paddington (like Brothers), and had many of her writings issued as cheap pamphlets. In October that year she announced that she would bear the second Christ. Though many of Brothers' followers came to her, she did not refer to him till 1806 when he was let out of prison. She refused to read his books. 'I never read any book at all; but write by the spirit as I am directed... All I know of Mr Brothers is what was explained to me from my dream.' She told Sharp that her dream was of wagons passing close by: which signified 'The Spirit of the Lord in the hearts of men to press her forward'. Next year she explained the details. God told her the wagon was Brothers: he was thus a way-clearer. 'I said that Brothers broke the ground all through; The heavy-loaded wagon so did go.' But in jail his mind, she said, was heavy laden and the powers of darkness tempted him to pride and envy of Joanna. Brothers replied in his *Dissertation on the Fall of Eve*. The woman clothed with the sun was not Joanna, but his own bride. She riposted that God was furious with Brothers for making him the author of Eve's temptation. 'The Bear shall meet him, and his Bones shall break.' She took over his idiom and saw her followers as the Jews. 'Deep are the Sorrows he would bring on man, had I not saved them by the Woman's hand.' Sharp, in his introduction to her *Divine and Spiritual Communications*, 1803, argued that as a woman Eve had brought the knowledge of evil into the world, so a woman must bring the knowledge of good.

Blake could not possibly accept such a redeeming role for woman, the mere emanation of the male. He had contempt for Joanna. 'Whate'er is done to her she cannot know . . .' But she now represented the main millenary trend among the craftsmen and the dispossessed. The numbers of her adherents steadily grew and she began to issue sealed letters to those whom she had formally accepted. Her verse is mostly rough doggerel, with elements of folk-poetry now and then showing up; at moments it rises to the level of homespun Blake:

> They patch the people up with lies,
> For to keep out the sun . . .
> Because their purse they all would save,
> And darken every mind.

Her way of interpreting the Bible and folk-themes is also of great interest in revealing a Blakean sensibility at her homely popular level.

11

Public Address, 1805–10

In January 1805 Blake was still acting as an agent for Hayley in London. He was seeing Phillips, who hoped to publish Hayley's works, but did not like to raise the question of the ballads himself. 'O that I could but bring Felpham to me or go to her in this World as easy as I can in that of Affection & Remembrance.' Hayley wrote to Phillips about the ballads and Blake thanked him for his 'generous manner'. He suggested that the copyright of the ballads should stay in Hayley's name, but 'Truly proud I am to be in possession of this beautiful little estate,' which he, Blake, expected to be profitable. The discussions with Phillips carried on for months, with Hayley insisting that Seagrave should be his printer. On 5 March Phillips stated that he agreed to Hayley's terms, adding, 'I am chiefly concerned for Poor Blake who has been sadly tortured by these untoward circumstances. I shall now direct him to proceed with his designs & engravings.' Hayley promptly replied that the terms set out by Phillips were not those that he, Hayley, had proposed. 'I am sorry the Impediments in our business have vexed Mr Blake but I must not permit my eagerness to serve one Friend to render me unjust to another.' Phillips caved in. No doubt he was thinking of the strike of 250 pressmen that was upsetting London printers. Despite his long dealings with Blake he mentions that he does not know his address.[1]

Hayley got Carr to break to Blake the news that Miss Watson was doing the Cowper plates. Carr reported, 'He observed that his feelings were not wounded, & that he was completely satisfied with your wishes'. On 25 April Blake himself wrote to Hayley, telling him that Fuseli was now Master of the R.A. and that Flaxman was to lecture on sculpture. The death of Banks had left the latter 'without a competitor' in his field. Blake goes on to talk of the printing strike and the fad for a boy-actor, Master Betty, and he makes conciliatory remarks about Miss Watson.

The Journeymen Printers throughout London are at war with their Masters & are likely to get the better. Each Party meet to consult against the other; nothing can be greater than the Violence on both sides. Printing is suspended in London, Except at private Presses. I hope this will become a source of advantage to our Friend Seagrave.

The Idea of Seeing an Engraving of Cowper by the hand of Caroline Watson is, I assure you, a pleasing one to me; it will be highly gratifying to see another Copy by another hand & not only gratifying, but Improving, which is better.

The Town is mad. Young Roscius like all Prodigies is the talk of Every Body. I have not seen him & perhaps never may. I have no curiosity to see him, as I well know what is within the compass of a boy of 14, & as to Real Acting it is like Historical Painting. No Boy's Work.

Here, in his only known comment on organised working-class action, he shows no interest except in so far as it affects Hayley's schemes. The linking of the grand style in art with that in acting brings out the strong theatrical concept in Blake's art which he inherits from the baroque world.

In another letter to Hayley, whose eyesight was failing, Blake promised to complete the plates by 28 May; but they are dated 18 June. Within a month the booklet was then published. On 4 June Blake wrote in dismay to say that he had belatedly done a plate for the ballad on the horse. 'Its omission would be to me a loss that I could not now sustain, as it would cut off ten guineas from my next demand on Phillips, which sum I am in absolute want of.' The plate, he says, is one of his best and has cost him immense labour. Phillips had also rejected Blake's advertisement for the booklet calling it an appeal to charity. To Hayley Blake had declared that whatever writings of his 'hereafter appear before the Public, they will fall far short of this first specimen'. He thus himself states that so far he has published no writings.[2]

The horse illustration, which Blake praised so highly, was unintentionally comic. Lady Hesketh found it 'a little Extra', and later Rossetti remarked that the horse was 'absolutely snuffling with propriety' and showing an 'intensity of comic decorum'. Soon afterwards, Lady Hesketh gave away her real feelings about Blake to Johnny J., 'My hair stands on end to think that Hayley & Blake are as dear friends as ever . . . I don't doubt he [Blake] will poison him in his Turret or set fire to all his papers, & poor Hayley will consume in his own Fires'. Hayley wrote her a lengthy defence of Blake, at the end declaring that he wanted to do him

all the little good in my power, & for extraordinary reasons (*that may make you smile*) *because* He is *very apt* to *fail in his art*:—a species of failing peculiarly entitled to pity *in Him*, since it arises from nervous Irritation, & a *too vehement desire to excell.*—I have every wish to befriend Him from a motive that, I know, our dear angelic Cowper *would approve*, because this poor man with admirable quickness of apprehension & with uncommon powers of mind, has *often appeared to me on the verge of Insanity*. But Heaven, who has graciously assigned to Him, as an invaluable Helpmate, perhaps the only woman on Earth, who could have suited him as a wife, will continue, I hope, to watch over this singularly Endangered mortal, unfit in truth to take care of Himself in a world like this!

Hayley here showed a genuine depth of insight into Blake's predicament, even if he did not know or understand the resources in poetry which in the last resort kept Blake sane. To his letter Lady Hesketh replied tartly with a hope that 'you may not be a sufferer from your goodness and unbounded Confidence'.

Hayley, not Blake, sent Flaxman copies of the ballads.* But a new and important commission came up for Blake from Cromek. Born in Hull, Robert Hartley Cromek was now about 35. A pupil of Bartolozzi, he had engraved much after Stothard, but bad health made him turn to publishing. Gilchrist says he had 'a nervous temperament and an indifferent constitution'. In October Flaxman told Hayley that Cromek had engaged Blake to make forty drawings for Blair's poem, *The Grave*, half of which Blake would himself engrave.[3]

On 21 November Blake wrote to Hayley about the commission, on which he had been working for two months. Cromek had set him to engraving twenty designs 'with the same liberality with which he set me about the drawings'. He, Blake, did not know how the ballads were going, but he had heard 'they were approved by the best, that is, the most serious people'. What is good must succeed at last. He and Catherine desired 'to be particularly remember'd by You & our Good Lady Paulina over a dish of Coffee'. He was handing the letter on to Cromek, who would include the Blair prospectus with it. He little knew that the prospectus, while citing many well-known artists as patrons, named the engraver as Luigi Schiavonetti, who had been a fellow-pupil of Cromek under Bartolozzi and who worked in a fashionable

---

* The Rev. J. Thomas, rector of Epsom, in late 1801 had visited Felpham and commissioned drawings from Blake. Now, one Sunday in September 1805, Nancy told her husband Flaxman that the Rev. Thomas had been near death and wanted to see them; he had asked to be lent her copy of Blake's Gray-illustrations, so that he might make some copies from it to keep with his *Night Thoughts*. 'He wishes to collect all B—has done, & I have a little commission to give to Blake for him.'

style of stippling. Later Stothard's son said that his father had been told by Cromek that Blake's work in the plates he had etched was done 'so indifferently and so carelessly' that he, Cromek, had to turn to Schiavonetti.* There must have been a rapid change of plans, for two prospectuses exist, both dated November 1805. One speaks of fifteen plates invented and engraved by Blake; the other of twelve engravings by Schiavonetti.

Early in December Flaxman, who now knew the facts, told Hayley 'Blake is going on gallantly' and 'has good employment besides', though he, Flaxman, feared he would not get all the advantages to be wished from the Blair because 'his abstracted habits are so much at variance with the usual modes of human life'. Hayley had replied cordially to Blake's letter, and on 11 December Blake wrote back in the last letter he seems to have sent to Felpham. He thanked Hayley for having conducted him 'thro Three years that would have been the Darkest Years that ever Mortal Suffer'd, which were render'd thro' your means a Mild & Pleasant Slumber'. Without Hayley he 'must have Perish'd'. But the dangers are now in the past. 'It will not be long before I shall be able to present the full history of my Spiritual Sufferings to the Dwellers upon Earth & of the Spiritual Victories obtain'd for me by my Friends.'

Recieving a Prophet as a Prophet is a Duty which If omitted is more Severely Avenged than Every Sin & Wickedness beside. It is the Greatest of Crimes to Depress True Art & Science. I know that those who are dead from the Earth, & who mock'd & Despised the Meekness of True Art (and such I find, have been the situations of our Beautiful, Affectionate Ballads), I know that such Mockers are Most Severely Punish'd in Eternity. I know it, for I see it & dare not help. The Mocker of Art is the Mocker of Jesus. Pray Present My Sincerest Thanks to our Good Pauline, whose kindness to Me shall recieve recompense in the Presence of Jesus.

* The prospectus included remarks by Fuseli (though unsigned) deploring the frivolity of the taste of the times, which merged refinement with corruption of manners and debased symbolism with stale emblems. Blake however did not draw on far-fetched symbols, mythology, Gothic superstition. 'His Invention has been chiefly employed to spread a familiar and domestic Atmosphere round the most important of all Subjects, to connect the visible and the invisible World, without provoking Probability, and to lead the Eye from the milder Light of Time to the Radiations of Eternity . . . Wildness so picturesque in itself, often redeemed by Taste, Simplicity, and Elegance, what Child of Fancy, what Artist would wish to discharge.' All classes of artists, 'from the Contriver of Ornaments, to the Painter of History, will find here Materials of Art and Hints of Improvement'. Schiavonetti's plates cost Cromek about £540; Blake might have expected £300 to £600.[4]

He sends thanks also to Seagrave (to whom he still owes money). He is returning the Romney works he holds; and he still has to add a few touches to the Shipwreck. The letter has a farewell note as if he knew the end of his relations with Hayley had been reached; he comes at last into the open in describing himself as a prophet. Yet in the midst of his outpouring of gratitude he can mention the work in which he bitterly depicts Hayley as Satan; and his expressions of goodwill turn into the revenge-fantasies of eternity, which make a mock of his creed of forgiveness.[5]

He had not been seeing Flaxman, for the latter wrote to ask Hayley if he would find out if Blake had time to engrave the designs for Hayley's *Hero and Leander*. Flaxman had not himself asked Blake as 'I would not have either his good nature or convenience strained to work after my designs'. The engravings were not done by Blake; but Flaxman, we see, kept his good will towards him to the end. During this year Malkin worked on the Memoir of his dead son. He felt an affinity between the boy and Blake in their art-attitudes, and in 1805 he gathered information from Blake about himself, which he put into a prefatory letter to Thomas Johnes of Hafod, translator of Froissart, which is dated 4 January 1805; about the same time he got from Blake a copy of *Songs of Innocence* for Johnes. He offered to write the notice for the Blair prospectus, which however Fuseli did.

Malkin's preface is the only sympathetic account of Blake of any length published in the latter's lifetime; and only here were some of Blake's poems brought before the general reader. Malkin cited six lyrics, two from *Poetical Sketches*, three from *Songs of Innocence*, and the *Tyger*. Of the illuminated books, he seems to know only *Songs*, and comments that it was meant to circulate 'only among the author's friends'. In citing *Holy Thursday* he says, 'The book of Revelation, which may well be supposed to engross much of Mr. Blake's study, seems to have directed him, in common with Milton, to some of the foregoing images'. Though he sees that Blake's influences went as far back as the Elizabethans, he asks the reader to decide if the poems' 'simplicity and sentiment at all make amends for their inartificial and unassuming construction'. Blake, we see, had not tried to interest him in the prophetic books. The reviewers of the memoir saw no value in the poems. *The British Critic* in September 1806 remarked that as an artist Blake was one of those 'who mistake extravagance for genius' and 'as a poet, he seems chiefly inspired by that,—Nurse of the didactic Muse, Divine Nonsensia'. *The Monthly Review* (October) thought the poems 'certainly very inferior to Dr.

Watts'. *The Monthly Magazine* (January 1807) considered they did not rise above mediocrity.

During the winter of 1804–5 Blake painted the vigorous *Famine and War* (a version of *A Breach in a City*, with Orc's body added to the pile of dead); and he drew *Let Loose the Dogs of War*. Perhaps also he rewrote Night VIII of the *Four Zoas* in denunciation of the betrayal of peace by leaders who only pretended 'repentance'. Recalling Milton's account of the devils' invention of gunpowder and cannon, he breaks out into his full vision of the metallurgical developments going on through war-pressure. Urizen gains new powers of destruction. 'Sparkles of Dire affliction issu'd round his frozen limbs Horrible hooks & nets in hollow globes & bor'd Tubes in petrific steel & rammed combustibles & wheels And chains & pullies fabricated all round the heaven of Los.' Well might Los–Blake feel the whole destiny of man threatened. 'All futurity Seems teeming with Endless destruction never to be repelld.' The application of Urizen's 'enormous sciences' to the invention of engines of death has also perverted the arts. Thus music becomes a means of inflaming people. Such a total perversion, says Blake, is necessary in a Britain aiming at world-empire.[6]

The year 1805 was on the whole disastrous for Blake. His connection with Hayley broke down. What had seemed an important commission from Cromek was spoiled by Schiavonetti taking over the engravings. Malkin handed over to Cromek the engraving of the frontispiece that Blake had designed. Even Flaxman seems to be drawing away. The only helpful person left was Butts, who in 1805 paid him 12 guineas (January) and £5 7s. (July), and who was to pay him over £400 in the next five years. During those five years, and the following five, Blake did no more trade-engraving.

As far as we know, little happened in 1806. In April Richard Brothers petitioned for his release; and Erskine, who had become Lord Chancellor after Pitt's death, ordered him to be freed despite the opposition of Dr Simmons. Brothers was looked after by a follower till he died in 1824. Blake sank to the point of asking Ozias Humphry to help him in getting permission to dedicate *The Grave* designs to the Queen. Humphry took the matter up, helped Blake to draft the request correctly, and gained the permission. In the dedication Blake called the Queen the 'Shepherdess of England's Fold' and bowed before his sovereign's feet.

A criticism of Fuseli's picture of Count Ugolino in *Bell's Weekly Messenger* annoyed him and in June he had a letter of protest printed in

Phillips' *Monthly Magazine*. This was the only time he ever managed himself to get anything of his own, prose or verse, printed in his lifetime, apart from the dedication to the Queen. He praised Fuseli's drawing, colour, expressiveness, and attacked the prevalent taste, citing a visitor who had said to him that Fuseli was 'a hundred years beyond the present Generation'. We feel in his words a strange self-identification with both Fuseli and Ugolino (a character in Dante's *Inferno*, who ate his own children out of hunger). Ugolino is 'a man of wonder and admiration, of resentment against man and devil, and of humiliation before God', who is shown in 'his passionate and innocent grief, his innocent and venerable madness and insanity and fury'.[7]

The Grave was being held up. Even in the summer Cromek was still chasing subscribers. In June Fuseli gave him an introduction to his patron, William Roscoe of Liverpool, who subscribed. But more troubles were coming Blake's way through Cromek. Blake had decided to make a bid for popular favour on his own. He drew Chaucer's pilgrims and decided to make a big engraving of his work. Why he chose such a theme is not clear. Perhaps the taunts at his wildness had made him want to tackle an earthy subject where the main interest lay in human characterisation. But he had long brooded on what constituted true character, and he may well have felt that a success with such a work would establish him as a master of history. But it is also possible that Cromek suggested the idea. In a letter to the poet James Montgomery, dated 17–20 April 1807, he remarks, 'I give myself great Credit for thinking of such a glorious Subject—it is true that it was sufficiently obvious—but, it is equally true that what is obvious is often overlooked'.* However, with such a wily character we cannot trust any statement; he may be protecting himself against accusations of having stolen the idea from Blake. In any event we can be sure he took the idea to Stothard, who began a work on the Chaucer theme; and Blake was soon convinced that both Stothard and Cromek were conspiring to cheat him. (Later, Stothard's son claimed that his father had done his work in 1805, but we cannot check this statement.) Gilchrist says that Cromek, calling on Blake, saw the *Pilgrims*

---

* In this letter Cromek expatiates at length on Blake as a wild and wonderful genius, who lives in fairy land, 'still believing that what has been called *Delusion* is the only *Reality*; what has been called Fancy & Imagination is the Eternal World! & that this World is the only cheat, Imagination the *only Truth!*' He speaks of his 'Noble though extravagant Flights' (probably *Poetical Sketches*), and goes on to address Montgomery in very Blakean terms. The poet 'is a Pilgrim & stranger upon Earth, travelling into a far distant Land . . .' In England is 'a vast formidable Party' whose aim is to depress true Art and Science, etc. He even uses the term '*hired* Miscreants'.

and asked for a finished drawing of the subject to be engraved. Blake was not to be caught a second time but considered that Cromek had given him a commission to execute the design. However, Cromek went to Stothard and commissioned an oil-painting on the theme (to be engraved by Bromley, though later Schiavonetti took over). Stothard agreed, knowing nothing of Blake's plans or the fact he had already circulated a subscription-paper among his friends. Smith merely says that Blake showed Cromek the designs sketched out for a fresco picture. Cunningham's version was that Blake claimed Cromek had commissioned him to paint the *Pilgrims* before Stothard thought of the subject. 'To which Cromek replied that the order had been given in a vision for he never gave it.'⁸

Under the pressure of these disappointments Blake grew ever more enraged and driven in on himself. Gilchrist tells us: 'Blake was at no pains, throughout this business or afterwards, to conceal his feelings towards Stothard. To the end of his life he would, to strangers, abuse the popular favourite, with a vehemence to them unaccountable. With friends and sympathisers, he was silent on the topic.' It is very unlikely that Stothard consciously stole from him, though he may well have been used by Cromek. We can smile at Blake's epigram on the latter: 'A petty Sneaking Knave I knew— O Mr. Cr[omek], how do ye do?' But his rage against Stothard is not so acceptable. 'S[tothard] in Childhood on the Nursery Floor Was extreme Old & most extremely poor. He is grown old & rich & what he will: He is extreme old & extreme poor still.' Stothard's 'heart is iron, his head wood, & his face brass'. Blake's moods grow even more unpleasant as he draws Flaxman in. Of the latter and Stothard he writes: 'I found them blind: I taught them how to see; And now they know neither themselves nor me'. Of Nancy he writes: 'How can I help thy Husband copying me? Should that make difference 'twixt me & Thee?' Cosway was one of those who about this time began to fear 'to associate with Blake'.⁹

We cannot date with any precision the worst things he wrote about Hayley, but doubtless they began about this time. 'Thy friendship oft has made my heart to ake: Do be my Enemy for Friendship's sake.' 'To forgive Enemies H[ayley] does pretend, Who never in his Life forgave a friend.' 'My title as a Genius then is prov'd: Not Prais'd by Hayley nor by Flaxman lov'd.' 'Of Hayley's birth this was the happy lot His Mother on his Father him begot.' 'I write the Rascal thanks till he & I With Thanks & Compliments are quite drawn dry.' This last couplet shows that even in the midst of his fulsome compliments to Hayley he knew that he was being hypocritical. Commentators have cited the lines that begin: 'Was I angry with Hayley who us'd me so ill, Or can I be angry with Felpham's old Mill?'—with the conclusion: 'At a Friend's Errors Anger shew, Mirth at the Errors of a Foe'—and have read them as meaning that he is angry with Hayley as a friend. But that is the opposite of what he says. He links Hayley with Flaxman, Cromek and the others against whom he felt an unslackening grudge. He says that he should mock and laugh at them all, and keep his anger for real friends in whom he feels an error.

The six lines *On H——y's Friendship* go far beyond an expression of passing irritability.

> When H——y finds out what you cannot do,
> That is the very thing he'll set you to.
> If you break not your Neck, 'tis not his fault,
> But pecks of poison are not pecks of salt.
> And when he could not act upon my wife
> Hired a Villain to bereave my Life.

The suspicions peeping out at the trial have hardened into definite convictions. He believes that Hayley stood behind the Scolfield episode. Hayley had clearly liked Catherine, and Blake had seen his attitude as an attempt to seduce her by playing on her need for security and charming her with his fine manners, so that she was less enclosed in Blake as an obedient emanation. Therefore Hayley, seen in all his malevolence, was the agent of the sedition trap. Blake is citing a line from his early ballad *Fair Elinor*. There a duke, apparently a friend of Elinor and her husband, hires a man to murder the latter. The severed head warns the wife: 'He seeks thy love—who, coward, in the night Hired a villain to bereave my life'. The ballad also has the line: 'A hired villain turned my sleep to death'. Note further how Blake uses the term 'hired' in attacking Reynolds with 'his Gang of Cunning Hired Knaves'. Reynolds himself was hired to depress Art; his hired knaves are responsible for Blake's poverty and neglect. Later, denouncing Cromek and his fellows he called 'for Public Protection against these villains'. Anyone who thwarted him was thus seen as a hired villain.

In regarding Hayley as the architect of the Chichester trial Blake is not making a passing comment. He also identifies him in the Notebook with Pick Thank, Bunyan's informer who accuses Faithful of seditious remarks against the Prince of Vanity Fair. In *Jerusalem* (42) Albion urges the dragoons of

Hand and Hyle to 'seize the abhorred friend' (Jesus or Los–Blake) and 'Bring him to justice before heaven here upon London stone,' the Druidic centre of war and sacrifice. All this while Blake is preaching an ethic of total forgiveness. The poet now is to be only a recorder. He may describe the crushing of oppressor and oppressed together (in the wine-press, 'call'd war on Earth', which is the printing press of Los), but he must not express wrath, perhaps not even 'the fury of Poetic Inspiration', till the day when the cry for freedom brings no violence. Then the universal brotherhood and mercy will give us 'powers fitted to circumscribe this dark Satanic death'. 'But how this is as yet we know not, and cannot know Till Albion is arisen; then patient wait a little while.' Wait on the Lord, as Erdman says, and trust in the Godwinian concept of historical inevitability. But when it is a matter of his own wrongs, or what he conceives to be his wrongs, Blake forgives nobody.

According to Gilchrist he even thought a curse had been laid on him. He had hung his first pilgrimage design over his sitting-room door. When Stothard's picture appeared, he took down the design; finding it nearly effaced, he assumed that some malignant spell of Stothard's had had this effect. So he assured his friends in telling the story. One of them (Flaxman) mildly expostulated that exposure to dust and air would anyway have affected the work in the same way. Butts later bought the design.

In this year, 1806, Butts paid Blake £21 10s. on 30 June; 5 guineas on 15 October.

The year 1807 was again a sad one for Blake. During the 1806–7 winter he went to the house of Thomas Phillips, R.A., at 8 George Street, Hanover Square, to be painted. Phillips was a talkative fellow, who liked a good story; and as his account of Blake comes through unreliable Cunningham, it must be taken as the sort of thing expected of Blake rather than as a verbatim report of what happened. Blake had insisted that Michelangelo painted an angel better than Raphael.

'Well, but' said the other, 'you never saw any of the paintings of Michael Angelo; and perhaps speak from the opinions of others; your friends may have deceived you.' 'I never saw any of the paintings of Michael Angelo,' replied Blake, 'but I speak from the opinion of a friend who could not be mistaken'. 'A valuable friend truly,' said Phillips, 'and who may he be I pray?' 'The archangel Gabriel, Sir,' answered Blake. 'A good authority surely, but you know evil spirits love to assume the looks of good ones; and this may have been done to mislead you.' 'Well now, Sir,' said Blake, 'this is really singular; such were my own suspicions, but they were soon removed—I will tell you how. I was one day reading Young's Night Thoughts, and when I came to that passage which asks 'who can paint an angel,' I closed the book and cried, 'Aye! who can paint an angel?' A voice in the room answered, 'Michael Angelo could'. 'And how do you know', I said, looking round me, but I saw nothing save a greater light than usual. 'I know' said the voice, 'for I sat to him: I am the arch-angel Gabriel.' 'Oho!' I answered, 'you are, are you: I must have better assurance than that of a wandering voice; you may be an evil spirit—there are such in the land.' 'You shall have good assurance', said the voice, 'can an evil spirit do this?' I looked whence the voice came, and then was aware of a shining shape, with bright wings, who diffused much light. As I looked, the shape dilated more and more: he waved his hands; the roof of my study opened; he ascended into heaven; he stood in the sun, and beckoning to me, moved the universe. An angel of evil could not have done that—It was indeed the arch-angel Gabriel. The painter marvelled much at this wild story; but he caught from Blake's looks, as he related it, that rapt poetic expression which has rendered his portrait one of the finest of the English school.

The portrait was engraved by Schiavonetti for *The Grave*; Phillips gave it to Cromek, says the *Antijacobin Review* in November 1808.

In this situation Blake reached an unusually deep trough of depression. He wrote in his notebook: 'Tuesday, Janry.20, 1807, between Two & Seven in the Evening—Despair'.

He tried again to assert himself in business dealings, asking four guineas from Cromek for the vignette to go with the dedication to the Queen. Cromek in May returned the sketch, saying that Blake had overpriced it and that in any event the dedication was wholly his concern, though he, Cromek, would have paid Schiavonetti ten guineas to etch the drawing. He went on to defend his actions at length. 'You charge me with *imposing upon you*.' In fact he had been imposed on by Blake. He gives examples. When he had first called on Blake, the latter was without reputation. He, Cromek, took on the Herculean task of creating a reputation for Blake. In that he had not only the public to contend with, but Blake himself, 'a man who had predetermined not to be served'. Such fame as Blake now owns, apart from his name for eccentricity, has been Cromek's creation. 'I also imposed on myself when I believed what you so often have told me, that your works were equal, nay superior, to a Raphael or to a Michael Angelo.' But the public woke him from 'this state of stupor, this mental delusion'.

Cromek goes on, 'I have imposed on myself yet more grossly in believing you to be one altogether abstracted from this world, holding converse with the world of spirits!—simple, unoffending, a combination of the serpent and the dove. I really blush when I reflect how I have cheated in this respect'. He had tried to help Blake by having his designs engraved by 'one of the first artists in Europe', so as to gain him both food and fame. When *The Grave* commission was offered, 'you and Mrs. Blake were reduced so low as to be obliged to live on half-a-guinea a week!' (We know that from January to October, 1805, Blake earned a least £98, that is £2 3s. a week; but he must have told Cromek that he was very hard up or Cromek would not have spoiled his own case by a misstatement.) Cromek next asserts that he paid for the drawings 'more than I could then afford, more in proportion than you were in the habit of receiving, and what you were perfectly satisfied with, though I must do you the justice to confess much less than I think their real value'.[10]

Cromek avoids the point that he called in Schiavonetti without telling Blake that he was to lose the money which would have come in from doing the engraving. His plea that he was carried away by Blake's self-praise may have some truth, though he is cleverly using Blake's words against him; and his devious, wily nature comes out in the proposition with which he ends his letter. If Blake can arrange to sell the drawings to a collector for sixty guineas, Cromek will hand them over to him after publication if twenty guineas (the sum he has paid for their use) is allowed him out of the sixty. That is, he would then have got the copyright for nothing. What Blake replied to him we do not know. He was doubtless too angry to say anything. Cromek had concluded by disingenuously and cruelly asking, 'Why shd you so furiously rage at the success of the little picture of "The Pilgrimage?" 3,000 people have now seen it and approved of it. Believe me, yours is "*the voice of one crying in the wilderness*!" '

Stothard's painting had been exhibited in a perfume shop in the Strand in May. A proposal to publish an engraving of it was inserted at the end of *The Grave*, which Blake would have much resented. The publicity given to Stothard's work must have increased his conviction of having been cheated of his due rights. Hoppner wrote an appreciative letter to Cumberland, which infuriated Blake when it was printed in Prince Hoare's *The Artist* and cited by Cromek in his prospectus. W. P. Carey wrote a *Critical Description* of the painting; he seems to have no awareness of Blake's grievance as he refers enthusiastically to *The Grave* designs. On 4 May Flaxman, who defended Stothard as no accomplice of Cromek, wrote to Hayley, 'at present I have no intercourse with Mr. Blake'.

On 14 October Blake wrote a letter (not printed) to Phillips's periodical protesting against the arrest of an astrologer. He told Phillips, 'I do not pay the postage of this Letter, because you, as Sheriff, are bound to attend to it'. He argues: 'The Man who can Read the Stars often is opressed by their Influence, no less than the Newtonian who reads Not & cannot Read is opressed by his own Reasonings & Experiments. We are all subject to Error: who shall say, Except the National Religionists, that we are not all subject to Crime?' He describes the surgeon who caused the arrest as acting 'with the Cold fury of Robespierre.'*

This year Blake got from Butts four sums: £28 6s. (March), £12 1s. 6d. (2 June), 15 guineas (13 July), 10 guineas (6 October). He had been experimenting with engraving on pewter, and what he called woodcut on pewter (also on copper): that is, he etched the white area instead of the black. On the back of a watercolour of the Fall of Man he wrote that it showed 'the birth of War & Misery; while the Lion seizes the Bull, the Tiger the Horse, the Vulture and the Eagle contest for the Lamb'. All harmony is lost. Blake also painted a small tempera of the Last Judgement for the Countess of Egremont, which elaborated one of *The Grave* plates; and he did his only lithograph, which shows Enoch, ancestor of Noah. Enoch and his two sons stand for 'Poetry, Painting, and Music, the three Powers in Man of conversing with Paradise, which the flood did not sweep away' (1810). About this time Blake also did his first set of illustrations for *Paradise Lost*.

He had met the Egremonts through Hayley, but now Ozias Humphry was the link. Humphry, Painter in Crayons to the King since 1792, was given in 1805 an annuity of £100 by Lord Egremont for his copy of a portrait made in Italy. Blake drew up an account of the picture for Humphry, who, liking it, asked for a copy for Lady Egremont, then another copy for the Earl of Buchan. Humphry wrote to the Earl that he thought the picture in many respects superior to Michelangelo's *Last Judgement*. Blake's account sees the New Jerusalem as 'ready to descend upon the Earth'.[11]

---

* Cumberland, in London early this summer, called on Blake. 'Blake made 130 drawings for Flaxman for 10.10 (116 drawings to Gray)—Blake has engd. 50 Plates of a new Prophecy! Intends to publish his new method through means [?] of stopping lights. I am to prepare my new Plan for really encouraging the arts by buying pictures—The new work seems to be *Jerusalem*, unless Blake really did ten more books to *Milton* and engraved part of them. Perhaps he did a shorter version of *Jerusalem*, then expanded it in the next decade or so. The earliest known copy of the prophecy has watermarks of 1818–20. On 5 December a copy of *Poetical Sketches* that had belonged to Nancy Flaxman was auctioned; it looks as if the Flaxmans had had enough of Blake.

In May 1808 Blake had two works at the Royal Academy, his first for eight years and his last: Jacob's dream and Christ in the sepulchre, guarded by angels. In June and July *The Grave* was announced and at last in August it was published at two and a half guineas, with 589 subscribers; some proof copies were priced at four guineas.* The book included an advertisement by Cromek, Fuseli's 1805 recommendation, and descriptions of the plates probably by Malkin. For frontispiece there was the engraving of Phillips' portrait, in which the head seems weaker than in the life-mask.[12]

A letter from Hoppner to Prince Hoare, apparently dated July, suggests that Cromek was considering the issue of some of Blake's illuminated works (probably *Songs of Innocence*) and in his canny way was sounding some influential persons. 'Respecting Blake's Poems, will you believe me? The merit was all vanished, in my mind at least, on reading them next morning. I therefore took no copy—but if you wish for them Cromek can now refuse you nothing.'† *The Grave* engravings with their nudes upset many people. Most disturbing was St Michael on the title-page, who descends head down with genitals hanging the wrong way round. The first review, by Robert Hunt in the Hunts' new periodical, *The Examiner*, on 7 August, discussed at length the impossibility of representing the spirit to the eye, and found 'much to admire, but more to censure in these prints'. The reunions in heaven were indecent; libidinousness intruded. The reason for the attack seems to be that the radical Hunts saw Blake as a Methodist enthusiast or some other sort of fanatic. They were running a series on 'the Folly and Danger of Methodism'. On 28 August Leigh Hunt compiled an account of the Ancient Redoubtable Institute of Quacks, in which the Painting Officers were Copley, Craig, Bourgeois, and Blake; the Poets included Wordsworth and Scott.[13]

The first article in the November *Antijacobin* made a long attack on Blake. The critic objected to the title-page and the attempt to represent spirits by domestic aspects of earthly life; despite touches of 'imagination chastened by good taste', the effect was of a morbid fancy. Blake, once a mediocre

---

* On 4 May Flaxman told Hayley that Raimbach, working on plates for Cowper's version of Milton's Latin poems, suggested Blake could do 'the outlines better than himself but it was not possible to take the commission from the person that brought it to town, besides at present I have no intercourse with Mr Blake'. Hayley, Miss Poole, Seagrave and other acquaintances were among *The Grave* subscribers.

† On 14 August Cromek sent a copy of *The Grave* to Cumberland, apologising for the omission of his name from the list of subscribers. He seems to have been a guest of the Cumberlands in Bristol. 'You are the only person in Bristol who thoroughly understands the Inventions of Blake ... Your Packet went to Blake. I sent him 2 Copies, but he has not had the common politeness to thank me for them.'

engraver, had turned to design, aided by 'visionary communications'. (The writer probably drew on the artist Phillips.) Even the little dedicatory poem was seen as an abortive attempt 'to form a wreath of poetical flowers'. Should Blake try more poetry, his friends were advised 'to restrain his wanderings by the strait waistcoat'. *The Monthly Review* on 1 December was kinder, seeing *The Grave* as 'one of the most singular works ever published in England' with its mixture of correctness of form, well arranged composition, and 'wildness of fancy and eccentricity'. The artist was said to gain his conceptions from 'Vision bright' coming on him like Milton's Muse: Blake had himself made the same comparison in his 1799 letter to Trusler.

Blake was in communication with Cumberland through the latter's sons, George and Sydney, who lived with Cromek at 64 Newman Street and worked in Whitehall at the Army Pay office.[14] They were interested in art and their father gave them a list of persons to see, which included Cosway, Phillips, Douce, and Blake. On 1 December he wrote that their sister Georgiana was coming with tracings of Raphael's paintings for Blake, which were of little value to him, being rude sketches only—'for those I keep for you are the best.'* On 19 December Blake sent him one of his letters of baseless optimism. 'New profits seem to arise before me so tempting that I have already involved myself in engagements that preclude all possibility of promising any thing. I have, however, the satisfaction to inform you that I have Myself begun to print an account of various Inventions in Art, for which I have procured a Publisher, & am determined to pursue the plan of publishing what I may get printed without disarranging my time, which in future must alone be devoted to Designing & Painting: when I get my Work printed I will send it you first of any body.'

Nothing whatever came of these hopes. Gilchrist says that he made many unsuccessful applications to the trade, and he used to say, 'Well, it is published elsewhere, and beautifully bound'. But we have no evidence that he ever tried to get any of his poems published. This year, 1808, he himself perhaps started printing *Milton*. From Butts he received five lots of money: £26 5s. (14 January), £10 (29 February), £10 (29 July), 5 guineas (3 November), 5 guineas (7 December).[15]

---

* George used the situation to ask Blake for a painting of the Holy Family. His father replied with a hope he hadn't asked 'very importunately—I must send him more of those heads . . . tell me what passed'. He wrote in apology to Blake and said a friend wanted a set of the illuminated books as complete as possible. He asked about the publication of Blake's new method of engraving. 'Send it to me and I will do my best to prepare it for Press'—otherwise it could go into *Nicholson's Journal* or the *Monthly Magazine*.

About this time he completed his annotation of Reynold's *Discourses*. As Reynolds represents the prevailing taste, he is seen as the cause of all that has gone wrong in the arts, and so of all social evil. 'The Whole Book was Written to Serve Political Purposes'. Mortimer and Barry were denied; 'Fuseli, Indignant, almost hid himself. I am hid'. Reynolds and Gainsborough 'Blotted & Blurred one against the other & Divided all the English World between them'. As usual he elevates Raphael and Michelangelo, but now he violently attacks Rubens, the Flemish, and the Venetians. The shadows of Rubens 'are of a Filthy Brown somewhat the Colour of Excrement'. It is hard to tell where he saw any such Rubens, but he is close to the facts in stating, 'His lights are all the Colours of the Rainbow, laid on Indiscriminately & broken one into another'. However, Rubens' rich and complex use of colour 'is contrary to The Colouring of Real Art & Science'. No wonder then that Blake never grasped the real adventure of art in his world or noticed the work of Turner.

He sees Titian's 'Harmony of Colouring' as destructive of art, and claims against Rubens and the Venetians that 'Shade is always Cold'. A subtle organic use of colour he sees as a mere 'General Hue over all', and, unable to grasp the way in which Rembrandt's art reveals the most delicate discrimination of individual existence in form, tone, colour, with all the elements merged in a living unity of a sort not dreamed of in Raphael, he declares, 'Rembrandt was a Generaliser'.

He applauds the copying of art-works. 'Servile Copying is the Great Merit of Copying.' 'Mechanical Excellence is the Only Vehicle of Genius.' 'Without Minute Neatness of Execution The Sublime cannot Exist! Grandeur of Ideas is founded on Precision of Ideas.' Upholding Outline, he still has a good word for the ancients who were 'attentive to Complicated & Minute Discrimination of Character; it is the whole of Art'. He attacks the glorification of generalised definitions or images which was typical of eighteenth-century outlooks, and defends the 'Minute Particular'.

But what makes nonsense of these enunciations is that he cannot recognise a master of the individual existence like Rembrandt, and deifies an artist like Raphael in whom form is very much more generalised. His own art-forms almost wholly lack the minute particular and are extremely generalised, derived from the copying of other art-forms, not from life itself with its endless variations of particular existence. To escape this dilemma he elevates the outline as a thing-in-itself which somehow cuts off an individual form from a universe that seeks to encroach upon it.

He had now decided on a bold stroke, a direct appeal to the public with an art show, and was advanced with his plans. For a catalogue and advertisement sheets he needed commercial printing; for the small jobs he used a workshop in his own street, for the catalogue he turned to D. N. Shury of 7 Berwick Street, Soho. His brother James did the dealing with Shury; the catalogue imprint stated 'for J. Blake, 28, Broad Street'. As Blake could not afford to hire a showroom, James agreed to hang the pictures in the old family house. Sixteen works were to be shown, including Blake's version of the Canterbury pilgrims. In an Advertisement he stressed *The Ancient Britons*, citing six lines from the Welsh Triads, and his invention of what he calls a portable fresco (the date 15 May 1809 was added in handwriting). He stated that his Designs, 'being all in Water-colours (that is in Fresco) are regularly refused to be exhibited by the Royal Academy, and the British Institution has, this year, followed its example'. So he invited the noblemen and gentlemen, who subscribed to the Institution, to see the excluded works, as well as 'those who have been told that my Works are but an unscientific and irregular Eccentricity, a Madman's Scrawls'.*

Blake misstates the facts. The R.A. did not exclude watercolours, and the previous year he had shown there two watercolours. If he sent in the *Ancient Britons* it was doubtless rejected, as had been James Ward's lurid *Serpent of Ceylon* five years before. In a shorter sheet he merely advertised the catalogue and 'the grand style of art restored'. The catalogue, priced at 2s. 6d., entitled the holder to enter the exhibition.[16]

It opened with a claim that Blake was in the line of Raphael and Michelangelo, and attacked Rubens and the Venetians. 'Mr. B. appeals to the Public, from the judgment of those narrow blinking eyes, that have too long governed art in a dark corner. The eyes of stupid cunning never will be pleased with the work any more than with the look of self-devoting genius.' There were sixteen works: the pictures of Nelson and Pitt, the pilgrims, Gray's *Bard, The Ancient Britons, A Subject from Shakespeare, The Goats, The Spiritual Preceptor* (from Swedenborg's *Visions*), *Satan calling up the Legions, The Bramins*, five works on Biblical themes, and *Jane Shore's Penance*. He mentions that the last item and the Shakespeare *Subject* were early works. In dealing with the Bard he replies to those who have made 'objections to Mr.

---

* It was probably in spring 1809 that a young Irishman, Martin Cregan, visited the Blakes. (He wrote about it some fifty years later.) 'I had the felicity of seeing this happy pair in their one apartment in South Molton st the Bed on one side and picture of Alfred and the Danes on the wall'—doubtless the *Ancient Britons*.

B.'s mode of representing spirits with real bodies', and in describing his *Ruth* he defends the bounding line, which he identifies with the artist's idea. He now depreciates the Greeks as mere copiers of the Asiatic Patriarchs.[17]

He heads the list with the works symbolically depicting Pitt and Nelson. Powerful works, they importantly reveal his state of mind at this phase. Since Nelson's death, and even before it, there had been calls for monuments in his honour. As far back as 1799 a committee of admirals and statesmen had asked for a monument to 'the Glorious Victories of the British Navy', and Flaxman commissioned Blake to engrave a prospectus of his designs to go before the committee for an allegorical naval pillar with Nelson on its pedestal. In November 1800 Hayley introduced Flaxman to Nelson as the sculptor who ought to make his monument. After Nelson's death the demand for a monument grew stronger. An Academy committee got the royal permission to design one that combined the arts of architecture, sculpture and painting. Benjamin West exhibited his *Death of Nelson*. In this situation Blake conceived *The Spiritual Form of Nelson guiding Behemoth*. Nelson stands on the monster in whose coils men are entangled, struggling in agony. A visitor to the exhibition would at best have seen the creature as representing the sea in all its terrors, which Nelson tames, at the same time destroying the enemies of England. If he looked hard at the details, he might have been puzzled that women too were being mauled and that Nelson stood both on Leviathan and on a fallen Negro, whose colour was contrasted with the gold tints of the hero. But we can be sure that the last thing he would have thought was that Blake was attacking Nelson, whose head was haloed, nor would he have wondered why the Negro, though outside the coils, was manacled. (The slave-trade, but not slavery, had been abolished in 1807.) Neither would he have been likely to notice that the main antagonist was not France (apparently the figure at the top clutching his shorn hair) but was Christ, flower-crowned and holding a sword. Indeed no one could have guessed that the figure was Christ; Blake carefully obscures the fact by using flowers (apparently lilies) instead of thorns for the wreath. In the preliminary sketch things are a little clearer. A lightning-bolt hits Nelson's right shoulder, knocking his head to the left, and another bolt flashes from the direction of Christ's sword. But even if the viewer had had this sketch before him, he would only have inferred that Nelson had a hard time defending Britain.

Does Blake give the least aid to the viewer in his Descriptive Catalogue? Not at all. In dealing with the pictures of Nelson and Pitt he makes yet another attack on Rubens and oil-painting, and depreciates Greek art as deriving from Asia. He describes the works as 'compositions of a mythological cast, similar to those Apotheoses of Persian, Hindoo, and Egyptian Antiquity, which are still preserved on rude monuments, being copies of some stupendous originals now lost or perhaps buried till some happier age'. He has seen the originals in vision, and he 'has endeavoured to emulate the grandeur of those seen in his vision, and to apply it to modern Heroes, on a smaller scale'. No one reading that could think he meant other than a whole-heartedly sympathetic apotheosis of the hero. There is not the least suggestion that even if Nelson does represent energy, it is fettered or distorted energy. The total acceptance of the war-hero is stressed by a call for state-support:

The Artist wishes it were now the fashion to make such monuments, and then he should not doubt of having a national commission to execute these two Pictures on a scale that is suitable to the grandeur of the nation, who is the parent of his heroes, in high finished fresco.

They are 'his heroes'.

There are even fewer clues as to his real feelings in *The Spiritual Form of Pitt guiding Behemoth*. Pitt, in his angelic nightgown and broad halo, hangs above the battle where Behemoth massacres the combatants. He is 'the Angel who, pleased to perform the Almighty's orders, rides on the whirlwind, directing the storms of war'. Not a hint that Blake considers war wholly abominable and Pitt a typically evil wielder of state-power. An indication of his direct reaction to events is given by his copying into his notebook from a newspaper *Lines Written on Hearing the Surrender of Copenhagen* by James Bisset (a radical bookseller and artist of Birmingham), in which indignation is expressed at Britain's underhand blow at Denmark for standing neutral in 1807. Bisset laments his shame at Albion, once Liberty's champion, now become a Tyrant hurling 'The shaft of war o'er a desolate world'. Blake added a sketch of a lurking assassin with a burning city at the back. (We must admit that Blake could be guilty of extreme equivocation. Thus he uses the name Jesus to Hayley as something that binds them, knowing quite well that Hayley's Jesus was 'his vision's greatest enemy' and represented what separated them.)

The Ancient Britons (lost) showed Arthur's last battle, from which only three Britons escaped; the three men were depicted life-size. They are the Most Beautiful Man, the Most Strong, and the Most Ugly, and they fight the

Romans. A long explanation repeats the idea of a lost higher civilisation, which had a single language and a single religion, that of Jesus (which Blake qualifies as the Everlasting Mercy; that is, as Antinomian). The 'reasoning historians' lack all the real clues to human development. Blake cites Milton as a fellow-believer in his ancient British history and Bryant as the expounder of mankind's original unity. He thus links all history, and particularly that of Britain, with his thesis of the fall into division, and sees his Giant Albion as the Greek Atlas, the Patriarch of the Atlantic, in the early happy days of unity.[18]

He claims to hold in his hands 'the British Antiquities', apparently in the form of visionary contemplations or fables. They include the Druid monuments, London stone, the pavement of Watling Street, the caverns of Cornwall, Wales, Derbyshire and Scotland, the elemental beings called fairies, the tales of Arthur and his promised return. 'Mr. B. has in his hands poems of the highest antiquity. Adam was a Druid, and Noah; also Abraham was called to succeed the Druidical age, which began to turn allegoric and mental signification into corporeal command, whereby human sacrifice would have depopulated the earth. All these things are written in Eden', which the artist inhabits. Eden in time will transform the earth back to its original shape.

The Strong Man represents the human sublime; the Beautiful Man, the human pathetic, 'which was in the wars of Eden divided into male and female'; the Ugly Man, the human reason. Originally they were one man. Blake has written under inspiration the tale of how the vision came about, 'and will, if God please, publish it; it is voluminous, and contains the ancient history of Britain, and the world of Satan and Adam'. The conflict of beauty and ugliness is overcome in strength; the Strong Man is 'a sublime energizer'. The full resolution of the triadic movement lies in fourfold Eden in the One Man.

The *Subject from Shakespeare* shows the Horse of Intellect 'leaping from the cliffs of Memory and Reasoning; it is a barren Rock; it is also called the Barren Waste of Locke and Newton'. *The Spiritual Preceptor* tells how 'The Learned who strive to ascend into Heaven by means of learning appear to Children like dead horses, when repelled by the celestial spheres'. The Horse of Instruction is useless by itself; the pedants of Reason obstruct those with true insight even after death with their reputations and erroneous teachings. *The Goats*, drawn from Hayley's missionary poem, shows goats stripping native girls of their vine-leaf dresses. This, an experimental picture, is

'Albion Arose'; engraving about 1800

Engraving by James Heath of painting by Francis Wheatley

en, on the highest lift of his light pinions he arrives
that eagle Gate. another Lark meets him & back to back
y touch their pinions tip tip: and each descend
heir respective Earths & there all night consult with Angels
Providence & with the Eyes of God all night in slumber
ired: & at the dawn of day send out another Lark
another Heaven to carry news upon his wings
s are the Messengers dispatchd till they reach the Earth again
he East Gate of Golgonooza, & the Twenty-eighth bright
k, met the Female Ololon descending into my Garden
is it appears to Mortal eyes & those of the Ulro Heavens
t not thus to Immortals. the Lark is a mighty Angel.

Ololon stepd into the Polypus within the Mundane Shell
y could not step into Vegetable Worlds without becoming
enemies of Humanity except in a Female Form
d as One Female Ololon and all its mighty Hosts
yearil: a Virgin of twelve years nor time nor space was
the perception of the Virgin Ololon but as the
she of lightning but more quick the Virgin in my Garden
are my Cottage stood for the Saturic Space is delusion

when Los joind with me he took me in his fiery whirlwind
Vegetated portion was hurried from Lambeths shades
set me down in Felphams Vale & prepard a beautiful
nge for me that in three years I might write all these
Visions
display Natures cruel holiness: the deceits of Natural
Religion
king in my Cottage Garden, sudden I beheld
Virgin Ololon & addressd her as a Daughter of Beulah
gin of Providence fear not to enter into my Cottage
at is thy message to thy friend: what am I now to do
it again to plunge into deeper affliction? behold me
dy to obey. but pity thou my Shadow of Delight
ter my Cottage. comfort her, for she is sick with fatigue

Blake walking in his garden at Felpham with Ololon descending
(taken from Blake's Milton page 40)

Robert Hartley Cromek, drawing by Flaxman

'The Spiritual Form of Nelson Guiding Leviathan'

Thus wept the Angel voice & as he wept the terrible blasts
Of trumpets, blew a loud alarm across the Atlantic deep.
No trumpets answer; no reply of clarions or of fifes,
Silent the Colonies remain and refuse the loud alarm.

On those vast shady hills between America & Albions shore
Now barr'd out by the Atlantic sea: call'd Atlantean hills:
Because from their bright summits you may pass to the Golden world
An ancient palace, archetype of mighty Emperies.
Rears its immortal pinnacles, built in the forest of God
By Ariston the king of beauty for his stolen bride.

Here on their magic seats the thirteen Angels sat perturb'd
For clouds from the Atlantic hover o'er the solemn roof.

America plate 10, Orc in his 'red flames' of Energy

'Newton'; colour print by William Blake

James Parker; drawing by Flaxman

'laboured to a superabundant blackness'. The Satan picture from Milton is also experimental. Such works 'have been bruized and knocked about without mercy to try all experiments'.

The four Biblical works dealt with Jacob's Ladder, angels hovering over Jesus in the sepulchre, soldiers casting lots for his garments, Adam and Eve finding Abel's body. Blake says that he would like to see them on an enlarged scale ornamenting church altars; and he calls on the State to finance such church art. (That is, he hopes to see his paintings in the churches which he has always denounced as centres of evil.) *The Bramins* shows 'Mr. Wilkin translating the *Geeta* [*Gita*], an ideal design, suggested by the first publication of that part of the Hindu scriptures'. Blake means Sir Charles Wilkins whose version of the *Bhagvat Geeta* appeared in 1785. There are several points at which Blake's mythology seems to draw on Hindu creation-myths. The Hindu creator spins out seven threads, which are later absorbed back. Urizen is seen as a great spider: 'O Spider, spread thy web'. A design in *Europe* shows the spider entangling man and nature in the web's meshes. Indeed Blake's whole concept of the Net of Religion has this sort of imagery behind it. The *Bedang Shaster* sees affection as threefold, creative, preserving and destructive. 'From the opposite actions of the creative and destructive quality in matter, self-motion first arose,' says the *Samsara*. Four persons are born of Brimha's breath, who together form a living body of permanent intellectual existence, and so on.[19]

The longest description is that of the picture of Chaucer and the twenty-nine Pilgrims. Blake analyses the characters and claims that character has a permanent aspect which asserts itself in all periods. Chaucer thus provides a social picture as relevant to the modern as to the medieval world; only the accidents vary. 'I have known multitudes of those who would have been monks in the age of monkery, who in this deistical age are deists.' A prospectus was available asking for subscriptions to the engraving of the picture. Blake seems to have meant to open the exhibition in mid-May, but delays may have held it up till September when its one and only notice appeared. It certainly stayed open long after what was announced as its closing date, late September. It attracted almost no serious attention, though a certain amount of people may have visited it out of curiosity and made it worth while for James to keep it on.

On 14 August young Butts wrote to his mother, who was at their country house at Epsom, that he had called on the Blakes and found them well. 'They intend to pay the promised visit to Epsom'. On 17 September came the one

8

review of the exhibition, by Robert Hunt in the *Examiner*. It was a violent attack, and began:

If beside the stupid and mad-brained political projects of their rulers, the sane part of the people of England required fresh proof of the alarming increase of the effects of insanity, they will be too well convinced from its having lately spread into the hitherto sober region of Art.

Thus Robert Hunt linked Blake's art with the madness of the war-policy, which in fact Blake too detested. *The Grave* made the Hunts think him an evangelical fanatic; now through the Pitt and Nelson pictures, and the text to them, they took him for a glorifier of reaction. His show consisted of 'a few wretched pictures' and the Catalogue was 'a farrago of nonsense, unintelligibleness, and egregious vanity, the wild effusions of a distempered brain'. He was 'an unfortunate lunatic, whose personal inoffensiveness secures him from confinement'. Robert Hunt had an easy task in representing him as a victim of megalomania by citing his self-praise and his abuse of Rubens.

We can hardly blame Robert when Blake had taken so much trouble to hide his real opinions and to make his pictures seem aimed at supporting war and reaction. He had even used Nelson's famous signal in what on the face of it was a call for State aid for art that idealised the war-party. 'England expects that every man should do his duty, in Arts, as well as in Arms, or in the Senate.' When we consider how strong were the forces of reaction against which the Hunts were fighting, we cannot wonder at their anger against an effort to divert the arts in the worst possible direction. Indeed it is very difficult to understand how Blake could have sunk all his principles so shamelessly as in the call to make the arts do their duty like the armed forces and the State. The exhibition was yet one more disaster for him, and we are forced to admit that with his devious tactics he deserved this time what he got. It is noteworthy that none of the illuminated books, not even *Songs of Innocence*, was exhibited and put on sale, yet what better chance ever came his way of bringing those books to public attention?

Whatever he might write about forgiveness, he never forgave anyone he considered, rightly or wrongly, to be his enemy; as we saw in his last letter to Hayley, he wanted them punished in eternity. He maintained a furious hatred of the Hunt brothers, which he expressed in a symbolic three-headed figure, Hand, in *Milton* and *Jerusalem*. This figure was based on the pointing-finger emblem used in the *Examiner*. Hand, separating from Albion's bosom in *Jerusalem*, becomes the Reasoning Spectre, the source of division in both individual and society. He absorbs the other sons and sprouts from his bosom the Polypus, which overspreads the earth; he is responsible for war and the Satanic mill of industrialism; he wants to devour Los and Albion, and even to destroy the Saviour. (How Blake could blame the Hunts for the war, when they were brave and consistent radicals, it is impossible to surmise. He hated them, they had attacked him, so they could be blamed for anything evil.) The triad of brothers is made up of Hand (the heartless head), Hyle (the headless heart), and Coban (apparently the ravening loins). When Hand first appears, in Milton, he has 'become a rock: Sinai & Horen is Hyle & Coban'—that is, the trio stand for the Law. They later surround Milton with a girdle. These passages in *Milton* were inserted after September 1809; the earlier attack on *The Grave* would not have driven Blake to such an infuriated retort. He thus incorporates Hayley (Hyle) with the arch-villain Hand.[20]

In October young George Cumberland visited the show and wrote to his father of the Catalogue, a great curiosity: 'He has given Stothard a compleat set down'. Cumberland asked for two copies and wrote in November that the catalogue was 'truly original—*part vanity part madness*—part very good sense'. How many pictures had been sold? How many persons subscribed to the Chaucer engraving? 'Tell him with my best regards that I was not among the Subscribers it was because I literally cannot afford to lay out a shilling in any thing but *Taxes & necessaries of Life*.' Blake sent a ticket to Ozias Humphry. He disagreed with Ozias that Florentine and Venetian art could coexist—a thesis he himself had set out earlier—and prophesied that Venetian and Flemish art would be destroyed.

This year, 1809, Butts paid him £21 (7 April), 10 guineas (10 July), 10 guineas (10 August), 10 guineas (4 October), and £20 (25 November).

In the spring of 1810 Crabb Robinson grew interested in Blake. Born in 1775, he was articled to a Colchester attorney, but between 1800 and 1805 he studied at various places in Germany, becoming acquainted with many of the great literary figures such as Goethe, Schiller, Herder and Wieland. He was then war correspondent for *The Times* in Spain, and on returning to London studied for the bar. He came on some Blake texts owned by a Miss Iremonger of Upper Grosvenor Street, whom he described as a Unitarian, a sort of free-thinker, and she introduced him to patrons of Flaxman, such as Thomas Hope.

In April Crabb Robinson went to Blake's show, which was still open

The Entrance was 2/d Catalogue included I was deeply interested by the Catalogue as well as the pictures I took four—telling the brother I hoped he would let me in again—He said—Oh! as often as you please'—I dare say such a thing had never happened before or did afterwards.

The paintings 'filled several rooms of an ordinary dwelling-house'. In June Crabb Robinson came again, bringing Charles and Mary Lamb. Southey also looked in at some time, his interest stirred perhaps by Robinson. Later Lamb spoke of the 'marvellous strange pictures, visions of the brain, which he [Blake] asserts that he has seen'; they were 'of great merit, but hard, dry, yet with grace'. He rated Blake's Pilgrims far above Stothard's. Southey wrote of the show in 1830 to Caroline Bowles, and in *The Doctor* (1834–7) cited much of Blake's account of *The Ancient Britons*, describing the designs as often hideous, but at times suggesting that 'nothing but madness' prevented Blake from being the sublimest painter of this or any other country. The important point is however that both Lamb and Southey saw only an oddity at the time and felt no impulse to write about Blake. Lamb's comments were dredged up in 1824 when he was not sure if Blake was still alive; Southey wrote well after Blake's death.*

Crabb Robinson's essay on Blake, printed in German in 1811, was generally sympathetic, but with the usual qualifications. Blake reveals the union of genius and madness, a condition of great psychological interest. His religious convictions have earned him the name of an absolute lunatic so that connoisseurs know nothing of him and well-wishers cannot help betraying pity while they express admiration. Robinson later repeats that his belief 'in the intercourse which, like Swedenborg, he enjoys with the spiritual world has more than anything else injured his reputation'. He notes the fixed ideas that Blake vehemently held, gleams of reason and intelligence amid aberrations, and a host of expressions more likely to be found in a German than an English writer. The poems are discussed. *Poetical Sketches* shows in the metre of its lyrics a total ignorance of the art, but the dramatic pieces have wildness and loftiness of imagination. *Songs of Innocence and Experience*

---

* In May Blake wrote in his Notebook, opposite a drawing of himself, '23 May 1810 found the Word Golden'. The name Golden Square was familiar to him from earliest childhood. His new discovery of the word (its inner significance) may be connected with his taking over of Brothers' idea of Jerusalem as a square construction. The Golden Square was Paradise.

has decorations varying between the monstrous hieroglyphs of the Egyptians and not ungraceful arabesques, with vivid colours.

The poems, he considers, deserve both the highest praise and the gravest censure. Some are childlike songs of great beauty and simplicity, while others are excessively childish. *Songs of Experience* is made up of 'metaphysical riddles and mystical allegories. Among them are poetic pictures of the highest beauty and sublimity; and again there are poetical fancies which can scarcely be understood even by the initiated.' Robinson cites some examples including *Holy Thursday*, *The Tyger* and *The Garden of Love*. He then mentions *Europe* and *America*, citing a few lines but finding only a 'mysterious and incomprehensible rhapsody'. He adds, 'These Prophecies, like the Songs, appear never to have come within the ken of the wider public'. His essay, the only attempt at all seriously to grapple with Blake's work in his lifetime, was unknown in England.[21]

About this time Blake met a young man, Seymour Stocker Kirkup. Writing in 1865–6 Kirkup said he could still recall the *Ancient Britons* well enough to draw it. He himself was a partisan of the colourists and thought Blake mad, but always treated him with respect and did not contradict him. 'He was very kind & communicative to me—& so I believe he was to everybody except Schiavonetti. I used to wonder [at] his praise of Fuseli and Flaxman, my two first masters, for their tastes were so different to his, wh. Fuseli especially disliked & he was a magnanimous fellow though a sharp critic.' Kirkup, thinking Blake mad, neglected the opportunities of meeting him which the Buttses threw in his way, though he saw him now and then from 1810 to 1816, when he left for Italy. 'I only heard of him as the engraving-master of my old school-fellow Tommy. They [Buttses] did not seem to value him as we do now.' He adds, 'His excellent old wife was a sincere believer in all his visions. She told me seriously one day, "I have very little of Mr. Blake's company; he is always in Paradise". She prepared his colours, and was as good as a servant. He had no other.' Blake, we see, was earning a little as a teacher; another pupil of his about this time was William Seymour, who seems to have paid 18s. a week.

Another side of Blake came up in a dispute with C. H. Bellenden Ker, who on 20 August wrote to Cumberland praising *The Grave*, which he was too poor to buy. He soon wrote again, in a sadder strain. Three years back, when his father hoped to inherit the Duke of Roxborough's estate, he, Ker, had asked Blake at his leisure to do two drawings, to be paid for when the estate was gained. Now Blake had unexpectedly sent the drawings with a bill for

20 guineas. Ker was thunderstruck, 'not Knowing Where in the World [to] get any money'. Cumberland failed to pacify Blake, who was harassing Ker in late August. Ker says, 'I wrote at last to propose 15 Gs.—no—then to pay the price any mutual friend or friends shd. put on them—no—then I proposed to pay 10£ first and 10£ 3 months afterwds. no—and then he arrested me—and then defended the action and now perhaps [he] will never get a shilling of the 20 L. [he ori]ginally intended to defraud me of'.²²

The case does not seem to have come to trial. Ker must somehow have raised the money; for later, telling Cumberland how he called on Stothard with a commission from Lord Digby, he said, 'Blake is more knave than fool and made me pay 30 Guineas for 2 Drawings which were never orderd and which were as [illegible] as they were infamously done'. Blake, it seems, rankling under his treatment by men like Cromek, was getting his own back on the inoffensive Ker. This year, 1810, he had from Butts: £21 (16 January), 10 guineas (3 March), £21 (14 April), 5 guineas (30 June), 15 guineas (14 July), 10 guineas (20 September), 10 guineas (18 December).

Blake still had hopes of his Chaucer print and he wrote a public address to go with it, which never got beyond his notebook. He once more attacked the Venetians and the Flemish, and praised himself. 'Mr. B.'s Inventive Powers & his Scientific Knowledge of Drawing is on all sides acknowledg'd.' Had he really brought himself to believe that? or did he hope by the confident remark to make others believe it? Engraving is a lost art in England because of 'an artfully propagated opinion that Drawing spoils an Engraver'. His own art, of which Heath and Stothard were awkward imitators, was that of Dürer and the engravers. The *Examiner* attack exemplified the way in which his character 'has been blasted these thirty years, both as an artist & as a Man'; but 'the manner in which I routed out the nest of villains will be seen in a Poem concerning my Three years' Herculean Labours at Felpham, which I will soon publish'. This poem must be *Milton*. He then goes on to pour out his resentments against the men who befriended him.

Secret Calumny & open Profession of Friendship are common enough all the world over, but have never been so good an occasion of Poetic Imagery. When a Base Man means to be your Enemy he always begins with being your Friend. Flaxman cannot deny that one of the very first Monuments he did, I gratuitously design'd for him; at the same time he was blasting my character as an Artist to Macklin, my Employer, as Macklin told me at the time; how much of his Homer & Dante he will allow to be mine I do not know, as he went far enough off to Publish them, even to Italy, but the Public will know & Posterity will know.*

Then he turns to firmer ground in attacking commerce and the cash-nexus. 'Resentment for Personal Injuries has had some share in this Public Address, but Love to my Art & Zeal for my Country a much Greater.' He attacks the monopolising trader 'who Manufactures Art by the Hands of Ignorant Journeymen'. Barry and Hogarth exemplified the independent artist. The art-establishment has brought it about that 'most Englishmen have a Contempt for Art, which is the Greatest Curse that can fall upon a Nation'. He himself has been starved out by 'Calumny & the Arts of Trading Combination'. Then he divagates into the claim that an artist who 'studies & imitates the Effects of Nature' is injuring his country. (We know he found that 'Models are difficult—enslave one—efface from one's mind a conception or reminiscence which was better'. He never asks if the conception should not be strong enough to stand up against nature. For him the artist should learn by copying other art-works.) He drives home his moral with a poem, 'Now Art has lost its mental Charms France shall subdue the World in Arms.' He himself was sent down at birth to renew the Arts in Britain. Then France will fall down and adore, and wars will end. But if Britain refuses the renewal that Blake brings, France will take over. He appeals to the Spirit who loves Britain, 'round which the Fiends of Commerce smile'. (*Smile* comes in to rhyme with *isle*, replacing the rhymes *shore-roar*.)[23]

This argument leads on to the question of employing artists in public works. Blake calls on the Society for the Encouragement of Arts to consider his Plan for 'Monuments to the dead'. As for himself, 'the Lavish praise I have received from all Quarters for Invention & drawing has Generally been accompanied by this: "he can concieve but he cannot Execute;" This Absurd assertion has done me, & may still do me, the greatest mischief. I call for Public protection against these Villains'. He ends by taking up Hogarth's phrase and extending it: 'Every Line is the Line of Beauty'. But this idealisation of the line as a thing-in-itself loses sight of Hogarth's idea of the line of beauty as expressing the movement and tension of forms.

* He discusses the engravers Woolett, Strange, Basire, and tells of an argument with the painter West, 'who hesitated & equivocated' about the labour and care used in different styles of engraving. West said there was more work in a print by Woolett than one by Basire. Blake says that Woolett could not draw a leaf, 'all his study was to make clean strokes and mossy tints—how then should he be able to make use of either Labour or Care, unless the Labour and Care of Imbecility'. He is defending his concept of sharp outlines or bounding lines.

About the same time Blake rewrote and printed the Prospectus for the Chaucer print. To this period also belongs the poem, 'I rose up at the break of day', in which he repudiates the struggle for money. He is nerving himself to accept the poverty which has been steadily enclosing him. He no doubt kept on writing epigrams against old friends, now become (in his mind) his enemies. Linnell states that later he saw Blake offer to shake hands with Stothard at a meeting of artists, but Stothard repulsed him. Also, that Blake called on him when he was ill and was refused admittance. Stothard's son, however, in 1863, denied these stories. 'On one occasion I was sent to Blake with a message from my father, when I found him living in a court off the Strand, and met him on the stairs, saying to me "he had a battle with the devil below to obtain the coals" which seemed to me to indicate madness.' This year Ozias Humphry died.

It was now, it seems, that Blake took up the 1773 engraving of Joseph of Arimathea and described the figure as one of the artists who built the cathedrals, 'of whom the World was not worthy'. He also wrote an elaborate account, *A Vision of the Last Judgement*, meant for the Catalogue but never printed. He defines the Judgement as the moment on earth when the Antinomian vision triumphs and the religious obsession with law and morality ends. The last days are characterised by a general contempt for 'Imagination, Art & Science, & all Intellectual Gifts, all the Gifts of the Holy Ghost'. Blake continually makes clear that for him the Last Judgement is not a theological concept, but represents an earthly resolution of the conflicts inside history, the conflicts of a fallen or divided society which must face and overcome itself or perish. 'A Last Judgement is necessary, because Fools flourish' and 'Poverty is the Fool's Rod, which at last is turn'd on his own back; this is a Last Judgement—when Men of Real Art Govern & Pretenders Fall'. The problem is to deepen consciousness, to extend the range of the realising imagination. 'The Treasures of Heaven are not Negations of Passion, but Realities of Intellect, from which all the Passions Emanate Uncurbed in their Eternal Glory . . . The Last Judgement is an Overwhelming of Bad Art & Science.'[24]

But his depressed state and his inability to see how the great change is to occur leads him to pessimism about politics.

I am really sorry to see my Countrymen trouble themselves about Politics. If Men were wise, the Most arbitrary Princes could not hurt them, If they are not wise, the Freest Government is compell'd to be a Tyranny. Princes appear to me to be Fools.

Houses of Commons & Houses of Lords appear to me to be fools; they seem to me to be something Else besides Human Life.

The last sentence is true enough of politics in the limited sense; but the passage as a whole shows as abstractly moral an approach to political issues as could be found in Locke or any of the scorned Deists. It ignores the processes by which systems grow free or tyrannical. In *Jerusalem* (52) Blake denounced this sort of separation of morals and politics as vicious nonsense. 'What is a church, & what is a theatre? Are they two & not one? Are not religion & politics the same thing? Brotherhood is religion, O demonstration of reason, dividing families in cruelty & pride.' Unable to accept this statement of the unity of the life-process, 'Albion fled from the Divine Vision', and in his Address Blake is fleeing from it too. In the poem Albion's flight marks a turning-point: he collapses and only his spectre remains active.

Blake over these years was being torn between a ferocious animosity to those he considered his enemies, and his efforts to school himself into a creed of universal forgiveness. Cromek's deceits and the failure of the exhibition gave full rein to his rages. The deaths of Schiavonetti in June 1810 and of Cromek in March 1812 seem to have aroused in him an unholy joy and a sense of magical power. He felt that he could kill off all his enemies or at least that God would do it for him. In *Jerusalem* Hand (the Hunts) is set for trial on the Anvils of bitter Death; he tries to protest, but trembles at the 'Mace Whirled round from heaven to earth'. He keeps on editing the *Examiner* till 'scorn of others & furious pride Freeze round him to bars of steel & to iron rocks beneath his feet'. Thus Blake mocks at the Hunt brothers, two of whom were jailed for their 'scorn' of the Prince Regent in 1813 and 1814, and had to do their editorial work from behind prison bars. That they suffered as radicals, as opponents of the war policy, does not affect Blake's hatred. He accuses them with complete irrationality of being the main forces of the war, building castles and fortifications, and forging 'bars of condens'd thoughts . . . Into the sword of war: into the bow and arrow: Into the thundering cannon and into the murdering gun'. Hand becomes imperial power: 'Lo! Hand has people Babel & Nineveh'. Hand becomes the central force of evil: 'The Wheel of Hand, incessantly turning,' determined to suppress Blake and carry on the war. To say there is here no personal rancour (as Frye does) is nonsense; it is precisely because the personal hate is so unbounded that Hand and the magnifications of Blake's enemies become symbolic figures and draw wide social forces into their damned being.

8*

One value to Blake of his vision of Hand as owning complete power to destroy or suppress is that he now has a perfectly adequate reason for not trying to publish anything. To do so would be to put him at once at the mercy of hired villains. Also, with Hand in power, nobody has ears to hear or eyes to see the truth. The government which the radical Hunts were attacking fades out as the guilty system. Blake–Los turns to building the City of Art, Golgonooza, as an escape from Hand.

In his mixture of abject fear of the Hunts and his magical sense of death-power, Blake denounces even poor Rose who defended him at the trial. In the verses, 'And his legs carried it like a long fork', he indulges in his power-fantasies as a dispenser of death, and writes, 'And Felpham Billy rode out every morn Horseback with Death over the fields of corn'—a reference to Hayley's riding accident—Death, 'who with iron hand cuff'd in the after-noon The Ears of Billy's Lawyer & Dragoon'. No difference is made between Rose and Scolfield as creatures of Hayley. In this poem Schiavonetti is called Assassinetti; Stothard is Stewhard and Flaxman is Jack Hemp, the Hangman. 'The Examiner, whose very name is Hunt, Call'd Death a Madman trembling for the affront, Like trembling Hare sits on his weakly paper On which he used to dance & sport & caper.' Hare is Hoare, whom Blake, unable to forgive his praise of Stothard, makes tremble at the games of Death.

We see then where the revelation at the Truchsessian Gallery has led Blake. It convinced him that he must put all his efforts into his art and that if he did so he would triumph. Hence the way in which he nerved himself to conceive and carry out the exhibition. But at the same time his increasing fears of attack by the watch-fiends and the opportunist element which crept in with his turn to Jesus made him compromise in this one attempt to appeal directly to the public with what could only be taken as support of the State and its war-basis. (The first intrusion of the opportunist element had been in his dedica-tion of *The Grave* to the Queen, but we might say that its ultimate roots lay in the touches of self-abasement which all along, as a craftsman hovering on the starvation-line, he had felt impelled to make to those on whom he financi-ally depended.) The defeat encountered at the exhibition was crushing and he never fully recovered from it. The next decade was one of great misery and depression for him, and it says much for his stamina that he was able to go on working at *Jerusalem* and etching it. The balm that Linnell brought him after 1818 helped him to get through his final years and do the drawings for Job and Dante; but the accounts of Hand and Hyle in *Jerusalem* show how painfully his mind kept on revolving round the failure of his hopeful exhibition. The attack in the *Examiner* was seen as the final act in a concerted, treacherous and murderous campaign that had been launched at Felpham.

As he retreated into a social ethic of forgiveness, his personal hatreds grew more exacerbated. Since he no longer exulted over the execution of kings for political crimes, he wanted to see them beheaded for patronising the art of which he disapproved. But now it all happened in the mind. In the Public Address he saw himself as a mental prince who should 'decollate & Hang' the souls of princes 'as Guilty of Mental High Treason' for turning to the wrong art. The political act was transformed into a purely mental one and related solely to the world of art. This changed attitude to politics was linked with the post-Truchsessian concept of himself as primarily an artist, not a revolutionary poet.

12

London and Jerusalem, 1811–20

Blake now sinks into almost total obscurity for several years. In 1811 Crabb Robinson continued to be interested in him, discussed him with some friends in January, and on 10 March showed the *Night Thoughts* to William Hazlitt, who saw no merit in the designs. Robinson then read him some of the *Songs of Innocence*. Hazlitt found them beautiful and 'only too deep for the vulgar'; Blake had no sense of the ludicrous, like God to whom all objects, even a worm crawling in a privy, were equally worthy. 'He is ruined by vain struggles to get rid of what presses on his brain—he attempts impossibles— I added—he is like a man who lifts a burthen too heavy for him; he bears it an instant, it then falls and crushes him. W.H. preferred the Chimney Sweeper.'

In late July Robinson was at a large party given by Lamb. He met Southey there. Southey had been at Blake's show, admired both his designs and poetic talents, but held him to be decidedly a madman. 'Blake, he says, spoke of his visions with the diffidence that is usual with such people. And did not seem to expect that he shod. be believed. He showed S. a perfectly mad poem called Jerusalem—Oxford Street is in Jerusalem.' (Southey had not understood Blake's idiom. The emanation Jerusalem is in Oxford Street.)

On 4 August Blake annotated an extract from *Bell's Weekly Messenger* about Peter le Cave, then in Wilton Gaol, who said that Morland had sold many of his (Peter's) paintings as his own. 'It confirms the Suspition I entertain'd concerning those two I Engraved from for J. H. Smith—That Morland could not have Painted them, as they were the works of a Correct Mind & no Blurrer.'[1]

The year 1812 is again almost a total blank. James Blake retired on a scanty independence and lived from now on in Cirencester Street. William exhibited four works with the Watercolour Society, of which he was a member: the pictures of Pitt and Nelson, the Pilgrims, and 'Detached Specimens of an original illuminated Poem, entitled "Jerusalem the Emanation of the Giant Albion" '. What pages, and how many, were thus shown, we do not know;

but the event, which brought no response, is noteworthy as the one time that Blake showed publicly even a couple of sheets of his prophecies.[2]

On 24 May Crabb Robinson walked out to Hampstead Heath with Wordsworth. The latter said that he thought Byron 'somewhat cracked', and this gave Robinson the chance to talk about Blake. He read some poems, no doubt again *Songs of Innocence*. Wordsworth was pleased with some and thought Blake had the elements of poetry, far more than Byron or Scott. But like Lamb and the others he was not enough interested to follow up Robinson's reading.*

The year 1813 is again almost a blank. On 12 January, after a lecture by Coleridge, Robinson talked at home with some friends, who knew nothing of Blake's poems. On 12 April Cumberland, on a London visit, 'Saw Blake who recommended Pewter to Scratch on with the Print—He is Doing Ld Spencer'—that is, engraving the portrait of the Earl by Phillips.[3]

We get some idea of how Blake felt about London in the account of Los's quest there in the second chapter of *Jerusalem*. Los sees everyone degraded and murdered, and roams about the city which he sees as 'rocks & precipices, caves of solitude and dark despair'. Watching brickmakers at work, he feels that 'the articulations of a man's soul' are treated as the clay is, stuck in a mould then knocked on to a board, till there are rows and rows of bricks ready to bake in the kilns and be used to 'build the pyramids'. Los seeks those responsible for the deadly work, but fails. And even if he did find them, he could not take vengeance, since the Divine Hand has so arranged things that the sinner will always escape and the revenger alone is 'the criminal of providence'. So he calls on Albion not to revenge his wrongs or he will be lost for ever.

Los traverses the outer villages, then comes into the city and sees 'every minute particular' or individual, 'the jewels of Albion, running down the kennels of the streets & lanes as if they were abhorred. Every universal form was become barren mountains of moral Virtue, and every minute particular hardened into grains of sand. And all the tendernesses of the soul cast forth as filth & mire Among the winding places of deep contemplation intricate to

---

* In December 1811 a pamphlet printed Chaucer's Prologue to his Tales in the original and in a modernised version; a part of Blake's engraving was used, with slight changes, and a vignette of his seems meant to show a part of Canterbury Cathedral. The preface, perhaps by Malkin, praised Blake's genius and fancy. Cromek died in 1812 and his widow sold the remainder of *The Grave*, with copyright, for £120 to E. Akkermann, who reissued the book.

where the Tower of London frowned dreadful over Jerusalem.' The edifice
of State power looks down on the people who are turned into refuse or
hardened out of humanity by the moral law.

Los's quest is a fundamental part of the theme of *Jerusalem*; for the frontispiece shows him crossing the threshold of an arched door into darkness,
holding a sun for light. His lifted hand suggests that he leads us into the
scene of action. Graffiti erased on the wall tell us that he enters the 'Void,
outside of Existence', which, thus tackled, becomes in time 'A Womb . . .
Albion's lovely land.' In the quest Los with his globe of fire searches 'the
interiors of Albion's bosom', to bring 'the tempters out'. Later we see the
traveller, who has found his own human form divine (undivided humanity),
springing up out of the tomb and looking forward. He begins to build the
new world, carrying the sun as a hod of mortar.[4]

All we know of 1814 is that Blake had a visit from Cumberland and a commission from Flaxman. In June Cumberland called to see the artist Cosway
at 51 South Molton Street, 'facing Poor Blake where he has been 3 Years'.
Afterwards he dropped in on Blake, 'still poor and Dirty'; in the evening he
visited Stothard who was 'still more dirty than Blake, yet full of Genius'.

Flaxman remained friendly to Blake. He mentioned him to Cary, Dante's
translator, who had spoken of the few English history painters. 'But Blake
is a wild enthusiast.' said Cary, 'isn't he?' Flaxman drew himself up. 'Some
think me an enthusiast.' Now, apparently on his own initiative, he asked
Blake to do the thirty-seven engravings from his Hesiod designs. Gilchrist
says that Blake did not take the kindly offer in good part. 'He would so far
rather have been recommended as a designer.' On 19 August Flaxman described
him as 'the best engraver of outlines' for dealing with a drawing of his (Flaxman's) monuments. The first Hesiod plate was finished on 22 September.[5]

We have seen how often Blake was dilatory with commissions; but he
probably worked hard enough at his own prophetic books. Indeed such work
may well have kept him from breakdown. Samuel Palmer once mentioned
to Blake a young artist who complained of illness. 'Oh,' said Blake, 'I never
stop for anything; I work on, whether ill or not.' Gilchrist says he kept a
manuscript by him as he engraved, now and then writing something down.
He also read as he worked, as plate-marks on his books testified.*

* 'He despised etching needles, and worked wholly with the graver in later years'
(Gilchrist). The Hesiod plates were etched; the Job plates, says Linnell, were wholly cut
with the graver.—His brother James, hard up, was one of the clerks under Butts in the
office of the Commissary General of Musters, though he does not appear in the accounts.

A few more details come up in 1815. In January Crabb Robinson was with Flaxman, who told tales of the credulous Sharp and remarked on Blake's refusal to listen to any other prophet. 'Blake lately told Flaxman that he had had a violent dispute with the Angels on some subject and had driven them away. Barry partook much of this strange insanity . . . excessive pride equally denoted Blake & Barry—Sharpe seems of a quiet & more amiable turn of mind'.

In April George Cumberland reported to his father that he and his brother had called on Blake and found him and his wife drinking tea, 'durtyer than ever'. He showed them his watercolour of the Last Judgement, so worked on that 'it is nearly as black as your Hat—the only lights are those of a *Hellish Purple*'. He was afraid 'they will make too great a man of Napoleon and enable him to come to this Country—Mrs B says that if this Country does go to War our K—g ought to loose his head'. We are reminded of the remarks that Scolfield alleged Catherine had made. Cumberland replied to his son, 'You have a free estimate of Blake—& his devilish Works—he is a little Cracked, but very honest—as to his wife she is the maddest of the two'. George was thinking of asking Blake's advice about engraving methods; his father told him, 'He will tell you any thing he knows'.[6]

Probably it was this spring that Blake went to the R.A. at Somerset House to draw the cast of the Laocoon for Rees' *Cyclopedia*. Fuseli came in and said, 'Why, Mr. Blake, you are a student? you might teach us'. About this time a young engraver, William Ensor, came to know Blake and made a pen-and-ink drawing of him that won the silver medal from the Society for the Encouragement of Arts, Manufactures, and Commerce. He may have bought work from Blake. A coloured set of *Night Thoughts* designs is inscribed: 'This copy was colour'd for me by Mr. Blake, W.E.' In this spring of 1815 Flaxman introduced Blake to Wedgwood, for whom Blake engraved pottery designs. On 29 July Wedgwood wrote approving a drawing but asking for a hole to be removed from the ladle. Blake did not reply till 8 September. Wedgwood accounts state that Blake had drawn a China-form fruit basket with stand, an oval cream bowl, an oval rose-top soup terrine, a butter-boat and so on. Two days later two items (basin and nurse-lamp) were credited to Mrs Blake. On 5 December Blake was intending to send drawings soon; on the 13th he sent some drawings and said he would soon complete drawings of all the articles he had. As he did not get payment, £30, for his engravings till 11 November 1816, we may surmise he was again dilatory.[7]

We get two glimpses of Blake in 1816. In July Nancy Flaxman wrote to her husband, asking how the Hesiod prints were getting on and telling of a clash between Blake and a friend who seems to be the Swedenborgian Charles Augustus Tulk. 'As I understand B— was very violent indeed beyond all *credence* only that he has served you his *best friend* the *same trick* [some] time back as you must well remember—but he [Tulk] *bought* a *drawing* of him. I have nothing to say in this affair It is too ticklish, only I know what happened both to yourself & me, & other people are not oblig'd to put up with Bs odd humours—but let that pass.' When we consider this episode together with the earlier harrassing of Ker, we see that under the strain of isolation and poverty Blake was liable to lose control of himself.*

Probably this summer he called on the bibliographer Thomas Frognall Dibdin to discuss the minor poems of Milton. Dibdin thought him a most extraordinary artist in his own particular element and admired his *Night Thoughts*, though he considered his Chaucer engraving inferior to Stothard's and felt that after the troubles with Cromek Blake 'seems absolutely to have lost his wits'. When they talked about Milton, Blake was soon 'far beyond my ken or sight', rapt in this third heaven. 'Never were such "dreamings" poured forth as were poured forth by my original visitor:—his stature mean, his head big and round, his forehead broad and high, his eyes blue, large, and lambent.' Dibdin asked Blake what he thought of Fuseli's *Lycidas*. Blake said that he didn't remember it, and Dibdin told him to study it for its poetic expressiveness. 'I learnt afterwards that my Visitor had seen it—but thought it "too tame".' Dibdin told Blake that 'our common friend, Mr. Maquerier, had induced me to purchase his "Songs of Innocence", and that I had no disposition "to repent my bargain" '.[9]

Blake had made twelve drawings to *L'Allegro* and *Il Penseroso* (on paper watermarked 1816), which he was doubtless beginning to engrave. Their style was gentler and more lyrical than the crisp precise style of those for *Paradise Lost*. He wrote a description of each drawing: 'The Lark is an Angel on the Wing . . .' In these days he seemed quite aloof from what was going on around him. In 1815 there was a revival and extension of the radical movement, to which the government responded with a national State of Alarm and a Seditious Meetings Act in March; in December came the Spa Fields riot.

---

* The Tulks had copies of *Poetical Sketches, Songs, No Natural Religion.* Tulk's daughter about 1860 gave a garbled account of her father's relations with Blake, whom she saw as 'much impressed with the Spiritual Truths in Swedenborg's Writings'. Her father rescued Blake and his wife from destitution.[8]

For the year 1817 we have the record of one meeting with Blake and a reference to him in print. John Gibson, a young sculptor from Liverpool (where Roscoe was his patron) called on Flaxman and Fuseli. 'I also presented myself without a note of introduction to Mr. Blake, after showing him my designs, he gave me much credit for the invention they displayed; he showed me his cartoons, and complained sadly of the want of feeling in England for high art, and his wife joined in with him and she was very bitter upon the subject.' (There had been a strong element of Satanism in Gibson's cartoon, *Fall of the Rebel Angels*, but Roscoe had drawn him into accepting the Greek Outline as the highest form of art.)

W. P. Carey's essay on West's *Death on the Pale Horse* was dated 31 December 1817. It dealt with the 'superior moral influence of paintings from *Sacred* history over those from *profane*', and expatiated enthusiastically on Blake's *The Grave*, praising the 'primitive simplicity of disposition and character' in the designs, united with 'bold and successful novelty, and a devotional grandeur of conception'. So little was Blake known that Carey had some difficulty in establishing that he was still alive and living in London. 'I have, however, heard enough to warrant my belief that his professional encouragement has been very limited, compared with his powers.'

How was Blake living? Tommy Butts may still have been his pupil and Butts may have bought a few drawings, but we have no records of payments after 1810. This year saw the Pentridge Rising, twenty-six prosecutions for seditious and blasphemous writings, and, in November, public hangings and quarterings.[10]

In 1819 Blake begins to come out of the shadows which have enclosed him since 1810.* He appears in an account by Lady Charlotte Bury of a dinner-party given by Lady Caroline Lamb, which seems to have occurred on 20 January this year. We have here the fullest picture by anyone of Blake in contact with other people.

Then there was another eccentric little artist, by name Blake; not a regular professional painter, but one of those persons who follow the art for its own sweet sake,

---

* The diary gives the date Tuesday, 20 January; and only in 1801, 1807, 1818, 1824 did that day fall on a Tuesday; Lawrence left England in 1818 and did not return till late March 1820. Also there are references to Lady Charlotte Lamb's scandalous novel, *Glenarvon*, 1816, and to Princess Caroline, who died 1821. Besides Blake a 'soft and sweet' miniaturist Miss Mee was present.

and derive their happiness from its pursuit. He appeared to me full of beautiful imaginations and genius; but how far the execution of his designs is equal to the conceptions of his mental vision, I know not, never having seen them. Main d'ouvre is frequently wanting where the mind is most powerful. Mr. Blake appears unlearned in all that concerns this world, and from what he said, I should fear he was one of those whose feelings are far superior to his situation in life. He looks care-worn and subdued; but his countenance radiated as he spoke of his favourite pursuit, and he appeared gratified by talking to a person who comprehended his feelings. I can easily imagine that he seldom meets with any one who enters into his views; for they are peculiar, and exalted above the common level of received opinion.

I could not help contrasting this humble artist with the great and powerful Sir Thomas Lawrence, and think that the one was fully if not more worthy of the distinction and the fame to which the other has attained, but from which *he* is far removed. Mr. Blake however, though he may have as much right, from talent and merit, to the advantages of which Sir Thomas is possessed, evidently lacks that worldly wisdom and that grace of manner which make a man gain an eminence in his profession, and succeed in society. Every word he uttered spoke the perfect simplicity of his mind, and his total ignorance of all worldly matters.

He told me that Lady C[aroline] L[amb] had been very kind to him. 'Ah!' said he, 'There is a deal of kindness in that lady.' I agreed with him, and though it was impossible not to laugh at the strange manner at which she had arranged this party, I could not help admitting the goodness of heart and discrimination of talent which had made her patronise this unknown artist.

Sir T. Lawrence looked at me several times whilst I was talking with Mr. B., and I saw his lip curl with a sneer, as if he despised me for conversing with so insignificant a person. It was very evident that Sir Thomas did not like the company he found himself in, though he was too well-bred and too prudent to hazard a remark upon the subject.[11]

We know nothing more of the relations of Blake and Lady Caroline.

Tulk, apparently reconciled with Blake, lent a copy of *Songs* to Coleridge who on 6 February wrote to H. F. Cary that he had been reading poems with very wild and interesting pictures. He called Blake 'a man of Genius—and I apprehend a Swedenborgian—certainly a mystic emphatically . . . verily I am in the very mire of commonplace common-sense compared with Mr. Blake, apo- or rather ana-calyptic Poet, and Painter!' Soon after he wrote at more length, finding faults and a few beauties in the designs. The faults were 'despotism in the symbols'. The forms have an effect of rigidity or of exossation [no bones]; the drapery is ambiguous. 'Is it a garment—or the

body incised and scored out?' Coleridge then listed the poems with marks as
to their excellence. He liked best *Divine Image, Night* and especially *Little
Black Boy*; he put next *Holy Thursday, Infant Joy* and *School Boy*. He
placed third *Laughing Song, Earth's Answer, Garden of Love, Tyger,* and
Little Boy Lost. The others still gave him great pleasure, though he liked
least *Chimney Sweeper, Voice of Bard, Blossom, Nurse's Song, To Tirzah,
Poison Tree* and *Little Girl Lost*. He would have liked the last-named poem
left out, not for its lack of innocence, 'but for the too probable want of it in
many readers'. His reaction is thus conventional and prudish. His long-
winded and pompous comment on *The Little Vagabond* shows how unable
he was even to begin to enter Blake's Antinomian world. He fears that the
poem will tempt weak minds to sink 'the Love of the eternal *Person* into *good
nature*', though he does even more disapprove of the 'the servile, blind-worm,
wrap-rascal Scurf-coat of FEAR of the *modern Saints*'.[12] Like Lamb,
Southey, Hazlitt and Wordsworth he saw in the last resort only an oddity,
which he made no effort to bring to the general public.*

In June Blake wrote to Dawson Turner, botanist and antiquary of Great
Yarmouth, with a list of his illuminated books. He has raised the prices:
America, Europe and *Urizen* now cost five guineas each; *Visions, Songs of
Innocence* and *Songs of Experience* three guineas each; *Thel,* two guineas and
Milton ten. 'The few I have Printed & Sold are sufficient to have gained me
great reputation as an Artist, which was the only thing intended. But I have
never been able to produce a Sufficient number for a general Sale by means
of a regular Publisher.' This is sales-talk. There is not a fraction of evidence
that the books ever earned him the least reputation or that he tried to sell
them publicly. He does not cite *Song of Los* or *Ahania,* of which he seems to
have printed only one copy each, or *The Book of Los* or *Marriage*.

The poem, *The Everlasting Mercy,* seems to have been written in 1818. It
shows no concern for the texts of the New Testament; Jesus is made a
replica of Blake himself. In his Notebook Blake wrote, 'I always thought that
Jesus Christ was a Snubby or I should not have worship'd him, if I had
thought he had been one of those long spindle nosed rascals'. The poem says

---

* Probably this spring appeared *City Scenes,* a book for children, anonymous (though
by Jane and Ann Taylor). Blake's *Holy Thursday* was cited, without his name. An engraving copied in larger size his etching of children walking two by two. The Taylors
did not live in London but may have known Blake; they had been trained as a fourth
generation of engravers and their grandfather knew Fuseli. In May Hazlitt in a lecture
cited Blake's comment on Chaucer as having numbered the classes of men, but did not
name him. Crabb Robinson had probably shown or given him the Catalogue.

'Thine has a great hook nose like thine, Mine has a snub nose like to mine'. The episode of the woman taken in adultery is used to prove that Jesus advocated free love, whereas in the New Testament the moral is that all are equally sinful and the woman is to go and sin (love) no more. The poem is one of great power in the rushing vehemence of the couplets, where the varying accents produce a richness and impact that is metrically without parallel in the uses of the form. Blake brings to a head the Antinomian picture of Jesus as the rebel defying all law and morality, and demanding universal tolerance and acceptance of people in their complex diversity, which he had first set out in the devil's reply at the end of *The Marriage of Heaven and Hell*.

About this time also he redid *The Gates of Paradise*, with deep changes of meaning. Stress is laid on forgiveness, with denunciation of the Jehovah who perverted all the teachings of Jesus: 'And the Dead Corpse from Sinai's heat Buried beneath his Mercy Seat'. Stress is also laid on the revolt against the female principle, with an attempt to relate the work to Blake's later mytho-logical systems, so that it expresses the struggle in and through the existing world, with the focus turned back from death into life.

In June occurred an event that had a profound effect on Blake's final years. Young Cumberland introduced him to John Linnell, aged twenty-six and already doing well as an artist. George told his father, 'They like one another much and Linnel has promised to get him some work'. Linnell was a Baptist who, after Blake's death, thought of turning Quaker, then ceased to belong to any group, though he held fast to his evangelical outlook. At root his piety was conventional and he never understood Blake, though he came to have a strong feeling for him and did much to make his last years tolerable. On 24 June he called on Blake with his portrait of a Baptist preacher, Upton, which Blake was to engrave. 'We soon became intimate.' Blake at the time had scarcely enough employment 'to live by at the prices he could obtain'. Linnell was 'somewhat taken aback by the boldness of some of his assertions'. Still, he never saw anything the least like madness. 'For I never opposed him spitefully as many did but being really anxious to fathom if possible the amount of truth which might be in his most startling assertions I generally met with a sufficiently rational explanation in the most really friendly & con-ciliatory manner.' In that account we read Linnell's own character. He was determined to accept Blake as a truly religious man who at times resorted to paradox in the face of a disbelieving world.

He introduce Blake to John Varley, whose pupil he, Linnell, had been from the age of twelve. Varley, some twenty years younger than Blake, was a founder of the Society of Painters in Watercolours and a capable landscapist. A big clumsy man, fond of boxing, careless and extravagant, he was always hard up and always in high spirits. His house was burned down three times and his son was a mental defective, but he saw all his troubles as necessary and crowning mercies. He loved anything mysterious, was a palmist and an astrologer, adept at predicting disasters for himself and his friends, and strongly attracted to all the visionary qualities in Blake, which he took quite literally. Linnell adds that even to Varley Blake would occasionally explain unasked how he believed that both Varley and he, Linnell, could see the same visions as he did; making it evident to me that Blake claimed the possession of 'the same powers only in a greater degree that all men possessed and which they undervalued in themselves & lost through love of sordid pursuits—pride, vanity, & the unrighteous mammon'.

Linnell took Blake round to see works of art. In July they went to Lord Suffolk's 'to see pictures', and in August to Colnaghi's. Occasionally Catherine was drawn in 'to take tea &c.' On 9 September Linnell called on the Blakes in the evening and two days later he brought Blake £5. Next day Blake brought a proof of the Upton plate and named £15 as the price for what he had done. 'Mr Varley and Mr Constable stayed with Blake.' Perhaps it was then that the episode recounted by C. R. Leslie occurred. Blake was looking through a sketchbook of Constable's and said of a drawing of an avenue of firs on Hampstead Heath, 'Why, this is not drawing, but inspiration,' and Constable replied, 'I never knew it before; I meant it for drawing'. In September Linnell went with Varley to the Blakes, and next day, 'Dr Thornton called & Mr Blake. Went with Mr Blake to Mr Varley evg.'. That evening Blake and Linnell worked out their accounts. Linnell was paid £42 10*s*. for the Upton plate, of which Blake got 15 guineas. (How slow Blake was on his engraving jobs is shown by the date on the finished plate: 1 June 1819.)[13]

The year 1819 saw Blake carrying on in close relation with Linnell and Varley, and soon as other young artists gathered round him the pattern was set which carried on till his death. These young men looked up to him, admired and humoured him, but failed truly to enter the world of his imagination. Their stories about him, told and retold, provided the basis for a Blake legend which tended to sentimentalise him into a pious eccentric, eliminating all the elements that bit deeply into life. Three of Linnell's notes show him in June and August taking Blake round to persons who might help him, a bookseller like Carpenter or James Holmes, a fashionable miniaturist. On 20 August they went to see a copy of Raphael's *Transfiguration* made by G. H. Harlowe, who had died in February. (This was the month of the Peterloo massacre; and the year saw a general attack on the freedom of the press, with seventy-five prosecutions.)*

On 11 October Blake wrote to Linnell arranging a meeting at noon on Thursday to see Thomas Heaphy, engraver and water-colourist. Round this time he began to make drawings of spirits for Varley. Clearly he was stimulated and flattered by Varley's unreserved belief in his visions, though he refused to share or accept Varley's astrological views. On the back of a drawing of Richard I the latter wrote: 'Drawn from his Spectre', added some astrological jottings, and went on, 'W. Blake fecit Octr. 14 1819 at 1/4 Past 12 Midnight'. Gilchrist says he drew two heads of this king, 'and each one is different'. On 18 October Blake drew the Man who built the Pyramids, 'Degrees of Cancer ascending'. Gilchrist says Blake made forty or fifty such sketches. Sometimes the spirit came at call, sometimes Blake had to wait; sometimes he paused, 'I can't go on—it is gone! I must wait till it returns'. 'It has moved. The mouth is gone.' 'He frowns; he is displeased with my portrait of him.' When next day criticisms were made of the drawings, Blake replied, 'It *must* be right; I saw it so'. He drew Saul in armour with an odd helmet, which, owing to the spectre's position, he could not see clearly. So he left the drawing unfinished till some months later Saul appeared again.

October 1819 saw several spirit-drawings. 'Wat Tyler By Wm Blake from his spectre as in the Act of Striking the Tax Gatherer on the head Drawn Octr 30 1819 at 1h. A.M.' But the drawings went on, now and then, for years. Varley writes: 'Head of Achilles drawn by William Blake at my request 1825'. There were heads of Corinna the Theban, Lais the courtesan, Herod, the man who taught Blake painting in his dreams, the taskmaster killed by Moses in Egypt, William Wallace with Edward I stepping in front of him. Varley talked to Cunningham about the seances: 'I was his companion for nine years. I have sat beside him from ten at night till three in the morning,

---

* On 22 June Cumberland wrote to his son: 'Tell Blake a Mr Sivewright of Edinburgh has just claimed in some Philosophical Journal of Last month as his own invention Blake's method—& calls it Copper Blocks, I think'. T. Sivwright of Meggetland (now an Edinburgh suburb) collected art-works, especially prints and made experiments. The Edinburgh *Philosophical Journal* (June to October 1819) had an account by W. Lizars of a new way of engraving on copper in *alto relievo*, with acknowledgements to to Sivwright for help.

sometimes slumbering and sometimes waking, but Blake never slept; he sat with a pencil and paper drawing portraits of those whom I most desired to see.' But Cunningham was an unscrupulous romanticiser. He gives a lurid account of the drawing of the Ghost of a Flea: 'a face worthy of a murderer, holding a bloody cup in its clawed hands . . . a kind of glistening green and dusky gold, beautifully varnished'. Blake cries, 'Here he is—reach me my things—I shall keep my eye on him. There he comes, his eager tongue whisking out of his mouth, a cup in his hand to hold blood, and covered with a scaly skin of gold and green.' Varley's own account of the episode in his *Zodiacal Physiognomy* has nothing melodramatic in it.[14] Blake made a drawing of the head and another of the full figure; neither of which show the cup. In a tempera painting there is a large bowl. In each work there are many differences about the head, so that Blake was certainly not drawing from a single head that he had seen or conjured up. Varley says that the sketches were made on sleepless nights, so that it has been suggested that Blake suffered from migrainous visions. Fleas and worse vermin would have been common in his dirty, cramped and cluttered room. But he seems to have based his drawing on the engraving of a flea seen under the microscope in Hooke's *Micrographia* (1665).

Blake may have exaggerated the extent to which he could summon and sustain images, but there can be no doubt that he owned the power to project in varying ways an internal image, and was thus what has been called an eidetic. My own feeling is that he developed the power of eidetic projection in the period of composing the *Four Zoas*, as a result of the extreme strain he felt at that period, the increase of mental dissociation, and the creative struggle to overcome that dissociation. Clearly it helped to sustain him by intensifying his conviction of a living world of the imagination; but it may well also in his later years have become disturbing and exhausting. Varley's account of his sleepless sessions does not suggest a happy use of the faculty.*

---

* I myself in 1931, after a fortnight or so of strict fasting, saw the Egyptian goddess Sekhmet at the end of the room, not a statue, but a living form in a very clear light; the image lasted long enough for me to have a good look at it. Jaensch thus defines eidetic images: 'Like ordinary physiological after-images, they are always *seen* in the literal sense. They have this property of necessity and under all conditions, and share it with sensations. In other respects they can also exhibit the property of images. In those cases in which the imagination has little influence, they are merely modified after-images, deviating from the the norm in a definite way . . . In the other limiting case, when the influence of the imagination is at its maximum, they are ideas that, like after-images are projected outward and literally *seen*.'[15]

Linnell says that it was Varley 'who excited Blake to see or fancy the portraits of historical personages'. Varley 'did not admit of the explanations by which Blake reconciled his assertions with known truth. I have a sketch of the two men as they were seen one night in my parlour near midnight, Blake sitting in the most attentive attitude listening to Varley who is holding forth vehemently with his hand raised. The two attitudes are highly characteristic of the men for Blake by the side of Varley appeard decidedly the most sane of the two.'

About this time Blake read Spurzheim's *Observations on the Deranged Manifestations of the Mind, or Insanity* (1817). Having been so often called mad, he bravely decided to see what the medical profession had to say of the condition. He was disturbed by the passage stating that 'Religion is another fertile cause of insanity'. He annotated, 'Cowper came to me and said: "O that I were insane always. I will never rest. Can you not make me truly insane? . . . You retain health and yet are as mad as any of us all—over us all —mad as a refuge from unbelief—from Bacon, Newton and Locke.' He defiantly uses the term mad for the man who rejects the prevailing ideas of reason. Having stared so long and diligently at Romney's portrait of Cowper as he transferred it to copper he would have had no difficulty in conjuring up the face.

In 1820 we gain a few slight glimpses of Blake. Linnell continued to take him round. On 24 April, 'Spring Gardens with Mr Blake met the Duke of Argyll & dunned him for money due on portrait'. He had painted the Duke, his wife and his brother in 1817, and apparently had not been paid. On 8 May he took Blake to the painter H. Wyatt; also to Lady Ford: 'saw her pictures'. Three days later he had tea with Blake and Varley. On 6 June Cumberland

went to Blakes and read the Courier to him about Queens arrival Mr Linel came in—& I recommended to him the Subject of Spring on a large scale—viz the whole of That Season from the first budding to the full leaf—with many anachronisms To introduce Fly fishing, Rooking Trees Lambing in watered Vallies— later Leaping on exposed Hills—Horse fighting for Mares—&c with showers. He likes the idea as does Blake.

The scandal of the divorce proceedings against the Queen in the House of Lords was providing the newspapers with much lively material, but Blake would not have been able to afford newspapers. (The *Courier* was editorially hostile to the Queen, whom the radicals supported.)[16]

On the back of a visionary drawing (Old Parr when Young) of August Blake wrote, 'Saturday Mr Pepper called/ Vincent/ Mr Sneyd'. The second caller was perhaps George Vincent, landscapist. Another visitor round this time was Thomas Griffiths Wainewright, born in 1794, who had been a pupil of Fuseli. In the September *London Magazine*, under the pseudonym Janus Weathercock, he published a letter to the editor, in which he described his vain efforts to 'procure crack-contributors'. Then he goes on about Blake in a humorous vein, perhaps hoping that the editor would smile on an essay about Blake and *Jerusalem*:

Talking of articles, my learned friend Dr Tobias Ruddicombe, M.D., is, at my earnest entreaty, casting a tremendous piece of ordnance,—an eighty-eight pounder! which he proposeth to fire off in your next. It is an account of an ancient, newly discovered, illuminated manuscript, which has to name 'Jerusalem the Emanation of the Giant Albion!!!' It contains a good deal anent one 'Los', who, it appears, is now and hath been from the creation, the sole and fourfold denominator of the celebrated city of *Golgonooza*! The doctor assures me that the redemption of mankind hangs on the universal diffusion of the doctrine broached in this M.S.[17]

In 1825 Blake did an elaborately finished version of the *Songs* for Wainewright, who later embarked on a criminal career by poisoning his sister-in-law and was deported in 1837 to Australia for forgery.

We saw that the previous September Blake had met Dr Thornton, Linnell's family doctor. Interested in botany, Thornton had drawn up for use in schools an edition of Virgil's *Pastorals*; and Linnell suggested Blake as illustrator. There were to be 230 drawings and Blake contributed six engravings from his own designs of busts of Virgil, Augustus, Theocritus, Caesar, Agrippa, Epicurus, a drawing after a Poussin painting and twenty original designs for woodcuts (of which he himself finally executed seventeen). By autumn 1820 the work was well under way, but on 25 September Thornton wrote to Linnell, dissatisfied with the woodcuts (the only ones Blake ever did) and suggesting they should be redone as lithographs. The Virgil head was thus redone, for on 2 October Thornton and Linnell went to see a proof of it at the Lithography Press in Westminster. On the 9th Blake went with Linnell to call on Thornton about these matters. The latter had been told by fashionable wood-engravers that Blake's style was hopelessly heavy for the day's taste, and he had had three of the designs recut in a thin conventional style. Blake's work was however saved by Thornton's presence at a discussion between Lawrence, James Ward, Linnell and others. The artists praised Blake's cuts highly, and the puzzled Doctor gave in. Apart from the three recut designs, Blake's work was used in the book.

The cuts show a twilight pastoral dream-world: a revival of Blake's earlier countryside of innocence in darkened tones. He was thinking nostalgically of Felpham and put on a milestone '63 Miles London'—the distance he must have often seen on milestones there. The cuts powerfully affected Samuel Palmer; indeed they may be said to have evoked his deepest aesthetic response and thus determined his life's work.[18]

About this time Blake annotated Bishop Berkeley's *Siris* (1746). He was unhappy about Berkeley's idealist abstraction of the soul. To the statement that God knows all things as pure mind and nothing by sense, he added, 'Imagination or the Human Body in Every Man', and went on to stress the significance of the senses. 'Imagination is the Divine Body in Every Man'. 'The All in Man. The Divine Image or Imagination. The Four Senses are the Four Faces of Man & the Four Rivers of the Water of Life.' When Berkeley cited Themistius that all things are in the soul and the forms are the beings, Blake commented, 'This is my Opinion, but the Forms must be apprehended by Sense or the Eye of Imagination. Man is All Imagination. God is Man & exists in us and we in him.' As always, for him Imagination means the power to grasp the life-process in its wholeness, in the unity of the concrete moment; but his own idealist side intrudes to make imagination the life-process itself. So he never deals directly with the opposition of the elevation of the Body as imaginative form and such statements as that 'the Natural Body is an obstruction of the soul or Spiritual Body'. He thus defines the body as the source of both division and alienation, and of energy and unifying comprehensions. Since he does not go on to realise how the senses are social products as well as products of organic nature, he can relate the two sides of his proposition only in terms of his symbolic imagery.

About this time he etched the plates *Laocöon* and *On Homer's Poetry* and *On Virgil*. His main aim was to attack war and to link it with both the cash-nexus and abstracting art. In the *Laocöon* he used the classical composition (which he had drawn in 1815) with his own symbolism. Laocöon becomes Jehovah or the Angel of the Divine Presence, the two sons are Satan and Adam, and the two serpents are Good and Evil. All five forms writhe together in struggle. Blake stresses the need for work, production. In art, 'If you leave off you are lost'. 'The unproductive Man is not a Christian, much less the Destroyer—that is, War, Money, Antichrist, (mechanistic) Science.' 'Spiritual War: Israel deliver'd from Egypt, is Art deliver'd from Nature &

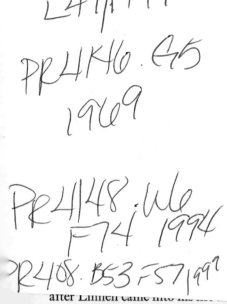

only in the struggle to liberate man from
represent the acceptance of things as they
comprehension of the whole living situa-

ught such trivial and vague glimpses of
pic *Jerusalem*, composing and etching and
pects by his wife. Here he attempted his
niverse in terms at once symbolic and
, philosophic and aesthetic. The first idea
o him at Felpham, and he did much work
oofs are watermarked 1807; the title-page
804; but he seems to have kept on extend-
nd, we saw, described in mid-1807 what
s, but the poem we have runs to a hundred
re not printed till 1818–20. Politically the
from Trafalgar to Waterloo. Probably only
after Linnell came into the ... 1818 did Blake regain the courage and confidence needed to start printing copies.

In the opening address to the public (written, he says, after his three years
slumber on the banks of the ocean: that is, after leaving Felpham) he describes the poetic form he had developed. What he says goes back to his
experiments with new forms about 1789, but he may well have felt that he
had now matured his method:

When this Verse was first dictated to me, I consider'd a Monotonous Cadence,
like that used by Milton & Shakespeare & all writers of English Blank Verse,
derived from the modern bondage of Rhyming, to be a necessary and indespensable
part of Verse. But I soon found that in the mouth of a true Orator such
monotony was not only awkward, but as much a bondage as rhyme itself. I therefore
have produced a variety in every line, both in cadences & number of syllables.
Every word and every letter is studied and put into its fit place; the terrific numbers
are reserved for the terrific parts, the mild & gentle for the mild & gentle parts,
and the prosaic for inferior parts; all are necessary to each other. Poetry Fetter'd
Fetters the Human Race, Nations are Destroy'd or Flourish in proportion as
Their Poetry, Painting and Music are Destroy'd or Flourish! The Primeval State
of Man was Wisdom, Art and Science.

Note the contradiction between the claims that the poetry was dictated and

; *Hist*

DA4
tructi
000.

w wor
oyed
ting
is can
status
le Kno
she co
itical
the e
s, Ire
s can
rpe's
(CH

that he carefully considered what form he would use. Though he exaggerates the precision with which rhythm and sound echo the sense, he is right to assert that he has achieved a new kind of expressive form, and his statement shows us the ideal he had set himself. The term 'orator' is of interest. No great poet ever wrote with less of an actual audience, and yet he sees himself as addressing a vaster audience than any previous poet. The concept of humanity takes on an enlarged and dynamic sense, in which he feels himself directly addressing all men, all nature. The form he creates is at all points linked with this new active sense of the audience. It needs to break all set metrical patterns, save at brief lyrical moments, and to find a new relation between common speech and rhythmical concentrations or expansions.

This new kind of verse is declamatory, with its system of rhythmic expressiveness suited to theme and emotion. It is both narrative and dramatic, with Biblical and Miltonic echoes, but turning to direct speech. Though the characters make short or long addresses or expostulations, we cannot say that they converse together, except in the Edenic vision at *Jerusalem*'s end, when unity and community are being established. Blake is not turning to common speech and idiom in a Wordsworthian way. Rather, his urgency, his keen sense of the dramatic occasion, tends to make him link his free accentuation with the natural stresses of speech. The oratorical or declamatory method, with its mixture of Biblical balances and passionate rhetoric, has in turn its link with music. One aspect of this is the use of tag-lines with varying effects. The repetitions have something of a Wagnerian motif in the midst of the surging rhythms, helping us to get our bearings in the mythological maze and providing fundamental clues as to what is going on. The musical aspect appears also in the way in what he calls the parts

become complexes of poetic sound. Blake uses them as patches of voice, called up irregularly on a moment-to-moment basis, and he does not gradually modify them from one to another as he would if he were subordinating them to the demands of linear narrative and thus creating tonal sections rather than interwoven tonal motifs. He achieves a dynamic much like that of music. (Frosch)[19]

We learn from the Linnells that Blake sang his lyrics till the end, and we find him going to opera with Linnell. His response to orchestral music seems recorded in passages of *Milton*, which tell of the 'softly lilling flutes' making sweet melody, 'the long sounding clarion', 'the double drum' (kettledrums), 'the shrill fife'. 'The crooked horn mellows the hoarse raving serpent, terrible but harmonious' (the serpent was a bass instrument). He describes a *contre-danse*: 'every one the dance knows in its intricate mazes of delight artful to weave; every one to sound his instruments of music in the dance, to touch each other & recede, to cross & change & return'. In *Jerusalem* he speaks of 'Harmonies of Concords & Discords, opposed to Melody'.

By the means we have noted he creates a sense of immediacy, as if the visionary happenings occur only at the very moment we read his lines. Further, the vision is something seen as well as rhythmically created; his verse-form is based in both the oral and the visual senses, which are affected again by the imagery he sets out as artist. The result is a fusion of elements that cannot be found elsewhere in anything like so sustained a way. The unity of poetry, music, art in his work represents the primal organisation of human faculties which he believes will be regained in the revolutionary future. The strange thing is that his poetic method, oriented outwards as if in direct contact with a mass-audience, is the creation of a man who in fact is talking always to himself: to angels or devils whom he needs to believe in as a projection of the missing audience which he feels to be potentially present.

Now for the poem itself. Its theme is the fate of Albion, the story of every-thing that has happened or will happen to men and women. Albion represents all Britons of all times, the geography of their island, their history, their total experience. But this character of his involves him in a yet fuller existence. In his address to the Jews Blake argues that Britain was the seat of the original religion of brotherhood and equality, which gave men a living sense of the cosmos and of their place in it. So Albion becomes the whole of humanity, from the earliest days; and the problem is how a fallen or divided people are to regain their wholeness, their free and undistorted awareness of the life-process.[20]

Blake takes over the idea of the New Jerusalem which was hailed in count-less evangelical hymns and sermons, and which was given its full contem-porary significance by Brothers. In the lyric that opens *Milton* Blake is saying that there is no need to go to Palestine, as Brothers demands; our problem is *here*, amid the dark satanic mills and the green pleasant land, to build Jerusalem. The reunion of Albion and Jerusalem means the creation of a free and fraternal Britain or world. 'Jerusalem is named Liberty among the sons of Albion.' (Brothers said of his Jerusalem: 'It shall be the land of true liberty'.) But to achieve unity we must understand the nature and causes of disunity, division, fall. So Blake sets out once again to show in yet fuller terms how the primal fall leads to incessant extension of division in society and inside the individual.

The story starts in Eternity, in fourfold reality, in a world where men still maintain a stable and harmonious relation with nature, their fellows and their own inner selves. This world we may say is early tribal society idealised as in legends of the Golden Age, Eden, a pastoral society without inner conflicts. The fall begins when Albion rejects Jerusalem as sinful: when the moral law intrudes to distort men's relationships and brings with it egoism, pride, power-lust. Albion asserts male power over the female, who breaks off wilfully. The female principle is divided against itself. Vala turns on her sister Jerusalem and causes Albion to drive her off. Albion grows sick. His perverted sons take over despite the efforts of his friends. Evil contagiously spreads. Only Los keeps on struggling for the right aims. Blake in his chastened post-1798 mood drops the imagery of a revolutionary uprising and turns more and more to Jesus as the type of self-sacrifice and forgiveness; at the same time he renews his emphasis on the need to overcome the Urizenic or Newtonian systems, the class-state and the moral or scientific abstraction.

In the second chapter Albion keeps on breaking up. But there cannot be a simple narrative account of such a process. Blake tries to define the effects radiating in all directions from the primal fall, the betrayal of human unity; also the futility and frustration of partial attempts to stem the evil, which result in new combinations of the old conflict. So, from this point till near the end, he strives to achieve both a narrative progression and a presentation of simultaneous events or processes. Nothing but a total response to divine mercy (a complete acceptance of human needs with all distorting egoisms eliminated) will arrest the disintegration and reconstitute Albion. Vala reasserts her domination of Albion and Los fights on. (We have already seen how Los searching London for Albion's error is very much Blake in his London wanderings.)

The third chapter carries on with the picture of entangled simultaneities of discord and unresolved conflict. Something of a narrative structure appears as Albion falls into his spectre's power so that his sons and daughters become spectrous beings abandoned to evil, while he himself, in his true being, lies asleep, paralysed. Jerusalem's separation is defined as her captivity in Babylon. Rahab-Vala controls Albion and enslaves the children that Jerusalem has borne him. The fallen sons and daughters bring war and human sacrifice into the world, building Stonehenge. The twelve daughters have names from British legendary history. Of the twelve sons at least eight are figures from Blake's Felpham's troubles: the soldiers, Scolfield and Cock; the officers, Hutton and perhaps Sleyd; the magistrates, Brereton, Peachey, Quantock; a lawyer, Bowen; and Hyle (the Greek word for Matter and Hayley in a Cockney pronunciation). Coban may be Cromek.

Much of the fourth chapter concerns the evil activities of the daughters, watched by ever-labouring Los. In the *Four Zoas* Blake and Catherine, Los and Enitharmon had achieved a full reconciliation, but now they fall again into discord till Los sees signs of hope in his furnaces. The Covering Cherub, who embodies all the evils of male aggressiveness and violence, advances on Jesus, but is annihilated. The fourfold vision triumphs. The harmony of man and the cosmos is re-established.

Both Blake and Brothers draw on Ezekiel and Revelation for their picture of Jerusalem as a city. Brothers stresses the square structure, giving his account in *A Description of Jerusalem*, 1801 (1802) and *A Letter to the Subscribers for Engraving the Plan of Jerusalem*, 1805.

The form is planned by God himself; and as he has ordained the government shall be in a king . . . His residence will be a noble palace, on the north side of the great central square that incloses the park, or Garden of Eden, for the public to walk in. The square is formed by a range of twelve private palaces on each side, including the king's, which makes forty-eight in all. Each palace is 444 feet long, with a space of 144 feet between each; to every one is a lawn in front, and behind is a spacious garden. What a noble square to excite admiration! Each side of it is near a mile and a half in length! Such is to be the centre of the future Jerusalem, and round it the city is to be built.

His vision, whatever its Biblical origins, is linked with contemporary schemes of town-planning and dreams of what was later to be worked out as the garden city. Blake is concerned with a living relationship to a changing universe, but he too bases his symbolism on the square, the Golden Square of his childhood developed into an image of the fourfold cosmos, which becomes man's ideal habitation. 'These are the Four Faces towards the Four Worlds of Humanity. In every Man... And every part of the City is fourfold; & every inhabitant fourfold . . . And every house fourfold'. Brothers says he would like to build his Jerusalem on both sides of the Jordan near the lake. Blake says: 'Jordan sprang from beneath its threshold, bubbling from beneath its pillars', when the Mighty Temple of Urizen was built.

The political issue pervading *Jerusalem* is that of peace and war. Blake preaches peace without vengeance. Since he ignores or frowns on all forms of social or political struggle, there is thus a general unity in the work, but at the cost of a certain grim flatness and lack of dramatic structure. Too much of the work consists of lists and blank statements more suited to a mythological textbook than an imaginative poem. Blake's isolation and personal despair limit the free range of his mind; he repeats previous formulations without new connections or illuminations. His efforts to broaden his concepts is liable to founder on the geographical and other catalogues. As in the *Four Zoas*, the main revelation is one of breakdown, division, disintegration, though the focus within which such processes are viewed is always that of unitary integrative development.

After the end of the peaceful Atlantic world came the Druid world of war and human sacrifice. Albion, embodiment of power-lust and the cash-nexus, is creating a world-empire, 'Shooting out fibres round the Earth, thro Gaul & Italy and Greece . . . to India, China & Japan'. Blake takes the London Stone (a supposed Roman milestone) as the central altar of Druidic sacrifice carrying on from old Jerusalem through the various stages of division; for him it is linked with Tyburn Tree and the stone where soldiers were shot in the north-east corner of Hyde Park. The reviewed soldiers are men doomed to sacrifice. From the Stone, the Druidic oak and gallows, the evil spreads throughout the world. (Blake in South Molton Street saw himself as at the centre of evil power.)

We can make out many references to the war-situation between 1804 and the battle of Waterloo in 1815, though there is no attempt at a chronological system. A few details of history trickle through. Bath is praised because of its pacifist preacher Richard Warner. Tharmas is sacrificed in Mexico because Spanish squads executed insurgents there in 1811 and 1813. Erin becomes prominent through Blake's sympathy for Catholic Emancipation and national independence. (It is tempting to think that Blake read an account of Byron's speech on Ireland in 1812 in the Lords.) The passage of the Slave Trade Bill of 1807 is hailed; and for once Blake forgets his quietist rejection of struggle. He attributes the Bill to the rising of Africa and the 'well-timed wrath' of the watchful brethren who 'cut his strong chains, & overwhelm'd his dark Machines in fury & destruction'. But people at home must not draw a lesson from all that. Albion must bide his time. The Notebook shows that Blake could still be heartened by such activities as those of Col. Wardle in his parliamentary exposure of the sale of army commissions; he sees in Wardle an attacker of the English nobility and gentry who buy the art-works he denounces.

The question of timing, of the need to wait and choose the right moment, set out in *Milton*, had grown ever more important for Blake. It had a great truth behind it, the realisation that wishful thinking was not enough and one must understand the phase of history in which one lived; but it also provided an excuse for doing nothing except brood in a corner as the witness whose testimony, unknown for the time being, would play an important part when Fate and Jesus decided to inaugurate a new stage.

Still, Blake kept looking anxiously for signs of the great change. Once more he falls back on the idea that the worst must happen first, the advent of Antichrist or the final Druidism, the extreme form of the Polyp of War, the full triumph of mechanistic science. Albion tries to tax all the nations. The stages are represented first by the taxes leading to the American revolt, then those stirring the French Revolution, finally by those that Albion has to impose to carry on his wars. 'The body of Albion was closed Apart from all Nations.' In modern terms, the full expansion of imperialism is reached. So 'Time was finished!' Britannia, become harmlessly revolutionary, leads Albion into Paradise, ends war by putting down the Druidic knife, and drops her role as the Jealous. Near the end, we noted, Blake described a fresh quarrel of Los and Enitharmon. Now the reunion is not described; instead we are shown Los's fight against both emanation and spectre. Despite his struggle the powers of evil dominate. The Covering Cherub gathers all the forces of aggression to attack him and his aiders, and to devour Albion and Jerusalem. Los stays divided, and by way of his spectre we return to his break with Enitharmon. Then comes the reversal of history. Enitharmon merely asserts, 'The poet's song draws to its period, & Enitharmon is no more'. She is absorbed into Los. Albion realises that all along Los–Blake has been his true friend; he sees the reality which Hand has hidden from him; and so everything is redeemed and transformed. What happens is not a wrathful Last Judgement, but the triumph of the poet's song, a harmonious regeneration of man and nature together.

For all its weaknesses *Jerusalem* is a not unfitting conclusion of Blake's prophetic vision. He expressed an ardent faith in revolutionary action in the Lambeth books, a huge vision of the condition of divided man in the *Four Zoas*, a revaluation of the English revolution and of the issues of contemporary culture in *Milton*, and then a critique of war as the final world-wide form of power-perversion and money-rule. At each stage he made a passionate fusion of his own personal dilemma and the position of world-conflict. The balance between the two aspects was continually threatened; a paranoiac

9

fantasy seemed to be about to take over and make the world-picture a mere projection of the confused and unresolved conflicts inside the poet; yet in the last resort the creative balance is achieved. We confront not only an unparalleled poetic universe of forms, images, symbols, but also a penetration into the processes of history which holds an ever-deepening meaning for all of us.

Take his treatment of Hayley and the Hunts. Hayley–Hyle represents the 'Affections rent a sunder & opposed to Thought'. Gwendolen subjects him to a series of operations that hide his organs: his heart behind his ribs, his tongue behind his teeth. She forms his kidneys and hides away his testicles 'of self interest & selfish natural virtue', compelling him into a shape of Moral Virtue against the Lamb. She thinks to reduce him to a babe on her breast, but he is only a worm; then, under Los's influence, she tries bitterly to 'form the Worm into a form of love'. Thus Hayley is made into a type of dissociated sensibility. No doubt he did typify many such aspects of the bourgeois consciousness of the day; but what drove Blake thus to pillory him was not his outstanding character in this respect. It was the fact that he, Hayley, had done his best to help Blake and had thus come to seem a supreme enemy.

The situation is different with Hand (the Hunts). They had indeed attacked Blake, but his hatred is so insensate that he makes them typify the very things which, at a much simpler level of understanding, they too hated and opposed. He ignores the fact that Leigh Hunt was sentenced to two years in jail in 1820 for an attack on royalty; and so on. His letter to Linnell in 1819 was written on the very day Richard Carlile's trial began, in which, among other things, he was indicted for publishing Paine's *Age of Reason*. Shelley, writing to Leigh Hunt on the trial, remarked, 'The tremendous question is now agitating, whether a military & judicial despotism is to be established by our present rulers, or some form of government less unfavourable to the real & permanent interests of all men is to arise from the conflict of passions now gathering to overturn them'. Blake seems untouched. Yet the strange thing is that in the last resort his symbolic definitions are not reduced to the personal limitations and distortions. The fears that at one level cut him off from his fellows somehow manage to reunite him with them at another and deeper level. In no other way could he have so powerfully grasped and expressed the tensions affecting everyone in the turmoiling situation.

13

Job in Captivity, 1821–5

In 1821 the Blakes moved from South Molton Street to 3 Fountain Court, off the Strand to the south.* The house was kept by Mr Banes (Baines), whose wife was a sister of Catherine. The Blakes had two small dark rooms on the first floor. Gilchrist hastens to say that the other lodgers were humble but respectable, and that children played in the court. Palmer tells of Blake leading a friend to the window and pointing to a group of children, 'That is heaven'. The redbrick house had a wainscoted staircase with a window on to the well-like backyard. The Blakes' front room window looked down on the court and its panelled walls were hung with Blake's works; here visitors were received. A door led into the smaller bedroom where a side window gave a narrow view of the Thames with its muddy banks and the distant hills beyond.

Here it was that Blake came to know the group of young artists, Samuel Palmer, George Richmond, Edward Calvert, Francis Finch, Frederick Tatham and others, who later tried to make the place out as much finer than it was, insisting that at the time the court was not as slatternly and noisy as it became. Tatham tries to enlarge the lodgings by speaking of two good-sized rooms and kitchens—by kitchens apparently meaning the one cupboard. Palmer romanticises by writing of the high, gloomy buildings, between which from his study window, a glimpse was caught of the Thames and the Surrey shore, and how they 'assumed a kind of grandeur from the man dwelling near them'. Not a sentiment likely to be shared by the man who was actually living there in poverty.[1]

In one corner of the main room was the bed, in another the fire at which Catherine cooked, at one side the table for meals and by the window the table at which Blake worked. Someone noticed there was no soap, and Catherine

* Linnell says the cause of removal was the departure of Martin, the landlord, who had a French wife, to France, but the Rates Books credit him with paying the rates for some more years. Rate Books show Henry and Mary Banes as rate-payers, 1820–9, at Fountain Court.

stoutly replied, 'You see, Mr Blake's skin don't dirt'. On the work-table, to
the right, was a pile of portfolios and drawings; to the left, a pile of books.
There was no bookcase and not many pictures on the walls. There were more
pictures in the second room, called the show-room, which was rather dark.
Among the sentimentalised comments by the visitors we find, 'Ah! that
divine window' and 'a strange expansion and sensation of FREEDOM in
those two rooms very seldom felt elsewhere'. A little girl who was brought by
her father recalled later only the beautiful things on the walls and Blake's
kind manner. But one visitor remarked, 'Poor dear man, to think how ill he
was used, yet he took it all so quietly'. Blake is said to have commented, 'I
live in a hole here, but God has a beautiful mansion for me elsewhere'. If he
did make that remark he was not speaking in the conventional piety of the
person recording it; he was referring to the world of his imagination.[2]

On 3 February Dr Thornton dined with Linnell, who took him along to
Fountain Court. Blake is not likely to have enjoyed the visit. (In 1827 he
annotated the Doctor's *New Translation of the Lord's Prayer* as 'Most
Malignant & Artful', calling him a Tory and one of 'the learned that Mouth'.)
Six days later Linnell began a small picture of his mother, and Blake called in
the evening. On the 12th Thornton's *Pastorals* was entered at Stationers'
Hall. Thornton tried to quiet his qualms about Blake's cuts by writing that
they 'display less of art than genius, and are much admired by some eminent
painters'. The young artists were delighted, and Palmer admired rapturously
the 'visions of little dells, and nooks, and corners of Paradise' with their
mystic and dreamy glimmer. The figures had 'that elastic, nervous spring
which belongs to uncaged immortal spirits'. This elastic quality, which makes
the figures seem to fly, bound, or float above earth, is linked with Blake's
rejection of Newtonian concepts such as gravity.* Calvert later told his son,
'They are done as by a child', often careless and incorrect, but with a spirit
in them 'humble and of a force enough to move simple souls to tears'.[3]

On Thursday, 8 March, Linnell took Blake to the British Gallery and then
home to dinner. On Tuesday the 27th he took Blake to Drury Lane to see
Sheridan's *Pizarro* and a piece by J. H. Payne, *Thérèse, the Orphan of Geneva*,
with music by Horn. In late April they went to the Water Colour Exhibition,
and he paid Blake £2. On 7 May they went to the Somerset House Exhibition,

---

* Compare the millenarian view set out by the Rev. T. Vivian in 1785: 'In this New
Heaven and New Earth, among other Changes, it is probable that the glorified Bodies will
not be confined to the Earth by the Principle of Gravitation, but be capable of visiting
distant Worlds with the Swiftness of Light which they may resemble.'

and on the 27th to Hampstead. No doubt Linnell was looking for lodgings, as next summer he took rooms in Hope Cottage in Hampstead for his wife and children. On Friday 8 June the pair went to Drury Lane again and saw a New Grand Serious Opera, *Dirce, or the Fatal Urn*, based on Metastasio's *Demofonte*, with music by Mozart, Rossini and others—with a farce, *The Midnight Hour*, to follow. Linnell says that Blake was a great laugher at absurdities. On Sunday 26 August they went to Hendon to see one of the three Woodburn brothers who had a well-known art collection.

Probably this summer Blake met the radical William Frend, an acquaintance of the 1790s, walking in the Strand with his daughter aged about eleven. She recalled how a man in a brown coat with uncommonly bright eyes stopped her father and shook hands. 'Why don't you come and see me? I live down there.' He pointed down a street that led to the river. They agreed to meet and then parted. The girl asked who the man was. 'He is a strange man, he thinks he sees spirits.' 'Tell me his name.' 'William Blake.'

About this time poverty reduced Blake to sell his whole collection of prints to Colnaghi, bookseller of Pall Mall East—'before I knew of his distress', says Linnell.* The latter seems to have been stirred to think up some money-making project for Blake. He had seen at Butts's place the twenty-nine Job drawings that Blake had made for him, and now he and Blake decided to reproduce them in a business collaboration. On Friday, 7 September, Linnell made a start by tracing outlines from the designs all day. On the 10th Blake worked all day finishing the outlines. Now the originals could be returned to Butts, from whom Blake borrowed a drawing of Cain and Abel. Linnell promptly made a copy of it. He also did two portraits of Blake.†

Some time this year Linnell's father, a picture-framer in Bloomsbury, framed a painting by Blake for Colonel Chichester of an estate near Barnstaple. It was one of his finest tempera works, painted on a thin gesso ground applied to stiff paper, with the colours worked up to a delicate finish. The central figure was based on shipwrecked Odysseus, but no doubt also on St John thrown up on Patmos. Man is a castaway on the sea of space and time,

---

* This year the *Night Thoughts* designs were offered for sale by one of the brothers of R. Edwards; the latter had gone off to Majorca in 1799 and given or sold them to his brother Thomas. They were described as 'In the Style of Michael Angelo' and priced at £300. Unsold, they were offered five years later for £50.

† On 8 September Blake was with Linnell all day with a Mr Read, probably the painter and engraver, D. C. Read of Salisbury. The Diary records Blake dining with Linnell on two Sundays, 11 November and 9 December; he visited Linnell on 27 October, evening. One portrait is dated 12 September.

surrounded by destructive and redemptive elements, witcheries and compulsions. He is about to make a decisive choice and alone of the figures turns his eyes to the spectator, drawing him into the turmoil of conflicting forces. At the same time he is moving outside the sphere of corruptive influences into the world of liberating action. The picture expresses the mood of revolt against the evil dominances which Blake had summed up in *Laocoön* and the statement against Homer and Virgil. It is a personal testament of reawakening, of renewed prophetic purpose.[4]

All the while the Blakes were getting poorer. Palmer says that Blake with a careful frugality worked on with serenity when there was only a shilling in the house. Once he spent one of his last shillings on a camel's-hair brush. But Gilchrist says that he refused to discuss money with Catherine, shouting at her, 'Oh, damn the money!' so that she was forced to bring their lack of it home to him by serving an empty platter at dinner-time. We also hear that she learned to keep a guinea secretly in reserve. A passage in Crabb Robinson's Diary (1826) shows what an anguish the very theme of money was to Blake. Robinson ordered a copy of *Songs* for five guineas. 'He spoke of his horror of money and of turning pale when it was offerd him—And this was certainly unfeigned.'

Linnell went on trying to help. On 8 May 1822 he took Blake to see James Vine, a Russian merchant living in Grevill Street, Brunswick Square, who ordered copies of *Thel*, *Milton* and *Job*. Next day Blake began copying the drawings he had made for *Paradise Lost*. Linnell applied on his behalf to the Royal Academy, using William Collins, an old friend of Cumberland; he also canvassed Lawrence and others. On 8 June the application came up, and William Blake, 'an able Designer & Engraver', was voted £25. On 1 July Collins wrote to Linnell saying that Blake need not apply personally, and Linnell collected the money for him.

Blake clearly disliked trade-engraving. We have seen how slow he was with Hayley. In the eight years between 1806 and 1814 he did only three outside jobs: one, together with Butts, in 1806, one in 1809, one in 1813. In the years 1815–20 he did nine engravings (two of them with others, Lowry and Linnell) and a number of etchings, eighteen for Wedgwood and thirty-seven for Flaxman's *Hesiod*. The etchings, though needing skill, consisted of outlines and were easy compared with engravings which involved complex tonal work.

On 13 July Linnell went with Blake to see Lawrence, perhaps to thank him for the £25. Lawrence is said to have liked Blake's work so much that he kept his watercolour, *The Wise and Foolish Virgins*, on his desk. Varley was introducing Blake into society. Once he took him to dine at Lady Blessington's house in St James's Square. Why Blake went to such a place it is hard to say. We are told that Lady Blessington kept 'a menagerie of small lions' and Blake appeared at her house 'in the simplest form of attire then worn, which included thick shoes and worsted stockings, nobody complaining of the strange guest's lack of refinement and gentlemanliness'. Catherine was not included in such visits or in the theatre-goings.*

Blake had read Byron's *Cain, A Mystery* (1821) and been strongly affected. Though he had read some Wordsworth with interest and revulsion, and presumably knew a little of Coleridge, it was Byron who moved him to attempt a dialogue. Byron showed Lucifer tempting Cain to kill his brother, and used Lucifer and Cain to denounce Jehovah for putting temptation in the way of Adam and Eve, and then punishing them. A key-text was that of *Genesis*, which in *Cain* is spoken by the Angel of the Lord: 'The voice of thy slain brother cries out, Even from the ground, unto the Lord'. The law exacting death for death is justified. But for Blake that law is the source of all evil, leading to human sacrifice, to Cain's City (civilisation built on blood-guilt), and to Christ crucified. So he composed and printed *The Ghost of Abel*, the last of his illuminated works, consisting of two pages. The voice calling for human blood is Satan's. Jehovah replies to Satan by sending him to eternal death, while a chorus of angels distinguish the Elohim of the Heathen who swore vengeance for sin (that is, the God of the Old Testament) from Elohim Jehovah clothed in the covenant of the forgiveness of sins.[5]

Thus as always Blake chooses what part of the Bible he likes and considers it the truth, while rejecting as evil the part he dislikes. He invents his own Jehovah, god of Inspiration and Mercy, and hands over most of the deeds of the Biblical Jehovah to Satan, Urizen, or the Angel of the Divine Presence. In *Milton* it is Satan who gives the moral law attributed in the Bible to Jehovah and declares, 'I am God alone'. Yet later in the same poem, in the events preceding the advent of Jesus, 'Jehovah was leprous; loud he call'd, stretching his hand to Eternity, for then the Body of Death was perfected in hypocritic holiness round the Lamb'.

Blake feels that Byron is a true prophet who merely needs some adjurations

---

* The date was before August 1822 when the Blessingtons went abroad. As the account was published in 1867 we can hardly trust its details. Perhaps it was really about this time that Blake went to Lady Caroline Lamb's party. This year Linnell took the Hampstead lodgings for his family at North End, Collins' Farm (kept by a dairyman).

to be set on the right path. 'To Lord Byron in the Wilderness: What dost thou here, Elijah? Can a Poet doubt the Visions of Jehovah? Nature has no Outline, But Imagination has.' For Blake Elijah is the bold speaker who comprehends 'all the Poetic Character'. Unfortunately he did not read Shelley's *Prometheus Unbound*; it would have been of great interest to hear his points of agreement and disagreement with Shelley's ideas and terms.

In 1823 the one important event was the contract for Job drawn up between Blake and Linnell on 25 March. Blake was to engrave ten of his designs, with Linnell paying him £5 per plate, or £100 in all, some of the money before completion of the set, the rest on completion. Further, Blake was to get another £100 from the profits 'as the receipts will admit of it'. Linnell was to provide the plates. On the back of the contract Blake acknowledged receipt of the first £5. The terms worked out as Linnell paying about a pound a week, as Butts had done. He gave Blake £54 in 1823; £46 7s. 9d. in 1824; £48 6s. 6d. in 1825. Blake began at once on the plates but did not finish the ten till early 1826.[6]

On 5 May, shortly before the R.A. show opened, Linnell went with Blake to Somerset House, and paid him £10. On 25 June the pair went 'to the British Gallery, &c.' This month Johnson published Hayley's *Memoirs*, which contained many references to Blake; and some time in the summer the phrenologist James S. Deville took a cast of his head. He chose Blake to represent the imaginative faculty. It was the first cast he made, and the mouth was given an uncharacteristic look of severity because Blake suffered much pain through the plaster pulling out a quantity of his hair. So Catherine disliked the cast, though Blake's friends approved of it.

In March 1824 the improvident friend of Linnell, William Dixon, wrote about a portrait he was sending to the R.A. and gave his best respects to Varley and Blake. Samuel Palmer took Blake in May to the Academy. Blake pointed out a scene from Walton's *Angler* by Wainewright and called it very fine.[7] Later Palmer wrote about how well he recalled 'Blake in his plain black suit and *rather* broad-brimmed, but not quakerish hat, standing so quietly among all the dressed-up, rustling, swelling people, and myself thinking "How little you know *who* is among you." '*

---

* This year, 24 January, Brothers died. Finlayson, his disciple, says: 'Holding his right hand in my right hand, he asked if my sword and hammer were ready'. An end that Blake–Los should have approved of.—Cumberland in March wrote twice to his son about the Blake plates which 'may require a little reentering the Lines'.

Gilchrist gives a full account of Blake's appearance in these years. At home he wore threadbare clothes, with trousers worn black and shiny in front, like a mechanic's. When he went out he wore black knee-breeches, black worsted stockings, shoes that were tied, and a broad hat. 'It was something like an old-fashioned tradesman's dress.' He was under five-and-a-half feet tall, broad-shouldered, with an upright carriage. 'He bore himself with dignity, as not unconscious of his natural claims.' His head was impressive, square and massive, with a piled-up brow, full and rounded at the temples, and wonderful eyes. His small nose gave an effect of fiery energy: 'a little *clenched* nostril; a nostril that opened as far as it could, but was tied down at one end'. His mouth was wide, the lips not full, but tremulous. His prominent eyes indicated his short-sightedness. 'He wore glasses only occasionally.'

On 6 March Linnell made a complete move to Hampstead, taking the Home Farm on Wylde's Estate, though he kept his place in London as a studio. Cumberland was at work on a sequel to *Thoughts on Outline*, in which he was to use four of Blake's 1795 plates. James Montgomery was publishing *The Chimney-Sweeper's Friend*, intended to arouse sympathy for the boys; and Lamb sent him Blake's lyric on the sweep. Bernard Barton, the Quaker poet, a contributor to the book, wrote to ask about Blake; and Lamb replied at length, unsure if Blake were still alive or in a madhouse, but talking about the plates of *Night Thoughts* (which he confused with those of *The Grave*) and the Broad Street show. 'His poems have been sold hitherto only in Manuscript, I never read them.' A friend (certainly Crabb Robinson) had got him the sweep poem. He, Lamb, had heard *The Tyger* recited and thought it glorious. The reciter would have been Robinson. Linnell later recalled hearing him recite it most impressively to a gathering at the Aders' table; he, Linnell, in turn learned the poem and used to declaim it.[8]

Blake was now walking out to Hampstead with some regularity. In June he gave a copy of his Catalogue to the elder Tatham, and on 2 August the latter wrote to Linnell to say that he and his son Frederick were coming to dinner. 'Can you engage Michael Angelo *Blake* to meet us at yr. Study, & go up with us?—Such a party of Connoisseurs is worthy Apollo & the muses.' Two days later the party came off, with Varley added. Perhaps Blake brought along his portrait-engraving of the Rev. R. Hawker (dated 1 May 1820) for Tatham, with a note from Catherine, in which she cited one of Lavater's Aphorisms: 'Mr C Tatham The humble is formed to adore; the loving to associate with eternal Love C. Blake'.

In *The Library Companion* of 9 August T. F. Dibdin wrote rhapsodically

9*

of Blake's *Night Thoughts*, his 'bizarre but original and impressive ornaments'. He loved to look at the designs 'amidst the wild uproar of the wintry
elements—when piping winds are howling for entrance round every corner of
the turreted chamber,' and so on. He added, 'Mr. Blake is himself no ordinary
poet'.

This summer, with the Job designs done, Linnell commissioned a set for
Dante. In return he was to go on paying Blake £2 or £3 a week, as he needed
money—Blake doing as little or as much as he liked in return, says Gilchrist.
To grapple the better with Dante, Blake set himself to learn Italian, and,
'helped by such command of Latin as he had, he taught himself the language
in a few weeks; sufficiently, that is, to comprehend that difficult author sub-
stantially if not grammatically, just as, earlier in life, he had taught himself
something of Latin, French, and even Greek'—we might add, Hebrew.[9]

On Saturday 9 October Palmer called on Linnell and they went to Blake.
He lay abed, with a scalded foot (or leg), working with books all round him,
'like one of the Antique patriarchs, or a dying Michael Angelo'. He was
drawing in a big folio book and said that he had begun with fear and
trembling. Palmer replied 'O! I have enough of fear and trembling'. 'Then,'
said Blake, 'you'll do.' He had done a hundred drawings abed in a fortnight,
Palmer thought.[10]

Palmer and Blake rapidly became friends, and Blake, passing through
Broad Street in his walks to Hampstead, picked him up there. 'As the two
friends neared the farm, a merry troop hurried out to meet them led by a
little fair-haired girl of some six years old.' She was Hannah, who later
married Palmer. 'To this day,' wrote her son in the 1890s, 'she remembers
cold winter nights when Blake was wrapped up in an old shawl by Mrs.
Linnell, and sent on his homeward way, with the servant, lantern in hand,
lighting the way across the heath to the main road.'

Now a fair-sized group of mostly young men had gathered round Blake.
Besides those already mentioned were H. J. Richter, James Holmes, Henry
Walter. Richter, a disciple of Kant, was older than most of the others, and
Blake may have known him some time, since he was taught by Stothard about
1788. Finch, some twenty-two years old, met Blake through his teacher
Varley. He thought Blake a new kind of man, wholly original; most men tried
to soften their extreme opinions, not to shock others, but Blake did the
contrary. More than any of the others (says Palmer) Finch accepted Blake's
visions and spirits. Calvert, born in 1799, was married and earning his living.
He may have heard of Blake first from Henry Walker or Palmer's cousin, the

stockbroker John Giles, who spoke excitedly of the divine Blake, who 'had seen God, sir, and had talked with angels'. Palmer seems to have introduced himself to Blake; and he and the others came to see Blake every month and to talk about art. Linnell rarely attended the meetings. The group referred to Blake's place as the House of the Interpreter. (Bunyan's Christian, on his way from the City of Destruction, visited that House after being told that the Interpreter would show him excellent things and help him in his quest for Mount Zion.) No doubt it was this name for his rooms that inspired Blake to make his watercolour series illustrating *The Pilgrim's Progress* and drew him to refurbish his engraving of 1794, *The Man Sweeping the Interpreter's House.*

The group called themselves the Ancients. The name came from Giles, who went into raptures over all things ancient and denounced modern art as too finished: 'no room to get a thought in edgeway'. At Shoreham, where the group also gathered, the villagers called them Extollagers while Linnell's landlady saw them as Academinions. Linnell stood outside the group with a certain disdain, irritated at 'real Greeks from Hackney and Lisson Grove'. Miss Linnell told how Calvert once showed her a drawing, remarking, 'These are God's fields, this is God's brook, and these are God's sheep and lambs'. Linnell broke in in exasperation, 'Then why don't you mark them with a big G?'[11]

How little these disciples understood or respected Blake's essential ideas is shown by their later remarks. Linnell wrote in 1855:

... it must be confessed that he said many things tending to the corruption of Xtian morals—even when unprovoked by controversy & when opposed by the superstitious the crafty or the proud he outraged all common sense & rationality by the opinions he advanced occasionally even indulging in the support of the most lax interpretations of the precepts of the scripture.

A few years later he wanted to censor much of Blake's writings. He disliked *The Marriage of Heaven and Hell*, marked one page for excision, and thought the whole book unfortunate. Without cuts it would be excluded 'from every drawing-room table in England'. He tried to argue that Blake took extreme positions only under provocation. He 'sometimes wrote under irritation. Nothing else would explain some things in the MS'. He wanted the censoring of all passages in which 'the word Bible, or those of the persons of the blessed Trinity, or the Messiah were irreverently connected'. In effect he wanted

Blake's whole Antinomian position, fundamental to his work, suppressed. Later we shall see how disgracefully Tatham behaved.

Dr Thornton was gathering material for a new Christmas annual, *Remember Me!* There were nineteen plates 'by Linnell, Blake, and other eminent artists'. The book came out in November. Blake's contribution was *The Hiding of Moses*, with comment by the Doctor or his daughter. Blake's nativity was given in *Urania, an Astrologer's Chronicle*. The writer knew of the Job designs, mentions the drawing of spirits, and refers to a long poem 'nearly finished, which he affirms was recited to him by the spirit of Milton'. The writer, probably a friend of Varley, describes the astrological forces that have produced Blake's 'extraordinary faculties and eccentricities'. He had been in Blake's company several times.[12]

In the period between June 1825 and Blake's death we have twenty-one of his letters to the Linnells, one to Maria Denman and one to Cumberland, though they are all slight in interest compared with the letters of the Hayley period. At the start of the new year Palmer reviewed his work since last July and remarked on the encouragement given by Blake. His 1824 sketchbook shows the sort of advice that Blake offered:

Remember that most excellent remark of Mr. B's—how that a tint equivalent to a shadow is made by the outlines of many little forms in one mass, and then how the light shines on an unbroken mass near it, such for instance as flesh, &c—This remark alone if generally acted upon would go a good way toward the much hoped for & prayed for revival of art.

We see that Blake attempted analyses of light which he did not seek to apply in his own work. He does not seem interested in showing the Ancients the one important collection of his paintings. Palmer tells us: 'Dear Mr. Blake promised to take me himself to see Mr. Butts' collection—but alas! it never came off.'

A copper-plate printer, Lahee, was drawn in to deal with the Job plates. The twenty-two plates were labelled 'March 8:1825', but they were not printed off and ready for another year. Linnell continued to see Blake, and in May took him to the R.A. exhibition.* But most of the summer Blake was ill, already suffering, it seems, from the gallstones and inflammation that caused

---

* On 10 January Linnell visited Blake to pay him £10; on 5 March they both were with Lahee. On 9 March Linnell writes, 'To Mr Blake Read Cafe Bollo &c.' Read seems to be the engraver met in 1821. On 8 April Linnell has: 'To City Blake'—he paid him £3 10s.[13]

his death. On 7 June, at night, he wrote to Linnell, whom, despite their close relationship, he still addressed as Dear Sir. He sent thanks for two pounds. 'As to Sr T. Lawrence, I have not heard from him as yet, & hope that he has a good opinion of my willingness to appear grateful, tho' not able, on account of this abominable Ague, or whatever it is.' He was working abed, affected by the cold weather: able to draw but not engrave. 'I am going on with Dante, & please myself.' In an oddly reactionary sentence he adds, 'I am sorry for Ld Ld'—apparently Lord Lilford, who died soon after, 'as also for the D of C'—the Dean of Canterbury. Not long after, on a Wednesday, he wrote that he had had a return of the old shivering fit, but hoped to be at Mr Laker's (Lahee's) next morning. Linnell seems to have found a buyer for his print of the Chaucer Pilgrims.

The illness must have carried on through July; on 6 August an undergraduate friend of Balliol College wrote to Linnell: 'I am sorry to hear poor Mr Blake is so unwell, and hope he may recover, again to use his pencil and graver'. Indeed Blake was up that day, going with Linnell to Mrs Aders at 11 Euston Square. She was the handsome and gifted daughter of Raphael Smith, mezzotint engraver, and had married a wealthy merchant of German extraction, who owned a fine collection of early Italian, Flemish and German paintings. Among them were two Van Eycks, two Van Leyders, four Memlings, and other important works by German painters of the Renaissance; the centre-piece was the head of John the Baptist attributed to Van Eyck (probably a copy by Petrus Christus).* At one of the Aders' parties (Gilchrist tells), where Flaxman, Lawrence and other artists were present, Blake was holding forth to a group in his usual quiet way: 'The other evening, taking a walk, I came to a meadow, and at the further corner of it I saw a fold of lambs. Coming nearer, the ground blushed with flowers; and the wattled cote and its woolly tenants were of an exquisite pastoral beauty. But I looked again, and it proved to be no living flock, but beautiful sculpture.' A lady, who thought the place a fine holiday-setting for her children, asked where it was. Blake touched his forehead, '*Here*, madam.' (The idiom of the remarks is not at all Blakean, but something of the sort might have been said.) The Aders' house was probably the scene of a story told by Palmer. 'Being irritated by the exclusively scientific talk at a friend's house, which talk had

---

* At one time Mrs Aders wanted Linnell to paint Coleridge, who addressed to her his poem *The Two Founts*. Lamb wrote verses to C. Aders on his art collection. Gilchrist's version of Palmer's story runs, 'I was walking down a lane the other day, and at the other end of it I touched the sky with my stick'. Cf. Blake's aphorism: One Thought fills Immensity.

turned on the vastness of space, he cried out, "It is false. I walked the other
evening to the end of the earth, and touched the sky with my finger".' It was
at the Aders' that the German painter Götzenberger met him. On returning
home, Götzenberger wrote, 'I saw in England many men of talent but only
three men of genius— Coleridge, Flaxman, and Blake, and of them Blake was
the greatest'.[14]

In the spring of this year the young artist George Richmond, about sixteen years, met Blake at the Tathams, 'and was allowed to walk home with
him'. He argued and was treated good-humouredly by Blake. Once, being at
a loss for a whole fortnight, he called and found the Blakes at tea. Telling
how he felt deserted by his power of invention, he was astonished when Blake
turned to Catherine and said, 'It is just so with us, is it not, for weeks together,
when the visions forsake us? What do we do then, Kate?' 'We kneel down and
pray, Mr. Blake.' Blake once told him, 'I can look at a knot in a piece of wood
till I am frightened at it.'

It was probably in September that Palmer took Blake and the Calverts to
his grandfather's house at Shoreham, Kent, some twenty miles from London,
travelling in a covered stage-wagon. The route ran from Charing Cross to
Tunbridge Wells. (Calvert's son suggests that Catherine was with them, but
she does not appear in the story.) The wagon was drawn by a ten-horse team,
caparisoned with hoops and bells, and with large flapping flanges. At last they
arrived at the gabled and thatched cottage, where, inside a huge chimney-
hearth in the beamed room, they found old Palmer in knee-breeches and
gaiters. The Calverts had a room in the cottage, but Blake was put up by a
neighbour and Palmer stayed at the village bakery. Next day they talked of
vision and inspiration, and old Palmer told of ghosts in a ruin nearby. They
decided to visit the ruin that night: which they did with candles and lanthorn.
There was a moaning wind and wavering shadows in the moonlight. Then a
tapping, grating noise was heard, which Calvert at last traced to a big snail
crawling up the glass of an oriel window.

Next day Palmer went off to meet some engagement in London, and in the
evening the others sat in the chimney-room. 'Presently Blake, putting his
hand to his forehead, said quietly: "Palmer is coming; he is walking up the
road." "Oh, Mr Blake, he's gone to London; we saw him off in the coach."
Then, after a while, "He is coming through the wicket—there!"—pointing
to the closed door. And surely, in another minute, Samuel Palmer raised the
latch and came in among them. It so turned out that the coach had broken
down near to the gate of Lullingstone Park.'

In October there was another adventure with a coach. Blake, as he told in a letter to Mrs Linnell, had gone to see her husband off in the Gloucester coach. They were so engrossed in talk inside that they failed to notice the coach had started off. 'We, with some difficulty, made the Coachman understand that one of his Passengers was unwilling to Go, when he obligingly permitted me to get off, to my great joy; hence I am now enabled to tell you that I hope to see you on Sunday morning as usual.' Two days later Mrs Linnell wrote to her husband that Blake expected to see them on Sunday: 'I have engaged Hannah to be with us also on that day.'

On these Sundays the children kept watch for the first glimpse of Blake. Hannah long remembered 'how, as he walked over the brow of the hill and came within sight of the young ones, he would make a particular signal'. Dr Thornton, another regular visitor, used to raise his hat on a stick. 'She remembers how Blake would take her on his knee, and recite children's stories to them all; recollects his kind manner; his putting her in the way of drawing, training her from his own doings.' In fact, all he seems to have done was to correct by a few touches a rough drawing she had made of a face. Linnell's part of the house was made up of five rooms, built later than the rest and lower in height, with separate entrance. The front looked south. Blake liked to stand at the door gazing out across the garden at the hill of gorse, or to sit in the arbour at the end of the garden, or to walk up and down as the cows were at their evening meal on the other side of the hedge. He was very fond of hearing Mrs Linnell sing Scottish songs, and tears came in his eyes with the first line, 'O Nancy's hair is yellow as gowd.' 'To the simple national melodies Blake was very impressionable, though not so to music of more complicated structure. He himself still sang, in a voice tremulous with age, sometimes old ballads, sometimes his own songs, to melodies of his own.' So writes Gilchrist, but the account handed down in the Linnell family was less idealised. Blake was remembered as grave and sedate, kind and gentle with the children; he took them on his knee and talked in a grave but amusing way. His eyes filled with tears at the songs.[15]

On 18 October Mrs Linnell reported that on Sunday morning Blake had come as usual, with good news about the *Job*. He had taken the prints to Flaxman, who bought a copy. 'His approbation Mr B thinks will be of considerable advantage.' She was copying something of Michelangelo, and Blake gave her a drawing-lesson. Just before dinner her father, Thomas Palmer, arrived, 'so that we had plenty of company till about six o'clock when they all departed'. About two days later she wrote to say that Blake had called again with an old sketchbook used when he was about fourteen. No doubt this was the visit that Gilchrist mentions when Blake delighted the children with a sketchbook in which was 'a finished, pre-Raphaelite-like drawing of a grasshopper'.[16]

Blake, we see, was constant in his Hampstead visits though he thought the region ruinous to health. One day when Mrs Linnell commented on its healthiness, he startled her by interjecting, 'It's a lie! It's no such thing'. One day at the Linnell's he met the painter William Collins who made some very rude remarks about 'enthusiasts', but had to admit that 'Blake had made a very gentlemanly and temperate return'. Some time later Blake encountered Collins in the Strand, with the pot of porter he was in the custom of fetching from a public-house for his dinner. They had met at some social gathering a few evenings before, and now Collins went to shake hands. But seeing the plebeian porter, he averted his eyes and went on.

Gilchrist, also somewhat put out by the porter, insists that only in his later years did Blake take it regularly. He sat and mused over the pint after his one o'clock dinner; but if he had wine at home, which was seldom, he disliked wine-glasses and drank good draughts from a tumbler. Once a nobleman sent him some oil of walnuts for experimenting with in his art, but he drank it all; and when the nobleman called to ask how the experiment went on, Blake had to admit what he had done.

In early November Blake was again ill abed, but hoped to get up next day. The weather was wet and the plates still unfinished. Mrs Aders was writing to Linnell, asking him to bring Blake along; and at least on 10 December he did dine at her house with Linnell and Crabb Robinson; in the evening Maria Denman and Miss Flaxman came in. Robinson noted that Blake was now old, pale, with a Socratic countenance of great sweetness but bordering on weakness except when his features grew animated; then there was an air of inspiration about him. Robinson admitted however that at first his expression was 'almost of fatuity'. He did his best to draw him out; and if he had not already known much of his ideas would at times have been at a loss to understand him. Blake had brought his Pilgrims engraving for the Aders and 'cordially praised' some compositions of Mrs Aders'. One figure in his engraving was like a figure in a painting in their collection. 'They say I stole it from this picture, but I did it 20 years before I knew of this picture— however in my youth I was always studying this kind of paintings. No wonder there is resemblance.' In fact the Pilgrims had been done fifteen years before. Robinson noted the contradiction between deriving his forms both from visions and from other art-works. He remarked that Blake spoke of his Spirit in the same way as Socrates, and asked what likeness was there between the two Spirits. 'The same as between our countenances.' Blake paused, then added, 'I was Socrates.' But went on as if correcting himself, 'A sort of brother—I must have had conversations with him—So I had with Jesus Christ—I have an obscure recollection of having been with both of them.'[17]

Blake then talked of everyone's coexistence with God and called Jesus Christ the only God, but added, 'And so am I and so are you'. Of Jesus' errors he said, 'He was wrong in suffering himself to be crucified He should not have attacked the govt he had no business with such matters'. We see how far Blake has gone in passivity; he now totally rejects the positions of *The Everlasting Gospel* where Jesus is praised for lack of gentleness and humility. 'I come your King & God to seize.' 'And in his hand the Scourge shone bright', and so on. Blake has changed his image of Jesus in order to justify his own withdrawal from politics out of terror of Hand and Hyle, the Hunts and Hayley, the government.

He now went on to attack education as the great sin of eating the fruit of the tree of knowledge of good and evil. Robinson noted the contradiction in his not liking to say outright that there was nothing absolutely evil in what men do, and his denial of evil's existence: 'as if we had nothing to do with right & wrong'. Blake liked the German term 'objectivity' when Robinson used it. 'Yet at other times he spoke of error as being in heaven, not only in the angels, but in God himself.' Turning to art, he said, 'When Michael Angelo or Raphael or Mr Flaxman does any of his fine things he does them in the spirit'. He said that he himself wanted no earthly fame or profit. He mentioned Dante and Swedenborg together. Robinson asked if he thought their visions of the same kind. 'As far as I could recollect he does—Dante he said was the greater poet—He had *political* objects. Yet this tho wrong does not appear in Blake's mind to affect the truth of the vision.' Blake attacked Wordsworth as a Platonist and said that a passage in the *Excursion* so shocked him that 'it brought on a fit of illness'. It was that in which the poet speaks of passing Jehovah, his shouting angels and empyreal thrones, unalarmed. (In 1814 Flaxman had told Crabb Robinson how he objected to this passage, and it was doubtless his comments that drew Blake's attention to it.) Blake now praised Boehme, attacked Bacon, Locke and Newton, and declared the earth to be flat.

Crabb Robinson wrote his recollections down the next day, and they constitute by far the most valuable record we have of the way that Blake talked, at least in his garrulous last years. 'The tone and manner are incommunicable. There is a natural sweetness & gentility about Blake which are delightful. And when he is not referring to his Visions he talks sensibly & acutely. His friend Linnell seems a quiet admirer.'[18]

Haunted by the conversation, Crabb Robinson called the following Saturday on Blake. 'I found him in a small room which seems to be both a working room and a bed room. Nothing could exceed the squalid air both of the apartment & his dress—but in spite of dirt—I might say, filth, an air of natural gentility is diffused over him, and his wife, notwithstanding the same offensive character of her dress & appearance, has a good expression of countenance.' Using Cary's translation, Blake was working on Dante, whom he declared 'an atheist—A mere politician busied about this world as Milton was till in his old age he returned back to God whom he had had in his childhood'. (This time Blake uses Milton to justify his own withdrawal.) He denied all education save that of the cultivation of imagination and the fine arts. Robinson pressed him on the subject of evil:

I asked wher. if had been a father he would not have grieved if his child had become vicious or a great criminal. He ansd. I must not regard when I am endeavouring to think rightly my own any more than other people's weaknesses. And when I again remarked that this doctrine puts an end to all exertion or even wish to change anything He had no reply.[19]

Blake denied the omnipotence of God. 'The language of the Bible on that subject is only poetical or allegorical.' Yet soon after that 'he denied that the natural world is any thing. It is all nothing and Satan's empire the empire of nothing.' Then he said: 'I saw Milton in Imagination And he told me to beware of being misled by his Paradise Lost. In particular he wished me to shew the falsehood of his doctrine that the pleasures of SEX arose from the fall—The Fall could not produce any pleasure'. Then 'he went off upon a rambling state in which I could not follow him. And again spoke of Milton appearing to him.' He declared that all men owned the faculty of vision, but lost it through lack of cultivation. Robinson decided to come again and read Wordsworth to him.

He came on 24 December and read Wordsworth's *Ode on Imitations of Immortality*. Blake again accused Wordsworth of loving Nature, the Devil's work. Asked if God could not destroy the Devil, he denied that God has any power. The parts of the Ode he most enjoyed were the most obscure and those that Robinson least liked or understood.

Blake's uncertainties are brought out by erasions he made on the plate of *Jerusalem*'s Preface. In the sentence, 'Dear Reader, forgive what you may not approve & love me for this energetic exertion of my talent', he scratched out *Dear*, *forgive*, and *love*. He made no effort to fill in the gaps, which he left in the most richly coloured copy. He deleted the names after Richard and John from a list of Kings who were 'to be in Time Reveald & Demolished'. The names that drew him too much into the present were Edward, Henry, Elizabeth, James, Charles, William, and George; he also cut out the names of prophets which had balanced with the king-list. His illuminated books, few as their copies were, might fall somehow into the hands of Hand. So his ideas must be hidden ever more obscurely in 'beautiful labyrinths' holding Oothoon (Liberty) at their centre 'in merciful deceit Lest Hand the terrible destroy'.[20]

Crabb Robinson's account of the conversations make painful reading. We hear indeed the voice of Blake, but with a weakened and confused note. He can no longer draw his ideas together in a vigorous Antinomian faith and defiance. As he said of Socrates and Jesus, 'I have an obscure recollection of having been with both of them'. The living connections seem lost in the past.*

---

* This year, 1825, Fuseli died; for long there had been no contact between him and Blake. James Blake's name drops out of the list of ratepayers of Cirencester Place; perhaps he was hard up or in bad health and took a smaller number of rooms; he may even have lived in Linnell's house.—Blake scratched out also in the Preface, 'The Antients entrusted their love to their writing, to the full as Enthusiastically as I have who acknowledge mine for my Saviour and Lord'.

14

Last Days, 1826–7

In the *Job* plates Blake made the last great expression of his vision of life; here indeed was the only case where he used his art in a continuous narrative that rivalled the prophetic books. He summed up his life and at the same time restated his basic ideas. As usual he considered the Bible a source of rough material to be reshaped and revalued. In the Bible Job is the subject of a sort of wager between God and Satan. Though he has done nothing wrong he is submitted to all sorts of miseries so that God can show Satan's error and emerge with enhanced glory. Blake could have nothing to do with such a theme. He used the episodes to depict the breakdown of the state of innocence, the tests and trials of the exposed individual in the world of experience, and his final rebirth of a new level of deepened understanding and secure relation to the cosmos.

The first plate shows Job in the state of pastoral innocence. Not realising the nature of this state, he hangs up the musical instruments of free self-expression on the tree and opens the Books of the Law, an obedient child. He makes God in his own image, a God of Law, and his eldest son begins to rebel. Job, accepting the Law, turns on his refractory sons; the unity of the family is destroyed. Disasters begin to heap up on him and his wife. He loses his four senses (sight, hearing, taste, smell) and his fifth sense (touch, sex) is corrupted. (In this plate, no. 6, the emblems below include the broken sheep-hook of Innocence.) Job curses the day of his birth; he begins to rebel. His friends argue with him and the just punishing God is represented as a sort of monolithic nightmare, with his arms bound. The friends now accuse Job and even his wife is shaken. At last the God in whom he has trusted is shown as a demon of law and hell, who begets what is to Blake the world of reason and nature, the existing divided world. Elihu expounds the greatness of God in terms of the stars (i.e. Newtonism). Job in his reaction at last realises what the true divine is, in the whirlwind of rapturous vision, and his wife is reunited with him. (The plate's number, 13, represents death and so rebirth.)

Job enters the fourfold world of his imagination, and realises the terrible forces of destruction in a fallen society (Behemoth and Leviathan), war and power-lust. He goes through a Last Judgement and achieves a world where the fall is ended. He finds true community. The three daughters (the arts) return and are told of his experiences, which become their material. The unity of the family is restored. Innocence is regained, now with full consciousness of the issues: the Law banished and the arts celebrating and revealing freedom and its meaning.

In the prints Blake has used elements from both the prophetic books and *Night Thoughts*. The picture is in the middle, with text above and below, and with decorations (now simple emblematic forms) around. Mannerist elongations of form and disregard of normal proportions are almost wholly discarded. As a result there is emotional concentration with compactness both of composition and individual forms, which make the set stand on its own.[1]

Early in January 1826 Mrs Aders asked Linnell how she could tactfully pay Blake for the books he had given; neither she nor Crabb Robinson had meant to get them for nothing. On the 6th the latter called on Blake with two subscriptions for *Job*, but did not record their conversation as it merely repeated what had been already said. The subscriptions cheered Blake. 'He spoke of being richer than ever in having learned to know me.' (He had embarrassed Robinson by telling Mrs Aders that the two of them were 'nearly of an opinion'. Robinson says that he himself had 'practised no deception intentionally unless silence be so'.) Blake complained of Wordsworth, while expressing admiration of him, and told how when commanded to write about Milton he had refused and was applauded. 'He struggled with the Angels and was victor—his wife joined in the conversation.'

Ten days later Blake wrote in the autograph album of William Upcott, illegitimate son of Ozias Humphry: 'William Blake, one who is very much delighted with being in good Company. Born Novr 1757 in London & has died several times since'. He cited four lines of a Michelangelo sonnet about ideal form, translated by Wordsworth, giving the reference to the 1815 edition of the latter's poems, of which he annotated a copy. He makes his usual attacks on nature and declared: 'I believe both Macpherson & Chatterton, that what they say is Ancient Is so. I own myself an admirer of Ossian equally with any other Poet whatever, Rowley & Chatterton also.' It is of interest to find him making this statement about Ossian at such a late date. An annotation to the *Excursion* shows that when Wordsworth writes of the individual mind as fitted to the external world, and that world to the mind, he assumes that Wordsworth means a static mechanical sort of fitting-together, something like a jigsaw puzzle, not a fusion of two formative processes.

Orders for *Job* were trickling in to Linnell. On 1 February Blake wrote saying he had forgotten to ask him to look in and take a mutton chop with him and Catherine before he went to catch the Cheltenham coach. After, Blake would then walk with him to the coach. On Sunday he would go to Mrs Linnell but leave before dinner; and he asked for a copy of *Job* to show Chantrey the sculptor. Meanwhile he was laid up with a cold in his stomach, blaming the Hampstead air, which always had this effect except in the morning. 'When I was young, Hampstead, Highgate, Hornsea, Muswell Hill & even Islington & all places North of London, always laid me up the day after, & sometimes two or three days, with precisely the same Complaint & the same torment of the Stomach, Easily removed, but excruciating while it lasts & enfeebling for some time after.' A few days later he wrote to Mrs Linnell with apologies for an unwritten letter and with the news that he had been to see her husband off in the coach from the Angel Inn in the Strand.

Crabb Robinson called on a Saturday later in the month and found Blake still worried about Wordsworth's lack of alarm at Jehovah. But he insisted that he himself read the Bible purely in the spiritual sense. Voltaire had been commissioned by God to expose the natural sense. 'I have had much inter-course with Voltaire and he said to me I blasphemed the Son of Man and it shall be forgiven me', but Voltaire's enemies blasphemed the Holy Ghost and it would not be forgiven them. Robinson asked what language Voltaire spoke in. Blake replied, 'To my Sensation it was English—It was like the touch of a musical key—He touched it probably French, but to my ear it became English'. Blake then told Robinson he had written more than Voltaire or Rousseau: 'Six or Seven Epic poems as long as Homer and 20 Tragedies as long as Macbeth'. He showed a work that he called his version of *Genesis* as understood by a Christian visionary. He read a passage at random, which Robinson found striking. He had decided to print no more (make no more illuminated books). 'I write when commanded by the spirits and the moment I have written I see the words fly about the room in all directions. It is then published and the Spirits can read.' As his manuscripts were no longer any use he had been tempted to burn them, but his wife would not let him.

Robinson said that she was right. 'You cannot tell what purpose they may answer unforeseen to you.' Blake liked that comment and said he would not destroy the manuscripts. He then brought himself to mention that Robinson's copy of the *Songs* would cost five guineas, and made his remark about the horror of money he felt.[2]

This month Robinson wrote to Dorothy Wordsworth a long account of Blake, mentioning his reaction to the Jehovah passage: he had been so upset that he nearly died of a bowel complaint. Robinson added that Coleridge had visited Blake, 'and I am told talks finely about him'; and he tried to draw in the Wordsworths by saying, 'You must see him one of these days'. No doubt it was at the Aders' house that Coleridge met Blake.

Probably this winter occurred an episode told by Calvert. There was a heavy tread on the stairs and a bump on the door. Blake rose somewhat disturbed as he never knew in what shape or manner his angels might appear, but it was only a coalman taking coals to a lodger upstairs. Thornbury, apparently citing the artist Leigh, says that Blake even saw the devil in his coal-cellar; and we heard earlier how Stothard's son found Blake fighting with the devil over coals.

The delays over *Job* may have been increased by the fact that the decorations had to be done direct on the plates; but at last the set was completed, dated March 1826. At the end of the month Blake wrote to Linnell about Robinson's order and said that he had again been very ill; he could now work but not venture out. If the weather was warm, he would come before Tuesday, 'But much fear that my present tottering state will hold me some time yet'.*

On 12 May Robinson gave a party which included Blake, the Flaxman's, the Masqueriers. He was surprised that Masquerier, a portrait-painter, took Blake's opinions 'as if they were those of a man of ordinary notions'—Blake however was 'not in an *exalted* state'. He denied any progression in art. Robinson noted that Blake appreciated Flaxman, but doubted whether Flaxman sufficiently tolerated Blake. They all stayed till eleven o'clock; and Robinson, determined to win Blake over to Wordsworth, decided to send him a copy of the latter's *Descriptive Sketches*.

A week later Blake had another 'desperate Shivering Fit,' which had come on the night before. In the morning, as he tried to rise, it attacked him with much pain and 'its accompanying deathly feel'. He would have to put off his Sunday visit to Hampstead.

---

* On 28 March Wainewright ordered the *Job* 'of our great genius Blake'. He had bought the *Milton* and wanted a list of the illuminated books. Next day he sent 5 guineas, praising the *Job* highly. On 17 May Linnell called at his father's, then at Blake's. On 12 and 13 July he again saw Blake.

On 13 June Robinson called on Blake and found him as wild as ever but there was no novelty in his remark that according to the Bible there had once been community of women. (Blake was in fact citing Matthew xix, 8, and twisting the text to make it mean the opposite of what it actually says.) He talked as usual of the spirits and asserted 'that he had committed many murders, that reason is the only evil or sin, and that careless gay people are better than those that think &c &c &c'.[3]

His health was worsening. In early July the sudden cold weather had cut up all his hopes 'by the roots'. With better weather he would come to Linnell by coach, with change of clothes, the Dante drawings, and one plate enclosed in the book. It seems that the Linnells had suggested he should leave Fountain Court and go to stay at Mrs Hurd's, where Linnell lodged before his Hampstead move. Blake demurred, 'Think of the Expense & how it can be spared, & never mind appearances'. Three days later he felt better and believed his paroxysms would not return. 'I thank you for the Receit of Five Pounds this Morning, & Congratulate you on the receit of another fine Boy.' On the 14th he wrote that he soon hoped to visit Hampstead despite his weakness, and enclosed receipts acknowledging that he had been paid for *Job* and that plates and copyright belonged to Linnell. No doubt it was about this time he gave Linnell the manuscript of the *Four Zoas*, which was thus preserved. There was something filial in Linnell's relations to Blake, but at the same time he was a good businessman. On 14 July, to make things unmistakably clear, he got a second receipt for the *Job*, which was witnessed by his nephew, J. Chance, print-dealer.[4]

Two days later Blake wrote an odd letter about the naming of Linnell's recently born son. He insisted that the boy must be named after Mrs Linnell's father, saying it would be a brutal act to do otherwise. 'It very much troubles me as a Crime in which I shall be the Principal.' He had been in a sort of delirium and pain 'too much for thought' since taking some medicine to which dandelion was added. But no sooner was bodily pain ended than there came the pain of mind over the boy's name.

Blake had certainly a very strong family feeling. We are told that in reading the account of the Prodigal Son he broke down on reaching the point of the son's return to the father. We can only surmise what would have been the effect if Catherine had borne children. Probably he would have been crushed by the responsibility and by the loss of her single-hearted devotion.[5]

On 29 July he wrote that no sooner did he feel better than he was afflicted with piles, but now the worst seemed over. However, 'I cannot yet tell when

I can start for Hampstead like a young Lark without feathers'. Two days later, Tuesday, he hoped to venture to Hampstead on Thursday in a cabriolet that would take him to the door. He was unable to walk, nothing but bones and sinews, 'all strings & bobbins like a Weaver's Loom'. But despite everything he was working on his Dante watercolours.*

In 1825–7 he made more than a hundred of these illustrations, of which he had engraved six at his death. Of Dante's world-view he strongly disapproved, seeing it as an acceptance of tyrannical purposes, of the rule of power, law and punishment. So he tended to treat Dante as cavalierly as he treated the Bible, especially when dealing with the cruelties of the *Inferno*. Technically he made some remarkable advances. He began with the broad washes normal in the medium, such as he had used in Biblical works for Butts, but he then went over the whole surface with small touches, at times returning and returning to the same area. Yet he kept a clarity amid the resulting richness, probably by waiting till the lower layers were fully dried before adding new touches. The result has been compared with Cézanne's watercolours. At the same time many of the compositions are imaginatively free and varied beyond those of any previous series, though others are only roughly indicated or crudely grotesque.

Probably in September 1826 he made his visit to the Calverts at Brixton. Late at night he and Calvert were trying an etching-ground and melting it, when the pipkin cracked and set the chimney in a blaze. His anxiety, says Calvert's son, 'was not for the fire, but that Mrs. Calvert, who had retired to bed, should not be alarmed'. The fire was easily put out.[6]

In late November Crabb Robinson wrote to Masquerier about a coolness that had arisen between him and Mrs Aders because she had heard of his asking the Flaxmans and the Masqueriers to his apartments without her. The Flaxmans insisted they had said nothing, 'and Blake I believe they have not seen Nor is he likely to have spoken of it'. He suspected the talkative Mrs Masquerier. Two weeks later Flaxman died. On 7 December Robinson called on Blake, curious to learn how he would take the news. 'It was much as I expected. Blake had himself been ill and his first comment was with a

* On 4 November Sir Edward Denny wrote to Linnell asking when the *Job* would be done, enclosing a letter to Blake with a request for *The Grave*. He had seen the unfinished *Job* plates at Linnell's. Palmer accuses Linnell of suppressing the letter to Blake and himself supplying *The Grave*, robbing Blake of the profit. But Linnell now owned the *Job* copyright and Blake no longer had any property in *The Grave*. Linnell knowing how ill Blake was, may have thought it best not to trouble him. Denny replied with thanks, finding *Job* a great work, and hoping for Blake's recovery.

smile, I thought I should have gone first.' Then he added, 'I cannot consider death as any thing but a removing from one room to another'. One thing led to another, says Robinson, and he fell into his wild rambling way of talk. Men are born with a devil and an angel: which Blake interpreted as body and soul. He did not seem to think favourably of the Old Testament, and he declared Christ to be one of the worst of men, taking much after his mother (the Law). Robinson asked for an example. Blake said that Christ had no right to turn the money-changers out of the Temple, and attacked all who sat in judgement on others. 'I have never known a very bad man who had not something very good about him.' He denounced the Atonement as a horrible doctrine, and brought out a copy of Fouqué's Gothic romance, saying, 'This is better than my things!'

In his quietist position he now rejects all the interpretations he has made of Jesus in his art and writings, seeing him as the Law of which he previously took him to be the arch-enemy. The cause of the change lies in his now rooted fear of political action. The comment on *Sintram* is of much interest. By thus comparing it with his own prophecies he infers that the latter are purely symbolic constructions. He is also perhaps comparing Fouqué's success in putting over his ideas and symbols in a public way with his own abandonment of all struggle to gain an audience.[7]

In January 1827 Linnell paid him two £5s and on 2 February he met the young Götzenberger. On the 7th Linnell again urged him to move to Cirencester Place, where he would have better quarters.* Soon afterwards Blake, acknowledging another £5, said that though still feeble he felt better in the warm weather. He was working on four Dante plates and asked to have the first two returned so that he might finish them enough for 'some shew of Colour & Strength'. He had thought and thought of the removal but could not prevent a state of terrible fear at such a step.

The more I think, the more I feel terror at what I wish'd at first & thought it a thing of benefit & Good hope; you will attribute it to its right Cause—intellectual Peculiarity, that must be Myself alone shut up in Myself, or Reduced to Nothing. I could tell you of Visions & dreams upon the Subject. I have asked & intreated Divine help, but fear continues upon me, & I must relinquish the step that I had wish'd to take, & still wish, but in vain.[8]

* On 27 January Blake wrote with extreme apologies for not having acknowledged £5: 'I am enough asham'd of [it] & hope to mend'. Robinson acted as translator with Götzenberger. 'Nothing remarkable was said by Blake—He was interested apparently by Götzenberger.'

Here we have an instance of his nervous fear, exacerbated by his enfeebled state, but revealing a characteristic element in his make-up. Meanwhile Linnell went on doing his best, not only to sell copies of *Job*, but also to find buyers for other works by Blake. In February he left the *Paradise Lost* drawings with Lawrence, offering them for £50. Lawrence turned the offer down, but commissioned copies of two works done for Butts, *The Wise and Foolish Virgins* and *The Dream of Queen Katharine*. Chantrey also refused the Milton drawings but gave £20 for a fine copy of *Songs*. Lord Egremont and others also bought copies of *Songs*. Gilchrist says that they were moved mainly by a charitable wish to help Blake.

Blake was now well enough to walk to Linnell's London place, and was working on the Dante plates. On 2 March James Blake was buried in Bunhill Fields. He had been living in Cirencester Place where William had feared to move. The records give his age as 71; but he was in fact 74. Blake had meanwhile sent *Job* to Cumberland in Bristol, who could find no buyers though he took a copy for himself. 'He tells me that it is too much Finish'd, or over Labour'd, for his Bristol Friends, as they think. I saw Mr. Tatham, Senr., yesterday; he sat with me above an hour, & look'd over the Dante.' Three days later he notified Maria Denman, Flaxman's sister-in-law, that he had found 15 proofs of the Hesiod; as he had duplicates, 'they are intirely at Miss Denman's service if she will accept them'. About this time Butts called on him and ordered a proof copy of *Job* for three guineas: 'this is his own decision, quite in Character'.

On 12 April he brought himself to reply to Cumberland. He had been near the gates of death and returned as 'an Old Man feeble & tottering, but not in Spirit & Life, not in the Real Man The Imagination which Liveth for Ever'. As for the Bristolians:

I know too well that a great majority of Englishmen are fond of The Indefinite which they Measure by Newton's Doctrine of the Fluxions of an Atom. A Thing that does not Exist. They are Politicians & think that Republican Art is Inimical to their Atom. For a Line or Lineament is not formed by Chance: a Line is a Line in its Minutest Subdivisions: Straight or Crooked: It is Itself & Not Inter-measurable with or by any Thing Else. Such is Job, but since the French Revolution Englishmen are all Intermeasurable One by Another. Certainly a happy state of Agreement to which I for One do not Agree. God keep me from the Divinity of Yes & no too, The Yea Nay Creeping Jesus, from supposing Up & Down to be the same Thing as all Experimentalists must suppose.

This important statement brings out how thoroughly he had grappled with the nature of Newtonian positions, of post-Galilean mechanistic science in general. His thinking in these matters is entwined everywhere in the cosmic and social definitions of the prophecies. The world brought about by Satan as he dominates, swallowing up Urizen, Vala and Orc, is one in which Newton's fluxional calculus becomes possible and necessary. That calculus draws together all that is most abstract and mechanistic in Urizen, all that is most delusive and confusing in Vala, all that is most frustrated and broken-down in Orc. A physicist has put the matter clearly:

Newton's fluxions connect the indefinite, indeterminate, and vanishing quality of temporal process with the static, inert 'places' of the moments of generation in Newton's space-like time. Newton's fluxions, in turn, make possible the revelation of the Satanic nature of the physical world by submerging the Urizenic-Orc-Vala components under the guise of mathematical system. Blake intimately connects the physical or 'corporeal' Polypus, which is a transformation of revolutionary activity into the subordinate activity of indefinite Newtonian physical change which has no real life, with the indefinite, constantly shifting and erratically fluctuating form of perception grounded in Vala. Newton's grounding the fluxions 'in the nature of things', thus inadvertently establishing the isomorphism between the indefinite-ness and incomprehensibility of mathematical and physical change in the fluxions and in nature is the mathematical version of Blake's union of Vala and Orc. Second, the connection that develops between Vala, the fluctuating form of perception, and the male spectrous component of Satan, the principle of mathematical abstraction and repression, can be seen in the way in which Newton's fluxions fuse the indefiniteness of temporal process with static definiteness, of spatial coordinates. (Ault)[9]

Thus Blake, working out the links between Satan, Orc and Vala, develops a system that reflects the elements combined by Newton in his system linking mathematics, perception and the physical world. When this abstract system comes about, Blake says, the process of integration, Jerusalem, is reduced to an evanescent shade. In the letter to Cumberland, just cited, he declares that the reaction in England against the integrations, the new element of community, in the French Revolution, has split the individuals apart in a way that makes them dead ciphers, lacking all true individuality, alienated and 'intermeasurable'.

Cumberland had asked if he had any of his printed works for sale. Blake replied that he had none left. He cannot now print except at a great loss. When he did print the books he had 'a whole House to range in', at Lambeth, but now he is 'shut up in a Corner' and forced to ask too high a price. He is now printing a copy of the *Songs of Innocence and Experience* for a friend at ten guineas, and the job will take six months. 'So I have little hope of doing any more such things.' His latest work is *Jerusalem*, which he could not ask less than twenty guineas for. 'One I have Finish'd. It contains 100 Plates but it is not likely that I shall get a Customer for it.' He adds a price-list: *America, Urizen, Europe*, six guineas each; *Visions*, five guineas; *Thel*, three guineas; *Songs*, ten guineas. As soon as he can he will produce a little card for Cumberland. 'I have been reduced to a Skeleton from which I am slowly recovering.' Flaxman is gone, but death means leaving 'the Delusive Goddess Nature & her Laws to get into Freedom from all Law of the Members into the Mind, in which every one is King & Priest in his own House. God send it so on Earth as it is in Heaven'.

Five days later Linnell took him to see Ottley, author of a *History of Engraving*; and afterwards he wrote to tell Linnell that he felt better and to thank him for £10 and 'the prospect of Mr Ottley's advantageous acquaintance'. (Ottley bought a plain copy of *Jerusalem* for five guineas.) 'I go on without daring to count on Futurity, which I cannot do without doubt & Fear that ruins Activity, & are the greatest hurt to an Artist such as I am'. But why does he doubt and fear so deeply if he truly thinks of death as walking into another room? 'As to Ugolino, &c, I never supposed that I should sell them [temperas]; my wife alone is answerable for their having Existed in any finish'd State.' (It is not clear whether he means that she has looked after the works, encouraged him to finish them, or done the finishing herself.) He was absorbed in his Dante work. 'I count myself sufficiently Paid If I live as I do now, & only fear that I may be Unlucky to my friends, & especially that I may be so to you.'[10]

On 3 July he wrote the last words of his that we have. 'I thank you for the Ten Pounds you are so kind as to send me at this time.' His Sunday journey to Hampstead had brought on a relapse. 'I find I am not as well as I thought. I must not go on in a youthful Style; however, I am upon the mending hand to-day, & hope soon to look as I did, for I have been yellow, accompanied by all the old Symptoms.' Linnell called at least twice during the month; and on 3 August he looked in to give Blake £2. Seven days later he found him 'not expected to live'. He made a very small sketch of him abed with a black skull-cap, his head sunk in a big pillow, his face thin and drawn, his darkened eyes hollow but alive. Blake was still working. A few days before he died he finished colouring a relief-etching, *The Ancient of Days* for Tatham.

In the early morning of 12 August Blake died, in his sixty-ninth year, of the troubles of gall and stomach which we have seen worsening in the last few years. As he weakened, he sang with rapture in his eyes. A woman neighbour, Catherine's only other companion, said, 'I have been in at the death, not of a man, but of a blessed angel'. Richmond came in just after he died, closed his eyes and kissed him.*

Blake had told Catherine that it did not matter where he was buried, but that it might as well be with the rest of the family, and that he preferred the service to be that of the Church of England. To meet expenses Linnell lent Catherine £5, which she repaid. He attended the funeral which was carried out by B. Palmer and Son of 175 Piccadilly, at the cost of £10 18s. This Palmer seems to have been Mrs Linnell's uncle; his bill was not paid till next January. Present at the funeral were also Calvert, Richmond, Tatham and a clergyman brother of his. No stone was set up on the grave.†

On 14 August Constable wrote to Linnell about Catherine: 'I hope our Charity will do something handsome for the widow'. His concern suggests that he knew Blake better than our sources imply. Linnell seems to have written to Princess Sophia, the King's sister, for she sent a gift of £100, which Catherine, politely but promptly, returned. With genuine dignity she said that she did not like to keep what she could do without, 'while many to whom no chance or choice was given might have been kept alive by the gift'. (So at least Swinburne tells us, drawing on Kirkup, whose source we do not know.) Linnell drew up a statement, which he took to Lawrence as President of the R.A. He also wrote to Wainewright, whose wife sent him their regrets. Richmond wrote to Palmer, who was out of town; he said that Blake at the end with brightening eyes 'burst out Singing of the things he Saw in Heaven'.

On 18 August *The Literary Gazette*, in an appreciative obituary, wrote of his art, often stressing his wretched living-conditions: 'his bed in one corner, his meagre dinner in another, a ricketty table holding his copper-plates, his

---

* So says Gilchrist, but Richmond in a letter three days later says nothing of having been in at the death. Doubtless there is not much we can trust in the edifying tales spread by the Ancients.

† There was an elm coffin covered with black flannel and black varnished nails, inscribed plate, three pairs of handles; a shroud, pillow and bed, two men to dress the corpse, use of a best velvet pall, six gentleman's cloaks, six crepe hatbands, three pairs of gloves, three men gowned as porters, hearse and pair, coach and pair, four men as bearers, etc., cost of refreshments for the men, grave-diggers, dues at the Fields, fees for clergymen.

colours, books . . . his ankles frightfully swollen, his chest disordered', yet all the while 'his eye undimmed, the fire of his imagination unquenched'. It paid tribute to Linnell for his aid and drew attention to Mrs Blake's condition. *The Literary Chronicle* on 1 September dealt mainly with Blake's drawing of visions. *The Monthly Magazine* for October compressed the account of *The Literary Gazette*, adding an incorrect birth-date. Cumberland did not hear of Blake's death till 23 October, apparently from some obituary. On 1 November *The Gentleman's Magazine* mentioned his illuminated books and his Catalogue, but said nothing of his poems. 'Flaxman pointed him out to an eminent literary man as a melancholy proof of English apathy towards the grand, the philosophic, or the enthusiastically devotional painter.' Blake had been allowed to exist in penury. *The New Monthly Magazine* on 1 December compiled its notice from *The Gentleman's Magazine*. And so, it appeared, Blake had been dealt with and disposed of for all time.[11]

Catherine had gone to the Linnells a month after Blake's death. She seems to have stayed at Cirencester Place till about June 1828. In January that year Crabb Robinson went to see her. 'The poor old lady was more affected that I expected yet she spoke of her husband as dying like an angel.' She was working as Linnell's housekeeper, with no property but a few of Blake's art-works. As the prints of the Pilgrims were still hers, Robinson bought two prints (one of them for Lamb) and his companion Field bought a third. 'Mrs Blake is to look out for some engravings for me hereafter.' Other friends and patrons also rallied. Lord Egremont called and asked, 'Why did he leave me?' That is, why did he leave Felpham? His words suggest that Blake had more contacts with Petworth than we know of; perhaps he had acted for a while as tutor there. Lord Egremont later paid eighty guineas for a watercolour of characters from the *Faery Queen*, a companion piece to the Pilgrims. Cary also bought a drawing, *Oberon and Titania*, and noted that Catherine was an excellent saleswoman, who did not make the mistake of showing too many things at one time. With Tatham's aid she coloured some of the prophecies, 'rather against Mr. Linnell's judgment'. She always spoke of Blake with trembling voice and tears in her eyes as 'that wonderful man', whose spirit was still with her, as he had promised in death. A writer in 1833 adds that Blake in spirit used to come and sit with her two or three hours a day, and she never agreed to anything till she had 'an opportunity of consulting Mr. Blake'.

In June she rented rooms at 17 Upper Charlotte Street, Fitzroy Square, which she kept until she died, though she spent part or much of the time with the Tathams. Late in October 1828 appeared J. T. Smith's *Nollekens and his Times*, with the first attempt at a biography of Blake. Smith wrote to Linnell, 'What I have said of your worthy friend Blake I am fully aware has been serviceable to his widow'. Before the year's end came Varley's *Zodiacal Physiognomy* with its section on Blake.

Catherine was showing all her stubbornness. When Linnell visited her on 27 January 1829 she informed him that 'Mr Blake told her he thought I should pay 3 gs a piece for the plates of Dante'. Tatham was also finding her difficult, but he wore her down. Joseph Hogarth wrote at the end of his copy of Smith's account of Blake:

Fred Tatham was Blake's executor and possessed several of his drawings, many of which I purchased from him. Mrs Blake was hardly the passive creature here described—at all events Tatham did not find her so for she was opposed to everything he did for her benefit and when she submitted to his views it was always with the words she 'Had no help for it'—till at last Tatham tired with her opposition threw the Will behind the fire and burnt it saying There now you do as you like for the Will no longer exists and left her. Early the following morning she called upon [him] saying William had been with her all night and required her to come to him and renew the Will which was done and never after did she offer any objection to Tatham's proceedings.[12]

Hogarth was repeating what Tatham had told him. There was no will, though, someone, perhaps Catherine herself, may have written down some dying wishes of Blake. She as widow inherited all his effects. Tatham declares that 'After having answered a few questions concerning his Wifes means of living after his decease, & after having spoken of the writer of this, as a likely person to become the manager to her affairs, his spirit departed like the sighing of a gentle breeze'. But he himself was certainly not present at the death; and Blake could not have designated him as the person to manage Catherine's affairs since it was to the Linnells she went. Tatham seems to have drawn her over to his side by playing on her suspicion and dislike of Linnell.

Now came Cunningham's *Life*, which stirred up fresh interest in Blake: for instance in the *Athenaeum* of 6 February 1830, the *Literary Gazette* of the same day, and the *Monthly Review* for March. More important was the essay on 'Blake's Inventions' in the March issue of *The London University Magazine*, with the first fully serious acclaim of Blake:

We may say, Blake in his single person united all the grand combination of art and mind, poetry, music, and painting; and we may carry the simile still further, and say, that as England is the least fettered by the minds of other nations, so Blake poured forth his effusions in his own grand style, copying no one . . . but breathing spirit and life into his works; and though shaping forms from the world of his creative and sportive imagination, yet he still remembered he was a moral as well an intellectual citizen of England, bound both to love and instruct her . . . This grand combination of art succeeded in every particular, painting being the flesh, poetry the bones, and music the nerves of Blake's work.

The figures surrounding and enclosing the poems, produce fresh delight. They are equally tinged by a poetical idea, and though sometimes it is difficult to understand his wandering flights, yet the extraordinary power developed in the handling of both arts astonish[es] as well as delight[s]. Here and there figures are introduced, which, like the spirits in Macbeth, pass quickly from the sight; yet they every one of them have been well digested in the brain of a genius; and we should endeavour rather to unlock the prison-door in which we are placed, and gain an insight into his powerful mind than rail and scoff at him as a dreamer and a madman.

Fraser's Magazine for March had a long essay, drawing on Cunningham, which concluded that Blake 'mistook the dreams of fancy for reality'. And in December Bulwer Lytton, who knew Varley, published a dialogue in the *New Monthly Magazine*, which however dealt mainly with Blake's art and the encounters with the dead.[13]

Meanwhile Linnell had agreed that the Dante materials belonged to Catherine after his own expenses had been met. In March he gave her an account, sending a copy to Tatham as if he accepted him as the guardian of her affairs. He seems to have omitted a sum of £10 8s. owing to Blake, but there may have been a lost separate account for the Dante works. The cost of the funeral and unpaid rent for Fountain Court were debited to Catherine; she was owed small sums for making proofs and for furniture sold. In any event it seems clear that Linnell was crediting her with as little money as he could. On 15 March Tatham wrote, objecting that Linnell had made tracings of the Dante drawings. 'The more I consider of it, the more covetous & unfair it appeared to me as it depreciates the drawings full 25 per Cent.' Catherine agreed with him.

Catherine's dislike of Linnell was strengthened. Tatham says he had defended Linnell to her, 'frequently to my own great annoyance'. He adds, 'She has as I now recollect mentioned her suspicions to me upon several occasions but I would not hear them'. These protestations do not carry much conviction; Tatham is more likely to have worked Catherine up further against Linnell. She now wanted to confront the latter, and Tatham told him, 'She wishes me to be present at the Interview'. Linnell wrote in defence of his actions, saying that Tatham might have waited till a purchaser of the drawings objected to tracings having been made by his children—'for they are partly done by them'. (In fact his Journal shows that he was himself hard at work on the tracings in January and February, and there is no mention of the children.) He claims that 'from no covetous feeling' he advanced Blake £305 15s., for which he had received no monetary return. But he forgets to bring in the £35 5s. he got for the engravings done by Blake of the portraits of Lowry and Upton. He next asserts that 'the Job only paid the expenses of printing & paper'. In fact the costs were £124 12s. 1d., and by the end of 1830 he had received £176 4s. 6d. from sales.

Catherine's suspicious dislike of Linnell is so strong that it is possible she with her frank nature is now blurting out things that Blake had said in his later years. We have seen how throughout his life he was liable to end with bitter resentment and suspicion towards the friends who helped him, especially if there were financial dealings.[14]

On 18 October 1831 Tatham wrote to Linnell, 'I have the unpleasant duty of informing you of the death of Mrs Blake, who passed from death to life this morning, at 1 past 7—After bitter pains, lasting 24 hours, she faded away as the whisper of a breeze'. The cause was a neglected attack of inflammation of the bowels. She had sent for the Tathams and instructed them to have her buried in Bunhill Fields, with the same arrangements as at William's funeral: asking that no one should see her after death and that a bushel of lime be put in the coffin. After bidding goodbye to her sister-in-law, she spent her last hours repeating scriptural texts and calling on William as if he were in the next room, to let him know she would not be long in coming. She died in Mrs Tatham's arms. Her funeral was attended by the Tathams, the Richmonds, the sculptor Denham, and the artist Bird.[15]

The continuing struggle between Linnell and Tatham throws light on the group surrounding Blake in his last years and on the fate of his artistic and literary remains. Who was to inherit Catherine's property? One would have expected it to go to Blake's sister Catherine or to Linnell. What happened seems simply that Tatham, for all his prim piety, made use of his strategic position to grab everything. In a letter to Sir John Sloane, trying to sell some of the works thus gained, he merely stated, 'I became possessed of all the residue of his Works being Drawings Sketches & Copper Plates of a very extraordinary description'. He even tried to wrest some of the Dante drawings from Linnell. In a letter of 1 March 1833 he asked for 'some settlement concerning the Dante'. Later Palmer's son said that his father must have taken the letter to Linnell, who gave a verbal answer, refusing to see Tatham and asking him to put in writing whatever he wished to say. Tatham made an evasive reply, 'It is not my intention in any way to commit myself in writing.' He asked for the name of Linnell's solicitor so that the latter might confer with his own solicitor: 'But upon this consideration that as you have refused to see me you must pay the costs of such arrangement'.

This note also seems to have been delivered by hand. Linnell ignored it as he did further messages brought by Palmer. His son says that the final message asked for a statement by Linnell renouncing any claims on Tatham —in return for which Tatham would give a statement renouncing any claims on Linnell. Linnell remarked that Tatham had now 'let the cat out of the bag', being afraid that he 'might be called to account about expropriating all Mrs. Blake's effects, &c.' He stressed the point that Tatham had produced no evidence beyond his own word that Mrs Blake had left him her property.

Linnell, in his efforts to make Tatham disgorge the Blake remains, got in touch with Blake's sister. Gilchrist gives this account of her in her old age:

She had in her youth, it is said, some pretensions to beauty, and even in age retained the traces of it; her eyes, in particular, being noticeably fine. She was decidedly a *lady* in demeanour, though somewhat shy and proud; with precise old-maidish ways. To this may be added that she survived her brother many years, and sank latterly, it is to be feared, into extreme indigence; at which point we lose sight of her altogether.

Linnell and Catherine took legal advice, but seem to have been told that no effective steps could be taken against Tatham. The latter no doubt heard of their failure and soon afterwards seems to have held a sale of Blake's effects. Besides the drawings he had proofs of engravings, copies of the prophecies, and plates from which in 1831–2 he printed copies of *America*, *Europe*, *Jerusalem*, and *Songs*: one copy each of the first two, three of the third, sixteen of the fourth. He did not print works like *Visions* or *Marriage of Heaven and Hell* in which Blake's attack on accepted values was obvious.

His unforgivable crime, however, was his destruction of a great many of Blake's manuscripts. Anne Gilchrist speaks of his holocaust of the manuscripts, though not of the designs, 'as I have heard from his own lips'. She further tells us of the Dante drawings:

Mrs Blake—who appears to have always much disliked Linnell—said that a considerable sum was still due on them: which Tatham claimed in her behalf (and afterwards on his own); hence arose a quarrel; and Tatham and Linnell have never spoken since. Now my Husband, who had sifted the matter, and knew both parties, thought Linnell an upright truthful, if somewhat hard man, and that towards Blake his conduct had been throughout admirable.

He also inclined to think, that Mrs Blake retained one trait of an uneducated mind—an unreasonable suspiciousness. But Tatham would of course be disposed to give an entirely different account of the affair. You know I believe the reason he assigns for the destruction of the manuscripts? Tatham was at that time a zealous Irvingite, and says he was instigated to it by some very influential members of the Sect on the ground that Blake was inspired, but quite from a wrong quarter— by Satan himself—and was to be cast out as an 'unclean spirit'. Carlyle says he is quite certain Irving himself never had anything at all to do with this.*

Calvert had heard of Tatham's intentions. He went to him and begged that Blake's works should be spared: 'notwithstanding which', says his son, 'blocks, plates, drawings, MSS., I understand, were destroyed'. Whatever the exact details, it is certain that Tatham destroyed a great deal of Blake material, no doubt mainly the manuscripts out of which he could make no money. We have seen how Blake boasted to Crabb Robinson of the vast extent of his writings, and Cunningham stated that he 'left volumes of verse, amounting, it is said, to nearly an hundred, prepared for the press'. We have the *Four Zoas* because Blake luckily gave the manuscript to Linnell; we have the early prophecies, *Milton*, and *Jerusalem* because he etched them. Otherwise they too no doubt would have perished in Tatham's pious holocaust. What we have lost we can never know.[16]

---

* Edward Irving was ordained to the ministry of the Church of Scotland; in London he preached the near approach of Christ's Advent and after publishing *Homilies on the Sacraments* was thrown out of the church. He founded a new communion, the Catholic Apostolic Church, the members of which were called Irvingites.

The Moravians or United Brethren

Their ancestry went back to the Hussites of Bohemia in the fifteenth century, who were however largely crushed by the Thirty Years War. A group from Moravia was reconstituted in the earlier eighteenth century on the estate of the Lutheran Count Zinzendorf in Saxony, and took a new turn. They were ardent missionaries and in 1749 the English Parliament recognised them as 'an ancient Protestant episcopal church'. Hurd in 1811 says that besides the chapel in Nevil's court, Fetter Lane, they had another in Chelsea, as well as congregations in many parts of England. There were Antinomian touches in their creed.

Regeneration is brought about suddenly, all at once. One moment is sufficient to make us free to receive grace, to be transformed to the image of the little Lamb. A person regenerated enjoys great liberty. He does what the Saviour gives him an inclination to do, and what he has no inclination for, he is not obliged to do. He doth what the Saviour makes him do, for he is the master, in whose power it is to make laws and to repeal them; who at all times can change the economy of salvation; make criminal what was virtuous, and virtuous what was criminal. It is wrong to say that a regenerated person doth any thing; properly speaking they do nothing. It is the Saviour that acts for them. He is with respect to the Saviour as a little child . . .

If Blake had been brought up in a Moravian atmosphere (see chapter 1 of our text), he would have been particularly responsive to pastoral imagery of the Lamb and to Antinomian elements in general. Hurd tells us: 'The *Herrnhuters* [Moravians] have this distinguishing character of fanaticism, that they reject reason, reasoning and philosophy. The children of God do not instruct themselves out of books . . .' Their ideas about sex were an excellent basis for Blake's later ideas and images:

The circumcision of the Saviour has, according to them, served to shew of what sex he was. It has likewise restored to honor that part of the human body, which as a consequence of Adam's fall, was become a disgrace to it; insomuch, that it is at present the most noble, and the most respectable part of a man's body. The sisters are exhorted never to think of it, but with sentiments of the most profound veneration. They are even thought to make a scruple of respecting men for any other reason. The organ of generation of the other sex is no less honourable.—It has been sanctified by the birth of the Saviour. We abate of the strength of our author's expressions whilst we abridge him, for fear of offending the modesty of our readers.

The ideas about souls and about Jesus as the universal husband, the one true male, could well have stirred Blake's imagination in a number of ways:

All souls are of the feminine sex... All that is of the male quality, and was adapted to our body, is detached from it as soon as it is interred. It belongs not to its natural and primitive state: it is an addition made afterwards: it is the seal of the office, which the male sex is entrusted with. For, our sex is an employment, an office. Jesus is the spouse of all the sisters, and the husbands, in the most proper sense, are his procurators, his agents ... The sisters are conducted to Jesus by the ministry of their husbands, who are thus their saviours in this world.

John Wesley, who had close contacts with them in early years, tells us that they rejected the works of the law, and made everything depend on total belief.

Their first mission was to the Negroes on the Island of St Thomas, where for a while they were as a result persecuted and jailed by the white settlers. They continued to be deeply concerned about Negroes as well as other heathens such as the Eskimos.

The Continuity of Antinomianism

First, some more examples of the strength of Antinomian doctrine in the period of the English Revoltuion. 'Many radicals taught that God or Christ were in all the saints, and that perfection was possible in this life. We are as free from sin and therefore from the Law, as Adam was before the Fall. Lieutenant Jackson believed in 1650 that he was "as perfect now as ever he shall be".' He thought that 'there is no God but what is in himself and whole creation, and that he is alike in beasts as in men.' Grindletonians, Winstanley, Dell, Erbery, Crab, Ranters, Quakers, all thought that sin had been invented by the ruling class to keep the poor in order. Murder, adultery and theft were not sins, thought a London lady whom Edwards reported in 1646. All the hell there was was the darkness of the night. 'The Leveller Walwyn accepted the label Antinomian' (Christopher Hill). William Erbery was said to have declared that he was as much God as ever Jesus Christ was. Clarkson wrote:

> Behold the King of Glory now is come
> T'reduce God and Devil to their doom,
> For both of them are servants unto me . . .
> Thy worship and thy God shall die truly.

Wesley in the next century kept encountering Antinomians. In his *Letter to the Moravians* written in September 1738 he says that three errors run through their books: 'Universal Salvation, Antinomianism, and a kind of new-reformed Quietism'. And he goes on, 'How can Antinomianism, i.e. making void the law through faith, be more expressly taught than it is in these words:—To believe certainly, that Christ suffered death for us,—This is the true means to be saved at once.' And he cites two more texts which state that salvation is for everyone that believes. In 29 May 1745, 'I talked at large with Howel Harris, not yet carried away by the torrent of Antinomianism. But how long will he be able to stand?' On 22 March 1746, at

Wednesbury, 'The Antinomian teachers had laboured hard to destroy this poor people.' Next day, Sunday:

I talked an hour with the chief of them, Stephen Timmins. I was in doubt whether pride had not made him mad. An uncommon wildness and fierceness in his air, his words, and the whole manner of his behaviour, almost induced me to think God had for a season given him up into the hands of Satan.

In the evening, I preached at Birmingham. Here another of their pillars, J—W—d, came to me, and, looking over his shoulder, said, 'Don't think I want to be in your Society; but if you are free to speak to me, you may.' I will set down the conversation, dreadful as it was, in the very manner wherein it passed, that every serious person may see the true picture of Antinomianism full grown; and may know what these men mean by their favourite phrase of being 'Perfect in Christ, not in themselves.'

'Do you believe you have nothing to do with the law of God?'
'I have not; I am not under the law; I live by faith.'
'Have you, as living by faith, a right to everything in the world?'
'I have. All is mine, since Christ is mine.'
'May you then take any thing you will, any where, (suppose out of a shop,) without the consent or knowledge of the owner?'
'I may, if I want it; for it is mine; only I will not give offence.'
'Have you also a right to all the women in the world?'
'Yes, if they consent.'
'And is not that a sin?'
'Yes, to him that thinks it is a sin; but not to those whose hearts are free.'

The same thing that wretch, Roger Ball, affirmed in Dublin. Surely these are the first-born children of Satan!

On 24 March 1753 he talked to Sarah B. at Birmingham.

Sat. 24. She said, 'I am in heaven in the Spirit; but I can speak in the flesh. I am not that which appears, but that which disappears. I always pray, and yet I never pray: for what can I pray for? I have all.'

I asked, 'Do not you pray for sinners?'
She said, 'No. I know no sinners but one, and the Devil is the other.'
I asked, 'Did not Adam sin of old; and do not adulterers and murderers sin now?'
She replied, 'No; Adam never sinned; and no man sins now: it is only the Devil.'
'And will no man ever be damned?'
'No man ever will.'

'Nor the Devil?'

'I am not sure, but I believe not.'

'Do you receive the Sacrament?'

'No; I do not want it.'

'Is the word of God your rule?'

'Yes; the Word made flesh; but not the letter. I am in the Spirit.'

Sun. 25. Upon inquiry, I found these wild enthusiasts were six in all; four men and two women. They had first run into the height of Antinomianism, and then were given up to the spirit of pride and blasphemy.

We cannot doubt that Blake had encountered men and women talking like this in London. The welter of dissident ideas, expressed in religious idioms, among craftsmen, tradesmen and industrial workers was very considerable in the 1790s. Thus a circle of what were called ancient Deists met near Hoxton and included intellectual and moral rebels of all sects and persuasions. 'Human learning was declaimed against . . . and dreams, visions, and immediate revelations were recommended as substitutes!' They believed in the foretelling of events and conversed with the dead. When the French Revolution came they were converted into 'politicians and inquirers after news' (Reid). Antinomian elements carried on to merge millenarian ideas with Owenite socialism. Owen himself in his lectures prophesied that 'prosperity would be let loose'; and ideas of sexual freedom came up. Zion Ward, who claimed to be the messianic Shiloh whose birth through Joanna Southcott had been announced, told the young people in his chapels: 'If you love one another, go together at any time without law or ceremony'. He also had a plan for a Land Colony 'where those who are willing to leave the world can love together as one family'.

There were followers of John Hutchinson, who was anti-Newtonian, attacked the *Principia* in his works (1749–65), and asserted that the Old Testament held all the elements of philosophy and physics. Hurd considered them an organised group as well as being spread 'amongst almost all the denominations of Protestants'. Hutchinson argued that the scriptures had 'never been rightly translated'. Moses knew all about the planetary system, 'and whereas Sir Isaac Newton instituted the notion of there being a vacuum in nature, he [Hutchinson] opposed it by asserting there was a plenum. That all heavenly bodies went round the sun by a sort of compressure.' (In *Milton* Blake furiously attacks 'the Newtonian Voids between the Substances of Creation', 'the Chaotic Voids outside of the Stars . . . measured by the Stars'.)

10*

Those of the lower sort, who reside in London meet, like the Muggletonians. We have been present at one of these meetings, in a club-room up stairs, at a noted public house in the Strand. The members consisted, for the most part, of discarded Methodists, Independents, and Sandemanians... In their public assemblies, one of them reads, and another explains a passage of scripture as well as he can; then a third prays; and then when they have drunk a little porter they are dismissed.*

* C. Hill, *Irreligion in the 'Puritan' Revolution* (Queen Mary College, London, 1974) 12, 9, 20; L. Clarkson, *A Single Eye*, 1650, Sig. A, 1v; Edwards, *Gangraena*, 1646, i, 21, 106f, ii, 21, and ii, 8; Wesley's Journal under the dates given; Hurd.

Appendix 3

The Book of Revelation: Blake and Coleridge

We have noted the new attitude to the Bible inaugurated by Lowth, which was carried on by Herder and Eichhorn in Germany. Even if Blake had not read Lowth, he would have been affected by his views through others, e.g. the account in the *Monthly Review* of A. Geddes' *Proposals and Specimens*, 1798, and the first volume of his Bible, praising him for treating the Bible as he would any other ancient literature. Geddes' project had been announced in 1786 and supported by Lowth among others; the first volume of his translation appeared in 1792. A Roman Catholic priest, he was suspended because of his writings, his *Critical Remarks* anticipating much of the German higher criticism. Radical in views, he published a poem in praise of the French Revolution, *Linton: a Tweedside Pastoral, Carmen Seculare pro Gallica Gente*, 1790. Blake, with his keen ear and eye for what was going on in spheres that interested him, would certainly have known something of what Geddes was doing.

The historical Jesus was tending to fade out in the gallery of mythological figures; Volney in his influential *Ruins of Empire* treated him as a myth. Following a suggestion by Herder, J. G. Eichhorn, in his *Commentary on the Apocalypse of John*, 1791, interpreted *Revelation* as a dramatic poem in the style of the Hebrew Apocalyptics, which depicted the events of the fall of Jerusalem in 168–9 A.D. He provided a breakdown of the work into three Acts and various Scenes: (1) Jerusalem falls (2) Rome falls (3) the Heavenly Jerusalem descends from above. Coleridge, strongly affected, planned an epic, *The Fall of Jerusalem*, 'the only subject now left for an epic poem of the highest kind'. Blake, we saw, drew on *Revelation* for much of the structure and concept of his *French Revolution*, and he continued to draw on it for his prophetic books. He approached contemporary history via the Apocalypses and *Revelation*, in which he found the dialectical pattern of conflict and resolution that alone seemed to him to make sense of human aspirations.

But he drew also on the rest of the Bible and on Milton for imagery of death–rebirth, creation–fall, transformation. He would have known the passage in Milton's *Reason of Church Government* which reviews the poetic genres of the Bible: *Job* as model of the brief epic, the *Song of Solomon* as 'the divine pastoral drama', and John's Apocalypse as 'the majestick image of a high and stately Tragedy, shutting up and intermingling her solemn Scenes and Acts with a sevenfold Chorus of hallelujahs and harping symphonies'. There had been much interest in Biblical criticism in the 1780s and early 1790s; but as the political climate darkened, that criticism came under the ban of all things radical, and in 1798–9 a plan for translating Eichhorn fell down through lack of subscribers.

We see how many of Blake's basic ideas were part of a general stream if we consider Coleridge, who planned to write his universal religious epic on the fall of Jerusalem as Dante had written a Catholic epic and Milton a Protestant one. From one angle this is just what Blake did. Coleridge praised the attitude to property among the Hebrew tribes and declared political liberty was the expression of true monotheism, which was still progressing towards the total abolition of property. By 1800 he turned on the rationalist elements in his thought represented by Newton and the Newtonian Christian apologists. What he now wanted was revelation. He took up the work of Berkeley and Cudworth, and sought for a new concept of witness and the visionary character. Dealing with miracles, he insisted that they were concerned, not only with physical laws, but also with laws anthropological and sociological. What was miracle in one society was nature in another. Thus he subjectivised nature and saw all events as mental; history was concerned, not with events in the abstract but with human nature. All event was interpretation. The historical event described by witnesses represented spontaneous myth-making. (The poet Klopstock had made a distinction between prophecy and event; but the new critics broke this distinction down till all history became prophecy.) Thus for a while it seemed that Christianity was once more secure. The question of historical truth did not matter; what mattered was prophetic revelation that became human truth. Herder, studying the Old Testament, concluded that every system was at root a mythology, and so a modern mythology was possible.

Thus Coleridge looked for his new mythology, not in ancient polytheism, not in animated physics (though he was much interested in Erasmus Darwin's work and in Schelling's *Naturphilosophie*) but in ancient history viewed from the perspective that Christianity was a mythology fundamentally the same in kind as any other Oriental religion. The impulse to new mythologies was entangled in the synthesising trends we have noted. Southey had a project for an epic on Mohammed, and William Taylor suggested as a joke an epic to be called *The Storming of Seringapatam*, which would merge Indian, Christian and Mohammedan mythologies. That there was a wide audience interested in comparative religion is shown by such works as William Hurd's *A New Universal History of the Religious Rites, Ceremonies, and Customs of the Whole World*, 1811, with its 858 double-columned pages, though, to save his book from causing offence, he treats Christianity as the one pure form. What came out of Coleridge's efforts was *Kubla Khan*, an expression of immediate prophetic witness. Blake alone tried to bring together all the elements we have been discussing, at the same time transforming the concept of religion by treating it consistently in terms of the human struggle for wholeness in the here-and-now.

Notes

With the vast amount of work done on Blake these Notes could have been expanded almost indefinitely. I have done my best to keep them down to the smallest compass that seemed adequate. The existence of Bentley's *Blake Records*, which sets out its material in chronological order has enabled me to omit a large amount of references that would have been otherwise necessary. The reader who wishes to follow up biographical material can do so easily by turning to *Records*. I must repeat here my debt to Erdman for the historical correlations. Abbreviations used are: B. or WB. for Blake; H. for Hayley; E. for Erdman (standing by itself it refers to the 1969 edition of *Prophet against Empire*); K. by itself for Keynes (2) and KS for his *Blake Studies*; BR for *Records*; MW for Mona Wilson's *Life*; FZ for the Four Zoas; J. is used for *Jerusalem*; and M. for *Milton*. Further abbreviations are listed before the Bibliography.

I. EARLY YEARS

1. S. Gardner 18–28 Miner(5) B.'s city-symbols: K. R. Johnston. See account of the Square in Dickens' *Nicholas Nickleby*, 1859, probably as it was in 1825 with many musical connections. Hartley's son lived there in 1797; Varley, Mulready etc. James Blake was born 26 Aug. 1731.

2. See BR for family, houses etc., the father 283. No basis for Ellis-Yeats story of Irish origin. James voted for Earl Percy and Lord Clinton, 1774; in 1780, 1784 for Fox, wasting second vote. The house was destroyed in 1963.

3. Lowery 14f, 210; Wright i 2; N. Bogen in E. 142. A Blake and wife was in List of Moravian Fetter-lane Chapel 1743. Mother: Fox 202.

4. Honour 113; BR 13; O. Crawfurd. Cosway at Pars: E. 3. Copies from *Ars Pictoria*, 1675: Baker (3). B. may have known engravings copied from Raphael's designs for the Vatican Loggie published 1772–7: Beer (2) 31.

5. Horace Walpole says, 1754, he was afraid to venture alone into the Abbey on account of the boys.

6. Garments: Paley in CW 119–39; Fox 80. Smith says Stothard admired the drawing of Queen Phillippa.

7. Gothic: D. Bindman. Tatham (BR 512) for predating of B.'s ideas. K. 593, 603.

8. Salviati Gioseffo Porta 1535–85. B. probably read of Druids in Stuckeley's *Stonehenge*, 1740; note Druidic idea in Robert's drawings, 1782. Joseph Lowery 19. A sister of Pars used the theme of St Joseph's Chapel. Glastonbury, 1774, on dinner-service for Russian Empress. Ossianic feeling of Blake's Joseph: Bindman (3) 15.

9. Bindman (2) 30f.

10. Egg, see Harper 296. K(3) 27; K. Raine (1). Note depreciation of colour in the outline-enthusiasts: Kant said colour was superfluous; Schiller, 'I cannot get rid of the idea that these colours do not tell me the truth. . . The pure outline would give me a much more faithful image.' See Honour.

11. E. 6.

12. Cf. Prelude to *Book of Los* with Joy, Envy, Eyeless Covet, etc. E. 468, for Gibbon.

13. Dorfmann (2).

2 ARTIST AND POET

1. BR 16f.

2. Nude: KS pl. 1.

3. Blunt (2) 6f. A. Kauffmann did an Edward and Eleanour 1776. 45–7, 66f, Rapin etc. Basire: Nichols iii 717; E. 53–5.

4. BR 454f, E. Pt. One; Bronowski 36; Wright i 8. Persons caught up: Postgate 229, cf. W. P. Frith, *A Vict. Canvas* (1937 ed. N. Wallis) ch. 13. H. Butterfield, *George III, Lord North and the People*, 1949, 263; D. M. Clark, *British Opinion and the American Revolution* (New Haven) 1930; E. P. Thompson 71f.

5. E. 11f; Nurmi 21; MW 51f. Engravings in Boehme's *Works*, 1764, 1772, 1781: E. 11.

6. Reaction of tradesmen etc. to American War, E. 12–7; E. 16–9.

7. E. 10f; Blunt (2) 5, 34f and (3).

8. BR 19f, cf. Hogarth's Peregrination and arrest in Calais.

9. B. (Like Steelyard) was well read in grave-literature, K. 52. Wright i 7 with tale (no source) of reaction to eloquence of Augustus Toplady. Sermons in Harvey's *Theron and Aspasia* on Judgement Day, and B.'s watercolour of c. 1810: E. 113f.

10. Barry: E. 37–45, 443, K. 446, 595, Barry's *Works* i 336. Wilkes and Nat. Gallery, E, 44. Barry was prof. of painting at R. A. since 1782, expelled 1799, died 1806. One Man: E. 10.

11. Vicar, J. Gardner, amateur landscapist: BR 23.

12. Lowery 42f; Harper 41f.

13. BR 27; E. 93 (Jane M.); KS 33 for price.

14. Early poems: M. Phillips; Tolley (2), spring; J. Miles (1) and (2); Hirsch; Gluckner (2); Hartman; Wickstead; Bass. *Gwin* and Chatterton: E. 250. Debt to Percy: Lowery 160. Pegge, *Archaeologa* iii for Percy's stress on high political and moral role of Saxon minstrel. Seasons and Milton: Gluckner (1), Damon (1) 91–6. Caduceus in Bryant and Spenser: Phillips 6. Shakespeare: Beer (2) app. 1. Edward III: E. 56. Breach: E. 75. Plague: E. 63. Many critics see subtleties of irony etc. where I see only a young poet struggling with diction and imagery hard to control. Note early drawings of Keys of Calais: E. 74.

15. Mad Songs: see J. L. (6). *Couch of Death*: E. 77–9. Thomson: Lowery 141–55. The Apology does not refer to lack of correction of proofs.

16. Lowery, 201; Bloom (1) 10, suggests *Samson* done about 1780; 63f, relation already to Milton? Hardly, I think. Phillips 13.

3. A LULL

1. Printshop: E. (9). *An Island*: M. W. England; Gardner; E. 92ff. Priestley: E. 107–9. Flaxman: Bentley (11), E. 110f. Cosway: Gardner 64, E. 96, 103. Huffcap: Whitfield. Etruscan Column: ? T. Astle, E. 31, or Brand, Harper 40, Damon, *Dict.* Foote: J. 52. Dr Clash: based perhaps on Foote's Dr. Catgut (*Commissary* 1765, revived 1782). Stinks: the jokes went on, cf Gillray's 'Scientific Researches! New Discoveries in Pneumaticks!—or—an Experimental Lecture on the Powers of Aair', 23 May 1802 (clouds of farts). Inflammable Gas may be W. Nicholson: BNX 51–2. Hollis and Milton: E. 34f. Sharp and animal elements in human face: W. S. Baker 25. Barry: Wright i15 and England 19. Mrs Barbauld: E. 123f. Darwin and *Botanic Garden*: Worrall.

2. England 23. The picture of the children goes back to Addison in *Spectator*. See Fauvet further, and Connolly. Gluckner (5); Gardner (2) 28. For Gass as W. Nicholson, see R. and M. Baine. Aradobo is one of the Edwards, E. (1b) 507.

3. KS 3; MW 23; L. Binyon; Todd; Symonds 363f, 391.

4. Catherine: Bogen (2) Catherine's forthrightness suggests Mrs Nannicantipot.

5. Robert: Gilchrist. Swinburne has tale (no source) of B. thrashing a man for maltreating a woman on or near St. Giles—he himself all the while outpouring 'a Tartarean overflow of execration. KS chs. i and xxiii; Wickstead (2). Taylor: J. King, also tale of Cumberland. B. was working with Stothard by 1779.

6. Harper, K. Raine, Perceval etc. Cupid and Psyche: Chayes, Raine (1) ch. 7 Smith says B. after this never attended any kind of church.

7. Sabri-Tabrizi 94–6, 14–24. Davies ch. ii. E. III, 138–46, 176 and (2). B. probably knew also Gibbon's attack on Warburton. Boehme: Nurmi, 28; Sabri-T. 89. Tulk: BR 38; MW 257. For Moravians; App. 2. Warburton: J: (5) 70.

8. Knowles 47, 54, 41ff, 301–4; dreams 325; against limits, 330; exalts nature,

311, 338. Mason: 356–8. Foul language: Richmond. Gilchrist says Fuseli and Flaxman declared time would come when Blake's first designs would be sought after as much as Michaelangelo's were.

9. Antal 85f. Fuseli admired Cowper above even Hayley or Darwin: Farington 28 May 1803.

10. BR 33; Blunt 58–63; Todd 397. Tatham, wrongly, says he used oils.

11. Ault 77f Hostility to New Church: G. Trowbridge, *Moving Light*, xxvi 1903 119; BR 35f; Fox 192. Nebuchadnezzar: E. 193; Hagstrum 66f.

12. Reason: Fisher ch. iv; Spragens 215, III; Burt, *Metaphysical Foundations of Modern Science*. Kepler, letter 9 April 1597; Locke, *Essay* II, viii 9f; Asa Briggs, *Age of Improvement* 1960; P. Brown, *The Chathamites* 1967, 75–88, 422 etc. B. took from Swedenborg the term States to define varying levels of development.

13. E. P. Thompson 69, 418; BR 553f. For Parker's print of Northcote's picture of 1688: E. (1b) 530. Smith, Robert's playfellow, says he was beloved as a boy by all his companions.

4. BREAKTHROUGH

1. Horne Tooke is on list of friends compiled by Linnell for Gilchrist: KS 244. Holcroft: MW 64. Note in 1791 Priestley addressed a series of letters to Swedenborgians, attacking their tenets. Frend: E. 158. Joel Barlow was there with Paine in early 1790s.

2. BR 40f. Erdman communication on cockades.

3. Wagenknecht; Hirst 23f. E. 243–7, 252; Witcutt, 120.

4. Ostriker. Hymns: Wesley (2) nos. 429, 104, 368; Wesley (1) iii 242; *Christian's Mag.* Oct. 1782; *Evangelical Mag.* Dec. 1794; Wesley (1) iv 306. Knox, 80, for Spence; such hopes carried on to Chartist days.

5. Hindmarsh 44; Thompson 52; Hurd 794 etc. He has also a section on Mystics, Hutchinsonian theories of fire and fluids had much effect from 1750s on the sciences of heat and electricity, and the roots of Dalton's theory have been found in H. chemistry.

6. Garett 150f; Reid 18f, 91f. Ward: Thompson 282f.

7. Morton (1) 43f, 51, 48f.

8. N. Bogen ed. *Thel*; E. (14) 33–41; Mellor; Heppner; Raine (1) ch. 4–5; Frosch 134, 50; E. (17). Not finished till 1791: E. (5) 713. Multiple perspective: Fox 8. Relation to Young's *Night Thoughts*: Tolley (5), note Young is mentioned in *Island*.

9. *Tiriel*. Note cut lines 362–74, related to George III: E. 135–8; Bogen (3). Essick (1); Raine (1) ch. 2 and (5); Beer (2) app. 2; Damon (1) 306; Gleckner (4). Snake: Hagstrum 89n. Ijim: Frye (1) 242. Written in 1790: E. 131–8. Hall; Bogen

(2). Names: Beer (2) 367. For Vale of Har and Vauxhall Gardens: Gardner 81. It is extremely unlikely as Bindman (3) argues that *Tiriel* was written in the mid-1780s, but it certainly is transitional between the prose-poems and direct Ossianic influence, and the Prophecies proper. Rose and Lily: note the ref. to the Rose and Lily Queen (Henrietta Maria) on tomb of Tradescants in church of St Mary's near Lambeth Palace: it could easily have been seen by Blake. Temple of Flora at Lambeth: E. (1b) 530, also P. Miner.

    10. Tiriel's kingdom: Essick; Mellor 19, 31 (serpents on Hela's brow).

5. MARRIAGE OF HEAVEN AND HELL

    1. Johnson and Paine: E. 112. Date: E. 152, also Bindman (3). For Johnson: Chard. Beer (1) ch. 5. For 1788 as new start: E. 117; K 781.

    2. Stars: Mellor 64f; E. 194; Paley (4) 99; Pachter 107. Clouds: Damon, *Dict.*; Halloran; Halliburton.

    3. KS 68f; Knowles i 172. B. did more drawings for M. W. than required. Good review in *Analytical Rev.* Jan. 1791: BR 38.

    4. Marriage: Devil's Party: Wittreich (1) 2 14 and (4); BR 317 Energy: Paley, ch. i; Taylor; Harper; Pierce; Raine (2) and (1); Damon (1) 37, 167 etc. Criticisms of Swedenborg: Sabri-T. 20f; Paley 7 for use and contradiction of phrase of Taylor's. Nurmi (6), Wagenknecht 199, 229; Raine (1) ch. 6; E. (20). Date, E. 152; *Argument*, E. 189.

    5. Schiller thinks in terms of Energy, working with such ideas as Transfer of Intensity: *Ueber die aesthet. Erzehuing des Menschen*, 1795. See Jung, *Contribs. to Analyt. Psych.* 1928 for him as forerunner of libido-theory. *Literary J.*, 1806, 446; sales, Baker, *Novel of Sentiment*, 1934, 173f. Note proneness of Shelley and Claire Clairmont to spectral visions; also de Quincy.

    6. *Evang. Mag.* 1794 393 and 114 (March). Wesley Coll. no 104.

    7. Seems sure B. did plates after Chodowiecki for version of Salzmaron's *Elements of morality* (for children).

    8. BR 46, 50–3; E (1b) 509. Tale of Wolcot scared by Opie and O. Humphry, E. 155, in 1795. Fuseli and Mary W.: Knowles and R. M. Wardle. B. seems to have explained some of his hidden meanings to Cumberland. Sharp: E. 35f, 154, 159f; BR 530. Note ref. to *Prologue for Edward the Fourth* in second version of *Our End is Come*, still 1793.

    9. Lambeth Assn.: *Trial of Thomas Hardy* ii 311f (1795) Taken in Short-Hand by Joseph Gurney. Franklin was member of London Corr. Society. See Trial ii 32ff for interrogation of Johnson about Barlow; Garrod 13. Work 1793: Stockdale, Gay's *Fables*; Bellamy's *Picturesque Mag.* i August; name in prospectus of Barlow's *Aesop*, no engraving with his name. Fuseli used his painting for his Milton Gallery

(in preparation at least since 1790). In Italy Flaxman made 3 sketches from memory of B.'s drawings.

10. *Tyger*: Mellor 12; H. Adams 65; Kaplan; Nurmi 37–9; E. 189 (date); Paley in Weathers 97–100. Various other essays in Weathers. Lord Abingdon: E. 238 *London*: E. ch. 13. Hirsch 265 sees as Urizen: typical effort to predate B.'s later symbols.

11. Hessians: *Trial of Hardy* i 120f, 180, 187; ii 301, 308f, 384. Germans were used in the American War; New Prussian exercises used in review, March 1792: E. 215.

12. Fayette: Kettle (2); E. 182–8; Mellor 41; Paley 261. E. 305 on brief appearance of Urthona, apparently already the productive worker (here a smith in his den); later he is B. himself toiling at his craft. Date of Argument: E. 189.

13. Gardner (2) ch. 3. E. ch. 10–11 for ref. to abolition debates; Vale of Leutha and Isle of Dogs, E. 237 Vien's painting: E. 241. Further on *Visions*: Wasser; Schorer 290. Ossian: Torman; Raine (1) i 398. Did he begin *Visions* 1791? May well have revised more than once.

14. Damon takes *Crystal Cabinet* to tell of love-affair in Lambeth, and relates it to *J.* 41: 15 and 65: 42; also *M.* 42: 33 and 13: 41. The harmony of Catherine and mistress could not last: see *J.* 19: 40 and 20: 1. Perhaps, but there is no proof of it.

15. BR 101f, 251; MW 75; Morton (1) 52; BR 238. Morton importantly shows the continuity of Ranter or Antinomian terms and ideas in Blake.

16. Note that Ossianic persons were seen as Spectres. Blair writes: 'The spectres of Ossian, which Dr. Drake said, seem to "rush upon the eye with all the stupendous vigour of wild and momentary creation," have their ghostly progeny on the thousand phantoms of a thousand castles. Thus he links Ossian and Gothic Novel: see Montagu Summers, *The Gothic Quest*, 47; Drake, *Lit Hours*, 1798, no. 6, on Gothic Superstition, links Ossianic and Gothic forms: 'Next to the Gothic in point of sublimity and imagination comes the Celtic . . .' Barham in *Ingoldsby Legends* links Ossian, Gothic, and the Evening Hour. Further: Douglas 15; Paley (1) ch. 8.

In general: Weiskel and review TLS 24 Dec. 1976 by Haughton. Bible etc.: Roston, 144f, 67, 86, 171; Frye, 108f; see Wordsworth, *Lyrical Ballads*, preface 1815, linking Bible, Milton, Spenser, as opposed to the classics. In Blake's *Visions* the first full expository vortex type of structure.

6. POLITICAL PROPHECY

1. America: E. 154 etc.; his use of Barlow with his 'Demon red' and so on, 250f. Gleckner; Raine (4); Fox, ch. i; Ostriker; J. Miles (2). Atlantis, from Plato or

Boehme: Raine (1) 423f; E. 33; Wicksteed (3) 48. Barry: E. 41. T. Day's *Ode for the New Year* 1776 and his name on gravestone, FZ IX, p. 4: E. 28.

Orc's name: Orc, whale, Orcus, *orca* as monster (Hoole's *Orlando Furioso*, 1783, for which B. made engraving. Not *cor*, heart, but *orcheis*, genitals. Orc as seed: E. 269.

2. Plate of Orc spreadeagled is suggested by Negro in Stedman plate, which B. seems to have engraved but felt unable to sign. Nature-Myth in preludes of *America* and *Europe*: E. 264. Erdman suggests the date of the passage about the shattered harp was 28 Jan. 1793 when Parliament voted for war with France (1b, 514).

3. Garrett 168–73; Altick 38; K. Thomas 128–45, 389–415. Quatrain: Bentley (3).

4. Gardner ch. 5; Mellor 15; Tolley (2)—Young: 'This particle of Energy divine.' Bottrall.

5. E. (4) for series of emblem sketches used for these. For Hunter as publisher: BR 213. Gillray: E. 202–5 ans (8). B. seems to have followed Gillray's work closely. *Gates*: Frye (5); Digby 5–53; Raine (1) ch. 9.

6. E. 201ff; ch. 9. Fulton may have known B., E. 210. Druidism already appearing in *Europe*, grew an ever more important matter for B. as the bloody war-ethic that broke the primeval Gospel of brotherhood. B. was affected by Norse Twilight of the Gods: Mallet i 104.

7. *Our End is Come*: K (7) pl. 10; E. 206–9. Close to political caricature: one copy was used as frontispiece to *MHH* and *Song of Liberty*. Newton with the Trump: E. 225, Frye 254. Irony as to Newton as a sort of god, 'Let Newton be!' The accumulation of error and evil leads to the point of breakdown-renewal. A joke aimed at Newton on *Revelation*.

8. Saurat; Hirst; James; Ansari; Fisch (1) 428. See *J.*, address to Jews. Zohar link with Gnostic views: Scholen 236–8. South: *Twelve Sermons* 1698; Bouchez and Roux, *Hist parl de la rév. fr.* 1834–8 xxxi 276.

9. Male emanation, Fox 217; three classes of men, not of women, 40. Altizer 48–56, 95–102; Wilkie 359–72: ironic treatment of epic view of women. Ololon: Fox, 219f; Mitchell (2) 305. Jesus and emanation: Fox 218. Phallic Woman: Hagstrum (5). Sandler 21 on Ololon in Eden as the 'spermatic stream of the Hermeticists'. Threefold: Fisher 12–16; Fox 124. Female Will: Damon, *Dict*. Britannia: *J.* 94: 26.

10. Urizen: Sutherland. Dialectics: opposites without resolution, see J. 10: 7–16 and 17: 33–9. Triads: three classes of men, heavens of Beulah, localities of Los's city, cosmogonies (J. 83). Cf. three gunas of *Bhagavat Gita* (Wilkins 1785 108). Abrams (1) 260 His only equilibrium in B.'s resolution.

Beulah: Perceval 52–9; Frye 227–35; Bloom (2) 16–29; Fox 202–4, 128–44; Fisch (3) 275; *Milton* 30–1. Changes according to altitude: *J.* 83: 43–5. Relation to Ulro: Fox 209; Perceval 71; Bloom (2) 22. Emanation of Eden: E. 202f. Duality: M. 27: 8–9.

Mitchell (2) 285 takes Eternals in M. as audience defining relation of audience and poem, now and then becoming Jesus to express their potential. Frosch 177: 'Eternal life consists in a particular rhythm of energy and repose.' See *J*. iii 54: 1–5. Eden: E. 309; Fox 195, 204. Los's earth: *FZ* i 11–13.

11. Bowlahoola: Fox 106–14. Body is built there and in A. by sons of Los: *M*. 26: 31–3. Damon (1) 420: digestive and nervous systems. Frye 260: stomach and heart. E. 432 bowels and alimentary canal of civilisation. Sandals: Fox 96–8, 91. Creation: Fox 5.

For Eden or Eternity, cf. Paracelsus, *Op. omnia* ii 573, Geneva 1658: 'There is also, according to nature, that thoughts make a new Heaven, a new Firmament, new energy, from which new arts flow (*promanent*) ... When anyone is engaged in creating something, he makes for himself a new heaven from which the work which he had undertaken progresses (*procedit*)': Fisher 7. The acceptance of Eternity as an idealist concept is exemplified by Nathan.

12. Spragens 214, 219.

13. Fairies: Adlard 55, 98, 100 (fallen angels), 101; *J*. 36: 35–8 and *M*. 31. Morris: E. 221. Albion was common term for England at this time but B. may have had in mind Milton, *Hist. of Britain* I ch. i: Fisher 221. *Materia prima*: Nanavutlty (3).

14. Ancient of Days: BR index; *P. L.* vii 224–8; *Proverbs* viii 27. Vision: cf. exaggerated tale BR 498, 54. Blake's picture of murderer among the stones is linked with Gillray's cartoon, 30 Dec. 1792, dealing with the Commons scene when Burke produced a dagger.

15. Blunt 62f. Butts: Bentley (9). Ozias H.; see B.'s letter June 1818.

16. Garrett ch. 8; R. Matthews ch. 3; A. Gordon; Balleine 27–36 Anecdote of Johnson and Erskine: Knowles i 203.

17. *Urizen* seems later in script than the *Song*. For *Song of Los*, E. ch. 14.

18. Fuzon: E. 314–16; *Ahania* 84. In *B. L.* ii 6, Los's fall and change to oblique is ref. to Epicurean swerve of atoms (Lucretius ii 292) that starts creation, assuring development through asymmetry: Frye, 257.

19. Kreiter; J. Oppenheimer. B. was also affected by E. Darwin. Hunter, *Essays and Observations*, ed. R. Owen, 1861. See Frye 257; not from *Timaios* as Harper thinks, 214. Hunter: Bentley (13) and (14) Seven days: Frye 258; Perceval 243; Gardner 87f. Worm: Gardner 93f. Series of drawings, *Vala MS* p. 26, illustrate account by Luvah of evolutionary stages of nature in relation to man. Structure: Gardner 83. Note Orc is also born of the forge; and B.'s unusual terms of lacteals.

20. Ault 183–6, also 99, 107f, and void, 5. Title-page of *Urizen*: Eaves. Note fusion of cross and tomb in Urizenic terms. Also Mitchell (3) *Visionary Forms Dramatic* 99, 194f; Pevsner (1) 117ff; Rosenblum (2) 154–9, 189–91. Warner (2) on figures of despair.

21. J. L. (4) for relation of mechanistic science and war. *FZ* viii 100, 102 and *M.* 10. Albion Mill: Blackstone 19; E. 396–9; Miner (2) 290.

7. NIGHT THOUGHTS

1. Godwin: BR suggests a date round 1804–5.

2. E. 297f; BR 50 n1. Young Hayley: Bishop 196f.

3. Blunt 58–83; Butlin (4); Binyon. Grotesque: Douglas. Worried at times: Wittreich (6) 41.

4. *Hecate* and Fuseli's *Silence*: see Douglas 12.

5. E. 297; BR 51; Schorer 413–25 for Blake's art as 'abstractions in a scheme designed to overthrow abstraction'. Blunt in general for Blake's art as based on borrowed elements.

6. E. 286–9 and (10); J. 59 (also Rahab and Tirzah as exploiters: M. 25). Hayley visited the asylum in 1793 and composed a hymn on the spot. Davies 33; Hayley (1) i 444f. Gardner 121f, 126 for propriety chapel built on green where children used to play (1793), cf. B.'s *Garden of Love*. Lambeth grave-robbers: E. 288.

7. Hoppner went on to ridicule Flaxman, whom Stothard defended. Testimonial: B.'s name follows Basire, Sharp, W. S. Blake (writing engraver). B. did frontispiece to Euler, *Elements of Algebra*, Johnson, 1797.

8. Young: J. L. (2). The *surréalistes* picked out Young as *the* English poet. Ouroboros: de Groot. Godwin: E. 157f. Gray: Grierson; Tayler; E. 348. For Edwards. E. (16) 506–8.

9. Blackmore, *Psalms* 1721 181, 263; *Job* 108.

10. Margoliouth; Bentley (4); E. (17) 112 and (1a) 295, 341; Raine (1) ch. 12–13; Stevenson (2); Beer (2) app. 3 and ch. 6; McNeil. Swedenborg: *True Christian Religion* ix no. 331. Hermaphrodite is twofold, self-dividing: *M.* 19: 32–4, cf. the Herm. shadow: 14: 37, cf. 9: 21–9 and 18: 19–25.

11. K. 607. Arthur: Bentley (4) 120.

12. J. P. Dumont, *Under the Rainbow* (Univ. Texas) 1976; P. Rivière, TLS 6 Aug. 1976, 992. In general J. L., *Short History of Culture*.

13. B.'s compass-points are not rigid: Fox 205–7. For scientific analysis of his systems: Ault. Blake seems to have read Newton's *Opticks* (double vision): Raine (1) i 420f. See also n. 7 ch. 9 here.

14. Busst for refs.

15. Late additions are esp. intrusive, e.g. use of Welsh place-names with Hebrew personal names: Night I. Or account of Rahab, VIII.

16. Hagstrum (2) 146 sees Jesus in frontispiece of *Songs of Experience*, but child has wings. cf. winged child in *The Gates* as regenerated man: Lister, 45. There is merely a glancing fancy.

17. Thompson, 195, 190, 192–4. Wright i 89. On Orc, Wagenknecht 295f is typical of idea that B. has worked-out systems.

18. Coppe, *Fiery Flying Roll* 1650, Pref. 2–3. Besides Morton, see Ranter texts at end of N. Cohn, *Pursuit of the Millenium*.

19. Tharmas: E. 298–301 for text; Daion, *Dict*; Raine (1) ch. 12–13; Frosch, see index. See Hayley's preface to his *Milton* (dated 29 Oct. 1795; second ed. 1976) on whether it was right to publish Milton's prose: Gibbon and Warburton thought it wrong. First ed. 1794 was watered down as publisher thought it too democratic: Hayley (1) i 450f.

20. Fisher (1) 7 on B. and Hegel; but his point brings out the closeness of B. and Marx. Altizer 207, 215.

21. J. L. (7). Dragon woman: Perceval 197–215; Nanavutty (3).

22. E. index under mills and wheels. Darwin on lava: E. 334, 30, 34, (1b) 511. Brass is of West, but Urizen takes it over (e.g. brass book and quadrant). Victims of industrialism: *FZ* VIIb 182, *J.* 65 : 24. Brass and iron together represent Brotherhood and Imagination fused and working harmoniously See *Levit.* xxvi 19.

23. Blunt 64–7, 76. Fears at this time: Southey in 1796, 'I have been in the crowd and have had my corns trod upon, and therefore I chose to take a snug bye path for the future': G. Carnall, *R. Southey and his Age*, 1960.

8. PASTORAL RETREAT

1. BR 62; Bronowski 75f; Bishop. Change in politics after 1798: E. ch. 14.

2. Gray: Tayler (Cat). Edda: E. 262, Schorer 405. Nat. Gallery: E. 364. Export of prints: E. 365. Hayley's Library: BR 69. Hayley attacks war: First Epistle, *Essays on Sculpture* 1800. Temper: BR 526.

3. Hawkins bought Bignor Park in 1806. Butts: PMLA lxxi 1956, 1052–66.

4. Riotous week: E. 345.

5. Bognor started some nine years before as watering-place; Hayley had sold his Eartham house to politician Huskisson.

6. Butts' poem starts with a Dryden line. Oct. 1800 B. refers to work 'the three Marys'. Note he addresses Butts 'Friend of Religion and Order'—though Order in this sense he hated. Little Tom: KS ch. 12. Extract of letter to Flaxman: K807. *Job*: 177f. Klopstock poem: probably stirred by H. showing him *The German Museum*, Aug. 1800 with comparison of English and German versions of Homer. B. may also have known the 350 odd lines of his Messiah translated in *Analytical Rev.* June 1791, ? by Fuseli. Nelson: E. 337.

7. H. to J. C. Walker on 23 July on B. at work: for this and other such letters see BR in chronological place. 6 Aug, H. to J. J. on Abbot portrait of Cowper for B. Secretary: BR 79 nl.

8. Letters 13 Aug., 3 and 5 Sept., BR 20–22.

9. E. ch. 19. Patience: cf. letter to Lady H. Jan. 1802, BR 82n. 'The unwearied engraver by your side', J. J. on 13 Oct.

10. Pitt's prescription: E. 367–9; belief in settled peace, 366; George III in *FZ*, E. ch. 20; Orc as Napoleonic serpent, E. 375. Thelwall's Ode on Peace in *Trident of Albion* (Liverpool, 1805). Note B.'s overvaluation of the King's interest in art.

11. H. on 18 Oct. to J. J. to come and see B.'s engravings; 21 Oct. J. J. sends 'kind remembrances to the Blake & his agreeable partner.' 1 Nov., H. to Lady H. for loan of Lawrence portrait for B., who is confident of 'a more satisfactory Engraving.' 2 Nov., J. J. on 'your patient and peaceful fellow Labourer.' 14 Nov., B. at work and H. to Lady H. who has acquiesced in 'the laudable wishes of the worthy artist.' More on 22 Nov.: 'our excellent Blake... He is in Truth an excellent Creature with admirable Talent.' 7 Dec., more on B. after arrival of portrait. William really died 27 Oct.

11. Fairy funeral probably at Felpham: MW 159. H. gave B. a copy of Rev. A. Hay's *History of Chichester*.

12. Holcroft, 246; E. 342.

13. E. ch. 21; Sloss and W. i 255n. Cf. *M.* 27: 8 and Swedenborg's idea that earthly wars represented in heaven the states of the church. E. links Golgonooza with Golconda (golden opportunity for artist) and Golgotha (for rebel). In idea of reversal, a heavy debt to the Eddas. Frye notes now B. founders as he nears apocalypse. Spectre: E. 374 and Mortimer's *Sir Artegall and the Iron Man* (exhibited 1778).

14. In 1809 (K 587) B. says he never passed a day without 'Labours on Copper' for forty years.

9. FELPHAM CRISIS

1. Blunt 69–71, with relation to earlier works.

2. Butts has suggested exhibiting two pictures. B. says, 'I will finish the other, & then we shall judge of the matter with certainty'. He puts the matter off. Hayley: praises B. in letter 23 March.

3. Letters 24–5 March to Flaxman, J. C. Walker on B. zealous at his side. On 23rd, J. J. on 'the admirable Blake.' cf. letter 2, 31 March. Again 10 April, J. J. and Carr on Blake. 26–7 March: Klopstock's death. H., learning German, translated for B. opening of third canto, *Messiah*. in which K. speaks of own death.

4. 20 May J. J. on B. See BR 96ff for Ballads.

5. Letter of J. J., BR 103f.

6. See BR for letters of J. J., Greatheed, Carr, Flaxman (about to go to Paris), Marsh mentioning B., July to November. Ballads handled in London by Evans of Pall Mall.

7. In poem (22 Nov.) he speaks of poem read by Hayley 'When my heart knock'd against the root of my tongue'. It may be the 200 lines of blank verse, 'Genesis, The Seven Days of the Created World', written out in B.'s hand. For single and double vision, see Gage, 374, citing Priestley. Gage also, 375–6, on Rainbow, and Hayley's *Life of Romney*, 1809, on Romney, Newton and Prism.

8. Lady. H. replies 23 Dec., BR 112, followed by letters from her and Carr in Jan. 1803: B; 'philosophical & ingenious'. Note letter to James refers to a previous letter (lost).

9. Ballad accounts: BR 116. April: J. J.'s letter; Greatheed at Felpham, perhaps settling accounts.

10. Cumberland and ten good rules: BR 118. Flaxman perturbed: BR 120. 'The Visions were angry with me at Felpham,' Gilchrist (1942) 161. Ladies disappointed: Lady H., BR 121.

11. Again the offer of exhibition: K. 826. I break B.'s statement into paragraphs.

12. I. A. Williams, *English Folksong and Dance*, 1935, 100.

13. Bronowski, 78f; E. 606, 411 on *J*. 7.

14. Scolfield remained a private till he died at Canterbury, 31 Jan. 1812 Note B. in *J*. 17 writes: 'Go thou to Skofield: ask him if he is at Bath, or if he is in Canterbury'. Scolfield had served in the Peninsular War, Sept. 1809 till Nov. 1811. Cumberland: BR 562. In Sept., J. J. on B.'s 'uncomfortable scrape', BR 131.

10. RETURN TO LONDON

1. Bronowski, 74; BR 122–46; Jenkins (1) and (2); KS ch. 14; Schorer, 354.

2. Letter 7 Oct. much on his Devil, 'good natur'rd'. Work: BR 136.

3. Work for Hoare, BR 179. Letters in Jan., Saunders and J. J. (Saunders a dealer with whom B. discussed the location of Romney works).

4. Poyntz: BR 100. More details BR 147, letters. B. hidden in verses: E. 410. Rose, 5 May 1804, to father-in-law: 'I was highly complimented by the Duke of Richmond for my Defence. of Blake. Bowen, prosecuting attorney? Jan. 1804, K. 835, B. praises picture by Tom Hayley.

5. Samuel Greatheed had been friend of Cowper: BR index. Feb. Letters: Lady H., Carr (on H.'s benevolent enthusiasm in the cause of oppressed innocence), J. J. on Rose; Letter 16 March: D. Braithwaite, who had been patron of Romney, called. BR 149f.

6. Greatheed on B.'s work: BR 151.

7. E. 418 on Fuzon and Robespierre; K. 357; M. 40; *FZ* VIII III: 1–5. Note 1809 painting, *The Whore of Babylon*. Cowper as B.'s spectre: Fisher 136f; Paley (4).

8. Flaxman may have tackled B. on the Stilettos, for he says it was only a poetic *jeu d'esprit*. Fear: E. 412. Lady H. delighted at Caroline Watson being used; BR 156.

9. Project of book for benefit of Rose's widow: MW 194. Dec., Hawkins out of town, Edwards too. Truchsessian Gallery: Commentators have been baffled by B.'s outburst. Sutherland, 245, links 1784 with death of B.'s father. Harper, 34f, sees if as the turn away from Greek art etc. at this moment and turn to Forgiveness. Blackstone, 120f, thinks in 1784 B. felt the full burden of marriage shackling him. Erdman sees the relation to the printshop.

10. Adlard for folk-roots. E. 468, 416–18 for Gibbon and Washington; Voltaire, 414. Democritus: B. did three engravings for Lavater's *Physiognomy* 1781, one of D. after Rubens. Self-castigation in treatment of Voltaire, etc., E. 422.

11. See J. 34 and 30. Kettle (1); Sutherland (2). The wilds are the dead world of money and mechanistic science.

12. Schaffer; Wittreicher (2).

13. Allegory (with Sublime) only once used approvingly by B. Hayley speaks of Spenser with 'allegory dresst with mystic art,' *Essay Epic* iii 393f. Fuseli sees epic as Sublime Allegory and Allegory as amalgamating the 'mythical and superhuman': Wittreich (5). England as chosen land in Areopagitica. Milton: Bloom (2), Saurat (1), Fisch (1), Damon (2) ch. 25. Damon sees affinity with T. Vaughan; Ololon rather as occult side of 17th c. Hebraism. Fisch 40. *Milton*: Fox (1) 223–38, 337, and (2); Bloom (1) 378; Fisch (1) and (2); Wagenknecht 215f, 239; Wittreich (1) 180. Robert Fox 226. Orc: Paley, 249–51; Fox 81. Vortex: Rose 71f; Frye 350; Bloom (1) 358f; Frosch 69–76; Ault, Index Vortex; Nurmi in Rosenfeld 303–19: Vortex as sole objective reality outside Eden, all that is real at mechanistic level, not the fourfold.

For Blake's symbolism of left and right, especially in connection with hands and feet, see Wickstead (2) and Damon *Dict*. Right is good, left bad. Thus when Job shares his last loaf with a beggar, the fact that he uses his left hand shows that he acts according to the Law, not out of love.

14. H. had his dark moments: in 1814 wrote to Mrs Flaxman that base slander is at work 'To wound him with a treacherous Dirk,' Bishop 329. Note Satan and Palambron are both sons of Los; *FZ* VIII 245–7, 356–63.

15. Politics: E. 423–6. Stevenson (1) 566–76 for omission.

16. Cosmology: Ault; Damon *Dict*.; Fox 205 etc. Symmetries in *Urizen*: Sutherland. Thyme: Fox 134–8; Frye 349; P. A. Taylor 56. Moment: Fox 151f. Bard's song, Fox 59f. Concept of States; E. 401. Lark and Nightingale in *Night Thoughts*, end of BK. 1; *L'allegro* and *Il Penseroso*.

17. E. (14) 233; Fox 227. Note pl. 7, females at top contrasted with males below.

In the conflicts there are doubtless quarrels between William and Cath. over her relations with Hayley.

Hermaphroditic shadow of Milton: Fox 67f; Frye 125; Bloom (1) 282f; Perceval 280; Damon (2) 412. Milton's prose: Frye, 159f; Blackmore, 139; E. 428; Crabb Robinson in 1825.

18. *Revelation*: Schaffer 26f, 57f, 316: romantic symbolism, 185. Sandler; Fox 185–7; A. Farrer; Mitchell (3) 287. See Appendix 3 and Farrer, ch. 9.

11. PUBLIC ADDRESS

1. Letters, Hayley and Phillips: BR 157–61, Feb. to March. 25 April Phillips writes that the paper has gone to Seagrave, hopes for 'a metropolitan & fashionable Air' in proofs.

2. Ballads: letters etc. BR 163f. Mr Thomas and purchases: BR 166. Gray a recent gift? *ibid.*: BR 166, 187. Flaxman paid about 1s. 10d. per drawing. Another *Comus* set bought by Butts: MW 367. F. made a design not used of Widow embracing the turf on husband's grave. In 1804 he recommended Cromek for the Romney Shipwreck, apparently not knowing it was given to B. (Cromek, 1804–5, lived nearly opposite F. in Newman St.) Nov., F. to H. on big chance for B. if 'he will only condescend to give that attention to his wordly concerns which every one also does that prefers living to Starving.' BR 167, Greatheed on the Ballads. Patrons: BR 169. Differences in 1808 edition.

3. BR 168 n.

4. Nov. 30. Cromek called on Farington with B.'s designs. On 1 Dec. Greatheed reviews Ballads in *Eclectic Rev.*, BR 172; Southey ridiculed in *Annual Rev.* 1805; another review 1807: MW 150, BR 177. 17 Dec., RB 173. Cromek in general: E. (1b) 517–21.

5. B. wrote of young Malkin's drawings: 'All his efforts prove this little boy to have had that greatest of all blessings, a strong imagination, a clear idea, and a determinate vision of things in his own mind.' The boy invented a land, Allestone, of which he made a map with sites like Bubblebob, Punchpeach, and wrote a history of the place. Blake's frontispiece: MW 191. Blake may have known him before he went to F. in 1800. Malkin was headmaster of Bury Grammar School and wrote *Scenery, Antiquities, and Biographies of South Wales*. For his friend Johnes and his Eden: E. (1b) 525; K (13).

6. Caroline Watson and Raimbach succeeded B. with Hayley. Politics; E. 397–401.

7. Ozias Humphry: MW 211, 376 and BR 178. 1806 saw B.'s engraving of Reynolds' *Graphic Muse* in Prince Hoare's book. E. had given Fuseli a copy of the *Gates* which on 22 Nov. 1806 he gave to girl, Harriet Jane Moore: BR 182 nl.

8. Stothard's son pointed out that his father 'had no time for going about and seeing what other artists were employed upon,' BR 179. For Montgomery letter, etc., see Bentley (13); E. (1b) 317–21.

9. E. 97; Notebook 37.

10. Cromek accuses B. of calling the Pilgrim theme low when what he said that Cromek's treatment of him was low. *Artist*, 6 June 1807; yet Cromek was trying to interest Hoppner in B.'s poetry (illuminated books).

11. BR 189, B.'s earnings 1805. B. was also connected with Countess of Egremont through Ozias H. (Did Turner see B.'s works at Petworth?) Enoch: KS 178, mistaken for Job.

12. 11 March. Flaxman to H. on Raimbach proof, BR 189. Before May, Cumberland again on B.'s method of stopping lights etc., also on getting B. commission for Antiquities 22 June he sent B. '4 Historical (drawings) and tracings of my own,' BR 190f. They seem delivered by Cromek.

13. Walker: probably for *Poetical Pieces* by the late Rev. Thomas Bradford, 1808.

14. *Antijacobin* says *Grave* drawings were submitted to public inspection at the R. A.; this seems incorrect, BR 200 7 Nov. Carey's pamphlet calls B. an 'extraordinary artist'. Cumberland: RB 211.

15. Hunter as publisher of B., RB 213. Cromek still offers *Grave* in December. This year H.'s edition of Cowper's Milton translations appeared. Young Cumberland, MW 376, when *Grave* went to press, five names were withdrawn from list of patrons, including those of Academicians Fuseli, Northcote, Opie; also those of two friends of Malkin, T. Hope and W. Locke. Malkin's name was omitted from the analysis, but Fuseli's panegyric was left.

16. The catalogue, it seems, started straight after Hoppner's puff, Aug.

17. Nelson monument: E. 336f, 441, 44–6. 448n. Note that Blunt does not accept E.'s analysis. B. and Lady Hamilton, *ib.* 337. Schorer 174; Paley (1) ch. 7, sees as demonic parodies, 195–9 cf. Wittreich (1) 68. Cf. with B.'s Nelson, Gillray's *Apotheosis of Hoche*: E. 452—also apotheosis of Napoleon, *Three Steps to the New Imperial Diadem*, published by W. Holland, 1804.

Behind B.'s arguments about the public use of art lie the struggles and proposals of Hogarth, Wilkes, Barry, and the large scale attempts by print dealers to establish Galleries etc. (Boydell, Macklin, Bowyer), together with Fuseli's attempt at a Milton Gallery. From 1801 the main exponent of an English Gallery had been Opie. He wanted a gallery where could be shown works depicting 'the heroes and heroic exploits of this country'. In 1802 there was a gallery in Berners St. supported by some R. A.s. Then in 1805 came the British Institution for Promoting the Fine Art, organised by rich patrons: see B.'s marginalia to Reynolds. In Jan. 1805 Prince Hoare proposed the publication of Opie's scheme. In Nov., with the death of Nelson, came proposals for a Naval Pillar, with Flaxman after the job and many artists making designs. In 1807 in his academy lectures Opie made call for public support and use of art, shocking Flaxman with his 'democratic spirit'. Prince Hoare took up the idea in the *Artist*, and called for a competition for 'an Historical Picture of Lord Nelson'. Opie died, exhausted by his labours at the lectures. B. must have followed all these developments and felt that the moment had come when he could put himself forward as the national painter. But his equivocations left him in the position where he attracted the *Examiner* attack. His fear of open exposure of war and power is shown by his comment on Fuseli's Milton, which he considers scared the king and nobles by their exposure as Satan. (Haydon who was coming forward to champion History was anti-republican.) Blake, we may note, came only marginally as an engraver into the schemes of the big print dealers mentioned above. Note Behemoth in *J.* 91, 'the war by land,' Bronowski 51f. There was a medieval tradition of Christ crucified on lilies: see glass in church of Long Melford, Suffolk. K. Raine and Lindberg see Blake as seriously glorifying Nelson and Pitt!—see E. (1b) 521.

18. *Ancient Britons*: their ruddy (almost vermillion) skin is compared with modern man who naked is like a corpse. B. was probably inspired by Red Indians: E. 42, MW 220–4. Perhaps behind it lay Barry's *Rise of America*. Hunt thought its colour like 'hung beef'. The size was 14 × 10 feet. Owen and Triads, BR 226, PP 283.

19. Nanavutty (2). Brimha prostrate before his own image: cf. Albion, *J.* pl. 29. Note birth of beings from different parts of the body, etc.

20. Hand: Damon, *Dict.* Young George replies, BR 200. Attack on Fuseli in *Weekly Messenger*: MW 209.

21. C. R. gets medium and number of pictures wrong: MW 221. Kirkup says B. positive in opinions; the fuller account states he did not try to force his ideas on anyone not accepting his position, BR 220–2. If the tale of thrashing the wife-beater was from Kirkup, it should be at this time, but it seems hardly likely B. would have had the strength. Darley on Seguier: BR 222.

C. R.: BR 224ff. Tale of Gabriel: BR 452. 28 April, with Dr Malkin. 7 May, Mrs Iremonger; 24–5 May, more talk on B.: BR 225f. See also E. (1b) 523; Phillips (2).

22. Ker: BR 228f.

23. Gilchrist (1942) 361; Notebook 42. Printer of Prospectus: G. Smeeton, 17 St. Martin's Lane. Public Address to be pub. as Anecdotes of Artists and Advertisement to the Pilgrims; but B.'s nerves could not stand a second exhibition. See below.

24. Allegories relate to Moral Virtues, which do not exist: K. 614. Cumberland: BR 212. Landor: BR 229.

Hayley: E. 428; M. 27 and J. 23, J. 7–8; E. 457–60; Frye 377; Wright ii 42f. Mental withdrawal: Schorer 361f.

12. LONDON AND JERUSALEM

1. Two Morland pictures engraved 1788. This year, Earl Spencer: MW 233. Rossetti MS has c. 1810: 'This day is Publish'd Advertizements to Blake's Canterbury Pilgrims from Chaucer, containing Anecdotes of Artists, Price 6*d*.' Nothing happened.

2. Cirencester Place: James in Rate Books 1818–25; he no doubt lived there till his death. Ackermann used the *Grave* plates for a Spanish poem, 1826: K. (1) 221. Relief etching like that of the first page of *America* is dated 1813. The president of the Watercolour Society (of which this was the fifth and last show) was M. Richter, brother of an important member of the London Corresponding Society.

3. 15 Jan. 1813 C. R. takes Blake's Young to C. Aikin. 26 April, auction, *Songs*: BR 232.

4. E. 468f and (10); Beer (2) 281–3, 361; Gardner (1) 142–5—B. thinking of *Antijacobin* attack 1806, 83, on Fuseli for the 'articulations' of the joints. *Gates* 14–15 and *Pilgrim's Progress* designs 10–11; *Urizen* 23 and 27.

5. III: BR 233, Nov. 1814 Joanna died: PP 286.

6. Second copy of *Vision of L. J.* described Jan. 1808 to Countess of Egremont. Note his own saying: 'First thoughts are best in art, second thoughts in other matters.' BR 236f.

7. Fuseli: BR 238; Gilchrist elaborates. Ensor: VR 239. Works of young George C., KS 245. Cumberland himself busy in Bristol. In 1810 a double leaf with Birthday Ode to friend Horne Tooke to go under bust of him by T. Banks in 1800. Cumberland etched a portrait of H. T.: *Book Collector*, Spring 1970 pl. xiii. In 1811 an account of seat of friend Right Hon. C. Long at Gromley Hill, revised edition 1816.

8. Dibdin thinks Cromek engraved Stothard's Pilgrims. Dibdin and Disraeli on B., BR 243, 289 (1835). B. in *Biog. Dict*, 1816 (BR 244) with mention of *Gates*, *Songs of Exp.*, *Europe*, *America*, *Catalogue*. Dibdin says that Phillips' portrait gives B. more 'elevation and dignity' than he owned. No basis for tale of Bedlam: MW 239, app. vi.

9. Tulk: BR 242, 250. Tulk also friend of Coleridge.

10. Copy of *Songs* inscribed 'Mrs Flaxman April 1817'. Gibson in London, March to Sept.; Kirkup at R. A. this year: MW 232, 378.

11. MW 277 makes it 1820; I follow BR 248f, and break into paragraphs, Taylor: ? source Malkin. Jane had heard of B. in 1810 (C. R. diary, 25 June). D. Turner: B. refers to the Ozias H. set. Nine years later comes a further increase in prices: letter to Cumberland 1827 with J. instead of M.

12. Not even Crashaw has the rush and substitutions of B. in his *Everlasting Mercy*. Note Coleridge in *Christabel* moving towards more freedom.

13. Had Linnell been teaching young Cumberland? See receipt 27 Dec. 1816:

BR 256, KS 214. Linnell had a daughter, Sept. 1818; Spring 1819, *Bibliotheca Britannica* prints what of B. was given in *Biog. Dict.* if 1816L BR 258f. Harlowe: KS 215f, Story ii 248. Cumberland: KS 245f, BR 214. C. Pye gave commentary on Lizar's article in *London J. of Arts and Sciences* 1820 i 55–8; his process would have produced something close to what B. got.

14. Story of Wallace and Edward I is in Sartain: BR 260f. Flea: KS ch. 17, Cornelius Varley's Patent Graphic Telescope for making copies of B.'s heads: Butlin (3).

15. KS 130: Dr C. Singer's theory. Jane Porter's *Scottish Chiefs*, 1841, for muddled account of B. and Varley. For Jaensch and further discussion of eideties, see Paley (1) 202ff; Coleridge, Beer (4).

16. BR 264; KS 216; Story ii 247.

17. Why name Ruddicombe? B.'s flame of hair long gone. W. on Fuseli: MW 261f.

18. Gilchrist musters testimonies as to B.'s sanity: Calvert, Fitch (who however saw him as 'perverse and wilful'), Varley, Butts, and probably Tatham: BR 268; MW 71. 1820, B. engraved portrait of Mrs Quentin, one of the Regent's mistresses, after Huet Villiers. Paddington: E. 473f on excavations; PP 275–8; J. 12 etc. In Dec. 1820 B. was among the artists recommending W. P. Carey for post of Keeper etc. of artworks.

19. Frosch 119–23, 198–200; Hollander; Damon (2a) 45, 57; M. 24 and 26; J. 74: 25. Love of old times: Descr. Cat. v. Shell-rings of music: Beer (2) 359.

20. E. 462–5, 484; Gibbon, 468; Cathedral Cities, E. (23). Note Waterloo is linked with Arthur's Last Fight. Tetrad: Harper (2). Structure, relation to Ezekiel: Bloom in E.'s ed. 833–4. FZ and Spaces: Wagenknecht, 259–61. Drama (fall, struggle, redemption, apocalypse): Frye 357. Rose (4) on the Four Zoas. Three ages of man: Kiralis. Three errors of the fall (misuses of body, mind, imagination) Mellor (2). Successive stages of fallen condition: Lesnick, 394. Foz, 13f; E. 462, 468f. 471; Wagenknecht, 250, 266. Length of poem: E. (4). Great importance of Druidic idea: Beer (2) 17–21; Fisher 34–46. (Note four levels of vision in Plato's allegory of the Cave.)

13. JOB IN CAPTIVITY

1. Martin: BR 563f. This year *Allgemeine Bibliog. Lexikon* mentioned B. (in English 1837): BR 270. B. in Germany: MW 385.

2. Palmer on love of Ovid with his copy of *Metamorphoses* after Guilio Romano on his wall, with Dürer's *Melancholy* close to his engraving table; his smile of welcome as the young men came in: BR 565. Soap: Richmond. In 1860 the front room was let at 4*s.* 6*d.* a week.

3. Vivian, 213. S. Calvert, 19. Early April, F. Douce got MHH from Dyer (probably Lamb's friend George). Note popularity of Italian writers among Romantics of 1820s; also interest in Dante: TLS 3 Jan. 1958; K 779, Cennini. Frend: BR 273, De Morgan 67f.

4. Young: BR 269. *Job*: KS 180. But for Linnell B. would have spent last years in making 'a set of Morland's pig and ploughboy subjects'—see BR 274. Paintings on glass: MW 385.

Arlington House picture: KS ch. 25; K. Raine (1) ch. 3; Mellor 256–70; Grant (2) and (1) 199; R. Simmons; G. W. Digby, 75; J. Beer (2) 289; A. S. Roe. Wickstead took it for vision of Kabbala: Adam Kadmon and his emanation at centre. Money: BR 275, 548. Lady Blessington: Stephens, 44.

5. Jehovah: M. 13: 24; FZ viii 405. But also Jehovah as Mercy: *Ghost of Abel*, J. 61:25 and 98: 23. See J. 39: 31 for great compliment to Byron. E. 393; Damon, *Dict.* Hate of Mechanics: BR 279. Nov. 1823, Cumberland's Essay on old engravers. 'Lent Blake my Catalogue to read.' which he returned: BR 279. Cast: BR 278f. In Nov. one of the *Job* plates was finished: BR 329.

6. Contract: BR 277; MW 281; KS 206. Sale: BR 279f.

7. A. H. Palmer says Palmer met Blake 9 Oct., but Gilchrist's May 1824 seems convincing. Gilchrist respectabilises etc.: B. was 'a gentleman, in a way of his own'. His eyes had 'a look of clear heavenly meditation'. No doubt on the same visit to the R. A. Blake remarked a copy of Leonardo's *Last Supper* and Fuseli's *Aegisthus*.

8. Cumberland again, 16 May: links B. and Schiavonetti in skill. Again 24 May and 17 June: KS 247. Says Stothard mannered and fine in contours only with drapery; praises B. On 21 June Dixon sends regards to Varley, B., Finch. September: BR 295.

9. Tatham, 2 Aug., on Michael Angelo Blake. Thomas Chevalier as friend of B. BR 288. Sept. 1824 Palmer to Linnell, he is drawing from nature: 'vision seems foolishness to me … Jacob Ruysdaal a sweeter finisher than William Blake.' BR 290. 'Love to the little ancients.' Elsewhere he calls B. the equal of Michaelangelo. Calvert about 1855 feels great force of M.A.s and B.'s 'great principles: Unbroken Masses; Unbroken Lines; Unbroken Colours': BR 290.

10. Palmer: BR 291, cf. Story i 231; Hardie 9f.

11. 'Fear and trembling': B. to Palmer: BR 291 n2. After the meeting, Palmer wrote in notebook: 'Look at Mr Blake's way of relieving subjects, and at his colour.' Palmer on B.'s art-views: BR 315, 382f, 291. A. H. Palmer 15, 27f. Gilchrist (1942) 299.

The group: Holmes, portraitist; John Varley brought in his brother Cornelius and brother-in-law Mulready (MW 299); no record of relations with Walter; Palmer and Richmond seem to have kissed B.'s bell-handle before pulling; Calvert, 'There was no assumption of occult mystery about Blake. All was serious reality, yet abnormal and strange to others.'

II

12. Bowdlerising: BR 318f *Remember Me!* reissued unchanged next year: BR 295f.

13. Probably the same writer on B. in *The Monthly Magazine*, March 1833: BR 298f. Cumberland, 5 April 1825, to his son about Moses, engraver; still thinks of B. for the plates: BR 300. Advice: BR 299, but note how B. claimed all shadows were cold. Butts Collection: BR 300.

14. Aders: BR 301f. 310; Passavant i 201–19. Richmond says he was only sixteen at the time: BR 293f.

15. Shoreham: S. Calvert 34–6. Hampstead: MW 296; BR 304f; Adlard 20; Ellis 424. Once B. drew himself: Story i 149.

16. Mrs L. spells *who* as *you*. Flea: KS 134f and Blunt 82.

17. Palmer says in talk B. was 'anything but sectarian or exclusive,' as a critic 'judicious and discriminating.' His 'conversation was so nervous and brilliant, that, if recorded at the time, it would have thrown much light upon his character.' He did not know that C. R. was recording it. BR 309.

18. 'I have conversed with the—Spiritual Sun—I saw him on Primrose Hill He said 'Do you take me for the Greek Apollo No I said' that (and Bl pointed to the sky) that is the Greek Apollo— He is Satan.' BR 313f. B. refers to Parnell's *Hermit* in a way that shows the poem had meant much to him. B.'s praise of Roman Catholic Church to Palmer: BR 321.

19. BR 311 for B.'s incorrect citation of the Bible. We may note he says Solomon married Pharoah's daughter. St Theresa: BR 321. Hagstrum (2) 146. On 20 Dec. C. R. argued with G. Hundleby about Wordsworth and B. James: BR 564.

20. Wilson Lowry, whose portrait B. engraved for Linnell, seems certainly the Lowry who engraved the Jerusalem Plans for Brothers: PP 273f; K. (4) p. 44. Note extent to which Spectre is Despair: Warner (2) 221. Erasures: Hoover 310; E. (21).

14. THE LAST DAYS

1. Earlier examples: Damon, *Dict.* 216f. The watercolours are very much weaker. *Job*: Damon (4); Warner (1) 222; Frye (4); Marqusee; Hofer.

2. Coleridge: MW 293; BR 325; Beer (3).

3. Sister Nativity, nun, wrote a book from spirit-dictation: review in *Quarterly Rev.* xxxiii, March 1826, 390 compares with plate of reunion of body and soul in *Grave.*

More references to B.: 10 April, Linnell to Lady Torrens; 11 April Daniell, undergraduate of Balliol to Linnell; 22 April, complaint from R. Balmanno; 27 April, engraver Haughton refuses set; 10 May, T. Edwards offers stock of Young for auction in Manchester; copy to Palmer; Hazlitt in *Plain Speaker*, i 223f (lumping B. with Sharp, Varley, Loutherbourg, Cosway): BR 328–32.

4. *Vala MS*: Ellis 411. B. adds (16 July) 'Fincham is a Pupil of Abernethy's; this is what gives me great pleasure. I did not know it before yesterday, from Mr Fincham'. Abernethy was surgeon in St Bartholomew's Hospital.

5. Probably later July Mrs Aders wrote to L. about C. R. being in town and eager for *Job* as she was for *Songs of Innocence*. She seems to pay for her *Job* on 29 July.

6. Roe, 33; Blunt, 89, with relations to Flaxman, pl. 59, 69, and medieval rondel, pl. 64. Probably late Dec. he wrote to Colnaghi with set of *Job* proofs and says he'll call in a few days. Perhaps this autumn Ackerman used *Grave* plates for poem by refugee Spaniard, José Joaquin de Mora who was trying to write in terms of 16th c. Spanish religious poetry: BR 33–5, K (1) 221. Mrs Collins recalls B. as 'that most delightful gentleman', BR 333.

7. On 5 Jan. Shorts, Salisbury dealer, said he could not find a buyer for *Job*: BR 337.

8. Unclear if move was to be to Linnell's quarters or those that James B. had occupied. Sales: BR 339, 400. Wainewright asks after B. and commends Linnell for his care of him. 'His Dante is the most wonderful emanation of the imagination that I ever heard of'. 22 Feb., R. Gooch, King's Physician, writes for *Job* for King's library, paid 10 gns. List of subscribers: KS 211f.

9. Ault, esp. 114f. He writes, 'Dear Cumberland'. Ottley: in 1833 Keeper of Books in B. M.

10. BR 346. On 16 Aug. L. sent. *Job* to Ottley.

11. Other notices: BR 361; *Annual Register* 1827. Robinson meets Palmer (Aug. 1836) of whom he was suspicious: BR 363. Chance at the Linnell place: KS 208n. Writers of 1833: BR 373f; *The Monthly Mag.* March 1853.

12. Ebert's *Lexikon* 1830: BR 375f, also 270.

13. KS 225f; BR 406f.

14. U.S.A. notices: BR 410.

15. Dante engravings: KS 228f. Garnet on Tatham: BS 417. Later reputation Hoover; Dorfmann. The author of the notice in the *London Mag.* seems Tulk: Dorfmann: 42f. Tatham seems to have written his Life to be bound in with copy of *J.* to make it more saleable. Palmer: Lister (2).

16. For an attempt to equate witchcraft beliefs, shamanism, and millenarian cults with schizophrenia: E. Leach, *Listener*, 17 July 1917. Hallucinatory state: A. Koestler, *The Act of Creation*, 1975, 322.

B. as precursor of *Art Nouveau*: Pevsner (2); Baurmann; Schmutzler; F. B. Smith, *Radical Artisan, W. J. Linton*, 1973, 196–8 and figure 5 (*Famine: a Masque*, 1875).

Bibliography

The following abbreviations have been used: BL, Blakestone; BM, Burlington Magazine; BN, Blake Newsletter; BNYPL, Bulletin N. Y. Public Library; BR, Bentley Records; BS, Blake Studies; CW, *see* Curran and Wittreich; ECS, Eighteenth Century Studies; E, Erdman (1a); EG, Erdman (3); ES, English Studies; G, Gilchrist Life 1880; G2, Todd ed. of Gilchrist 1942; HB, Hilles; HLQ, Huntingdon Lib. Quarterly; JWCI: Journal of Warburg and Courtauld Institute; K. Keynes (2); KS, Keynes (3); M. Margoliouth; MLQ, Modern Language Quarterly; MP, Modern Philology; MW, Mona Wilson; PMLA, Publications Modern Language Assn. of America; PP, Paley and Phillips; PQ, Philological Quarterly; R, Rosenfeld; RES Review of English Studies; SEL, Studies in English Literature; SIR, Studies in Romanticism; SP, Studies in Philology; WB, William Blake.

When no place of publication is given, read London.

ABRAMS, M. H., (1) *Natural Supernaturalism in Tradition and Revolution in Romantic Lit.* (N.Y.), 1971 (2) ed. *English Romantic Poets* (OUP), 1960.

ADAMS, H., (1) in Weathers, 52–66 (2) *Blake and Keats* (Ithaca), (3) *WB: A Reading of the Shorter Poems* (Seattle), 1963.

ADLARD, J., (1) *The Sports of Cruelty*, 1972 (2) BS, Spring 1969 (3) ES, xlv, 460–2, 1964.

ALTICK, *The English Common Reader*.

ALTIZER, J. J., *The New Apocalypse: The Radical Christian View of WB* (Michigan), 1967.

ANON (1) *Cornhill Mag.* xxii, Aug. 1875, 157–68 (2) *Literary Memoirs of Living Authors*, vols., 1798 (3) TLS 7 Oct. 1926, 680 (4).

ANSARI, A. A., in R, 199–220.

ANTAL, F., *Fuseli Studies*, 1956.

AXON, W. E. A., *T. Taylor*, 1890.

BAKER, C. H. Collins, (1) HLQ *Bull.* x, 1936, 127 (2) with R. R. Wark, *Cat. of WB's works in the Huntingdon Lib.* (San Marino), 1957 (3) *HL Bull.* iv, 140–1, 359.

BAKER, W. S., *W. Sharp, Engraver* (Philadelphia), 1875.

BAINE, R. and M., BNL X 1976 51–2.

BALLEINE, G. R., *Past Finding Out* (J. Southcott), N.Y., 1956.

BARRY, J., (1) *Account of a Series of Pictures in the Great Room of the Soc. of Arts*, 1783, (2) *Inquiry into the Real and Imaginary Obstructions to the Acquisition of the Arts in England*, 1775 (3) *Works*, 1809 (4) *Lectures*, ed. R. N. Wornum 1848.

BASS, E., EG ch. 9.

BAURMANN, R., *Archit. Rev.*, cxxiii, 1938, 369–72.

BEER, J., (1) *Blake's Humanism* (Manchester), 1968 (2) *Blake's Visionary Universe* (Manchester) 1969 (3) PP, 231–59, (4) *Coleridge the Visionary*, 1959.

BENTLEY, G. E., (1) *Blake Records* (OUP) 1969 (2) *Tiriel* (Oxford), 1967 (3) SIR vi, 1966, 48–57 (4) *Vala* (Oxf.), 1963 (5) BNYPL, xli, 1957, 539–60 (6) with Nurmi, *A Blake Bibliography* (Minneapolis), 1964 (7) *N. and Q.*, 1954, cxcix, 528–30 (8) BN, ii, Dec. 1968, 41–5 (9) PMLA, lxxi, 1956, 1052–66, (Butts) (10) *Studies in Bibliog.*, xix, 1966 232–43 (11) ib xii 1959 165 (12) *N. and Q.* ciii, 1938, 168 (13) BNYPL, lxvii, Sept. 1963, 443–54 (13) *Princeton Lib. Chronicle*, xxxv, 1974, 321–4.

BERGER, P., *WB, Poet and Mystic*, N.Y. 1915.

BINDMAN, D. (1) BM, cviii, Oct. 1966, 522 (2) PP, 29–49 (3) *Blake as Artist* 1977.

BINYON, L. (1) *The Followers of Blake*, 1925 (2) *Engraved Designs of WB*, 1926 (3) *WB. . .Woodcuts*, 1902 (4) WB, 1906 (5) *Illustrations to Book of Job*, 1935.

BISHOP, M., *Blake's Hayley*, 1951.

BLACK, C., *The Cumberland Letters*, 1912.

BLONDEL, J., WB (Paris) 1963.

BLOOM, H. (1) *Blake's Apocalypse* (N.Y.), 1963 (2) *The Visionary Company*, 1962 (3) *The Ringers in the Tower* (Chicago) 1971 (4) HB (5) In Abrams (2) (6) *Poetry and Repression*, 1976.

BLUNT, A. (1) *England and the Mediterranean Tradition* (Oxf.) 1945 (2) *Art of WB*, 1959 (3) JWCI ii 1938 53–63 (4) *ib.* vi 1943 225–7 (5) and 190–212 (5) *Intro. to Cat. of Works of WB in Tate Gallery*, 1957 (6) JWCI ii 65ff.

BOASE, T. S. R., *B. M. Quarterly* xx 1945 4ff.

BOGEN, N. (1) ed. of *Thel* (2) *Satire Newsletter* v 1968 114 (3) BNYPL lxxiii 1969.

BOLT, S. F., *Politics and Letters* i 1947 9–14.

BOTTRALL, M., *Songs of Innocence and Exp.* 1970.

BRAY, MRS A. E., *Life of T. Stothard* 1881.

BRIGGS, A. E., *Connoisseur* xiv 1907 95 (Butts).

BRIGGS, ASA, *The Chathamites*, 1967.

BROWN, A. R., BM lxxvii 1940 8off.

BRUCE, H. L. (1) MP Feb. 192 6 xiii (2) *WB in this World*, 1925.

BUCKLEY, V., *Melbourne Critical Rev.* vii 1969 3–21.

BURDELL, O., WB, 1926.

BURKE, J., in *In Honour of Daryl Lindsay* (Melbourne) 1964 ed. Phillip and Stewart.

BUSH, D., *Science and English Poetry* (N.Y.) 1950.

BUSST, A. J. L., in *Romantic Mythologies*, ed. I. Fletcher 1967.

BUTLIN, M. (1) *Blake-Varley Sketchbook of 1819*, 1969 (2) *Works of WB in Tate Gallery*, 1957 (3) PP ch. xiv (4) R. 109–16.

BUTTS, MARY, *The Crystal Cabinet*, 1937.

CALVERT, S., *A Memoir of Edward Calvert*, 1893.

CHARD, L. F., BNYPL lxxix 1975 51–82.

CHAYES, I. H., EG ch. lo.

COLBY, E., *Life of T. Holcroft*, 1925.

COLLINS, BAKER C., HLQ iv 1941 359f.

CONNOLLY, T. E., BS vi 1975 179–87.

CONWAY, D., *Writings of Paine*, 1892.

COXBY, A. C., *T. Stothard*, 1906.

CRAWFURD, O., *The New Quarterly Mag.* ii 1874.

CUMBERLAND, C. (1) *Thoughts on Outline*, 1796 (2) *Outlines of the Ancients*, 1829 (3) *Some Anecdotes of the Life of Julio Bonasoni* 1793.

CURRAN, S. and J. WITTREICH, *Blake's Sublime Allegory* (Univ. of Wisconsin) 1973.

DAMON, S. FOSTER (1) *Blake Dictionary* 1973 (2) *WB, his Philosophy and Symbolism* (Boston) 1924 (2a) reprint (Gloucester, Mass.) 1958 (3) *Blake's Grave* (Brown Univ.) 1963 (4) *Blake's Job* (Brown Univ.) 1966.

DAVIES, J. G., *The Theology of WB*, 1948.

DAVIS, A. P., *Isaac Watts* (N.Y.) 1943.

DE MORGAN, S. E., *Threescore Years and Ten*, ed. M. A. De Morgan, 1895.

DIBDIN, T. F., *Reminiscences of a Literary Life*, 1836.

DIGBY, G. W., *Symbol and Image: WB* (Oxf.) 1957.

DORFMANN, D. (1) *Blake in the 19th c.* (Yale) 1967 (2) BNYPL lxxi 1967 216–44.

DOUGLAS, D., *Balcony* (Sydney, N.S.W.) Summer 1967 9–33.

DOWDEN, E., ed. *Corresp. of R. Southey with Caroline Bowles*, 1881.

DUNCAN-JOHNSTONE, L. A., *A Psychological Study of WB*, 1945.

EASSON, R. R., with Essick, *WB Book Illustrator* (Illinois) 1970.

EATON, D. I., *Politics for the People* i no. 12 1793.

EAVES, M., PP ch. xi.

EHRSTINE, J. W., *WB's Poetical Sketches* (Washington State Univ.) 1967.

ELLIS, E. J. (1) *The Real Blake* 1907 (2) with Yeats, *Works of WB*, 1893.

EMERY, C., *The Marriage of Heaven and Hell* (Univ. of Miami Crit. Studies i) 1963.

ENGLAND, M. W., in Erdman (3) 3–29 (2) BNYPL lxx 1966.

ERDMAN, D. (1) Blake: *Prophet against Empire* (Princeton) 1954 (1a) *ib.* Garden City 1969 (1b) *ib.* 1977 (2) *Comp. Lit.* v (Swedenborg) (3) ed. with J. E. Grant, *Visionary Forms Dramatic* (Princeton) 1970 (4) ed. with D. K. Moore, *Notebooks of WB*, 1973 (5) *Poetry and Prose of WB* (Garden City) 1965 (6) *Concordance* (Cornell) 1966 (7) Text in Stevenson (8) *Art Q.*, xii 1949 165–70 (Gillray) (9) PQ xxviii 1949 465–70 (lo) MP xlviii 1951 184–92 (Lambeth) (11) *English Institute Essays*, 1950 (N.Y.) 1951 199–223 (12) PQ xxxi 1952 337–43 (13) JWCI xv 1952 242–52 (13a) *Keats-Shelley J.* ii 1953 61–71 (14) *Illuminated Books* (OUP) 1975 (15) R. 395–413 (16) *Library* 5th s. xix 1964 112–29 (17) BN ii 13 Sept. 1968 24 (18) BNYPL lxxii 1968 518–21 (19) SIR, Blake Issue 1977 (Song of Los) (20) PP 162–207 (21) *Studies in Bibliog.* xvii 1964 1–54 (22) Speech 23 April 1976 (typescript communicated) (23) *J. of English and Germanic Philol.* lxx 1966 606–12.

ESDAILE, K. M., *The Library* v 1 July 1914 229–56 (Crabb R.).

ESSICK, R. N. (1) PP 50–65 (2) BS v (1) 1972 (3) ed. with J. La Belle, *Night Thoughts* 1975 (4) ed. *The Visionary Hand* (Los Angeles) 1973 (5) see Easson.

FARINGTON, L., *Diary*, ed. J. Greig 1922–3.

FARRER, A. (1) *A Rebirth of Images: The Making of St. John's Apocalypse*, 1949 (2) *The Revelation of St. John the Divine* (Oxf.) 1964.

FAUVET, P., *Red Letters* no 6, 1977.

FINLAYSON (FINLAYSON), J. *The Last Trumpet and the Flying Angel*, 1849 (1850).

FISCH, H. (1) R. 36–56 (2) *Language and Style in Milton*, ed. T. H. Shawcross and R. Emma, N.Y. 1967 (2) *Jerusalem and Albion*, 1964.

FISHER, P. F. (1) *The Valley of Vision* (Toronto) 1961 (2) PQ xl 1951, 1–18.

FLAXMAN, J., *Lectures on Sculpture*, 1838.

FOUCAULD, M., *Madness and Civilisation*, N. Y., 1965.

FOX, S. (1) *Poetic Form in Blake's Milton* (Princeton) 1976 (2) BS ii (1) 21–2.

FROSCH, T. R., *The Awakening of Albion* (Cornell) 1974.

FRYE, N. (1) *Fearful Symmetry* (Princeton) 1963 (2) in Pinto 97–137 (3) MLQ xxi 1953 57–67 (4) R. 221–34 (5) *Some British Romantics*, ed. J. V. Logan and J. E. Jordan (Ohio) 1966 3–40 (6) *Eng. Inst. Essays* ed. A. Downer (Columbia) 1951 170–96.

GAGE, J., JWCI xxxiv 1971 372–6.

GANZ, P. L., *The Drawings of H. Fuseli*, 1949.

GARDNER, S. (1) *Blake*, 1968 (2) *Infinity of the Anvil* (Oxf.) 1954.

GARNET, R. (1) *The Hampstead Annual* 1903 (2) *WB Poet and Painter* 1895.

GARRETT, Clarke, *Respectable Folly* (John's Hopkins) 1975.

GEORGE, M. D., *Cat. of Political and Personal Satires in BM* (8 vols.) 1935–47.

GILCHRIST, A. (1) *Life of WB*, 1863 (2) 1880 (3) ed. Todd 1942.

GILCHRIST, H. H., *Anne Gilchrist*, 1897.

GILHAM, D. G., *Blake's Contrary States* (O.U.P.) 1966.

GLECKNER, R. (1) SEL v 1965 533–51 (2) *The Piper and the Bard* (Detroit, Wayne)

1959 (3) R. 321–32 (4) PQ 1957 xxxvi 192–210 (5) *Mod. Lang. Notes* lxxi 1958 412–15 (6) SIR v (1) 1–15.

GORDON, A., *Dict. Nat. Biog.* Brothers.

GRANT, J. E. (1) BS I 1969 Spring (2) SIR x 1971 (3) BN xvi 1971 (4) Erdman (5) (5) CW 141–202 (6) EG 304–25 (7) R. 333–47.

GRIERSON, H. J. C., *Blake's Designs for Gray's Poems*, 1922.

GRIGSON, G. (1) *Archit. Rev.* cviii 1950 220 (2) *S. Palmer: The Visionary Years*, 1947.

GROOT, H. B. DE, *Eng. Studies* 50 (Oct. 1969) 553–64.

GURNEY, J., *The Trial of Thomas Hardy for High Treason* (4 vols.) 1794.

HAGSTRUM, J. H. (1) *WB Poet and Painter* (Chicago) 1964 (2) PP 129–56 (3) HB 311–30 (4) R 368–82 (5) CW 101–8.

HALL, M. S., BNYPL lxxiii 1969.

HALLIBURTON, D., SIR v 1966 158–68.

HALLORAN, W. F. (1) EG 30–56 (2) BNYPL xii 1968 3–18.

HANSON, T. W., TLS 8 Aug. 1942 396.

HARDIE, M., *S. Palmer* 1928.

HARPER, G. M. (1) *The Neoplatonism of WB*, 1961 (2) R. 235–55.

HARTMAN, G. H. (1) R. 57–68 (2) *Beyond Formalism* (Yale) 1970.

HAVENS, R. D., *The Influence of Milton on English Poetry* (Camb., Mass.) 1922.

HAYLEY, W. (1) *Memoirs of the Life and Writings*, ed. J. Johnson, 1823 (2) *Life of G. Romney*, 1809.

HAYTER, S. W., *New Ways of Gravure*, 1949.

HELMS, R., SIR 12 (2) 1974 127–40.

HELMSTADTER, T. H. (1) in Essick (4) (2) SIR lo 1971 199–212 (3) BS v 1972 105–39.

HENDERSON, M. S., *Constable*, 1905.

HEPPNER, C., in Sutherland (3).

HERZING, T. W., BS vi (1) 1973 19–34.

HILLES, F. W. and H. BLOOM, *From Sensibility to Romanticism* (O.U.P.) 1965.

HINDMARSH, R., *The Rise and Progress of the New Jerusalem Church*, ed. E. Madeley, 1861.

HIRSCH, E. D., *Innocence and Experience* (New Haven) 1964.

HIRST, D., *Hidden Riches*, 1964.

HOARE, PRINCE, *Academic Annals*, 1805.

HOBSBAWM, E., *Labouring Men*, 1964.

HOFER, P., *Illustrations to the Book of Job*, 1937.

HOLCROFT, T., *Life*, ed. Elbridge, 1925.

HOLLANDER, J. in HB.

HOLLOWAY, J., *Blake: The Lyric Poetry*, 1968.

HONOUR, H., *Neo-Classicism*, 1968.

HOOVER, S. R., PP ch. xvi.

HUNGERFORD, E. B., *Shores of Darkness* (Columbia) 1941.

HURD, W., *A New Universal History of the Religions, Rites, Ceremonies, and Customs of the Whole World* (Newcastle) 1811.

IRWIN, D., *English Neoclassical Art*, 1966.

JAENSCH, E. R., *Eidetic Imagery* (N.Y.) 1930.

JAMES, L. DE WITT, *WB and the Tree of Life*, 1956 (1971).

JENKINS, H. (H. Ives), (1) *Nineteenth Century* lxvii 849–61 (2) WB 1925.

JOHNSON, M. L., BS vi (1) 1973 11–17.

JOHNSTON, K. R., EG 413–42.

JONES, M., *N. and Q*. n.s. xvii 1970 314.

JONES, R. M., *Mysticism and Democracy in the English Commonwealth*.

KAPLAN, F., SEL vii Autumn 1967 617–27.

KETTLE, A. (1) *Arena* 3 1950 46–52 (2) *Mainstream* (N.Y.) Nov. 1957.

KEYNES, G. (1) *Bibliog. of WB* (N.Y.) 1921 (2) *Writings of WB*, 1957 (3) *Blake Studies* (O.U.P.) 1971 (4) *Blake's Separate Plates* (Dublin) 1956 (5) *Notebooks of WB*, 1935 (6) *WB's Watercolour Illustrations to the Poems of T. Gray* (Chicago) 1972 (7) *Pencil Drawings of WB*, 1927 (8) *Gates of Paradise* 1965 (9) *Blake's Laocoon*, 1977 (10) *Illustrations to Young's Night Thoughts* (Camb., Mass.) 1927 (11) *Blake* (N.Y.) 1964 (12) *Engravings of WB*, 1956 (13) *Book Collector* xix 31–65.

KING, J., SIR xi 1972.

KING, R. W., *The Translator of Dante: The Life of H. F. Cary*, 1925.

KIRALIS, K. (1) in Pinto 139–62 (2) *Journal of Eng. Lit. History* xxiii, June 1956, 127–43.

KIRSCHBAUM, L., *Essays in Criticism* xi 1961 154–62.

KNIGHTS, L. C., *Sewanee Rev.* lxxix 1971 371–92.

KNOWLES, J., *Life and Writings of H. Fuseli*, Esq., 1831.

KNOX, T. R., *Past and Present*, no 76, 1977.

KREITER, C. S., SIR iv Autumn 1964 110–18.

LESNICK, H. (1) EG 391–412 (2) BNYPL lxxiii (1) Jan. 1969 49–55.

LINDBERG, BO, *Book of Job* (Acta Acad. Absensis) vol. 46.

LINDSAY, JACK (1) WB, 1928 (2) 2nd ed. 1929 (3) *Life and Letters*, Feb. 1947 110–24 (Young) (4) *Modern Quarterly Miscellany* (Ossian) (5) *Blastpower and Ballastics*, 1974 (6) as in (3) April 1947 (7) *Loving Mad Tom*, 1929 (8) *Origins of Alchemy* 1970 (9) Essay in *Poetical Sketches* (Scholartis Press) 1929.

LISTER, R. (1) WB (N.Y.) 1968 (2) PP ch. xv.

LOWERY, M. R. (1) *Windows of the Morning* (New Haven) 1940 (2) *Library* 4th s. xvii 1936 354–60.

MCNIEL, H. T., EG 373–91.

MALLET, P. H., *Northern Antiquities*, transl. T. Percy, 1770.

MARGOLIOUTH, H. M. (1) *WB's Vala* (Oxf.) 1956 (2) *Rev. Eng. Studies* xxiv 1948 312–16 (3) in Pinto 193–204 (4) WB 1951.

MARQUSEE, M., *The Book of Job* (N.Y.) 1976.

MASON, E. C., *The Mind of H. Fuseli*, 1951.

MATTHEWS, R., *English Messiahs*, 1936.

MAUNG BO-HANN, *WB, his Mysticism*.

MELCHIORI, G., *Michaelangelo nel Setticento Inglese* (Rome) 1950.

MELLOR, A. K. (1) *Blake's Human Form Divine* (Univ. California) 1974 (2) SEL xi (3) Autumn 1971 592–620.

MILES, J. (1) PP 86–95 (2) *Eras and Modes in Eng. Poetry* (Calif.) (2) 1941 (1957).

MINER, P. (1) BNYPL Dec. 1963 639–42 (2) R. 256–92 (3) *Texas Studies in Lang. and Lit.* ii 1960 198ff (4) BNYPL, lxii 1958 535–50.

MITCHELL, W. J. T. (1) ECS iii 1969 83–107 (2) CW 281–301.

MOORE, D. E., *Annotated ed. of WB's Europe*, Diss. State Univ. of N.Y. (Stony Brook) 1952.

MORRIS, E., JWCI xxxiv 397–9.

MORRIS, H. N., *Flaxman, Blake, Coleridge and Other Men of Genius Influenced by Swedenborg*, 1915.

MORTON, A. L. (1) *The Everlasting Gospel*, 1958 (2) *The World of the Ranters*, 1970 (3) *The Matter of Britain* 1966.

MOSS, W. E., BN 2 Sept. 1968 19–23.

MURRAY, R., SIR 13(2) 1974 89–104.

MURRY, J. M. WB, 1933 (and 1936).

NANAVUTTY, P. (1) JWCI xv 1952 238–61 (2) in Pinto 165–82 (3) R. 293–302.

NELMS, B. F., EG 336–58.

NICHOLS, J., *Lit. Anecdotes*, 1815.

NORMAN, H. J., *J. of Mental Science*, April 1915.

NURMI, M. K. (1) WB, 1975 (2) BNYPL April 1964 249–56 (3) in Weathers 34–51 (4) PMLA lxxi 1956 660–85 (5) R. 303–18 (6) *Blake's M.H.H., a Critical Study* (Kent, Ohio) 1957.

OPPENHEIMER, J., *J. of Hist. of Medicine* i 1946 41–5.

OSTRIKER, A., *Vision and Verse in WB* (Wisconsin) 1965.

PACHTER, H. M., *Paracelsus* (N.Y.) 1957.

PALEY, N. D. (1) *Energy and Imagination* (Oxf.) 1970 (2) PMLA viii Dec. 1966 540–1 (3) with M. Phillips, ed. *WB, Essays in Hon. of Sir G. Keynes* (Oxf.) 1973 (4) in Weathers 80–103 (5) ECS i 1968 (6) R. 131–57 (7) BN 3, 15 Dec. 1967, 15–8 (8) ed. *Twentieth Century Interpretations of the Song of Los* (Eaglewood Cliffs) 1969.

PALMER, A. H., ed. *Life and Letters of S. Palmer*, 1892.

PANOFSKY, D. and E., *Pandora's Box* (N.Y.) 1962.

PARSONS, C. O., *Art Quarterly* xxvi 1968 300.

PASSAVENT, M., *Tour of a German Artist in England*, 1836.

PAUL, C. K., *W. Godwin*, 1876.

PAULSON, R., *Listener* 2 Aug. 1973 140–2.

PEVSNER, N. (1) *The Englishness of English Art* (N.Y.) 1956 ch. 5 (2) *Pioneers of Modern Design* 1968 90–3.

PHILLIPS, M. (1) PP ch. 1 (2) RES, xxvi 1975 19–33.

PIERCE, F. E., PMLA xliii 1928 1121–41.

PINSON, K. S., *Pietism as a Factor in the Rise of German Nationalism* (N.Y.) 1934.

PINTO, V. DE SOLA, ed. *The Divine Vision*, 1957.

PLOWMAN, MAX, TLS 18 Nov. 1926. A selection of writings? *See* Keynes.

POLLIN, B. (1) BNYPL lxxvii 1968 507–17 (2) *ib.* lxxiii 1969 25–7.

POSTGATE, R. W., *That Devil Wilkes*, 1929.

POVEY, K., TLS 1926 782.

PRICE, N., *To the Palace of Wisdom* (N.Y.) 1964.

QUASHA, G., EG 263–84.

RAIMBACH, A., *Memoirs*, 1843.

RAINE, K. (1) *Blake and Tradition* (Princeton) 1968 (2) *Sewanee Rev.* lxxi 1963 352–450 (3) JWCI xx 1957 318–37. (4) R. 383–92 (5) HLQ xxi 1957 1–36.

REEVES, M., *The Influence of Prophecy in the Later Middle Ages: A Study of Joachimism* (Oxf.) 1969.

REID, W. H., *The Rise and Dissolution of the Infidel Societies of the Metropolis*, 1800.

RIFFATERRE, M., in J. Ehrmann, *Structuralism* (Garden City) 1970.

ROBINSON, H. Crabb, *Blake, Coleridge etc.* ed. E. Morley (Manchester) 1922.

ROBINSON, J. E., *Arts and Decorations*, Jan. 1908, 100–5 30.

ROE, A. S. (1) *Blake's Illustrations to the Divine Comedy* (Princeton) 1953 (2) R 158–95.

ROSE, E. J. (1) BS i 1968 18–38 (2) *J. of Aesthetics and Art Hist.* xxiii 1964 173–83 (3) *Hartford Studies in Lit.* ii 1970 (4) *Bucknell Rev.* ii (3) 1762–3 35–54 (5) CW 83–99 (6) SEL v 1965 587–606.

ROSENBLUM, R. (1) in *Romantic Art in Britain*, ed. F. Cumming and A. Staley (Philadelphia Mus. of Art) 1968 (2) *Transformations in Late Eighteenth Century Art* (Princeton) 1967.

ROSENFELD, A., ed. *Blake Essays for S. F. Damon* (Providence, R. I.) 1969.

ROSTON, M., *Prophet and Poet* (Boston, Evanston) 1956.

RUSSELL, A. G. B. (1) *Letters of WB, with Life by F. Tatham*, 1906 (2) *Engravings of WB*, 1912.

SAMPSON, J., *Poetical Works of WB*, 1905.

SANDLER, F., BS V 1972 13–57.

SARTAIN, J., *Reminiscences of a Very Old Man* (N.Y.) 1900.

SAURAT, D. (1) *Blake and Milton*, 1935 (2) *Blake and Modern Thought*, 1929 (3) MP xxiii Nov. 1925.

SCHIFF, G., *Zeichnungen von J. H. Fuseli* (Zurich) 1959.

SCHMUTZLER, R., *Archit. Rev.* vol. 117, 1955, 109–6 and vol. 118 1955 90–7.

SHAFFER, E. S., *Kubla Khan and the Fall of Jerusalem* (C.U.P.) 1975.

SIMMONS, R. E. (1) with J. Warner. SIR X 1971 (2) EG ch. 7.

SINDEREN, A. VON, *Blake the Mystic Genius*, 1949.

SLOSS, D. J. and J. P. R. WALLIS, *The Prophetic Writings of WB*, 1926.

SOUPPAULT, P. (1) WB (Paris) 1928 (2) Transl. J. L. May (London) 1928.

SPRAGENS, T. A., *The Politics of Motion*, 1973.

STEDMAN, J. G., *Journal*, ed. S. Thompson, 1962.

STEPHENS, F. G., *Memorials of W. Mulready*, 1867.

STEVENSON, W., *Divine Analogy: A Study of the Creation Motive in Blake and Coleridge* (Salzburg) 1972.

STEVENSON, W. H. (1) *Blake, Complete Poems* 1971 (2) BM i (3) 1967 13–16 (3) *ib.* March 1968.

STORY, A. T. (1) *Life of WB*, 1892 (2) *James Holmes and John Varley*, 1894 (3) *Life of John Linnell*, 1892.

STOTHARD, R. T., *Athenaeum* Dec. 1863.

SUTHERLAND, J. (1) EG 244–62 (2) *J. of Eng. Lit. Hist.* xxii 136–47 (3) ed. *Colby Lib. Quarterly*, June 1977.

SWINBURNE, A. C., WB 1868.

SYMONS, A., WB, 1907.

TAYLER, I. (1) *Blake's Illustrations to the Poems of Gray* (Princeton) 1917 (2) EG 285–303.

TAYLOR, G. J., SIR 13(2) 1974 141–5.

TAYLOR, P. A., BS iv (1) 1971.

TAYLOR, R., *The Political Prophecy in England* (Columbia) 1911.

THOMAS, K., *Religion and the Decline of Magic*, 1971.

THOMPSON, E. P., *The Making of the English Working Class*, 1968.

THOMPSON, S., *J. C. Stedman*, n.d. (Stapleford, Notts.).

THOMSON, J., *The National Reformer*, n.s. viii, 14 Jan. 1866.

TIMBS, J., *English Eccentrics*, 1898.

TODD, R. (1) *Tracks in the Snow*, 1946 (2) ed. Gilchrist, 1942 (3) *Print Collector's Quarterly* xxix 1948 25ff (4) *WB the Artist*, 1971.

TUVESON, E. L., *Millenium and Utopia* (Berkeley) 1949.

VIVIAN, T., *The Book of Revelation . . . Explained* (Plymouth) 1785.

WAGENKNECHT, D., *Blake's Night* (Harvard) 1973.

WARDLE, J., SIR 13(2) 1974 147–54.

WARDLE, R. M., *Mary Woolstonecraft* (Lawrence, Kansas) 1951.

WARK, R. R., HLQ V 1953 83–6.

WARNER, J. (1) *Blake's Visionary Forms Dramatic* (Princeton) 1970 (2) PP ch. x.

WASSER, H. H., MLQ ix 1948 292–7.

WEATHERS, W., *WB, The Tyger* (Columbia) 1969.

WEISKEL, T., *The Romantic Sublime* (John's Hopkins) 1976.

WESLEY, J. (1) ed. *A Collection of Moral and Sacred Poems* (Bristol) 1744 (2) *A Collection of Hymns, for the Use of the People Called Methodists* (8th ed.) 1793.

WHALLEY, A., *Poetic Process* (Cleveland, N.Y.) 1967.

WHITE, H. C., *The Mysticism of WB* (Wisconsin Studies in Lang. and Lit. 23) 1927.

WHITLEY, W. T. (1) *Art in England* 1800–30 (Camb.) 1928 (2) *Artists and their Friends in England* 1700–95, 1928.

WICKSTEAD, J. (1) TLS 18 Feb. 1972 (2) *Blake's Vision of the Book of Job* (2nd ed.) 1924 (3) *WB's Jerusalem*, 1953 (4) *Blake's Innocence and Experience*, 1928.

WILKIE, B., EG 359–72.

WILLIAMS, I. A., BM 1960 246–50.

WILSON, MONA, *Life of WB* 1948.

WIMSETT, W. K., *New Lit. Hist.* i 2 (*Winter*) 1972 215–36.

WIND, E. (1) JWCI i 1937 183 (2) *ib.* ii 1938 18–27.

WITCUTT, W. P., *Blake A Psychological Study*, 1946.

WITTREICH, J. A. (1) *Angel of Apocalypse* (Wisconsin) 1955 (2) SP lxix 1972 (3) *The Romantics on Milton* (Cleveland, London) 1970 (4) Intro. to W. Hayley's *Life of Milton* 1870 (Gainesville, Fla.) (5) BN iii 1969 3–4 (6) *see* Curran.

WOLFE, T. P., *Hudson Rev.* xx 1967–8 810–4.

WORRALL, D., BNYPL 78 (1975) 397–417.

WRIGHT, T. (1) *Life of WB* (Olney) 1928 (2) *WB: The Heads of the Poets* (Olney) 1925.

YEATS, W. B., with E. J. ELLIS, *Works of WB*, 1893.

Index

Index